WOMEN IN A CELTIC CHURCH
IRELAND 450–1150

Women in a
Celtic Church

Ireland 450–1150

CHRISTINA HARRINGTON

OXFORD

UNIVERSITY PRESS

OXFORD
UNIVERSITY PRESS

Great Clarendon Street, Oxford OX2 6DP
Oxford University Press is a department of the University of Oxford.
It furthers the University's objective of excellence in research, scholarship,
and education by publishing worldwide in

Oxford New York

Athens Auckland Bangkok Bogotá Buenos Aires Cape Town
Chennai Dar es Salaam Delhi Florence Hong Kong Istanbul Karachi
Kolkata Kuala Lumpur Madrid Melbourne Mexico City Mumbai Nairobi
Paris São Paulo Shanghai Singapore Taipei Tokyo Toronto Warsaw

and associated companies in Berlin Ibadan

Oxford is a registered trade mark of Oxford University Press
in the UK and certain other countries

Published in the United States
by Oxford University Press Inc., New York

British Library Cataloguing in Publication Data
Data available

Library of Congress Cataloging in Publication Data
Harrington, Christina.
Women in a Celtic Church : Ireland 450–1150 / Christina Harrington.
p. cm.
Includes bibliographical references and index.
1. Women, Celtic—Religious life—Ireland—History. 2. Women in
Christianity—Ireland—History. 3. Celtic Church—History. 4. Ireland—
Church history—To 1172. I. Title.
BR737.C4 H37 2001 274.15'02'082—dc21 2001033969
ISBN 0-19-820823-5

1 3 5 7 9 10 8 6 4 2

Typeset in Baskerville by
Jayvee, Trivandrum, India
Printed in Great Britain
on acid-free paper by
T.J. International Ltd.,
Padstow, Cornwall

Acknowledgements

ONE OF THE most enjoyable rewards of completing a research project is the opportunity to acknowledge those who have supported its creation. Scholarship is largely a solitary endeavour, so the help received is often indirect. As a result some to whom acknowledgements are due may not know how important their contributions have been.

For the financial backing and time necessary to complete the typescript, my first appreciation is to the Department of History at St Mary's College, Strawberry Hill, and also to Queens University, Belfast, for their award of a University Research Fellowship. My colleagues at St Mary's, in particular Sue Doran, Chris Durston, and Maria Dowling have been marvellous.

Being based in London has allowed me to be part of that alchemical alembic of historical endeavour, the Institute of Historical Research. The senior members of the Early Medieval Seminar have consistently fostered younger scholars, myself included, and I must mention by name Jinty Nelson, Michael Clanchy, Alan Thacker, Susan Reynolds, Matt Bennett, David Ganz, and my own former supervisor, Wendy Davies. From the IHR, too, have emerged some of my most treasured friendships. Gathering variously in the tea room, the Museum Tavern, the Rising Sun, Russell Square, and Da Beppe Italian restaurant, 'the gang' have many times offered suggestions and encouragement. My affectionate thanks to them all, in particular Guy Halsall, Geoff West, Andrew Wareham, Paul Kershaw, and Charlie Insley.

At Oxford, Thomas Charles-Edwards has been tremendously helpful and saved me from numerous blunders, for which I am ever grateful, as I am for his introducing me to the beneficial effects of drinking Lapsang Souchong tea when struggling with Old Irish texts. At the University of Pennsylvania over a decade ago Ann Matter introduced me to medieval religious women and their universes and encouraged my pursuit of the subject.

Behind-the-scenes help was provided by numerous people with their respective skills and expertise: on the computer, Mark Rimmell; on deadlines, Sarah Morgan; for their aid with texts, rare books, and manuscripts, the librarians of University College London, The British Museum, Queens University in Belfast, Senate House, and the IHR. For enlightening thoughts on particularly ambiguous Latin passages, Jason Davies of UCL and the Wellcome Institute. For such crucial gifts as thoughtful conversations and restful holidays, Sue Hurst, Peter Oates, Pete Townshend, Kate Moxham, Ronald Hutton, Colin Chapman, and Hillary Wiesner.

The *Conventus Nemorensis Bricketensis*, who support great work in a host of spheres, know their contribution to my endeavours, and have my deep appreciation.

Finally, with acknowledgements I cannot begin to catalogue, this book is for Hillary Wiesner.

C.H.

London
2001

Contents

List of Maps

Figures

Abbreviations

For full references please see Bibliography

AClon	Annals of Clonmacnois
AFM	Annals of the Four Masters
ALI	Hancock *et al.*, *Ancient Laws of Ireland*
AU	The Annals of Ulster
ATig	Annals of Tigernach
BL	British Library
BNE	Plummer, *Bethada náem nÉrenn*
CCSL	*Corpus Christianorum, Series Latina*
CIH	Binchy, *Corpus Iuris Hibernici*
Dictionary	Royal Irish Academy, *Dictionary of the Irish Language*
Heist	Heist, *Vitae Sanctorum Hiberniae*
Hibernensis	*Collectio Canonum Hibernensis*
JRSAI	*Journal of the Royal Society of Antiquaries of Ireland*
Kenney	Kenney, *The Sources for the Early History of Ireland*
MGH	*Monumenta Germaniae Historica*
Onomasticon	Hogan, *Onomasticon Goedelicum*
Pa1/Pa2	The First and Second Synods of St Patrick, in Bieler, *Irish Penitentials*
PG	*Patrologia Graeca*
PL	*Patrologia Latina*
PRIA	*Proceedings of the Royal Irish Academy*
PVSH	Plummer, *Vitae Sanctorum Hiberniae*
SEIL	Binchy *et al.*, *Studies in Early Irish Law*
Thes. Pal.	Stokes, *Thesaurus Paleohibernicus*
UJA	*Ulster Journal of Archaeology*
USMLS	Ulster Society for Medieval Latin Studies
ZCP	*Zeitschrift für celtische Philologie*

Introduction:
The Irish Holy Woman and her
Modern Inquisitors

ACADEMIC HISTORIOGRAPHY I: EARLY MEDIEVAL NUNS

Christian religious women in the early Middle Ages have been the subject of a steady flow of work over the past century. The first major work was Lina Eckenstein's 1896 general introduction, *Women Under Monasticism: Chapters on Saint-Lore and Convent Life between AD 500 and AD 1500*, which put medieval female religious life in the period onto the map for the English-speaking world.[1] It was among German scholars, though, that the subject really took off, and the two questions which preoccupied them were the organization and importance of the double monastery, and the meaning of the different categories of women religious mentioned in the early medieval sources. On the latter, K. H. Schäfer concentrated in a 1909 book, defining all early medieval nuns as 'canonesses'; he was rebutted within two years by A. H. Heineken, who demonstrated by contrast their great variety. In the 1970s M. Parisse took up the problem of canonesses and was followed in the 1990s by Andrea Hodgson; Anglo-Saxonists too have addressed it.[2] As for the issue of the double house, Hilpisch published his influential book on the subject which laid down the classic position in English: this was that the double house (by which is generally meant a monastery with both monks and nuns but headed by an abbess) was essentially a nunnery with worker-monks to perform male-only tasks. Mary Bateson and A. Hamilton Thompson reiterated and perpetuated this model, but it received a devastating critique by Andrea Hodgson in the 1980s.[3]

---

[1] Cambridge, 1896.

[2] K. H. Schäfer, *Die Kanonissenstifter im deutchen Mittelalter: Ihre Entwicklung und innere Einrichtung im Zusammenhang mit dem altchristlichen Sanctimonialentum* (Stuttgart, 1907). A. H. Heineken, *Die Anfänge der sächsischen Frauenklöster* (unpub. Phil. Diss.; Göttingen, 1909), 188–9, 114. For this part of the historiographic overview I am indebted to Dagmar Schneider's, 'Anglo-Saxon Women in the Religious Life: A Study of the Status and Position of Women in an Early Medieval Society' (unpub. PhD thesis; Cambridge, 1985), 9–37. M. Parisse, 'Les chanoinesses dans l'Empire germanique (ixe–xie siècles)', *Francia* 6 (1978), 107–26.

[3] S. Hilpisch, *Die Doppelklöster; Entstehung und Organisation* (Münster, 1928). M. Bateson, 'Origin and Early History of Double Monasteries', *Transactions of the Royal Historical Society* NS 13 (1899), 137–98. A. Hamilton Thompson, 'Double Monasteries and the Male Element in Nunneries', Appendix 8 to *The Ministry of Women: Report Commissioned by a Committee Appointed by the Archbishop of Canterbury* (London, 1919), 145–64, as well as his 'Northumbrian Monasticism', in *Bede: His Life, Times and Writings* (Oxford, 1935), 60–101, at 79–83.

   Scholars of Frankia gave the field of religious women a third preoccupation, namely, how the status of nuns changed over time. The most important work in this field, still influential today, is Suzanne Wemple's *Women in Frankish Society*, which claimed to show that Merovingian period as a heyday for religious women which came to an end with the Carolingian reforms.[4] Though the thesis was adopted by Jane Schulenberg and several others, it came under severe criticism from others on several accounts, and it has since been shown that the Carolingian reforms provided no such turning point in feminine monasticism as Wemple postulated.

   Since the early 1980s, most work on Carolingian religious women has concentrated on family politics and wealth; as a result we now appreciate that powerful abbesses and their nunneries owed their eminence more to their dynastic connections than to any inherent respect for women or nuns. We also see more clearly how nunneries were tools in the plans of dynastic schemers.[5] Karl Leyser's analysis of female monasticism in the tenth century in Saxony exemplifies this approach: he showed that the female houses of his study were so successful because noble families needed places in which to protect female relatives from the marital advances of male kinsmen and thus to limit the number of contestants for the family wealth.[6] The post-Wemple generation working on Frankish religious women have also eschewed broad generalization. This is the message of Janet Nelson's and Karl Leyser's work, but others, too, have provided examples. Jane Martindale looked at what we can learn from a single, intriguing case of a nun in early ninth-century Frankia, stressing the importance of the secular context, and Hlawitschka considered the composition of Remiremont, taking one place to work on in detail.[7]

   The nuns and abbesses of Anglo-Saxon England have been treated with as much enthusiasm as have their Frankish sisters. A solid tradition of scholarship on both women generally and religious women in particular is found there, characterized by a long awareness of the prominence of Anglo-Saxon abbesses and of the eminence of English double houses in the earlier Anglo-Saxon period. In the context of the social history of early England generally, historians have noted the scholarly and educational achievements of

---

   [4] S. Wemple, *Women in Frankish Society: Marriage and the Cloister 500 to 900* (Philadelphia, 1981).

   [5] A. Hodgson, The Frankish Church and Women, from the Late Eighth to the Early Tenth Century: Representation and Reality' (unpub. PhD thesis; University of London, 1992), 148–65. For critiques of method and of the use of evidence upon which the theory depends see, in addition to Hodgson's thesis, J. Nelson, 'Women and the Word in the Earlier Middle Ages', in W. Shiels and D. Wood (eds.), *Women in the Church* (Studies in Church History 27; Oxford, 1990), 53–78.

   [6] K. Leyser, *Rule and Conflict in an Early Medieval Society: Ottonian Saxony* (London, 1979).

   [7] E. Hlawitschka, 'Beobachtungen und Überlegungen zur Konventsstärke im Nonnenkloster Remiremont während des 7.–9. Jahrhunderts', in G. Melville (ed.), *Secundum regulam vivere: Festschrift für P. Norbert Backmund* (Windberg, 1978), 31–9. J. Martindale, 'The Nun Immena', in Shiels and Wood, *Women in the Church*, 27–42.

English nunneries.[8] Change over time also concerns the Anglo-Saxonists: the English Benedictine reforms of the tenth century seem to have seriously diminished female religious life, but there is little agreement as yet as to the extent or cause of the apparent plummet. Here, too, one can see the trend towards small-area, focused case studies in the work, say, of Stephanie Hollis.[9]

For regions such as Italy and Spain, only recently have early medieval religious women begun to receive attention.[10] The explosion of early twentieth-century German writing failed to prompt church scholars to look to women as a subject, so at present the state of study is much less developed. Returning to the Irish case, we find that it, like Italy and Spain, is a latecomer to the field. Much can be learnt from the Frankish and Anglo-Saxon precedents, not least in the sorts of questions that may usefully be asked of Ireland. Indeed, there must be some comparability of queries if we shall ever be able to make informed generalizations about the West as a whole, even if that conclusion is that one *cannot* in fact generalize. Were there different grades or sorts of religious women? To what extent were they creatures of their families' political ambition? How often, if ever, were they strictly enclosed? Did women under vows ever continue to control wealth? Did powerful abbesses owe their power to royal or noble status rather than *ex officio*? Did the number of female houses decline over time? Were female houses more vulnerable to dissolution than male ones? Were double houses anything other than nunneries with male workers attached? In this study of Irish holy women, even where adequate answers cannot be provided, these issues will be broached.

ACADEMIC HISTORIOGRAPHY II: THE EARLY IRISH CHURCH

Ireland from conversion to colonization (*c*.400–*c*.1200), termed variously Early Christian Ireland, Early Ireland, Celtic Ireland, Dark Ages Ireland, and most acceptably 'Early Medieval Ireland' has received significant scholarly attention for several centuries, and perhaps no facet of it more than its church. From James Ussher onwards, historians have been fascinated by Ireland's conversion to Christianity. Several of the questions asked in this tradition implicitly touch

---

[8] G. Browne, 'The Importance of Women in Anglo-Saxon Times', in his *The Importance of Women in Anglo-Saxon Times . . . And Other Addresses* (London, 1919), 11–39. H. Leibell, *Anglo-Saxon Education of Women: From Hilda to Hildegarda* (New York, 1922). M. Byrne, *The Tradition of the Nun in Medieval England* (Washington DC, 1932), outlining the portrayal of nuns and abbesses in early Anglo-Saxon writers. More recently, the monograph of Christine Fell, Cecily Clark, and Elizabeth Williams, *Women in Anglo-Saxon England and the Impact of 1066* (London, 1984), contains a chapter on women in religious life (ch. 6, 109–28). For a survey of scholarship from the nineteenth century through to the mid-1980s, see Schneider, 'Anglo-Saxon Women', 9–37.

[9] S. Hollis, *Anglo-Saxon Women and the Church: Sharing a Common Fate* (Woodbridge, 1992).

[10] e.g. M. Cabré y Pairet, '"Deodicatae" y "deovotae": La regulación de la religiosidad femenina en los condados catalanes', in A. Muñoz Fernández (ed.), *Las mujeres en el cristianismo medieval: Imágenes teóricas y cauces de actuación religiosa* (Madrid, 1989), 169–82.

upon the subject of nuns, but have been treated without regard to them. Bring-ing women religious into scholars' consideration of wider ecclesiastical matters is a logical next step. The main questions tackled in this field of scholarship merit consideration as well.

The first of these is a traditional assumption about the Irish church, namely that it was part of 'The Celtic Church', a group of national churches which were sufficiently homogeneous in structure, liturgy, practice, and outlook to merit being classed together as a single unit. This view was demolished in the course of the 1970s and 1980s, as various historians pointed out that there were variations among Celtic societies and their churches, and noted that regional variation existed among churches in the West generally. Thus the standard view at present is that in the early middle ages there was not a Celtic cultural unity, and, further, no such thing as 'The Celtic Church'.[11] The most obvious prac-tical implication is that evidence from other Celtic areas can no longer be applied to Ireland, and, conversely, that conclusions about Ireland cannot be extrapolated to the other Celtic areas, whether in ecclesiastical or other matters.

Another strand in the historiography concerns Ireland's monasticism. Ireland was one of the earliest places outside Egypt where it flourished, indeed the Irish took their monasticism to numerous places across northern Europe in the course of the sixth and seventh centuries. Historians of the early twentieth century called the early Irish a 'monastic church', for it had no diocesan structure and the power-brokers were abbots, not bishops as was the norm else-where. This thesis was modified to acknowledge first that the very earliest period of Christianity there (i.e. fourth and fifth centuries) had apparently been diocesan, and secondly that bishops did continue to hold some spiritual powers even after the ascendancy of monasteries and abbots in the sixth century.[12] Within the general subject of Ireland's monasticism there are a number of aux-iliary topics which have commanded attention. One of these concerns change over time, namely that monasticism, having flourished and gained strength over the course of the sixth century, had become highly secularized, in some cases at least, by the eighth. The trend continued, the *Céli Dé* movement notwith-standing, through to the twelfth. 'Secularized' in this context means that many abbots no longer lived the monastic life; that monasteries were at times involved in the dynastic wars of their patrons; that many churches (monastic and other-wise) were controlled by laymen simply for gain. In this period in the case of male houses, there was sometimes a division of abbatial tasks—one 'abbot' would become the monastic estates manager, while another would lead the monks in

---

[11] W. Davies, 'The Myth of the Celtic Church', in N. Edwards and A. Lane (eds.), *The Early Church in Wales and the West: Recent Work in Early Christian Archaeology, History and Place-names* (Oxbow Monograph Series 16; Oxford, 1992), 12–21, with references.

[12] On early diocesan structure followed by a rise in monastic power, the work of Kathleen Hughes is important; for the continuing powers of bishops see Sharpe's and Etchingham's work particularly their interpretation of the text *Riaghail Phátraic*.

their religious life. The question remains to be asked: what happened in female houses—do we ever have a female lay abbot or estates manager? Was the head of religious life always female, or could it ever be male? With regard to dynastic rivalries, do we ever find female houses going to war as male houses sometimes did? And did ruling families attempt to control female establishments by different means than they did male ones? Or were the tactics essentially the same?

Lay-controlled churches and monasteries are known across early medieval Europe under the term 'proprietary church' or *eigenkirche*. The extent and meaning of this trend as it developed in Ireland has come under recent question, with challenges to the idea that such establishments were products of simple economic self-interest, were usually short-lived, and failed to provide pastoral care to their communities.[13] It remains to be explored whether any of these assumptions apply to female houses—whether they were set up by men or by women. That is to say, were female houses more likely to be proprietary? Were they more likely to be short-lived? Did female houses ever provide pastoral care to the community? Is there any evidence that nuns of small houses ever controlled their own finances?

Another monastic question centres on the monastic federations (called *paruchiae* by scholars of the generation of the 1950s and 60s). These networks of hegemony were formed by leading churches such as Armagh, Iona, and Clonmacnois; scholars inquire into the means by which these were extended, the extent and kind of obligations the tributaries owed to the head house, and the ways the federations bolstered their wealth and prestige. Promoting a patron saint was a political act; by doing so a monastery hoped to attract more dependent houses, more visiting pilgrims, and more wealth. If the dynasty that supported or 'owned' a monastery was successful, the success was attributed in part to the saint, and this included success in war. Saints who gave their protégés success on the battlefield were sure to gain new adherents in such a war-ridden society as early Ireland.

The female saint who has received the most attention is, unsurprisingly, Brigit. She was remembered as the founder of Kildare, a very wealthy and successful double-monastery with a confederation of dependent churches. Numerous hymns and poems praising her survive, and even in the twelfth century the visiting English aristocrat Gerald of Wales saw fit to describe the monastery. In the late nineteenth and early twentieth centuries, the era in which the search for survivals of pre-Christian religion was respectable in academe, Brigit was treated foremost as a Christianized goddess, a figure who may have had no historical reality as a human mortal. Scholarly and popular works of *c*.1910–40 portray her as an ideal of Christian female domesticity—she produced food, was kind to animals and hung her cloak on a sunbeam; alternatively they ignore her altogether. The questions which remain to be answered centre on

---

[13] J. Blair and R. Sharpe (eds.), *Pastoral Care Before the Parish* (Leicester, 1992).

the way in which the gender of the saint affected the cult. Did the Irish treat female saints differently from male ones? Were monasteries with female patron saints politically disadvantaged? Did female saints have attributes distinctly feminine?

The last area of Irish ecclesiastical historiography which bears mentioning in an introduction concerns asceticism. The early Irish saints, i.e. the missionaries-*cum*-monastic founders of the fifth and sixth centuries, have enjoyed a long reputation as great ascetics. Probably since the Bollandists published their great volumes of Lives they have been known for their feats of self-mortification. The well-known examples are their long fasts, their standing in freezing rivers, their extended vigils and, above all, their avoidance of women. Even when academics identified eighth-century 'secularization', they continued to hold as highly ascetic the early period, *c.*400–600. The modern reputation is due largely to writers of the nineteenth and early twentieth centuries, often male clerics, who scoured the Lives for anecdotes which proved the early church to be exceptionally admirable in religious terms. It is true that the Irish had in the early middle ages something of a reputation, at least in some places at some times, but the modern writers exaggerated the degree of male asceticism in the Lives, particularly the avoidance of women. The Lives written before the tenth century almost never speak of the early male saints avoiding the opposite sex: it is a later *topos*. Thus it is useful to consider the hagiographers' ideas on female impurity, the extent to which male ecclesiastics perceived nuns as a threat, and the possible reasons for the shift in tone in the Lives in the tenth century.

ACADEMIC HISTORIOGRAPHY III: EARLY IRISH WOMEN

In 1936 Rudolf Thurneysen and Daniel Binchy, with a handful of others, produced a volume of essays on the legal status of women, *Studies in Early Irish Law*. The first concerted attempt to understand the role of women in marriage, in property and at law, it forced readers to the conclusion that Irish women in the earliest period for which we have written evidence, *c.*700–900 were legally inferior to men in all areas of public life and in many areas of private life as well. Furthermore, it demonstrated that marriage laws had become more, not less, generous to women, which suggested that before Christianity arrived the plight of married women had been even worse. Binchy and his fellow contributors made it clear that there was no legal evidence for any sort of ancient Irish *Mütterrecht*. One legal tract, *Cáin Adomnáin* (the Law of Adomnán), written near the turn of the eighth century, famously alleged that the pre-Christian status of women had been deplorable and owed it to Christianity to bring women out of the gutter. In the light of the finding of the 1936 studies, this fanciful allegation now recounted a more plausible line of progression than that of a native matriarchy turned Christian patriarchy.

It can hardly be appreciated how much these findings challenged a prominent school of thought at the time, according to which all societies were originally matriarchal and/or goddess-worshipping, becoming increasingly patriarchal over time. The 'evolutionary' model made famous by Sir James Frazer in his *Golden Bough*, asserting that pre-Christian Europe had matriarchal roots and a primal religion of the worship of a single Great Goddess, was widespread in academe.[14] Among Irish scholars the most prominent scholar embracing such an approach was the prodigious editor, translator, and archaeologist, R. A. S. Macalister, though there were others.[15] By finding evidence which looked as though it denied the applicability of this stage-progression model to Ireland, Binchy and Thurneysen changed the direction of Irish scholarly approach to the pre-Christian past: they ended any possibility of Irish scholarship going down the road of seeing the past in matriarchal terms, and they indirectly threw into question suppositions about the common methodology of the day, namely using folklore and myth as 'survivals' of the pagan era.

Never universally accepted, survivalism had long been on the point of extinction among Celticists in the 1970s when of all the extant early medieval texts only the sagas and law tracts were held to have an identifiable pre-Christian stratum. This seemed at the time reasonable, as the Irish did have a long tradition of oral learning and classical authors had observed that Continental Celts at least did not commit important matters to writing; by the 1980s, though, it was agreed that even the sagas could not be used as evidence for the pre-Christian era because anthropologists showed that even oral societies drastically change stories and histories in their retellings over even a few decades—and the Irish tales purported to describe an era not just a few decades earlier, but 600 to 800 years previous. It was increasingly realized, too, that the saga writers were influenced by literary models, so they may have been modelled largely on, say, Homer. The last serious survivalist work in the academic community was Kenneth Jackson's study of the Ulster Cycle, *Window on the Iron Age* (1963), which was received with harsh criticism for its methodology. Since then, only the law tracts, written down *c*.700, are treated as reflectors of pre-Christian society, because it is recognized by anthropologists that customary law (which the Irish tracts record) changes extremely slowly, though increasingly there is suspicion that the 'earlier' and 'later' strands, which Binchy claimed he could identify, might not be so clearly delineated, and also that the influence of Christian values on the texts is more pervasive than previously recognized.

In a few corners of academe the twin bastions of late-Victorian anthropology, survivalism and presumed pagan matriarchy, live on. There was Jan de Vries's

[14] R. Hutton, 'The Neolithic Great Goddess: A Study in Modern Tradition', *Antiquity* 71 (1997), 91–9, which contains a thorough outline of the historiography of this thesis among archaeologists and, to a lesser extent, historians.
[15] R. A. S. Macalister, *Archaeology of Ireland* (2nd edn.: London, 1949), 355–63; H. J. Massingham, *Through the Wilderness* (London, 1935); J. MacCulloch, *The Celtic and Scandinavian Religions* (London, 1948), 42.

Keltische Religione, published in 1962, which saw in the early Irish church the last traces of a European-wide matriarchy and vestal priestess cults. It was followed by Jean Markale's *Les Femmes des Celtes* (1974), also a work scholarly in ambition if not in achievement, which like de Vries's book claimed to show that Celtic women enjoyed great status until Christianity eroded their position, and indeed that goddess-worshipping matriarchy was Ireland's original socio-religious structure. Fifteen years after Markale, Mary Condren published *The Serpent and The Goddess: Women, Religion and Power in Celtic Ireland*.[16] Her early Irish church was one in which Brigit-the-Goddess was transmogrified into Brigit-the-Saint, in which male church authorities gradually edged out the peaceful and woman-centred values of the previous religion until, by the twelfth century, Ireland was as violent and patriarchal as anywhere else in Europe. She, like de Vries and Markale, followed the Cambridge Ritualist school of thought which was certain that Europe was originally matriarchal and goddess-worshipping, that in the Iron Age it was partially patriarchal, and that Christianity completed the patri-archalization. The chronology of Condren's transitions is inconsistent and hard to follow because her rules of evidence differ from those of the modern main-stream scholar's: she follows the Ritualists' rules, under which goddess-oriented or matriarchal elements in texts must, by force of evolutionary logic, be older than those showing worship of male deities, violence, and male rule. *The Serpent and the Goddess* has influenced popular histories such as Peter Berresford Ellis's recent *Celtic Women*, for whom Condren is an oft-cited source, most significantly an authority for the 'fact' that Ireland was originally a goddess-worshipping matriarchy and for the basic view of the early Irish church as one in which the dying embers of goddess-worship can be perceived.

Mainstream Irish scholarship, having abandoned the evolutionary model, has produced much very good and interesting work on early medieval women.[17] Philip O'Leary has written on the honour of women in the tales. Queen Medb has been fascinatingly reassessed by a number of historians, who have argued that she appears to be an anti-heroine, representing as a female war-leader an inversion of the proper cosmic order. Among the more recent developments in the study of Irish law of women are an increasing understanding of the terms of marriage law and, with one article now published on the subject, the study of the law as it applied to females in the professions. This tradition of work, largely legal and literary, has implications for the study of religious women. Historians concerned with Irish female status will want to know whether there are changes over time in nuns' status which may or may not correspond with the increased status of wives. Were nuns treated at law like married women, for after all they

---

[16] San Francisco, 1989.

[17] e.g. P. O'Leary, 'The Honour of Women in Early Irish Literature', *Ériu* 38 (1987), 27–44; M. Ní Brolcháin, 'Women in Early Myths and Sagas', *Crane Bag* 14 (1980), 12–19; P. Ford, 'Celtic Women: The Opposing Sex', *Viator* 19 (1988), 417–38.

were betrothed if not actually married to Christ? Were they classed with professional women? Were they treated as ecclesiastics or as laity? Turning from the legal questions to those raised by the study of the literature, it may well be asked whether religious women, like those women in the tales and other narrative texts, were able to give increased honour to the men in their families through their wealth, eminence, spiritual power (in the women of the myths it is beauty rather than holiness). Did laymen look toward the religious women in their kindreds to enhance their own status? Are any strong female religious women actually perhaps anti-heroines as was Medb? Where are religious women in the cosmic order? By rounding out our picture of early Irish women to include those who lived the religious life, the complex and nuanced landscape of early Irish gender is appreciated all the better.

POPULAR PERCEPTIONS AND NON-SPECIALIST HISTORIOGRAPHY

When one mentions the phrase 'early Irish holy women' to the non-academic enthusiast of things Celtic, it conjures up exciting images of pagan priestesses, amazonian warriors, powerful goddesses, and Christian saints; it prompts phrases 'Celtic matriarchy', 'Culdee Christians', and above all 'Celtic Christianity'. The general reader is presented with a veritable industry of Celtic spirituality which has literary, religious, and ethnic dimensions.

Popular writing, so scorned by scholars, has created a situation in which most intelligent non-specialists hold out-of-date views about early Christian Ireland, especially about the status of its women and the nature of its religion. The fact that this could be the case for so popular a subject as early Ireland is curious, and demands some explanation. The cause, at the simplest level, is a divergence between popular and scholarly writing on matters Celtic which has been increasing since the Edwardian period. The abyss between the Ivory Tower dweller and the Waterstone's Bookshop browser has never been wider. There was a time when cutting-edge academic work was read by the man on the street: and that time was about 1890–1930. Then, much Irish scholarship was published in book form, rather than being more focused on journal articles as it is now. The style of much of it was sufficiently accessible for the layman. Moreover, its discoveries were of common interest, because at the time there was a great popular interest in ancient religion, in matters of sex and gender, and in ancient mythology. Furthermore, the 'survivalist' method, in which traces of the distant past were sought in the contemporary customs, was inherently attractive to the ordinary reader. The subject also touched upon the literary fashions of the day: the Irish Literary Revival was happening and folklore studies were in their ascendancy. It was this era which produced J. Bonwick's *Religion of the Ancient Celts* (London, 1894) and G. Stokes's *Ireland and the Celtic Church* (London, 1892), along with studies alleging continuities from paganism to the near-present, such as

W. B. Yeats's *The Celtic Twilight* (London, 1893) and W. Wood-Martin's *Traces of Elder Faiths of Ireland* (London, 1902).

Popular and academic trends gradually diverged, though through the 1930s there appeared books on Celtic history and mythology whose approach was largely Victorian in its underlying assumptions and whose methodology supposed the usefulness of late sources for early events: one can cite Gougaud's *Celtic Christianity in Celtic Lands* (published in English in 1932) and Eoin Mac-Neill's *Celtic Ireland* (1921). But on the whole academic writing had moved away from its populist phase, and was increasingly abstruse. Scholarly involvement with Irish nationalism faded, and so one large popular audience thus disappeared from the collective academic mind, an audience for which it had produced numerous works, translations, and interpretations. Then there were the methodologies themselves: increasingly shy of using the swashbuckling tales of cursing saints, bold queens, and pagan druids as historical documents, scholars turned to less story-like sources in their work, and the published results were correspondingly less appealing to the man in the street. The commoner was marginalized from the collective project of scholarly history in another way, too, for no longer were memoirs of folk customs of grandparents' childhoods relevant to the projects of historians as they had been to Evans-Wentz, to Wood-Martin, to Yeats. The very media were also part of the trend, for journals more than books became the favoured medium of scholarly publishing, and academic journals are not found on bookshop shelves where the non-specialist goes to engage with the Celtic past.

The continued popular interest in matters Celtic meant that many older books remained in print or were reissued, even though they were out of date in terms of approach, interpretation, and conclusion. The lack of accessible publications on early Ireland by professional scholars left a vacuum which semi-scholarly and popular historians have filled: one can cite not only Condren and Markale, as above, but also Ward Rutherford, John and Caitlin Matthews, and those who come from overtly particular spiritual traditions. These writers depend upon what scholarship they can get, assimilate, and understand: overwhelmingly this is survivalist, mythologically-based history of the Victorian and Edwardian period. These writers in turn create generations of Celtophiles whose beliefs, acquired in good faith from books they believe reliable, include ancient Celtic matriarchy, early Christian nature-worship, and Amazonian Irish warrior queens. The popular historians also feed the novelists, science-fiction and fantasy genre writers. It is telling that for the generation who were in their twenties during the 1980s there was no more influential portrayal of early Celtic Church than Marian Zimmer Bradley's fantasy novel, *The Mists of Avalon*, in which the Great Goddess's priestesses at Glastonbury fought against the incoming Christian missionaries who sought to bring not only the Christian God but the rule of males over females. Scholars, rather than stepping into the fray to fight for the mass readership, have removed themselves from the battlefield.

This dichotomy has had a practical impact on some niches of modern religious life. 'Celtic spirituality' has been going in one form or another for the whole of the twentieth century, and the image of the 'Celtic religious woman' features in all of them. The various groups whose worship, liturgy, and theology is defined thus are built upon those very same translations and Victorian-era interpretations, in two ways most noticeably: in their beliefs that the early Irish church was characterized by a great many survivals from the pagan period, and that the Celtic character was inherently more mystical than its Anglo-Saxon or Roman counterpart. The Celtic temperament was then classed as 'feminine, poetic, imaginative, mystical' in contrast to the Anglo-Saxon, which was 'masculine, logical, rational', a belief seen in Fiona Macleod's *The Immortal Hour* and in the writings of H. J. Massingham. In very few areas of modern life is scholarship so influential on so many people's daily religious life—but it is Victorian scholarship, not contemporary work.

MODERN CELTIC CHRISTIANS

The modern Celtic Christianity movement is not an organized one, but rather consists of groups within established churches across various denominations. It speaks to those for whom none of the available contemporary versions of Christianity offer full satisfaction in their current form. A prime example in the British Isles is the Celtic Christian retreat centre on Iona, founded in 1938 by the Revd George Macleod, which has its own liturgical forms, worship groups, and literature. In the south of England, Glastonbury boasts the thorn tree said to have been planted by Joseph of Arimathea and the Chalice Well centre, built around a well which yielded in 1907 a goblet said to be that used by Christ in the last supper: Celtic Christian pilgrims abound all year round.[18] In America the Celtic Christian movement is transmitted in large part by the school led by the ex-Dominican mystic Matthew Fox, best known for his 1983 book *Original Blessing*.

Today's Celtic Christians believe that native pre-Christian Celtic culture lent the earliest insular Christianity a particularly beneficent quality, one worth reviving today. The key qualities attributed to it are an incarnational attitude to God and Christ, i.e. a sense that God is in all aspects of nature and is rightly sought there, and that God may be addressed intimately; a Thoreau-like return-to-nature mysticism is attributed to those saints who inhabited such

---

[18] Glastonbury became a Celtic Christian centre in 1907 when a local clergyman, John Goodchild 'helped' some young people discover in a local holy well a chalice which he claimed had been proved by experts to be the chalice used by Christ at the last supper. Though the chalice had been planted there by the vicar himself, he disguised the fact successfully enough for Glastonbury to become famed for something more than the alleged burial place of King Arthur and Guenevere, for more than the thorn-tree planted by Joseph or Arimathea—that is, for being the resting place of the Holy Grail. The buildings surrounding the well were formed into a spiritual retreat (P. Benham, *The Avalonians* (Glastonbury, 1993), 5–52).

untamed islands as Iona or Skellig Michael. There is a fondness for the early medieval tales in which the pagan Irish are alleged to have foretold the coming of Christ to these islands, and some go so far as to believe that in some way the Celts were prepared for the new religion and thus welcomed it. Another purported result of the intermixing of native Celtic religion with the New Religion was a deep reverence for the divinity in women, which was expressed in their especial devotion to St Brigit as well as to the Virgin Mary. Brigit, as cited in early Irish texts and in later Scottish folklore, is the Mary of the Gaels—their own Blessed Virgin. Brigit, too, is in some legends the midwife of Christ, an Irish-woman present at the messianic events in Palestine.[19] Kildare, the site of Brigit's church, is a modern Celtic Christian centre for pilgrims and spiritual retreat.[20] Their historical assumptions are manifestly derived from those of an earlier era: i.e. that the nature of Celts was emotional, mystical and thus possessing 'feminine' qualities, and that that native Celtic spirit had survived into its early church.

Today's academics can be derisive of modern Celtic Christianity, but it must be remembered that such Christians rely heavily upon the writings of their own early twentieth century leaders and the authorities the latter had cited. They presume in good faith that older works ought to be valid still. Beyond that, the conclusions of Frazerians appear commonsensical. At the turn of the year 2000, Celtic Christians are often as frustrated with the academics as the academics are with them. But lest scholars believe that they themselves have no remaining connection with predecessors who held such views, they would do well to remember the Introduction of Charles Plummer's 1922 volume, *Irish Saints' Lives*, still the standard edition and translation of many Irish *Lives*. It is a hundred-page listing of pagan 'survivals' in the Lives, framed absolutely according to Victorian principles of the 'nature cult' school.

WOMEN'S SPIRITUALITY, FEMINIST SPIRITUALITY

A second group attracted to the religious women of early Christian Ireland is the Women's Spirituality movement and its close and indeed overlapping sister-movement, Feminist Spirituality.[21] These are two parts of an inchoate yet influential collection of authors, ritual groups, and feminist study centres that began

---

[19] A. Duncan, *The Elements of Celtic Christianity* (Shaftesbury, 1992); I. Bradley, *The Celtic Way* (London, 1993); E. de Waal, *The Celtic Vision* (London, 1988); M. Maher (ed.), *Irish Spirituality* (Dublin, 1981); E. Toulson, *The Celtic Alternative* (London, 1987); J. Mackey (ed.), *An Introduction to Celtic Christianity* (Edinburgh, 1989).

[20] M. Minehan, 'Kildare Today: Continuing the Brigidine Tradition', in P. Clancy (ed.), *Celtic Threads: Exploring Our Celtic Heritage* (Dublin, 1999), 161–70, and P. Clancy, 'Brigit, Muire na nGael: The Eternal Feminine in the Celtic Tradition', ibid. 33–50.

[21] On the development of the movement, C. Spretnak (ed.), *The Politics of Women's Spirituality: Essays on the Rise of Spiritual Power within the Feminist Movement* (Garden City, NJ, 1982).

in the 1920s and 30s with Esther Harding's *Women's Mysteries*, published in 1929, which owed much to the ideas circulating in the evolutionary Cambridge Ritualist group, particularly Jane Ellen Harrison and James Frazer. Robert Graves's 1948 book, *The White Goddess*, applied the goddess-worship and pagan-survival assumptions to Celtic myths, and gained a vast popular following. This, with Marija Gimbutas's fervid publicization of the ancient matriarchy thesis, helped give birth in the 1970s to the 'feminist spirituality' movement. Adherents of this movement seek personal religious inspiration from goddess images across a wide range of ancient cultures, from Sumerian to neolithic to Greek. Like the Celtic Christians, they depend upon the thesis that all religions began as devotion to an all-encompassing mother figure and that ultimately all goddesses are but aspects of a Great Goddess. Turning Frazer on his head without realizing it, they see the phase of religious development predating scientific understanding (especially of sexual reproduction) as a religious Golden Age because, being as yet un-masculinized, it must have been peaceful; being universal, it must have encompassed all Europe. Following Jane Ellen Harrison and those derived from her, they say this *Mütterrecht* came to an end by invasion which introduced war and patriarchy, which gradually eradicated all but mythological traces of the idyllic past.[22] Women forging a spiritual life from these beliefs see themselves as recovering scattered threads of a once-unified whole, re-weaving them into a functioning cloth that can serve as a garment for today's women. Texts such as the Ulster Cycle tales, and the Mabinogion, are analysed in 'evolutionist' fashion: signs of goddess-worship are assumed to be 'early' or 'ancient'; warlike elements and heroic elements are deemed later overlays. The early bits are extracted and preserved for modern use and modern inspiration, while the warlike ('later') strands are discarded as, frankly, bad. Warrior goddesses such as the Morrigan are seen as twisted Indo-Europeanizations of earlier peaceful goddesses, travesties of the original. Exemplifying this approach is Merlin Stone's 1976 *Paradise Papers* and Monica Sjoo and Barbara Mor's 1987 tome, *The Great Cosmic Mother: Rediscovering the Religion of the Earth*. Practical guidance on how to build a spiritual life on these premises has been given in a number of books from the 1970s onward, but among the most influential have been Z. Budapest's *Holy Book of Women's Mysteries* (1980) and Starhawk's *Spiral Dance* (1979). In terms of practice, groups in this tradition are generally women-only, non-hierarchical, consensus-based, and fluid. In the British Isles and Ireland they often meet at Neolithic sites such as Silbury Hill, Newgrange, and Glastonbury Tor to reverence the universal Great Goddess, the primordial nature whom they believe to have been the object of European-wide worship in the Stone Age.

At times there is open hostility among the feminist proponents of ancient matriarchy towards mainstream historians. Academics, it is alleged, have suppressed the fact of ancient matriarchy and Goddess-religion by unjustly

---

[22] Hutton, 'Neolithic Great Goddess', with references.

discrediting the evolutionary ethnographers of the early years of the twentieth century. It is profoundly unlikely that relations will improve at any time in the near future, though there is increasing opposition to the 'Great Goddess Thesis' from within feminism as well as from without it.[23] In the small corner that is Irish religious history an important inroad has been made by Lisa Bitel, who comes from the feminist scholarship tradition but who now uses the same sources (secondary as well as primary) as more mainstream scholars.

NEO-PAGANS, MODERN DRUIDS

The third group of non-specialists who take an interest in the religious women of early Ireland are modern pagans, and most especially those who practice a revived druidism. Several sociological studies in the US assert that paganism is the fastest growing spiritual path in North America, and in the UK it is estimated that there are about 100,000 pagans.[24] The origins of the revival lie at the turn of the century, with middle-class people of the sort active in the Folklore Society, well educated, schooled in the classics featuring alluring gods like Pan and Venus, people enamoured of the idea of a rural fertility cult. Frazer's progression of evolutionary stages made sense to them, but the part that appealed was not the first, Goddess-only phase, but the era when men and women performed a sacred marriage as equals. Following Frazer, Harrison, Yeats, and others, they pieced together a picture of a period when the Goddess of nature, whose primary symbol was the moon, mated with a God of Nature who was represented as divine a king or a horned Pan-figure; the result, theologically, was a fertility-oriented nature pantheism. In the 1930s and 40s, a few individuals pieced rituals together and gave groups of interested friends encouragement in getting started.[25]

[23] Criticizing the Great Goddess thesis generally, L. Motz, *Faces of the Goddess* (Oxford, 1997); E. Klein, *Feminism Under Fire* (Amherst, NY, 1996); D. Patai and N. Koertge, *Professing Feminism: Cautionary Tales from the Strange World of Women's Studies* (New York, 1996); Hutton, 'Neolithic Great Goddess'. Criticizing feminists' adoption of Bachofen's religious stages of development, S. Binford, 'Myths and Matriarchies', in Spretnak, *Politics of Women's Spirituality*. Feminist criticisms of the matriarchy thesis: M. Massey, *Feminine Soul: The Fate of an Ideal* (Boston, 1985); J. Bamberger, 'The Myth of Matriarchy: Why Men Rule in Primitive Society', in M. Rosaldo and L. Lamphere (eds.), *Woman, Culture and Society* (Stanford, 1974), 263–80; S. Tiffany, 'The Power of Matriarchal Ideas', *International Journal of Women's Studies* 5, no. 2 (1982), 138–47.

[24] On paganism in Britain, G. Harvey and C. Hardman (eds.), *Paganism Today* (London, 1995); G. Harvey (ed.), *Contemporary Paganism* (New York, 1997). On paganism in the United States, M. Adler, *Drawing Down the Moon* (Boston, 1986).

[25] For the most recent, and definitive study of modern paganism, see R. Hutton, *The Triumph of the Moon* (Oxford, 1999) which treats the role of Frazer, Harrison, and many of the other authors mentioned in this section. On the current Celtic manifestations, see Marion Bowman's work, especially 'Cardiac Celts: Images of the Celts in Contemporary British Paganism' (in Harvey and Hardman, *Paganism Today*, 242–51) and 'Contemporary Celtic Spirituality' (in A. Hale and P. Payton (eds.), *New Directions in Celtic Studies* (Exeter, 2000), 69–94).

Modern paganism is profoundly evolutionist in origin and, in the widest sense, will always be so, for it has a sense that it is retrieving elements Western society believed it had outgrown. Pagans make connections between psychic intuitiveness and goddess-worship, as did Frazer, and between nature-worship and goddess-worship, like him again. Where pagans depart from Frazer and are instead romantics, is in the value-judgement of the evolutionary process. It was, pagans say, a false sense of maturation which led to the abandonment of magic, poetry, reverence for nature and the feminine aspect of divinity—it can and should be revived. Certainly this new paganism, complete with liturgy, coherent groupings, and an evolved ethical philosophy, could never have been imagined by Frazer: rational Westerners living in the twenty-first century should by his account be moving from a mature transcendental monotheism towards scientific atheism.[26]

Since the 1930s and 40s, modern pagans have looked to Ireland and Wales as two of the last surviving pagan cultures in Western Europe and, simply, as those nearest home. To them, as to many, the Irish sagas appear to speak of a pagan world in which both the women and the men were strong, vibrant and, at their best, honourable, and free of prurience about matters sexual: Queen Maeve (Ir. Medb) to them demonstrates in their eyes an equality of male and female even in such a traditionally male sphere as war leadership. The four pagan Celtic quarter days are their main holidays, an adoption they view as a natural re-sacralization of native holy days. In conjunction with one of these days, Imbolc (1 February), they have taken a special interest in the goddess Brigit, and most pagans know her as the patroness of medicine, crafts, and poetry. Brigit is the only woman of the Celtic church who interests them, because she is the one clearly pagan goddess whose cult appears to have survived into the Christian era; her pagan temple practices seem to have continued uninterrupted at Kildare. In other words, the early Christian woman in Ireland is interesting only insofar as she remained at least partly pagan. Influential were the writings of Lewis Spence, author of the 1911 pagan survivalist academic study *The Mysteries of Britain: Secret Rites and Tradition of Ancient Britain*, a work which can serve to illustrate the kind of thinking by which the Irish saint Brigit (and indeed much later Christian figures) are reclaimed as wider European deities with long survivals.

Coventry was formerly situated near the southern boundaries of the great British tribe of the Brigantes, the presiding deity of whom was the goddess Brigantia or Brigiddu, the same, as has been indicated, with the Irish Brigit, later Christianised into St. Bridget. She was also known as Danu or Anu, and is undoubtedly identical with that Black Annis who was supposed to lurk in the Dane (or Danu) hills in Leicestershire.[27]

---

[26] On the belief in magic by modern British pagans in the late twentieth century, T. Luhrmann, *Persuasions of the Witches' Craft* (Oxford, 1989).

[27] L. Spence, *The Mysteries of Britain: Secret Rites and Tradition of Ancient Britain* (London, 1911), 174.

In modern scholarship most if not all of the connections Spence made are considered too tenuous to be asserted, and look profoundly dubious. For all that, his survivalist, folklorist, and heavily pagan approach was alive and well in the 1990s in the neo-pagan journals of Britain and the United States.

Because scholars are prone to scoff at Celtic Christians, religious feminists, and modern pagans, it bears reiterating that a spiritual movement's validity is not dependent on the historical accuracy of its origin myths; Judaism and Christianity have both managed very well in spite of the Bible's highly unlikely version of very early history. Nor is it cause for academic triumphalism, for scholars should be chastened to remember that the current situation has arisen because somehow the Victorians and Edwardians managed to reach 'the man in the street' in a way more recent generations, including theirs, have not. If the non-specialist still holds old views, today's scholars must bear the lion's share of the blame.

SOURCES AND PROBLEMS

A few words about the sources and their problems may be helpful. The main point to make is that those relevant to early Irish religious women are wide-ranging in type and form. For the earliest church, covering the fifth and sixth centuries, there are the two texts of St Patrick, the *Confessio* and the *Epistola*, and the early penitentials, which are priests' guides to the penances to be set for a wide variety of sins committed by the faithful. For the seventh to ninth centuries useful material is found in the Lives written in those centuries, the Irish laws, the canons of the *Collectio Canonum Hibernensis*, rules and monastic customs, annals, martyrologies, some biblical exegesis, hagiographic poetry, hymns, litanies, and there is even one fragment of a consecration rite. For the tenth- to twelfth-century period there are a great many Lives in both Irish and Latin, legal glosses, glosses on hagiographical poems and on the martyrologies, theological tracts, and apocryphal texts.

Though plentiful, the material presents a variety of difficulties. To begin with, the sources are extremely patchy over time: material of one sort may be relatively abundant in one period but scarce or absent in another; the legal evidence is a case in point. Furthermore the evidence is discontinuous, so while one may make observations about, say, the provision of sick-maintenance for virgins in the eighth century, there is no material on it for any time earlier or later. Then there is the perennial problem of dating the texts, which in the case of early medieval Ireland is particularly acute. Many texts, or sections thereof, are of unknown or disputed date, and scholarly estimates can vary by up to two hundred years. An historian using a multitude of texts in a wider analysis relies heavily on the current state of scholarly estimates and analyses of editors. Richard Sharpe's

seminal work on the Hiberno-Latin Lives, published in his *Medieval Irish Saints'
Lives*, now allows some texts: (those in what he denotes the O'Donoghue group,
abbreviated Φ), to be placed in the seventh- or eighth-century period. Sharpe
also identified the texts of a copyist-redactor working *c*.1200, identified as 'D',
whose habits of copying included making few changes to his exemplars; thus
Latin Lives which are 'D texts' can safely be assumed to be very close to their exemplars, which must, in turn, have been composed no later than the twelfth
century. The plethora of versions of anonymous Lives of Irish saints can lead to
confusion, so references identify those which are Φ texts and D texts, whilst
others are identified by manuscript origin, so as to minimize the problems of
identification. The bibliography also lists Lives individually with these tags.

There are also problems of genre. Some source difficulties are particular to
type: laws are by nature normative and prescriptive, and there is often an absence of evidence concerning their application. They may reflect more theory
than practice, and so are best interpreted primarily as indicators of attitude and
philosophy. Lives pose particular problems as they purport to describe events of
the past and can be formulaic and at worst are riddled with standard *topoi*. It is
now agreed that they reflect their author's own environment much more than
they do that of the imagined past. Theological tracts are inherently theoretical
and are not directly descriptive of the context in which they were written. Genre
is, in other words, always an issue.

The sources also present difficulties due to the terminology they use for religious women. There are numerous words for 'nun' in early medieval texts from
Ireland, both in Irish and Latin. In the Latin there are not only *sanctemonialis*,
puella sancta, *famula*, and *filia*, but also the unadorned term *virgo* and the simple
puella. In the Irish one finds not only *caillech*, *noeb-ingen*, *noeb-húag*, but also the un-
embellished terms *óg* and *ingen*. Some pose difficulties due to the breadth of
meaning of the word: for example, *ingen* which in a non-religious context means
simply 'girl' or 'daughter' but in a religious sense means 'nun' or 'religious virgin'. In the Lives even so exalted a saint as Brigit is sometimes addressed '*A ingen*'
by those making supplications to her. In Latin texts the same problem is faced,
with the term *puella* being applied equally to female saints, normal mortal nuns,
junior nuns, and non-religious girls. Another problematic term is *caillech*,
literally 'veiled one'. It derives from *caille*, meaning 'veil', in turn derived from
pallium, the Latin for 'cloak'. *Pallium* was the common term for a woman's veil up
to the seventh century in the West. In Ireland *caillech* was applied to both nuns
and old women on account of the fact that both were veiled. When the reader
of an Irish text comes across the word, determining its sense is not easy, especially in poetry, where there has been much controversy over its interpretation.[28]

---

[28] M. Ní Dhonnchadha, '*Caillech* and Other Terms for Veiled Women in Medieval Irish Texts', *Éigse*
28 (1994–5), 71–96.

'Virgin' (*virgo* or *óg*) also presents uncertainties. The word described at least two sorts of women: those unmarried women who were simply sexually inexperienced, and those women who had taken up the religious life (and who might or might not be physically 'intact'). Fortunately it is only rarely hard to ascertain whether the authors were referring to holy women or to unmarried laywomen. But the early medieval Irish on occasion also used the virginal terms for nuns who had actually had sex with men. Thus the extent of the biological basis of the virgin's status must remain an uncertainty. The virgin represented the highest level of female sanctity, and it was virgins who were female saints. But females who had borne children might also be saints and occasionally got counted as holy virgins on this account; for example, on a list of *noeb-huaga* (holy female virgins) one finds 'Eithne, mother of Columcille'. Eithne is but one of several women saints who gained a place amongst the 'holy female virgins' by giving birth to a holy son.[29] The word *óg*, which is both a noun and an adjective might refer to a virginal old man as being *óg* (virginal).

There are also unusual terms whose meaning is uncertain, for example *mac-caillech*, which literally means 'young nun'. It has a male counterpart, *mac-cleirich*, 'young cleric', which has been translated in some texts as 'novice'. Yet in some of the vernacular laws it would be most logical to think it meant virginal nuns, a type of nun which held a higher status than others in law. There has also been debate over the meaning of *clentella* which appears once in the early penitentials and though it refers to a cleric's 'wife' the connotations remain uncertain: was the woman herself under holy vows, was she still legally a wife, was it permitted for her to have conjugal relations with the cleric, and had they necessarily united before he took orders?

Despite various imponderables, the careful historian can tread a path through the mire of ambiguous terminology. In many cases the context of a passage makes it evident whether the woman in question was a dedicant of God. Indeed if one is aware of the possibility of uncertainty in the language one can discard for use in evidence those passages in which there is no resolution by context, and that policy has been adopted by this author. In some cases it is known that a given woman was a 'religious' of some variety, but her precise status none the less remains opaque through lack of further evidence. In uncertain cases the most sensible policy is to suggest possibilities but to avoid reliance upon speculation.

Finally, a few notes on editorial conventions. Among editors of Old and Middle Irish texts there have been a variety of systems for denoting grammatical changes in word forms. Because the sets of rules vary greatly, almost to the point of being particular to the individual editor, regularization would involve

---

[29] *Comainmnigud Noem Herend so sís* (D. Brosnan, *Archivium Hibernicum, or Irish Historical Records* (Maynooth, 1912), 353–60, at 358).

'correction'. Hence the Irish quotations in this book are presented in the form in which they appear in the edition used. The apparent lack of consistency which results is none the less necessary given the linguistic tradition of the field. Church and river names in the early middle ages very often survive into the present in a modernized form, so it is most common for editors to use the more familiar style; I have followed this practice and extended it, partially translating into English the names of other geographical features for the benefit of the reader unfamiliar with Old and Middle Irish ('Mag Breg' is presented, for example, as the 'Plain of Brega'); the Irish or Hiberno-Latin form is given in parentheses. Personal names are even more problematic in early Ireland. Most saints have two, if not three names: the name at birth normally gives way to a 'name in religion'; the latter, however is often replaced in texts with a diminutive form or another nickname, but the practice is inconsistent. Thus for example, St Carthach was nicknamed Mochuda; some Lives call him by one name, others by the other. Lives written in Latin normally Latinize the formal name. Readers foraying for the first time into the hagiographical texts will do well to have to hand the guide to the Lives in the back of Richard Sharpe's *Saints' Lives*, which cross-references formal Irish, Latin, and nicknames, giving the saints' feast days to clarify even the most troubling identity problems. Where relevant in this study, alternate names are given in the notes and bibliography. Many saints' names live on in modern Ireland, but among scholars a form of Old Irish spelling is normally retained—except for the case of Patrick and Columba, whom to call 'Pátraic' and 'Colum Cille' would be an affectation. This practice has been followed. The reader unfamiliar with rules of pronunciation is unlikely to recognize 'Coemgen' as 'Kevin', but this is probably the most extreme example, and it is hoped that accessibility has not been sacrificed.

PART ONE

The Conversion Period:
The Fifth and Sixth Centuries

Religious Women in the Conversion Period
*c.*AD 400–600

Sometime in the latter half of the fifth century, a British missionary living in pagan Ireland wrote in a letter which survives to this day, 'The sons and daughters of the Irish kings are giving themselves to be monks and virgins of Christ— I cannot count their numbers.' The author was Patrick, latterly the patron saint of Ireland.

To this missionary, this fact was important enough to him to be repeated twice in his memoirs. It is with these two writings, the *Epistola* and the *Confessio*, that the history of Christian female religious in Ireland commences, though we know Patrick was not the first missionary working there. Patrick's proud announcement lets us know that as early as his day the pagan Irish were seeing their young women converts to the new religion doing such things as renouncing marriage, shunning sex, and idealizing poverty. They must have seemed unimaginably peculiar.

The ideal starting-point of a study of Irish religious women, rather than to simply march forward in time from Patrick, would be to consider the native society into which Christianity obtruded: the pagan religion, the status of women, and the roles of female religious professionals. Against such a background we could more fully appreciate the following, Christian period—the powers religious women enjoyed, the strictures they had to follow, the way secular society regarded them, and how their nunneries were treated. This procedure, which has been extremely valuable in the study of early Christianity in the late antique world and in Germanic areas, is well-nigh impossible for Ireland because the sources are so limited. The Irish left no texts from the pre-Christian centuries. Patrick is not only our first Christian writing from Ireland, he is the first person of *any* religion to leave a surviving narrative text. The classical authors, so useful for studying Celtic society elsewhere, are simply absent when it comes to Ireland. No travelling Greek left a first-hand account of his travels, and no Roman armies attempted to extend their empire there. For Gaul and Britain the Romans left colourful accounts telling of the native society, its religion and the women's activities in it, but for Ireland, nothing.

The Irish themselves did leave ogam stones, but these, rather than being records of ancient mysticism or magic as commonly believed, are simply brief memorial notices from the fifth to seventh centuries AD, the period during Christianization. In fact, ogam script itself was only developed in this period, and it was based on the Latin alphabet. The writing of documents commenced in real volume in the seventh century when Irish society was almost wholly Christianized; all the writers were Christian and all were probably churchmen. These authors were unfortunately uninterested in writing the history of their pagan past. They did compose a handful of short annal entries for years pre-dating the fifth century, but mostly they wrote biblical commentary, prayers, hymns. The earliest saints' Lives, dating to the seventh century, contain a few anecdotes purporting to describe certain features of pagan Ireland, but only a few, and a further problem is the fact that these texts were at least partially modelled on non-Irish exemplars. The sagas and tales of native heroes of the pagan past, which do feature accounts of the pagan past, are also problematic, for they too are Christian compositions and their descriptions of the pagan religion are far from contemporary.[1]

For all this, the early medieval Irish portrayals of the its past are still worth noting at the outset of a study of Christian female religious, for at the very least they shed some light on how the early Christian Irish imagined the role of the female in religion in 'the old days'—what they thought the virgins, holy widows and other Christian *professae* had replaced. And, within extremely cautious bounds, we can make very general statements about gender in pre-Christian Irish religion and society.[2] Firstly there is the issue of deities. Our earliest witness is Patrick, and he made only one observation: 'they worship the sun'. All other signs, however, point to a religion with a pantheon of goddesses and gods, made up of extremely localized cults. Irish political units were very small, and other Celtic areas (and Germanic ones, for that matter) seem to have been similarly composed. Few indeed were pan-Celtic god names, and even with these the archaeological record suggests that different areas associated different attributes to them. Many deities were associated with natural features in the landscape; rivers appear to be especially linked to female deities. A link between goddesses and water is seen in also in Celtic Britain and Gaul at such places as Bath and Burgundy's *Fontes Sequanae*. The Irish gave some goddesses war attributes, of which the prime example is the figure of the Morrigan who appears in a range of early medieval Irish writings; in these, in the form of maiden, hag, or

---

[1] The earliest were written down in the 7th or 8th cent., and many as late as the 10th and 11th. For the non-specialist the most accessible translations are in J. Gantz (trans.), *Early Irish Myths and Sagas* (Harmondsworth, 1981), T. Cross and C. Slover (trans.), *Ancient Irish Tales* (London, 1936), and T. Kinsella (trans.), *The Táin* (Oxford, 1979).

[2] For a concise survey of the problems of goddess-worship and gender in religion in Iron-Age Ireland and the British Isles, with references, see R. Hutton, *Pagan Religions of the Ancient British Isles: Their Nature and Legacy* (Oxford, 1991), ch. 6.

scald-crow, she helped or hindered warriors in battle and she made prophecies about the future.[3] Sources from elsewhere suggests war goddesses were a wider Celtic phenomenon, as in the accounts of Boudicca's revolt, in remains around Rennes, and in the iconography of some continental Celtic coins.[4] Irish goddesses in the later Irish texts sometimes appear in triplicities, e.g. the three Brigits, the three goddesses who gave their names to Ireland, and the three Machas; some think Celts generally triplified their goddesses, but this is not a fully accepted theory. A divine couple presiding over fertility, a god-and-goddess pairing, is also found in some Celtic areas: outside Ireland there are Celtic sculptural representations, and in Ireland there are the Middle Irish tales which do suggest something of the sort: a royal candidate caused the Stone of Destiny at Tara to cry out if she accepted him; the female figure Sovereignty mates with a mortal king, though it must be remembered that these stories are from the eleventh century and reflect political preoccupations of that century.[5] Other goddesses were associated with particular wild animals, a phenomenon not particular to goddesses, but two birds, in Ireland at least, have particularly strong associations with the female deities: the crow and the crane.[6]

We can learn virtually nothing about Irish Iron-Age goddesses from sculptural remains. The abstract stone heads and roughly-hewn inscribed monuments which remain cannot be firmly dated; perhaps they were erected in the years before Christianization, but they could be from the fifth to seventh centuries. Given this, it is hard to know what to make of the fact that all are either androgynous or male. Sheela-na-gigs are now dated to the twelfth century Romanesque period, and have been demonstrated to be very Christian creations; it did become a good-luck practice for the people (all of whom were Christian) to touch them, and it is that last fact which made scholars think for a while that they had roots in the pagan era. Unlike many ancient societies, the pre-Christian Irish left very few representations which are identifiably female.

The existence of Irish female deities does not of itself tell us that women were powerful in pagan society. The evidence from Ireland does not support Jean Markale's assertion that there was between the sexes 'an equality in which each could feel comfortable'.[7] In fact, all the evidence which survives shows that Ireland on the eve of Christianization was patriarchal and had been so indefinitely. Patrick when a slave had a male slave-owner, and the other authority figures he

[3] For scholarly treatments of the war goddess in the early middle ages, see M. Herbert, 'Transmutations of an Irish Goddess', in S. Billington and M. Green (eds.), *The Concept of the Goddess* (London, 1996), 141–51; and J. Carey, 'Notes on the Irish War Goddess', *Éigse* 19 (1983), 263–75.

[4] Green, *Celtic Goddesses*, 34–5. See also, importantly, Hutton, *Pagan Religions*, with references.

[5] For an older view see P. MacCana, 'Aspects of the Theme of King and Goddess in Irish Literature', *Études Celtiques* 7 (1955–6), 76–114, 356–413, and *Études Celtiques* 8 (1958–9), 59–65. More recent, and treating the political context, is M. Herbert, 'Goddess and King: the Sacred Marriage in Early Ireland', in L. Fradenburg (ed.), *Women and Sovereignty: Cosmos* 7 (1992), 264–75.

[6] Bird references: Green, *Celtic Goddesses*, 128–30.

[7] Quoted in P. Berresford Ellis, *Celtic Women: Women in Celtic Society and Literature* (London, 1995), 267.

mentions are also male; young women, in contrast, he portrays as being forced into arranged marriages by their fathers. The Irish law tracts (written in the early eighth century and generally understood to represent native Irish society in broad outline) also show men as dominant: women had lower honour prices than men, and were normally unable to speak or act for themselves in business or law unless supervised by a male 'head', such as a father or guardian. A 1936 study showed that women's authority within marriage actually improved during the Christian centuries;[8] at the end of the seventh century the abbot of Iona formulated a statute to protect women (along with priests and children) from being abused and forced to participate in warfare—the abbot claimed the pagans had had this evil custom which he was finally eradicating.[9] In the sagas, desirable women are sometimes sassy and outspoken but never coarse or over-bold; women were not leaders with the exception of Queen Maeve or Medb of Connaught, who went to war against Ulster, but recent scholarship has shown her to be an anti-heroine. In spite of all this, Irish women were not without status. They had legal rights, were entitled to compensation when their honour was damaged, could sue their husband for dishonour, could instigate divorce proceedings, and were known to enter professions.

If we know little about women in pagan Ireland, we know even less about women in Irish pagan religion. The Victorians and Edwardians were more confident than today's scholars, as they felt safe in presuming that a universal neolithic matriarchy underlay the later paganism, and felt equally certain that modern folklore and medieval romances could be used in the project of reconstructing women's role in Celtic paganism. It does seem evident that in pre-Christian Ireland some women had been recognized as 'religious professionals' associated with druids. Druids were the priestly caste whose activities, from what can be inferred, involved magical rites, prophecy, eulogizing, satirizing, judging, blessing, and cursing. They appear to have served in the households of tribal kings and been involved in political matters as advisers to them. In eighth-century law, women in a range of high-status professions were accorded a high level of autonomy and legal competence, and the list included some who performed druid-like activities: female miracle-workers, female war-mediators, female druids, and female poets (the *fili* were a profession derivative of druidry with very high status and quasi-magical powers attributed to them). Females engaging in druidic arts are found in early medieval tales including *The Wooing of Etain* where a queen Fuamnach used magic against her rival, having learnt it

[8] D. Binchy *et al.* (eds.), *Studies in Early Irish Law* (Dublin, 1936), henceforth abbr. *SEIL*. Robin Chapman Stacey has cast doubt on the means by which the chronology was formulated: language which seems earlier may in fact be simply more 'high flown'—with two forms of composition due to the fact that much law was conducted in quasi-ritual, poetic performances. Thus it is safest to say the tracts contain both harsher and more generous versions of the marriage laws.

[9] *Cáin Adomnáin* (K. Meyer (ed. and trans.), *Cáin Adamnáin: An Old Irish Treatise on the Law of Adamnán* (Anecdota Oxoniensa 12; Oxford, 1905)).

from her druid father. That women were associated with magic is seen in the oft-cited prayer in which the petitioner implores the Christian god to save him from the spells of women, smiths, and druids. Most explicitly, the law tracts also refer to female druids (*ban-drui*) and their status and obligations. For all this, the signs suggest that females were the exception in that profession. In the Irish tales, druids are male; in the earliest saints' Lives they are also male; in the Roman sources describing druidism elsewhere (i.e. Britain and the Continent) they are male too, the only exception being from an area in central Europe which had women called *dryades*. In a small-scale society like early Ireland, those few women who did become druids probably did so through family connections.[10] In mythological fragments from the eighth century onwards are scraps on one goddess, Bríg or Brigit, adviser to the great judge Sencha, and on the doings of the Túatha Dé Danánn, a mythological race renowned for their druidic arts. These few bits, all late and none from the pagan era itself, have drawn the attention of a great range of scholars who have speculated on the relationship between the semi-druidical goddess Brigit and the same-named saint.

It has been suggested repeatedly for over a century, to the point of its becoming a folk truth, that Ireland had female druidical colleges in the pagan period. Most Victorian scholars were inclined to believe that all-female druid centres not only existed, but that they were subsequently transformed into nunneries. M. Brenan in his *Ecclesiastical History of Ireland* (1864) asserted plainly that Kildare was a female 'druidic college'.[11] The view's attractiveness remained strong to T. F. O'Rahilly in the 1940s, Jan De Vries in the 1960s, Jean Markale in the 1970s, and Mary Condren in the 1980s.[12] The history of the idea of Kildare as a druidic college or pagan temple has long been on the wane. It did survive in academe into the twentieth century, but diminished as scholars increasingly shied away from a historiography of survivalism.[13] As a result of the plethora of older scholarly claims for the druidical pre-history of Ireland's female monasteries, popular writers consistently describe Kildare in particular as a thinly-Christianized pagan priestess centre—a portrayal particularly popular among neo-pagans and feminists.

The historians who put forward this interpretation did so on several grounds. First there was precedent: Celts did have all-female sanctuaries according to the classical writers Pomponius Mela (describing an island off Brittany) and Strabo (describing an island of priestesses in the Loire).[14] How this proved their existence in pagan Ireland was tenuous. Brenan, for instance, was convinced by the

---

[10] For *dryades*, with full quotes from the sources Vopiscus and Lampridus, see T. Kendrick, *The Druids: A Study in Keltic Prehistory* (London, 1928), 95–7, 219.

[11] J. MacCulloch, *Religion of the Ancient Celts* (Edinburgh, 1911), 42; M. Brenan, *Ecclesiastical History of Ireland* (Dublin, 1864), 28.

[12] T. F. O'Rahilly, *Early Irish History and Mythology* (Dublin, 1946), 128; Condren, *Serpent and Goddess*, 65–78.

[13] MacCana, *Celtic Mythology*, 34.

[14] Pomponius Mela, *Chorog.* book 3, ch. 6; Strabo, *Annals*, book 4, ch. 4.

fact that Brigit's saints' Lives say she had eight companions, making up a party of nine, and this happened to be the same as the number of Celtic priestesses on Pomponius's island. Then there was the matter of the perpetual flame kept at Kildare, assumed to have been a survival from pagan times.[15] It was first and most famously reported by the twelfth-century traveller Gerald of Wales in his topographical account of Ireland. According to him, it was in a special enclosure, tended by a rota of nuns so that it never went out, and men might not enter the enclosure or approach it. Gerald's description of it implies that he thought the perpetual fire to go back to Brigit's own day. Though the Kildare flame will be returned to in a future chapter, some points are relevant here. That the classical writers give no accounts of Celtic priestesses or divineresses elsewhere (and certainly not in Ireland) tending a sacred fire might have given pause but did not, for it was a universal assumption of the 'evolutionists' that any devotion to elements of nature must, perforce, have pagan roots. MacCulloch was one author who found a Celtic parallel in the flame at the temple of Sulis Minerva in Bath, which led to his supposition that Brigit was the same deity as Sul and was the Irish Minerva.[16] Superficial similarities with the Roman vestal cult implied to some that that cult had made its way to Ireland, or that female vestal cults were part of the common Indo-European heritage.[17] The Kildare flame, and the other minor traces which were employed to prove the existence of Irish women's druidical centres, appear much less persuasive to the modern scholar. The classical accounts are now recognized as deeply problematical and quite possibly fictitious, the regional variety among Celtic societies is now appreciated (preventing us from extrapolating the Bath evidence to Kildare), and fires are no longer seen as proof of fire-worship. Most damningly, the late date of the fire's first recorded existence is of supreme importance, for the modern scholar is trained against presuming long-term survivals. The early saints' Lives of Brigit (and the late ones, for that matter) say nothing of a druidic background to the site; in fact, they give the impression that the site itself was insignificant, because Brigit settled in two other places first, and the actual process of setting up the Kildare settlement receives no attention. Turning to archaeological evidence we find that there has never been an excavation at Kildare to search for a pre-Christian layer which might demonstrate settlement there during the late Iron Age. The notion, then, though not disproved, by contemporary standards has no evidence in its support.

Beyond these few points, little can be added on the subject of native Irish religion and the role of women in it. Women could be active in at least some aspects of religion, including some magic and possibly other roles as well, though what these may have been we cannot surmise on the basis of the material we now have.

[15] E. MacNeill, *Celtic Ireland* (Dublin, 1921), 48; O'Rahilly, *Early Irish History*, 128; Brenan, *Ecclesiastical History*, 29; MacCulloch, *Celtic Religions*, 42.

[16] J. MacCulloch, *Celtic and Scandinavian Religion* (London, 1949), 27–8.

[17] e.g. O'Rahilly, *Early Irish History*, esp. 38, 128.

THE EARLIEST CHRISTIANS

It was into Irish pagan society, so scarcely perceptible, that Christianity first took root. The earliest settlements, by all reasoning, must have been on Ireland's Eastern coast. When this took place is not certain, but it probably occurred shortly after the Roman Empire, deeply established in southern and central Britain, converted to Christianity in the earlier fourth century. At that time there was some contact of various sorts between western (Romanized) Britain and eastern Ireland. There were raids, so Ireland's earliest Christians might have been Britons captured by pagan Irishmen and taken back to Ireland. Ireland's first Christians might alternatively have been Christian British emigrants who had moved to Ireland voluntarily to escape the disruptions of late Roman Britain. Or, they might have been Irish people who had converted while visiting Britain. Yet another possibility is that they were a conclave of Irish who had been converted by very early British missionaries who had come across the Irish Sea to them. Whatever their origins, the Christians of Ireland were numerous enough by AD 431 to require their own bishop.[18]

Popular esoteric ideas on the earliest Celtic church are more exciting than this, of course. The insular Celtic world (Scotland, Ireland, and Britain) has since the Enlightenment occasionally claimed a very early church, a church with the antiquity and thus authority of the church of Jerusalem. The British legends of Joseph of Arimathea are the best-known contemporary claim, and hinge on the supposed early arrival and mission of one man (the said Joseph) to Britain shortly after Christ's crucifixion; he allegedly established a church which had none of the faults, variously defined, that by contrast arose in the Roman ecclesiastical institutions. This early-established church is most often cited in the current day by Celtic Christians, who like to mention not only Joseph's thorn tree (still growing in Glastonbury) but also the words placed in the mouth of a sixth-century British literary figure Taliesin by a later author, which appear to support the claim: 'Christ the Word was from the beginning our teacher, and we never lost his teaching. Christianity in Asia was a new thing, but there was never a time when the druids of Britain held not its doctrines.'[19] The esoteric account of early insular Christianity, though attractive, is unsupportable. The earliest Irish Christians in Ireland were not, from what we can tell, semi-druidical in their reverence for nature—nor were they adherents of a church that pre-dated that of the Roman Empire. Their Christianity seems to have come from Wales and Britain, yes, but a Wales and Britain that was Christian because of, and not independently from, the Christianization of the Roman Empire.

---

[18] According to the Gaulish chronicler Prosper of Aquitaine, in this year Pope Celestine sent Bishop Palladius to 'the Irish believing in Christ'.

[19] I. Bradley, *The Celtic Way* (London, n.d.), 6.

THE SOURCES FOR FEMALE RELIGIOUS IN THE FIFTH
AND SIXTH CENTURIES

Mercifully for the historian, Patrick's *Confessio* includes discussions of the conversion of women and the conduct of female converts, so it is possible to speak
of women converts to Christianity as early as the fifth century. There are two
other relevant sources as well, 'The First Synod of St Patrick' (most commonly
and henceforth abbreviated PaI), and the Penitential of Finnian. All three have
many concerns other than women religious, and the relevant parts are frustratingly brief. PaI is a body of church canons which, though attributed to a synod
of Patrick, cannot be presumed to have links with him, nor to have been as early
as the fifth century. The Penitential of Finnian is the earliest datable penitential
tract, authored in the sixth century. From these scraps one can make a few tentative statements about the types of profession which had reached Ireland at
that time, as compared to the varieties of female religious life elsewhere in
Europe. Observations may be made about the ethos surrounding the lifestyles
such female religious were to follow, as the material sheds a few rays of light on
the sources behind the early Irish conception of female sanctity.

Patrick and Women

Patrick's chapter on the conversion of women runs as follows:

Et etiam una benedicta Scotta genetiva nobilis pulcherrima adulta erat, quam ego bap-
tizavi; et post paucos dies una causa venit ad nos, insinuavit nobis responsum accepisse
a nuntio Dei et monuit eam ut esset virgo Christi et ipsa <et> Deo proximaret. Deo gra-
tias, sexta ab hac die optime et avidissime arripuit illud quod etiam omnes virgines Dei
ita hoc faciunt—non sponte patrum earum, sed et persecutiones patiuntur et impropre-
ria falsa a parentibus suis et nihilominus plus augetur numerus . . . praeter viduas et continentes. Set <et illae> maxime laborant quae servitio detinentur; usque ad terrores
et minas assidue perferunt; sed Dominus gratiam dedit multis ex ancillis suis, nam etsi
vetantur tamen fortiter imitantur.[20]

And there was also a blessed lady of native Irish birth and high rank, very beautiful and
grown up, whom I baptized; and a few days later she found some reason to come to us
and indicated that she had received a message from an angel of God, and the angel had
urged her to become a virgin of Christ and to draw near to God. Thanks be to God, six
days later she most commendably and enthusiastically took up that same course that all
virgins of God also do—not with their fathers' consent; no, they endure persecution and
their own parents' unfair reproaches, and yet their number grows larger and larger (and
we do not know the number of our family of faith who have been reborn there), not to

---

[20] *Confessio*, ch. 42. (A. Hood (ed. and trans.), *Patrick: His Writings and Muirchú's Life* (London, 1978),
23–34). On the *Confessio* on mission, see M. Herren, 'Mission and Monasticism in the Confessio of
Patrick', in D. Ó Corráin, L. Breatnach, and K. McCone (eds.), *Saints, Sages and Storytellers: Celtic Studies in
Honour of Professor James Carney* (Maynooth Monographs 2; Maynooth, 1989), 76–85.

mention the widows and the continent. But it is the women kept in slavery who suffer especially; they even have to endure constant threats and terrorization, but the Lord has given grace to many of his handmaidens, for though they are forbidden to do so, they resolutely follow his example.

Patrick encouraged vows of chastity. In doing so he was typical of his age, and typical of the church leaders in the Christian West. The *topos* of the virgin who converts to the ascetic life of Christianity was transmitted across the West in a variety of texts. Jerome and Augustine wrote of young women who struggled with their families to undertake the virginal profession. Both Church Fathers and uncanonical Christian writers saw celibacy as an 'ontological status that raises humans to semi-divine status'.[21] There was a widespread and long-lasting belief that 'those who lead a life of virginal perfection in the present life attain to, or even surpass, the angelic mode of existence'.[22] Ambrose put it that 'in holy virgins we see on earth the life of the angels we lost in paradise'.[23] They looked to the Bible for confirmation of this view and found:

The children of this world marry and are given in marriage: but they that shall be accounted worthy of that world and of the resurrection from the dead shall neither be married nor take wives. Neither can they die any more: for they are equal to the angels and are children of God, being the children of the resurrection.[24]

The female virgins' semi-divine status posed a problem. The Bible was very clear that women by nature were inferior to men. Church Fathers wrestled with the paradox, and in the end came to a set of theological solutions; these emphasized that even as a holy virgin a woman had to obey male authority just as did other women. Some young women wanted to become virgins but their fathers forbade it, they admitted. They should use persuasion rather than disobedience to further their cause.

Patrick, then, is a far cry from patristic orthodoxy on gender when he praises the noble daughters for disobeying their parents in refusing to marry, and when he lauds the female slave for disobeying her owner.[25] How can one understand the encouragement he gives to women to contravene social authority? On one level, he was emphasizing that he converted people from all social classes, that he was carrying on the egalitarian spirit of Christianity. But more than that, he stresses that women, even the most repressed of them, could and should resist

---

[21] E. Clark, 'Introduction to John Chrysostom, "On Virginity, Against Remarriage"', repr. in id., *Ascetic Piety and Women's Faith, Essays on Late Ancient Christianity* (Studies in Women and Religion 20; New York, 1983), 229–55, at 236.

[22] J. Bugge, *Virginitas: An Essay in the History of a Medieval Ideal* (Archives internationales d'histoires des idées, series minor, 17; The Hague, 1975), 30. He later adds, 'Medieval monastic literature is shot through with the idea that the monk in his cloister leads a life that is essentially in anticipation of the angelic life in heaven. The notion prevails from the earliest days of Egyptian monachism down to the twelfth century and beyond' (p. 32).

[23] Ambrose, *De institutione virginis*, ch. 104 (*PL* 16. 319–48).

[24] Luke 20: 34–6. Cf. Matt. 22: 30, Mark 7: 25.   [25] *Confessio*, ch. 42.

male authority if it interfered with their undertaking ascetic Christianity: let the slave woman defy her master, the noblewoman her parents.[26] The solution to Patrick's seeming heresy lies in an examination of his models. He, rather than looking to the Fathers, seems to be looking to a different genre which dealt with the female virgin. The stories of the martyr saints, contained in the Apocryphal Acts and in a range of Christian legends compiled and circulating across the West in the mid-fifth century, were filled with stories of disobedient virgins inspired by a male apostolic missionary. By that time they had popular currency across Europe: they were copied widely and were well-known.[27] The Christian holy women of the Acts resist their pagan male guardians, usually their fathers and fiancés, but sometimes their husbands, to keep their virginity. Most often they go to their death, or are willing to do so, to keep their Christian virginal vow.

Another angle on Patrick's passage on virgins is highlighted by his mention of the slave women. Slave women were, for Patrick, worthy of especial mention; he made a point of saying that women slave converts also pursued the Christian life even in the face of great opposition. He made no mention of male slaves, even though he himself had been one, suggesting that he is here using women to 'think with'. Two reasons for this are possible. Firstly, the *topos* of the female Christian slave was to be found in the apostolic romances, particularly strongly in the martyrdom of Perpetua, for example, and Patrick may have known of the story. Or he may have been making a rhetorical point about the power of his proselytizing. It was a universal belief in late antiquity that the female sex was physically and spiritually as well as socially weaker than the male. Furthermore, due to their biological constitution, as then understood, they were more sexual. Thus when the Christian faith gave women strength generally, and strength to resist sex in particular, it was a way of giving credit to the supernatural power of the new faith. Patrick used the example of the slave woman to show that his missionary activity had brought even the weakest in Irish society to the new such that they—even the slave women—gained both strength of character and strength over their female sexuality. Patrick comes across as a man who wishes to convince his reader that he, like the apostles of the Acts, had virgin martyrs among his followers, and that his missionary powers were great enough to inspire even the powerless to a steadfast adherence to Christ.

[26] The account shares a certain amount of common ground, in this respect, with such virgin martyr accounts as that of Perpetua and Felicitas, a pair of female Roman martyrs who died together—one was a noble lady, and the other her servant woman.

[27] One of the most evident proofs of the widespread dissemination is the abundance of 'reluctant-bride' *topoi* in local saints' legends across the Christian West. Augustine in the fourth century found it necessary to remind his readers that they were non-canonical: *De natura et origine animae*, ch. 1 (as cited in D. Elliott, *Spiritual Marriage: Sexual Abstinence in Medieval Wedlock* (Princeton, 1993), 28). On fifth-century dissemination, E. Junod and J.-D. Kaestli, *L'Histoire des Actes Apocryphes des apôtres du II au IX siècle: le cas des Actes de Jean* (Cahiers de la Revue de théologie et de philosophie 7; Geneva, 1982), 102, which also outlines the evidence for this argument.

WOMEN IN THE MONASTIC VOCATION IN THE FIFTH
AND SIXTH CENTURIES

Patrick's texts leave hints about how the monastic profession generally developed in Ireland, the interpretation of which have been debated for decades.[28] It is a matter relevant to the study of women in the earliest Church, because women are traditionally classed as being part of the monastic movement. In the passage quoted above, Patrick recounts helping a woman become a virgin dedicated to God. Preceding that passage he had written: 'sons and daughters of Irish under-kings are seen to be monks and virgins of Christ' (*filii Scottorum et filiae regulorum monachi et virgines Christi esse videntur*), and later speaks of Irish 'Christian brethren and virgins of Christ and religious women' (*fratribus Christianis et virginibus Christi et mulieribus religiosis*).[29] As indicated earlier, what he proposed, indeed encouraged, for women was a lifestyle absolutely typical of Western Europe in his day. The formal office of the virgin had arisen early and gradually in the Christian Mediterranean. As early as the second century some young women were preserving their virginity as private dedications to God. By the late third century, the consecrated female virgin was already a well-established member of the Christian community, and 'virginity' had already come to mean a permanent and special state, not an ephemeral condition preceding marriage.[30] 'By the late fourth century . . . virginity and widowhood were . . . now "professions" for which a solemn pledge was taken.'[31] By the fifth century it had acquired a complex of connotations: personal sacrifice, apotheosis, spiritual fecundity, and marriage to God.[32] Living arrangements, and the regimen or rules by which the virgin might live, coalesced more slowly than the vow and the dedication, and were subject to much more regional and temporal variation. When Patrick was writing, the critical feature of the holy virgin was her vow of chastity. Sometimes this was accomplished during a veiling ceremony. An early description survives from the fourth century, where Jerome describes a rite in which the virgin, witnessed by her companions, presented herself to her bishop and he, in turn, placed a veil over her with words of commendation. Though we have no way of knowing, it is likely that Patrick in the fifth century was performing a similar, simple ceremony for his virgins.

Scio quod ad imprecationem pontificis flammeum virginalem sanctum operuerit caput; et illud apostolicae vocis insigne celebratum sit: Volo autem vos omnes virginem castam exhibere Christo.[33]

---

[28] D. Dumville, 'The Floruit of St. Patrick—Common and Less Common Ground', in Dumville, *Saint Patrick*, 13–18, at 16.
[29] *Confessio*, chs. 41, 49. *Epistola*, ch. 12 (Hood, 35–8). The *Epistola* adds *enumerare nequeo*.
[30] J. McNamara, 'Muffled Voices: The Lives of Consecrated Women in the Fourth Century', in J. Nichols and L. Shank (eds.), *Distant Echoes: Medieval Religious Women*, i (Kalamazoo, Mich., 1984), 11–31.
[31] Clark, 'Introduction', 233.
[32] For an in-depth study, L. Legrand, *The Biblical Doctrine of Virginity* (London, 1963).
[33] Jerome, *Ep.* 130, ch. 2 (*PL* 22, cols. 1107–24).

I am aware that the bishop has with words of prayer covered her holy head with the virgin's bridal-veil, reciting the while the solemn sentence of the apostle: 'I wish to present
you all as a chaste virgin to Christ.'

It is noteworthy that a woman could become a holy virgin without any formal
consecration, or could become one *before* a formality took place: she could
take a vow alone and without permission, and it would be binding and valid.
Canonically, the virginal dedication was like marriage: it was only necessary for
the participants to consent; there need be no priest or ceremony.[34] Unilateral
vows of virginity were definitely in practice across the West, as the synodal
legislation attests. For much of the West, the woman who took the vow was
bound by her decision in that its manifestation was a change of dress, the most
common means by which she announced her new status to the world. For
example, chapter 4 of the council of Barcelona (599) clarified the rule on rape: if
a man raped a woman who dressed herself as a virgin it was very serious, and not
like raping a lay woman. The same canon also stressed that if the victim chose
to stay with her attacker (suitor, perhaps?) she received a severe penance, i.e. she
could not renounce her identity as a nun. In Spain, at least, the self-dedication
of virgins continued into the seventh century and as late as that their unilateral
adoption of the veil constituted an irrevocable dedication to chastity: a council
of Toledo had spelled out that a woman who had herself taken to wearing the
Christian virgin's costume had no more right to give up the virgin's life than the
one who had been formally consecrated.[35] Innocent, though, in his decretal of
404 did distinguish between the self-dedicated and the ritually consecrated; if a
virgin left her vocation to marry, she could reconcile herself to God through
penance if she were self-dedicated, but if she had been ritually consecrated she
was condemned to permanent excommunication.[36] There were attempts to in-
stitutionalize the process by which one became a virgin, due in no small part to
the problems and confusion. In Spain, for example, in AD 300 a council ruled
that a woman undertaking to become a virgin was required to take a *public* pact
to that effect.[37]

In Ireland, we have some early synodal legislation, but it sheds no light on the
matter, save to say that a virgin's vow was irrevocable—the means by which she
took it are not elucidated. However, it is reasonable to surmise that in Ireland,
as elsewhere, no formal rite was required. Our earliest witness to the veiling of
religious women dates from the earliest Lives of St Brigit, namely the Life by
Cogitosus and the *Vita I*: those two attest to both the self-dedicatory option and

---

[34] R. Metz, 'Le statut de la femme en droit canonique médiéval', *Recueils de la Société Jean Bodin* 12
(1962), 59–113, at 84.

[35] Toledo (638), ch. 6; III Carthage (397), ch. 104 in the *Collectio Hispana*.

[36] Decretal of Innocent, chs. 19–20 (*PL* 67, col. 245).

[37] *Concilium Eliberitanum*, ch. 12 (*PL* 84. 301–10). José Fernandez Caton considers the text to indicate a
public contract, and therefore to represent a new departure from previous commitments to chastity,
which had been private (*Manifestaciones asceticas en la iglesia hispano-romano del siglo IV* (León, 1962), 53).

the consecration ceremony performed by a bishop. In her seventh- or eighth-century *Vita I* an unconsecrated Brigit and female companions were presented to bishop Mel as 'holy virgins (*sanctae virgines*) who wish to take the veil of virginity from you'.[38] In a much later Life Samthann is referred to as *sancta virgo* before her parents decide to let her take the veil.[39]

It would be interesting to know if female child oblation was practised in early Christian Ireland. The fifth- and sixth-century Irish material, scant as it is, gives us no suggestion of it for either sex, but nor can we argue from silence that it was not practised. For other reasons, though, it seems unlikely to have been current at the time. First, most Christians, including virgins, must have lived at home because it was only the sixth century which saw the rise of women's monasteries, and even in the seventh the large ones were few in number. Second, the eighth-century canonical texts prescribe that a girl was eligible for consecration only at the age of marriageability.[40] At that age, however, the penitentials do leave oblation open as a possibility, though they do not address the question directly, for they specify that a daughter was to obey her father.[41] Speculation on these matters is fruitless owing to the lack of evidence on the question of parental involvement in girls' vow-takings in the fifth and sixth centuries.

Because in the early middle ages, particularly by the fifth and sixth centuries, many religious women did not live in organized coenobitic monasteries, the matter of authority over virgins could be problematic. In Gaul and Spain we know that the bishop of the region in which they lived had overseeing responsibilities for them. This relationship was most straightforward when a virgin lived at home. In those situations where there was an organized house of nuns, headed by an abbess, that authority was mediated somewhat. However, the abbess herself was overseen, in theory at least, by the bishop. For Ireland, however, the few surviving texts allow us to say nothing with certainty. Patrick or other early bishops would appear to have been the ultimate if not direct supervisors of fifth-century virgins, from what we can gather from the tone of his text and the deductions from the simple fact that there were few if any other types of

---

[38] *Vita I* of Brigit [Latin], ch. 18 (J. Colgan, *Triadis thaumaturgae acta* (Louvain, 1647), 527–42).

[39] Life of Samthann [Latin], chs. 1–2 (C. Plummer (ed.), *Vitae Sanctorum Hiberniae* (Oxford, 1910), ii. 253–61). Both volumes of Plummer's edition of the Latin Lives henceforth abbreviated *PVSH*.

[40] *Bretha Nemed déidenach*: 'at a proper age a girl should be betrothed to God or Man' (*CIH* 1111–38, at 117.24–5; originally edited by E. Gwynn in *Ériu* 13 (1942), 1–60, at 22). It is also discussed in F. Kelly, *A Guide to Early Irish Law* (Dublin, 1988), 78, 268–9. In the *Senchas Mór*, a gloss states that 'the woman of choice' (*bé togai*), when she comes to the age of choosing for herself, is allowed to decide whether to marry or become a nun (N. Power, 'The Classes of Women Described in the *Senchas Mór*', *SEIL*, 81–108, at 107–8).

[41] Pa2, item 27: *Quid vult pater efficiat virgo, quia capud mulieris vir. Sed quaerenda est a patre voluntas virginis, dum Deus relinquid hominem in manibus consilii sui* (Bieler, *Irish Penitentials*, 184–97). The idea that man is the head of woman is a biblical one, reiterated in Patristic writings, and the sentiments of the statement are quite normal for the time. For example, Isidore of Seville says that woman is made in the image of man, whilst man is made in the image of God, and thus women must naturally submit to man (*Sententiae*, book 1, ch. 11). The passage uses *virgo* in a generic way; the term does not uniquely designate the virgin dedicated to God in this or any later era in Ireland.

senior ecclesiastical figures then. As for the sixth century, when monasteries grew in number and when we may presume with some certainty that the first female communities were established, we can hardly assume that the bishops maintained anything like organized power over virgins. They appear not to have had organized control over anything else whether it be dioceses, missionary activities, or education.[42] We do best to envision virgins in a variety of situations, supervised by any one of a number of type of supervisors, or none. The earliest Lives, which the next chapter covers in great depth, would appear to bear this out: one finds virgins under the authority of senior females, monks, priests, bishops, and under no one's authority but their own. Just as Ireland's overall ecclesiastical situation had an *ad hoc* quality to it during this period, so too must this part of it.

PERMANENCE AND LAPSES

Ireland by the sixth century probably considered irrevocable all dedications to chastity. At the time of the writing of the First Synod of St Patrick in the sixth or seventh century, a virgin who renounced her vow of virginity was to be excommunicated:[43]

Virgo quae voverit Deo permanere casta et postea nubserit carnalem sponsum excommonis sit donec convertatur; si conversa fuerit et dimiserit adulterium penitentiam agat et postea non in una domo nec in una villa habitent.[44]

A virgin who has made a vow to God to remain chaste and afterwards has taken a spouse in the flesh, shall be excommunicated until she changes her ways; if she converts and dismisses the adulterer, she shall do penance; and afterwards they shall not live in the same house or in the same village.

Though not copied directly from a Gallic or Spanish council, this Irish ruling is very much in the general spirit of the Western church, for not only is the basic

---

[42]   There is a long historiographical debate on the extent of episcopal power in the earliest church, but most relevant here, outlining the debate and providing references to earlier work, is C. Etchingham, 'Bishops and the Early Irish Chuch: A Reassessment', *Studia Hibernica* 28 (1994), 35–62.

[43]   The text survives in a unique 9th-cent. copy written at Tours; it is found in the company of other Hiberno-Latin matter in Cambridge, Corpus Christi College, MS 279. Bury and Bieler maintained a 5th-cent. date, Binchy argued for the 7th, and Hughes put forth a case for the mid-6th; in a more recent generation, Richard Sharpe has again dated them to the 7th. Binchy, 'Patrick and His Biographers', 45–9, and, changing to accept a possible 6th-cent. date, 'St Patrick's "First Synod"', *Studia Hibernica* 8 (1968), 49–59; L. Bieler, 'Patrick's Synod: a Revision' in *Mélanges offerts à Mlle Christine Mohrmann* (Utrecht, 1963), 96–102; id., 'Interpretationes Patricianae', *Irish Ecclesiastical Record* 107 (1967), 1–13. For a recent overview of the history of the debate and a view on the problem of dating the text, see D. Dumville, 'St Patrick at his "First Synod"?', in Dumville, *Saint Patrick*, 175–8.

[44]   Pa1, ch. 17 (Bieler, *Irish Penitentials*, 54–9). Kathleen Hughes thought that the absence of a regulation in Pa1 on clerical celibacy meant that conjugal relations were still permitted at the time of the synod. It may simply mean, though, that other issues were more pressing. (K. Hughes, *The Church in Early Irish Society* (London, 1966), 51.)

reaction similar, but also the insistence on separation afterward.[45] It was doubt-less inspired by overseas synods, but is noticeably milder, as normally such a woman had no option of penance. The synod of Mâcon (581–3), was being ex-ceptionally generous when it allowed that an exceptionally remorseful ex-nun could serve a long, hard penance under a bishop.[46] Some continental synods tried to stop the problem from happening in the first place, as did the council of Agde (506), which forbade the veiling of religious women before the age of forty, on the grounds that they were less likely to abandon the vocation.[47] The Irish canonists, though, made no preventative legislation and the penalty is comparatively light: Pa1 excommunicated the woman only until she changed her ways. It insisted upon penance, but did not specify its duration; the phrasing does not suggest that this penance would keep the woman from the altar for as long as, say, seven or ten years. She was excommunicated *until* she changed (*donec convertatur*). Even if this ruling is as late as the seventh century (some have sug-gested that many entries in the text may be from then), the notion itself was def-initely in Britain in the sixth. One finds the sixth-century British churchman Gildas excoriating the ruler Maglocunus for going back on monastic vows, vows which made his subsequent marriage illegal. It may be recalled that Gildas had contact with, and influence on, Finnian and Columbanus in Ireland.[48] Else-where, too, the impermanence issue had been the matter of legislation and rules.

Finnian's Penitential, written either at Moville or at Clonard, is dated firmly to the sixth century. It also deals with the issue of the fallen virgin:

Si mulier maleficio suo partum alicuius perdiderit, dimedium annum cum pane et aqua peniteat per mensura et duobus annis abstineat a vino et a carnibus et sex quadragissi-mas <ieiunet> cum pane et aqua. Si autem genuerit, ut diximus, filium et manifestum

---

[45] e.g. Orleans (541), ch. 29.

[46] In Gaul: Arles (442–506), ch. 52, self-vowed girls who subsequently married were excommunicated and had to undergo penance; Venice (461–91), ch. 4, those vowed to God who married were excommu-nicated on grounds of adultery; Tours (567), ch. 21, holy virgins and widows were excommunicated on grounds of adultery; Mâcon (581–3) ch. 12, a nun who married was normally excommunicated for life; Edict of Clothar (614), ch. 18, marriage was forbidden to girls who had vowed themselves to God. In Spain: Braga (572), ch. 31, the *devota* who married was anathema, receiving absolution only on her deathbed; Barcelona (599), ch. 4, ordered excommunication for girls who dress as virgins but then marry. The four extant early British synods did not address the issue, i.e. Synod of the Grove of Victory, Synod of North Britain, Gildas's Preface on Penance, and Excerpts from a Book of David (all in Bieler, *Irish Penitentials*). Early ecclesiastical councils: Chalcedon (451), ch. 16 (*PL* 67. 174) rules that virgins and monks who marry are to be penalized with full excommunication, though a bishop may show lenience at his discretion. Innocent's Decretal (404), chs. 19–20, offers forgiveness through penance to self-dedicated virgins who marry but denies it to those ritually consecrated (*PL* 67, col. 245). Ancyra (314), ch. 38 follows the church fathers in calling marrying virgins bigamists (*PL* 67. 155); see also Gangra (343), chs. 67–71 (*PL* 67. 158).

[47] Agde (506), ch. 19.

[48] Gildas, *De Excidio Britanniae*, ch. 35 (M. Winterbottom (ed.), *Gildas: The Ruin of Britain and Other Works* (Arthurian Period Series 7; London, 1978), 13–79). For the influence of Gildas on Finnian and Colum-banus, see Sharpe, 'Gildas as a Father of the Church', in M. Lapidge and D. Dumville (eds.), *Gildas: New Approaches* (Studies in Celtic History 5; Woodbridge, 1984), 193–205.

peccatum eius fuerit, vi. annis, sicut iudicatum est de clerico, et in septimo iungatur altario, et tunc dicimus posse renovare coronam et induere vestimentum album debere et virginem nuncupare. Ita clericus qui cecidit eodem modo in septimo anno post laborem penitentie debet accipere clericatus officium sicut ait scriptura: *Septies cadit iustus et resurgit*, id est post <septem> annos penitentie potest iustus vocari qui cecidit et in octavo non obtinebit eum malum, sed de cetero seruet se fortiter ne cadat.[49]

If a woman destroys by magic the child she has conceived of somebody, she shall do penance for half a year with an allowance of bread and water, and abstain for two years from wine and meat and fast for the six forty-day periods with bread and water. But, as we have said, she bears a child and her sin is manifest, six years, as is the judgement in the case of a cleric, and in the seventh year she shall be joined to the altar, and then we say her crown can be restored and she may don a white robe and be pronounced a virgin. So a cleric who has fallen ought likewise to receive the clerical office in the seventh year after the labour of penance, as the Scripture says, 'Seven times a man falleth and riseth', that is, after seven years of penance he who fell can be called just and in the eighth year evil shall not lay hold on him, but for the remainder [of his life] let him preserve himself carefully lest he fall.

The woman regained her status as a virgin (a vowed virgin) by, it seems, a re-enactment of her original consecration; not only was she 'joined to the altar' (the normal phrase signifying the end of penitential status) but she again wore a white robe. The male cleric was permitted, for his part, to receive the clerical office in his seventh year of penance for sin.[50] If a cleric lapsed but once and in secret, he did not lose his office even temporarily, according to chapter 10 of Finnian. The seventh-century Penitential of Cummean simply reiterated Finnian's chapter 21, saying that the penance for a virgin who commits fornication was the same as that of a cleric: a year on bread and water if no child was produced, and seven years of the same if one was.[51] It is worth digressing to comment on the restoration of virginity, the other feature of this entry. The idea of *coronam renovare* baffles the modern imagination, and those patristic authorities who wrote about it considered it an impossibility, though they did speak in general terms about the ability of a lapsed virgin to expiate completely her sin. Finnian, in the latter tradition, is betraying a deep belief in the efficacy of penance. The ruling for the reinstatement of clerics has precedents in the late antique Mediterranean writers Fulgentius, Cassian, and Caesarius of Arles, and it looks very much as though Finnian believed that virgins should be treated in an equivalent manner. This tells us something interesting about how virgins were placed within the church structure, as well as the extraordinary efficacy which the Irish ascribed to acts of penance.

---

[49] Penitential of Finnian, chs. 20–1 (Bieler, *Irish Penitentials*, 74–95). From the context I think it is clear that Finnian has used *mulier* initially to describe the vowed virgin who has lapsed, and that it is not ordinary laywomen who have their virginity restored.
[50] Ibid.   [51] Ch. 2, item 17.

BRITISH MISSIONARIES, IRISH MISSIONARIES: WOMEN SPREADING THE WORD

The ethos apparent in the earliest Irish material, fragmentary as it is, suggests that religious virgins were not held back from participating in missionary activity. There is evidence against an ethos of strict enclosure in Ireland, and there are no extant regulations constraining such activities.[52] And, in the Lives of the seventh century (as well as later ones), female saints and their virgins are portrayed as active in converting the Irish pagans. The earliest known missionaries in Ireland were foreign (mostly British), but in the sixth century we begin to get a swell of reported native Irish missionaries, remembered as saints and portrayed in the Lives as leaders of monks and often attributed with episcopal status. Their obits grace the pages of the early entries of the annals, though sometimes the notices were placed there retrospectively. A number of Irish women are counted among the Irish missionary saints of the early sixth century. The annals of Ulster record (retrospectively) the obits of saints Brigit (AD 524, 526, 528), Ita (AD 570), and Monenna (AD 517), who are reported as the foundresses of the nunneries of Kildare, Killeedy, and Killevy respectively. These women served as evangelists to their own people; whether they modelled themselves on a British inspiration to do so we cannot know, for no record survives of female missionaries going from Britain to Ireland.[53] All early Lives show Irish protagonists as spending much time travelling, spreading the Christian message and founding churches.[54] Together this material gives the strong impression that women were integrally involved in the spread of the new religion.

TYPES OF HOLY WOMEN IN THE FIFTH AND SIXTH CENTURIES

Virgins

In *Confessio*, chapter 42, after relating the tribulations of virgins, Patrick adds: *nihilominus plus augetur numerus . . . praeter viduas et continentes*. Women at various stages of life, he informs us, were undertaking religious professions of virginity, widowhood, and continence within marriage. By expressing it in this way, Patrick was betraying his familiarity with a standard late antique schema of human classification called the 'threefold scale of perfection'. The 'scale of

---

[52] Whereas in Spain and Gaul the restrictions in the legislation are numerous, and the absence of them in Ireland, I would argue, is significant, in light of the other, positive, indications in the extant sources.

[53] Ch. 1 of the 7th-cent. Additamenta to Tírechán mentions two British Christian women, mothers of missionaries, who travel in Ireland; however, they are not described as missionaries themselves (Bieler, *Patrician Texts*, 122–80).

[54] These include Cogitosus' Life of Brigit, the Memoirs of Tírechán, and an anonymous Life of Brigit, often called the *Vita I*.

perfection' had its origins in gnosticism but became widespread in late antique intellectual circles of all religious and philosophical persuasions. Essentially it said that there were three grades of spirituality, and each grade was defined 'by the degree of asexuality it demonstrated'.[55] There were a few variations on the specific membership of the grades, but the essential feature of the top grade was that it consisted of those who were furthest removed from attachment to the world and sexuality. The lowest grade consisted of those closest to, or still engaged in, a sexual life; the middle grade was made up of those in some intermediate state, usually those who had been sexually active but had given it up.[56] Christian thinkers very early on adopted the system as a way of describing the three levels of status available to Christian believers. This they did by bolting it on to Jesus's parable of the sower. In the parable, as it appears in Matthew 13: 18–23 and Mark 4: 3–9, the word of God was seed which fell (respectively) upon hard, thorny, and good earth. Christian converts were all 'good earth' because they accepted the seed (the Word) and nourished it within themselves; but their fruitfulness varied, for some brought forth more, and some less, fruit.[57]

In late antiquity the scale was a 'mainstay of Christian thought on sexual questions'.[58] In the second century Tertullian and Irenaeus had launched the typology by dividing mankind into three categories, 'spirituals', 'psychics', and 'materials'.[59] Cyprian, interpreting the seed parable in the third century, asserted that the hundredfold were martyrs, and the sixtyfold virgins.[60] Thus the three levels of parabled fertility were joined onto the three levels of sexual renunciation among Christians: virgins, widows, and the married. Jerome wrote at length on these three types in his *Adversus Iovinianum*, the purpose of which was to defend the principle that virgins, widows, and the married were ranked in holiness, refuting Jovinian who had dared to suggest they might all be equal in the eyes of the Lord. He also employed it in *Commentarium in Mattheum* and in his *Epistola* 22.[61] Augustine, too, used and defended the hierarchy.[62] For the Fathers, and indeed for most of Western Europe, it was a device by which authors discussed the nature of virginity, and female virginity in particular. This

---

[55] Bugge, *Virginitas*, 67.   [56] Ibid.

[57] 'But he that received the seed upon good ground is he that heareth the word and understandeth and beareth fruit and yieldeth the one and hundredfold, and another sixty, and another thirty' (Matt. 13: 32); 'and some [seed] fell upon good ground and brought forth fruit that grew up and increased and yielded, one thirty, another sixty, and another a hundred . . . And these are they who are sown upon the good ground: they who hear the word and receive it and yield fruit, the one thirty, another sixty, and another a hundred' (Mark 4: 9, 20).

[58] On the threefold schema see M. Bernhards, *Speculum virginum: Geistigkeit und Seelenleben der Frau im Hochmittelalter* (Cologne, 1955).

[59] Irenaeus, *Adversus haereses* bk. I, ch. 7 (*PG* 7. 517–20). Tertullian, *Adversus Valentianos*, chs. 17–18.

[60] Cyprian, *De habitu virginum*, written c.AD 249, ch. 21.

[61] *Adversus Iovinianum*, bk. 1, ch. 3. Jerome also uses it in *Commentarium in Mattheum*, bk. 2, on Matt. 13: 5–8, and throughout *Ep.* 22.

[62] Augustine's three tracts, *De sancta virginitate*, *De bono viduitatis*, and *De bono coniugali* are framed on the schema, and aimed to rebut Jovinian. For use of the parable, see *De sancta virginitate*, ch. 46, and *De bono coniugali*, ch. 8.

was its most common use, though it was on occasion used by writers wishing to stress that even the married are acceptable in God's eyes, in spite of their lack of sexual renunciation.[63] Only in one type of situation were the attributions altered: in times of persecution. In such periods Christian writers placed martyrs among the hundredfold.[64] As the world of late antiquity gave way to that of the early middle ages, the schema remained useful and was widely employed, both in Ireland and in other parts of the West, in its 'normal' form, in which the virgins are the hundredfold, widows the sixtyfold, and the married the thirtyfold. It received its widest circulation, probably, in Jerome's famous *Epistola* 22 to Eustochium on female holy life, where he speaks of virgins having the 'crown' and widows having the 'second degree of chastity'.[65] Patrick, then, knew it and used it, which informs us that he was familiar with patristic ideas on the 'correct' relationship between sexual activity and spiritual ranking, and that his high valuation of chastity was framed by Western ecclesiastical thinking. We might add that it survived in use in Ireland long after Patrick. The sixth-century Penitential of Finnian says of married people:

Si cum bonis operibus expleant matrimonium, id est cum elimosinis et mandatis Dei implendis et vitiis expellendis, et in futuro cum Christo regnabunt cum sanctum Abraham et Isaac et Iacob Iob Noe omnibus sanctis, et tunc accipiant xxxm fructum quem Salvator in evangelio enumerans et coniugiis deputauit.[66]

If with good works they fulfil matrimony, that is, with alms and by fulfilling the commands of God and expelling their faults, and in the life to come they shall reign with Christ, with holy Abraham, Isaac, Jacob, Job, Noah, all the saints; they shall receive the thirtyfold fruit which the saviour in the Gospel, in his account, has set aside for married people.

In the seventh century the 'threefold scale' continued in use. In the Second Synod of Saint Patrick (henceforth Pa2) the chapter entitled *De Tribus Seminibus Evangeliorum* runs:

Centissime episcopi et doctores, quia omnibus omnia sunt; sexagissimum clerici et viduae qui contenentes sunt; xxxmi layci qui fidelis sunt, qui perfecte Trinitatem credunt. His amplius non est in messe Dei. Monachus vero et virginis cum centissimis iungamus.[67]

The hundredfold are the bishops and teachers, for they are all things to all men; the sixtyfold are the clergy and the widows who are continent; the thirtyfold are the layfolk who are faithful, who perfectly believe in the Trinity. Beyond these there is nought in the harvest of the Lord. Monks and virgins we may count with the hundredfold.

---

[63] Two good studies of *virginitas* are Bugge, *Virginitas*, and L. Legrand, *The Biblical Doctrine of Virginity* (London, 1963).

[64] Bugge, *Virginitas*, 67, with patristic references.   [65] Jerome, *Ep.* 130, ch. 15.

[66] Penitential of Finnian, ch. 46.

[67] Pa2, ch. 18. Note: Bieler inserted *et* after *viduae*, to make the line read *clerici et viduae <et> qui contenentes sunt*; given that the thirtyfold are mentioned separately immediately after this, and given the patristic basis of the schema, I disagree with his interpolation.

The seventh-century *Liber Angeli* or 'Book of the Angel' and the eighth-century litany *Ateoch frit* also contain formulations of the 'threefold scale'.[68] Whenever it appears it is a witness to a line of thinking in which the virgin was the equal of the bishop and the monk, was lower than no one, and was higher than everyone else. This principle goes back to Patrick, where it was first expressed on Irish soil, with especial reference to women.

Holy Widows

Patrick proclaimed that among his Christian Irish were widows and *continentes*, sexually continent Christians. This boast cannot be taken at face value to mean that there were professed Christian widows in his day, as he was employing a rhetorical formula when speaking of them. The early penitentials (Finnian's, Columbanus's, and Cummean's) do not mention holy widows at all. Nor do the canons of Pa1 or for that matter the later Pa2. The earliest appearance of a holy widow is in the *Vita I* of Brigit, in which the young saint was said to have been cared for by such a woman, who lived on her own near to Brigit's parents' home. It is clear that vowed widows did exist in Ireland from the seventh century, though there is much about them we cannot know. It is sufficient to simply note here that the very prominent evidence of widows in Gaul and Spain in these early centuries did not translate into an equal prominence in Ireland. Possibly there were holy widows as early as the sixth century, but no textual trace survives; or possibly such widows were included in the legislation under the general heading of *virgines* (as was the case in a few late antique sources); or there may not yet have been in Ireland any formal status accorded to widows dedicating the remainder of their lives in chastity to Christ.

Married Religious Women

The Irish material gives the impression that married laywomen were not a special category in the minds of the authors. They fell in with the general group, 'married laypeople'. The married Christian was, in the threefold grading system, the Christian who rendered the thirtyfold fruit, and reaped the thirtyfold reward for his or her faith. Doctrine, by the fifth century, affirmed that the sexually active Christian, if lawfully married, was entitled to have sex. Married love (and sex) had been partially redeemed primarily by Augustine. Marriage, though not best, was reinforced as good. This reinforcement was necessary partly because the sex act was viewed with such general distaste by those with an ascetic bent. The writers of the penitentials wrestled with the dilemma posed by

---

[68] 'I entreat Thee by all holy virgins . . . I entreat Thee by all penitent widows . . . I entreat Thee by all the folk of lawful marriage . . .' (*Ateoch frit hule noeb-inghena ógha . . . Ateoch frit na huile fhedbai aithrigecha . . . Ateoch frit huile lochta in chomamais dligtheig . . .*) (C. Plummer (ed. and trans.), *Irish Litanies: Text and Translation* (Henry Bradshaw Society 62; London, 1925), 30–45).

married people, and their solutions took the form of restrictions on when, how, and how often they could have sex.[69]

Most of the Christian Irish anti-sex rules for married people centre on those occasions when it was religiously inappropriate: i.e. holy days and religious periods such as Lent. Since sex was considered anti-spiritual in its effect on the human psyche, it was deemed inappropriate, if not ritually unclean, to engage in it at 'holy' times. In addition, a married person's penance for some sins, such as rape, included a prohibition against sexual relations with the spouse.[70]

In Gaul in particular there was a great enthusiasm for promoting the chaste marriage, to the extent that it became something of a standard formula in hagiographic and eulogistic writings. It seems there was no parallel in Ireland. Patrick praised *continentes* but 'continence' in contemporary Western literature could refer to those who followed a regime of limited sexual activity. Neither Irish canonists and penitential authors, nor seventh-century hagiographers, take up the theme of the married couple who, inspired by God, forsake all sexual activity and live as spiritual brother and sister. In Finnian full marital chastity is put forth as a permanent proposition for couples in only two specific situations. The first was in the case of barrenness:

Si qui<s> habuerit uxorem sterilem non debet demittere uxorem suam propter sterilitatem suam, sed ita debet fieri, ambo manere in continentiam suam, et beati sunt si permanserint casti corpore usquequo iudicaverit Deus illis iudicium verum et iustum.[71]

If anyone has a barren wife, he shall not turn away his wife because of her barrenness, but this is what shall be done: they shall both dwell in continence, and blessed they are if they persevere in chastity of body until God pronounces a true and just judgement upon them.

The second type of celibate marriage of which Finnian spoke of is clerical marriage, a distinct topic in itself.

Priests' Wives

Patrick and other missionaries worked to increase the number of priests in the Irish countryside, as a clergy was essential to the survival and growth of Christianity. A man, to be eligible for ordination, did not need to be single at this time in the West, and by all accounts most priests were married. In Ireland as elsewhere there is much we cannot know about the wives of priests. Finnian's

[69] J. Lynch, *Godparents and Kinship in Early Medieval Europe* (Princeton, 1986), 267. See also P. Payer, 'Early Medieval Regulations Concerning Marital Sexual Relations', *Journal of Medieval History* 6 (1980), 353–76.

[70] e.g. Penitential of Finnian, chs. 36, 37.

[71] Ibid., ch. 41. Cf. Penitential of Cummean, ch. 2, item 28 (Bieler, *Irish Penitentials*, 108–35).

Penitential, the earliest Irish witness to the priest's wife, does however indicate that the Irish approach to the wife of the cleric can be placed well within the Western Christian tradition of the day:

Si quis fuerit clericus diaconis uel alicui<us> gradus et laicus ante fuerit <et> cum filiis et filiabus suis et cum clentella habitet et redeat ad carnis desiderium et genuerit filium ex clentella propria sua, ut dicat, sciat se ruina maxima cecidisse et exsurgere debere; non minus peccatum eius est ut esset clericus ex iuventute sua et ita est ut cum puella aliena pecasset, quia post votum suum peccaverunt et postquam consecrati sunt a Deo et tunc votum suum inritum fecerunt. III. annos peniteant cum pane et aqua per mensura et alios .iii. abstineant se a vino et a carne et non peniteant simul sed separantur, et tunc in vii anno iungantur altario et accipiant gradum suum.[72]

If anyone is a cleric of the rank of deacon or of any rank, and if he formerly was a layman, and if he lives with his sons and daughters and with his mate, and if he returns to carnal desire and begets a son with his own mate, as he might say, let him know that he has fallen to the depths of ruin and ought to rise; his sin is not less than it would be if he were a cleric from childhood or he sinned with a strange girl, since they have sinned after their vow and after they were consecrated to God, and then they have made void their vow. They shall do penance for three years on an allowance of bread and water and shall abstain for three years more from wine and meat, and they shall not do penance together, but separately, and then in the seventh year they shall be joined to the altar and shall receive their rank.

The Irish were typical in giving the wife a special name and status. In Gaul there were women called in canonical legislation *presbyterissae* and *episcopae*, and it is generally agreed that the terms refer to the wives of presbyters and bishops respectively.[73] Though these terms appear very infrequently indeed, and it is not appropriate to ascribe to these women clerical powers of the presbyterial and episcopal offices, the fact of the special terminology is worth noting. For in Ireland, too, the name of the priest's wife was an issue in this same period. The language which Finnian applies merits note. It is clear that the *clentella* is the cleric's wife: by eschewing *uxor* or *coniunx* the author shows, I believe, that the post-ordination relationship was not one of normal marriage. But why did the Irish use *clentella*, which seems to be unique in the West as a term for the priest's wife? Bieler convincingly argued that it is a Latinization of the Old Irish *ban-chéle*, female companion or partner.[74] Columbanus adopted Finnian's term, 'correcting' it to *clientela*, but Gildas and the early Irish canonist of Pa1 did not, using *uxor* instead. Kathleen Hughes noted this and used the fact to argue that the canons were, like Gildas's text, earlier than Finnian's Penitential: *uxor* must be earlier than *clentella*, she argued, because the former implied to her full marriage where

[72] Penitential of Finnian, ch. 27.
[73] B. Brennan, '"Episcopae": Bishops' Wives Viewed in Sixth-Century Gaul', *Church History* 54 (1985), 311–23.
[74] Bieler, *Irish Penitentials*, 243–4.

the latter distinguishes against it. Furthermore, she asserted, ascetic standards rose in the sixth century.[75] But an earlier date for the canons is not necessitated by the use of *uxor*. The canonists, if writing in the seventh century, may simply have been relying on Gildas rather than Finnian and Columbanus for their terminology. Another possibility is that Finnian's term for the cleric's wife was not universally adopted: clerical marriage (with full sexual union) certainly did continue. Yet another possibility is that the Irish canonical writers were following the lead of Gaulish and other Western canons which continued to use *uxor* for priests' wives (including chaste ones) with no hesitation whatsoever.[76] Máirín Ní Dhonnchadha has recently argued this point about *clentella* in Finnian, drawing on parallels with the Bigotian Penitential:

Christian thinking promoted the idea of equality of both partners in marriage and, more to the point here, in a celibate union. The terms *uxor* and *coniunx* would have been inappropriate for a 'former wife' in such a union. Since *céle* in the sense of 'wife' is not attested in Old Irish, I suggest that *céle* in the sense of 'fellow, companion' may have funcioned as the source for *clientella*, diminutive of *clienta*.[77]

Turning to the main thrust of Finnian's injunction, the insistence on clerical celibacy fits well into what was happening at the time in Western Christendom generally. Though it is absolutely clear that the vast majority of priests remained married with children right through the early middle ages, at the time Finnian was writing there was, in Gaul and North Africa, a concern among church authorities to try to promote celibacy for the clergy. The fact that Finnian in Ireland was promoting the same thing suggests he may have been in touch with wider Western authorities and, as an ascetic himself, would certainly have endorsed the campaign.

A brief digression will suffice to illustrate the details of this trend. A vow of chastity for clerics was required for the first time in AD 401 at Carthage. A campaign for clerical celibacy was escalating in the West in the sixth century.[78] Gregory of Tours, for example, romantically exalts the chastity of the marriages of the bishop Riticius of Autun and bishop Amator of Auxerre, along with those of other clerics.[79] From about 500 it was a standard idea that a man who was already married could become a priest, but not vice versa, although this was not

---

[75] 'The early [5th-cent.] Irish church certainly required monogamy from all its clergy, but it may have made no serious attempt to impose complete continence. This was the work of the ascetics of the later sixth century' (Hughes, *Church*, 52).

[76] On different grounds from those treated here, recent scholars have been less convinced of an early 6th-cent. date for the canons, with Richard Sharpe (for example) arguing strongly for a 7th-cent. date.

[77] M. Ní Dhonnchadha, '*Caillech* and Other Terms for Veiled Women in Medieval Irish Texts', *Éigse* 28 (1994–5), 71–96, at 87. This article also demonstrates convincingly that *caillech* was a term used for wives in many contexts in texts across several centuries in early medieval Ireland.

[78] Barstow, *Married Priests*, 27–8.

[79] *Liber in Gloria Confessorum*, chs. 74, 77 (B. Krusch (ed.), *MGH, Scriptores rerum Merovingicarum* 1, part 2 (Hanover, 1885), 744–820).

universally (or even widely) adhered to.[80] The married man could be ordained providing he and his wife agreed to live together chastely.[81] In fact, it was forbidden for a cleric to abandon his wife; thus insisted the Apostolic Canons in the fourth century, Leo I in the fifth and Gregory the Great in the sixth. Subsequent canonical collections such as the *Dionysio-Hadriana*, *Hispana*, Regino of Prüm, and Burchard of Worms continued along the same line.[82] Some councils tried to keep a strong hold on *how* the couple lived together by stipulating separate bedrooms, or, failing that, separate beds, and sometimes by threatening degradation or deposition if lapses occurred.[83] It was not until the eleventh-century reforms that priests were told to send their wives away, and then there was extensive resistance.[84]

Finnian's passage hints that the vow of the husband's ordination involved both the man and his wife. In his edition, Bieler changed *post votum suus* to *post votum suum* on account of the plural verb.[85] If he is correct that the original meaning was indeed plural, and I think he is, we can say that in yet another respect Finnian is taking precedents from other areas of the Christian West. In some areas the wife had a part herself in her husband's ordination ceremony: the Council of Orange (AD 441) stipulated that a clerical wife had to take a vow of chastity known as a *conversio*. The Council of Agde (AD 506) stressed the mutuality of marriage and required the wife's consent, insisting that the ordination could take place only if both had been equally changed (*pariter conversi fuerint*); the wife then might receive a special blessing and would thenceforth wear special clothing.[86] It seems most likely that in Finnian's sixth-century Ireland wives at least took a vow of celibacy together with their husbands as part of the ordination rites. This seems even more likely when we consider that in subsequent centuries the priest's living companion was sometimes termed *caillech*—the standard term for 'nun' which literally means 'veiled one'.[87]

If Finnian's entry implies that clerical couples lived in the same household, then so too does a canon in PaI, which insists that a priest make sure his wife veils her head, because it is he who is made responsible for making sure his

---

[80] Conciliar legislation and papal rulings of the 5th and 6th cents. are both numerous and inconsistent on this subject, and thus I here generalize. For a detailed treatment of legislation see C. Frazee, 'The Origins of Clerical Celibacy in the Western Church', *Church History* 41 (1972), 149–67, esp. at 156–7.

[81] But at least two councils insisted on actual separation: Lyons (AD 583), ch. 1. Gerona (AD 517). The Council of Agde also requires the woman to enter a convent.

[82] Elliott, *Spiritual Marriage*, 86–7. The apostolic canons were a popular apocryphal collection from the second half of the 4th cent., which was translated into Latin *c.*500 and included in the *Dionysiana*, which in turn served as a source for the influential Carolingian *Hadriana*.

[83] Auxerre (AD 561–605), ch. 21; Orleans (AD 541), ch. 17; Tours (AD 567), ch. 20.

[84] For example, the Council of Bourges in 1031 required priests to send away their wives, and the ruling aroused a great deal of controversy.

[85] 'My translation of *suus* throughout this passage has been prompted by the plural forms of the verb. It is, then, implied that both husband and wife had to take vows of virginity on the former's ordination.' (*Irish Penitentials*, 244).

[86] Chs. 9, 16. Discussion in Barstow, *Married Priests*, 33.   [87] Ní Dhonnchadha, '*Caillech*'.

wife is properly attired.[88] In addition to making a case for the existence of clerical cohabitation, this canon takes us back to continental rules for priests' wives. The Irish cleric's wife may well have acquired her veil as a sign of her celibate status, just as did her Gallic counterpart described in the Council of Agde.

All the early evidence, sparse as it is, points to a clergy which could live with a spouse married before ordination, and which normally did live with one afterwards. The wives seem to have taken a special vow, held a special title, and worn a distinctive dress or veil. An injunction to chastity was found in Ireland as it was elsewhere in the West in the same period, and whilst we cannot know if chaste cohabitation was widely adhered to, certainly later it was not. In both the canonical aspiration and the long-term ignoring of it, the Irish Church seems very typical of Western Churches generally.

Deaconesses

In the Christian church in Gaul there were women called deaconesses, whose ecclesiastical function was to assist in preparing female converts in their catechism and to assist during their baptismal rites. The canonical legislators during this era were concerned to eradicate the office. There is no evidence that this office ever existed in Ireland: it is not referred to in the contemporary texts discussed above nor in any later sources.

CONCLUSIONS

The new religion must have looked quite odd to the majority of the non-converted population, what with its single male deity, its idealization of chastity, and its dedication to following the religious customs of faraway lands. The position of women in the new religion may not have been profoundly different from what it was in the old one, in that, while the majority of leaders were male and official rites were conducted by men, there were still roles for women and high status was still available to exceptionally gifted females.

As for the possibilities in the new religion itself, from Patrick's own writing it seems clear that even in his own day, with virtually no institutions in place, Irish women could dedicate their virginity to God. In this Ireland was a later reflection of what had been the case earlier in Gaul and still earlier in Egypt and Syria—namely that the female virginal office got going well before coenobitic communities were established for them. As elsewhere, the profession was supposed to be permanent, and penalties were issued for those who lapsed. The

---

[88] Pa1, ch. 6: *Quicumque clericus ab hostiario usque ad sacerdotem sine tunica visus fuerit atque turpitudinem ventris et nuditatem non tegat, et si non more Romano capilli eius tonsi sint, et uxor eius si non velato capite ambulaverit, pariter a laicis contempnentur et ab ecclesia separentur.*

model which informed female asceticism in Ireland probably came from Britain, the source of most of the missionaries, and that church in turn was heavily influenced by Gaul. As the penitentials hinted, though, the builders of the new Irish church adopted foreign ideas about women and holiness more selectively than has hitherto been imagined, opting consistently for a more generous attitude towards the female sex than had the Church Fathers and foreign synods whose deeds and writings were their blueprint.

2

Christian Virgins and their Churches in the Sixth Century: The View from the Seventh

Somehow between Patrick's era and *c*.600 there came into existence places where consecrated women could live in community under an abbess. At the turn of the seventh century, many doubtless still lived in their home environments, as they had in Patrick's day, but many did not. In the course of the fifth and sixth centuries hundreds of churches and monasteries were established, so that by *c*.600 there existed across Ireland small women's 'churches' and a handful of flourishing nunneries. This chapter considers how these places came into existence, looking in particular at the role of those great evangelizing women founders who subsequently were revered as saints, as well as at those male missionaries who helped devout female Christians to establish the small churches at which so many lived. The sources are limited, consisting of archaeological remains and, of written material, only saints' Lives. Nevertheless, a picture emerges, albeit an incomplete one.

SIXTH CENTURY WOMEN'S PLACES IN THE ARCHAEOLOGICAL RECORD

There do exist, and have been excavated, archaeological remains of early, small ecclesiastical sites. In almost all cases, the earliest levels (fifth and sixth centuries) are not churches but cemeteries.[1] It seems that in many places which became churches, the first Christian activity on the site was burial, and later, above the burials, were built first shrines, then churches. Charles Thomas emphasized this, and it has become a well-known model of development for such sites.[2] In

---

[1] 'Excavation can reveal that such churches if built (say) in the late 7th century, are likely to be sited unwittingly and directly above burials of the 6th or even 5th century' (C. Thomas, *Celtic Britain* (London, 1986), 136). Scholars such as Nancy Edwards see the rise of saints' cults as a 7th-cent. phenomenon. (See N. Edwards, *The Archaeology of Early Medieval Ireland* (London, 1990), 105–6, where she also suggests that enclosures and *valla* round ecclesiastical sites arose no earlier than the 7th cent.). Charles Thomas shows in his work on slab shrines and other special graves a conviction that from the earliest days the saint was an instrumental figure in ecclesiastical site development (C. Thomas, *Early Christian Archaeology of North Britain* (Oxford, 1971)).

[2] Thomas, *Celtic Britain*, 136.

this model, the earliest construction is a burial ground, with one of the burials being a 'special grave' identifiable by a surround of some sort. The special grave was subsequently built up by a small shrine (sometimes a slab-shrine) and later by an actual wooden church building; the latter often dug into some of the other early graves, presumably unwittingly.

But where are the 'first-generation' churches and monasteries, those which the hagiography insists were constructed during the lifetime (and under the auspices) of such missionaries as Patrick, Ita, Monenna, Brigit, and a host of other male saints? Quite simply, if they exist they have not been found, or they have not been identified as such. Archaeologists note that near some of the early burial grounds are found residential huts, whose residents have so far remained uncertain. One is forced to wonder, though, if perhaps the dwellers of these primary-level huts were 'saints', i.e. holy people, ascetics, monks, and virgins. Perhaps these are the small places founded by Patrick, Mathona, and their like. Until archaeologists identify these places, there will remain a dichotomy between the archaeological and the historical 'portraits' of this phase of ecclesiastical development.

The success of Thomas's model and the general historical emphasis on the diocesan structure of the early church are two factors which have combined to make archaeologists tend to label early burial grounds as lay or community cemeteries, even when they also feature an oratory and/or dwellings. This is even more the case when a female burial is amongst those in the primary level. Thomas wrote in 1971 in *The Early Christian Archaeology of North Britain*:

At this stage of development, particularly in remoter regions, it is not of course always possible to distinguish at once between an enclosed developed cemetery (with a stone chapel and a handful of little round huts) and a small eremitic monastery. Only a careful excavation could produce the evidence to satisfy a purist as to this fine distinction; the presence or absence of lay persons (women and children) buried in the cemetery.[3]

By presuming that any female remains are, by definition, remains of a member of the laity, Thomas overlooks burials of vowed virgins, holy widows, and ecclesiastical families.[4] Certainly the presence of an infant's remains would suggest that a cemetery served the laity, but the mere presence of a female is not such an indicator.

One particularly interesting case is that of Church Island, off the west coast of Co. Kerry in the southern part of Dingle Bay. It is an ecclesiastic site whose earliest level consists of a residential dwelling, an oratory, and a few graves among which is a female burial.[5] The excavator dated the burials to probably the sixth

---

[3] Thomas, *North Britain*, 68.

[4] On identification problems see also A. Hamlin, 'The Early Irish Church: Problems of Identification', in N. Edwards and A. Lane (eds.), *The Early Church in Wales and the West* (Oxbow Monograph 16; Oxford, 1992), 138–44.

[5] Excavated by Professor M. J. O'Kelly in 1955–6. See M. O'Kelly, 'Church Island near Valencia, Co. Kerry', *PRIA* 59C (1958), 57–136.

century.[6] He and subsequent archaeologists have interpreted this site to be a male hermitage with a cemetery serving a lay community, on the basis that the cemetery includes a female body. Kelly made this assertion in the initial article, and it was followed by Thomas (who describes the place as a first-phase lay cemetery) and even more recently by Nancy Edwards who says 'the fact that a female grave was included amongst the Phase I burials suggests it was a community cemetery'.[7]

This conclusion does not follow, and scholars might do well to reconsider it. The woman in the cemetery at Church Island might not have been a laywoman: as very good textual evidence makes clear, not all sixth-century women were of the laity. She might have been an ascetic and the site at Church Island might have been a small mixed-sex religious community. She might have been a virgin who lived in chastity (or near enough) with several holy men. Alternatively, she might have been a sister or daughter in an ecclesiastical family whose site it was, i.e. a biological family for whom the upkeep of a church was an hereditary profession. Or she might have been a priest's wife, and her husband the priest of the site. Any of these situations could have enabled the woman to be a resident of the Church Island site during her lifetime, and could have made her a candidate to be buried there upon her death.

Until and unless female burials are considered as possibly belonging to religious virgins, clerical wives, or family members of hereditary churches, it is hard to see how the burials of religious women will be recognized. Certainly they were buried somewhere, and a great deal might be learnt about their places, making a valuable contribution to scholarly understanding of fifth- and sixth-century nuns and their lives.

THE WRITTEN SOURCES

If the usable material remains are scanty, so too are the written ones. The saints' Lives of this century are the only substantial, possibly useful, textual source for the foundation of female houses. They pose problems, of course. A hagiographer, even when writing during the lifetime of a saint, did not aim to write history but rather to demonstrate God's power. Moreover, storytelling devices were employed to enhance the plot, and entire episodes were sometimes copied wholesale from extant texts. The structure of saints' Lives was largely formulaic, too, many early medieval ones owing a large debt to Jerome's, Cassian's, and Athanasius's Lives of early Church Fathers. Moreover the political agendas underlying the writing of most Lives meant that the facts were skewed to elevate the status or wealth of the institutions of which the saint was patron—usually the

---

[6] Thomas, *North Britain*, 69.
[7] O'Kelly, 'Church Island', 60; Thomas, *North Britain*, 72; Edwards, *Archaeology*, 117.

redactor's own church. Hagiographical problems intensify when we come to the treatment of women. Men wrote virtually all, if not all, of the texts, so female characters are perceived only through male lenses, and further, they may illustrate principles rather than real women.[8] This problem has already been encountered in Patrick's *Confessio*. It is even more evident in the seventh century that ecclesiastical writers were aware of, and used, Christianity's symbolic language; Hiberno-Latin glosses and exegetical tracts of this century are filled with biblical symbolic metaphors.[9] A woman character in a Life could thus be intended as a metaphor.

In spite of these problems, the counter-arguments remain stronger. Only the hagiography deals with places holy women lived, and the seventh-century Lives were composed less than a century after the events they describe. If it is acknowledged that the texts may well owe a good deal to literary models, it will be productive to attempt to identify the latter, and to consider how the redactors used those earlier archetypes. The problems which drive some away from using hagiography at all can instead be borne in mind as *caveats*.

There are a handful of seventh-century Irish Lives, of which two have been mentioned already. Brigit's Latin Life by Cogitosus was written by a religious resident of the monastery of Kildare in the third quarter of the seventh century. Its purpose was the aggrandizement of Kildare, but there appears to be no special pleading.[10] It is a highly articulate, formally written piece in excellent polished Latin. Whilst scholars such as Bieler have argued for a date close to 650, Richard Sharpe has left the dating more open, to 'not later than 700'.[11] The so-called *Vita I* of Brigit is a long and fascinating Life. Written in much less polished Latin, it appears to have little in common with Cogitosus and is of con-troversial date, being from either the seventh or the eighth century.[12] In recent

---

[8] 'Historians can learn something from the anthropologist's idea that women are "good to think". That is to say, women have diverse, and opposed meanings inscribed upon them, and lend themselves to such multiple interpretations in ways that men do not. It is no coincidence that favourite subjects of Christian monastic spirituality should be the bride/soul/Church of the Song of Songs and the composite image of Mary, virgin-mother, sinner/saved' (Nelson, 'Women and the Word', in Shiels and Wood, *Women in the Church*, 53–78).

[9] M. McNamara, *The Apocrypha in the Irish Church* (Dublin, 1975; repr. with corrections, 1984); E. G. Quin, 'The Irish Glosses', in P. Ní Chatháin and M. Richter (eds.), *Irland und Europa: Die Kirche im Frümittelalter* (Stuttgart, 1984), 210–17; M. Herbert and M. McNamara, *Irish Biblical Apocrypha: Selected Texts in Translation* (Edinburgh, 1989).

[10] L. Bieler, 'The Celtic Hagiographer' in L. Bieler, *Ireland and the Culture of Early Medieval Europe*, ed. R. Sharpe (Variorum Reprints; London, 1987), 251. The Cogitosus Life exists in some 65 primary manuscripts, including two 9th-cent. manuscripts from northern France (Reims Bibl. Mun. MS 296 and Paris BN Lat. 2999) and two northern French copies of the 10th and 11th cents. The standard edition is J. Colgan, *Triadis thaumaturgae acta* (Louvain, 1658), 135–41. A less satisfactory edition is that in *PL* 72. 775–90. An English translation is published by S. Connolly and J.-M. Picard, 'Cogitosus' Life of St Brigit', *JRSAI* 117 (1987), 5–27.

[11] R. Sharpe, '*Vitae S. Brigitae*: The Oldest Texts', *Peritia* 1 (1982), 81–106, at 86.

[12] An early date was proposed by M. Esposito and has been defended by Sharpe; see M. Esposito, 'On the Earliest Latin Life of St. Brigid of Kildare', *PRIA* 30C (1912), 307–26; id., 'On the Early Latin Lives of St. Brigid of Kildare', *Hermathena* 49 (1935), 120–65; and Sharpe, '*Vitae S. Brigidae*'. For arguments

years, the debate has been furthered by Richard Sharpe and Kim McCone.[13] Though there are other points, the dating debate has hinged on how the text treats the relationship between Kildare and Armagh; as the two churches were at odds for much of the seventh century. Brigit's *Vita I* must date either from before the worst of the conflict or after it, not least because Patrick accords to Brigit equal status in a particularly fulsome passage. Sharpe's and Esposito's position is in many ways the more attractive, especially in light of the Latinity, but the case for the eighth century is a strong one. The text survives in about twenty-five Continental manuscripts, and the manuscript tradition goes back to the ninth century, the oldest and most authoritative manuscript being of possibly southern German provenance.

The remaining two Lives are not of Brigit but of Patrick. The Memoirs of Tírechán, found solely in the Book of Armagh, recount the activities, primarily the travels, of Patrick; appended to it are charter-like addenda, traditionally called the Additamenta. Tírechán aimed to build up Armagh's claim to episcopal supremacy, so he attributed to Patrick the foundation of hundreds of churches whose actual origins may have had nothing to do with him.[14] Muirchú's Life of Patrick casts the saint as a powerful magus overcoming the native pagans; no virgins appear in it.[15] It is necessary to mention also an eleventh-century Latin Life of the virgin saint Monenna, foundress of Killevy in south-west Ulster (Ir. Cell Shléibe Cuillin) by one Conchubranus.[16] Mario Esposito claimed that identifiable sections of it are verbatim copies of a seventh-century exemplar which he dated to between AD 600 and 624.[17] The argument is attractive, but insufficiently secure to warrant using the allegedly early chapters except as provisional supplementary evidence.

It is from this handful of material, then, that the historian must assemble a

favouring a later date see F. Ó Briain, 'Brigitana', *ZCP* 36 (1977), 112–37; Bieler, 'The Celtic Hagiographer', 246–53; K. McCone, 'Brigit in the Seventh Century: A Saint With Three Lives?', *Peritia* 1 (1982), 107–45. Also see D. Ó hAodha, 'The Early Lives of St Brigit', *County Kildare Archaeological Society Journal* 15 (1971–6), 397–405. For a brief summary of the debate see R. Sharpe, *Medieval Irish Saints Lives: An Introduction to Vitae Sanctorum Hiberniae* (Oxford, 1991), 15.

[13] Sharpe, '*Vitae S. Brigitae*'; McCone, 'Brigit'. Sean Connolly in his translation of Cogitosus says the *Vita I* is 'almost a century' later than Cogitosus' Life which (following Bieler) he puts at shortly after 650 ('Cogitosus' Life of St Brigit', 5).

[14] There is a discussion of the text in *Kenney*, no. 127, giving it the dates 670 × 700; also discussed in L. Bieler, ed. and trans., *The Patrician Texts in the Book of Armagh* (Scriptores Latini Hiberniae 10: Dublin, 1979), 35–43, with dating on 41–3.

[15] Muirchú, Life of Patrick, ed. and trans. in A. Hood, *Patrick: His Writings and Muirchú's Life* (London, 1978), 61–81; also in Bieler, *Patrician Texts*, 61–121.

[16] Conchubranus' Life is found in a single manuscript, Cotton Cleopatra A.ii, ed. and trans. USMLS, 'The Life of Saint Monenna by Conchubranus', *Seanchas Ard Mhacha*, 9.2 (1979), 250–73; 10.1 (1980–1), 117–41; 10.2 (1982), 426–53. It was also edited by M. Esposito in *PRIA* 28C (1910), 197–251.

[17] 'The Sources of Conchubranus' Life of St Monenna', *English Historical Review* 35 (1920), 71–8; for his dating of the exemplar, see 76. Seventh-cent. passages were identified as those which, *inter alia*, refer to Ireland as *Scotia* rather than *Hibernia*, and partly by identifying as contemporary an appended abbess-list of which the final name was that of an abbess of the early 7th-cent.

picture of how women's communities came into existence in the course of the sixth and very early seventh centuries.

PERIPATETIC FOUNDATION

The first thing to say is that the Lives consistently claim churches and monasteries were founded by peripatetic missionary leaders; they are also consistent in saying that these leaders tended to found numerous places rather than just one. They tend to report that places were established on lands donated for the purpose, normally by local magnates and on lands of their kindred. In Muirchú's Life for example, Patrick travelled extensively requesting land for churches.[18] In Tírechán's memoirs, he travelled almost continuously with brief stops to baptize, ordain, and establish churches.[19] It has been said that the geographical areas in which missionary-founders worked can be roughly deduced from the locations of their alleged foundations, but a problem lies in the fact that a place-name or legend can be generated by later devotion. Moreover, saints were sometimes credited with founding places by mother-churches trying to extend claims over them, a trick seen most clearly in Tírechán.[20] For all this, no one challenges the idea that the basic method of foundation was peripatetic. Exaggerated claims are thought to be just that: exaggerations, not inventions out of whole cloth of a foundation method which had never existed.

It is against this background that the foundations of holy virgins must be seen. In short, the seventh-century Lives depict women's places as being founded in the same way. Within this, one finds both women founding autonomously and men founding places for them. It is to these two means, both involving the ubiquitous topos of saintly wandering, that we now turn.

Women Founding Autonomously

In the seventh-century documents, when women act on their own to found female monasteries, they act very much like the male founder saints. The female saint travels frequently, travels considerable distances, and does so without receiving censure, criticism, or even comment. She preaches to pagans, acquires followers, befriends bishops and other saints, performs miracles, receives land from nobles, and sets up churches. Brigit's long *Vita I* emphasizes strongly the saint's travels, which took her to a variety of churches and to other regions.

[18] Muirchú's Life of Patrick, book 1, chs. 24, 26; book 2, chs. 2, 3, 4.
[19] Tírechán, Memoirs, chs. 9–13, 16, 17, 19–23, 26–8, 30–42, 44–7, 48–51 (Bieler, *Patrician Texts*, 122–80).
[20] A. Firey, 'Cross-Examining the Witness: Recent Research in Celtic Monastic History', *Monastic Studies* 14 (1983), 31–49, at 43. For a study focusing on popular devotion, see P. Ó Riain, 'St. Finnbarr: A Study in a Cult', *Journal of the Cork Historical and Archaeological Society* 82, no. 236 (1977), 63–82.

Cogitosus's Life of Brigit, for example, though it says little on the surrounding context of the saint's miracles, does refer obliquely to Brigit's missionary travels in chapter 22.

In these accounts, the female foundress is not reliant on her immediate family. Indeed, the parents are often seemingly absent. Occasionally the Lives mention parents as being financially supportive to the woman's foundation activity, but when this is so, the family is not given particular praise or credit. Brigit's *Vita I* exemplifies this particularly well. When she was to be consecrated, Brigit travelled on her own initiative to the region of the Uí Néill, taking three girls with her, where she received the veil along with eight other virgins. Immediately after the ceremony the parents of the other girls encouraged her to set up a community:

Tunc et aliae virgines octo acceperunt velamen simul cum sancta Brigita. Et illae virgines cum suis parentibus dixerunt, 'Noli nos relinquere sed mane nobiscum et locum habitandi in his regionibus accipe'. Tunc mansit cum illis sancta Brigita.[21]

Then the other eight virgins accepted the veil as had holy Brigit. And these virgins with their parents said, 'Do not leave us but stay with us and accept a place to live in these parts'. Then saint Brigit stayed with them.

The role of Brigit's own parents in this is nil, and Brigit is portrayed as possessing the authority necessary to accept in her own right the land and other resources offered by the virgins' parents. Indeed the role of the parental donors is somewhat perfunctory, as though once the requisite resources were gained, the saint could herself establish the community. In short, the important person here is Brigit, not the parents. A similar tone is found in the Cogitosus Life, which recounts how Brigit supposedly founded Kildare. The monastery was founded out of public demand, it says, with people of both sexes pledging their vows to Brigit.[22] Thus a seventh-century churchman imagined that in the century preceding him a holy women, a consecrated nun, could have developed a national following and built herself a large monastery for followers of both sexes. He relates this without explaining to his readers how a nun could have acquired the land or the temporal authority to do so. Consecrated women mentioned in passing are also attributed with the ability to found places on their

---

[21] Ch. 18. The 9th-cent. Life of Brigit, *Bethu Brigte*, gives another account of her first place and does mention parents; in ch. 16, Brigit's father, finally persuaded to let her take the veil, says 'Take the veil, then, my daughter, for this is what you desire. Distribute this holding to God and man' (*Gaib-siu tra calle, ammo ingen, ar is ed t'accobar. Fodail dano in trebad-sa do Dia 7 duiniu*). Some time later she did so, but had to travel with two other maidens through unsafe territory to get to the bishop who would perform the rite. Ch. 20 relates that *post haec obtuilit pleps locum ubi nomine Ached hI in Saltu Avis. Illic aliquantulum temporis manens, tres viros perigrinos ibi manere cogebat 7 obtulit eis locum* (D. Ó hAodha, *Bethu Brigte* (Dublin, 1978)).

[22] Cogitosus's Preface to his Life of Brigit, ch. 4: *Haec ergo egregiis crescens virtutibus, et per famam bonarum rerum ad eam de omnibus provinciis Hiberniae innumerabiles populi de utroque sexu confluentes, vota sibi voventes, voluntarie suum monasterium, caput pene omnium Hiberniensium Ecclesiarum, et culmen praecellens omnia monasteria Scotorum, cuius parochia per totam Hibernensem terram diffusa, a mari usque ad mare extensa est, in campestribus campi Liffeim, supra fundamentum fidei firmum construxit.*

own initiative. A passage in chapter 46 of Brigit's *Vita I* tells of an unnamed *virgo Dei* who travelled out of her own region to raise funds to buy land for a foundation. The author thus imagined it a plausible story to tell of a non-famous virgin travelling round Ireland attempting to raise funds and ultimately gaining sufficient donations to purchase property. In Tírechán's Memoirs of Patrick we meet another female foundress, the virgin Mathona, who set off on her own to found her own monastery after serving time with Patrick and his follower Benignus. In this case, Tírechán credits the nun with the initiative for founding a church and, as is so common, the origin of the resources required is not mentioned.

Et venit apud se filia felix in perigrinationem nomine Mathona soror Benigni successoris Patricii, quae tenuit pallium apud Patricium et Rodanum; monacha fuit illis et exiit per montem filiorum Ailello et plantauit aeclessiam liberam hi Tamnuch, at honorata fuerat a Deo et hominibus.[23]

And a blessed maiden came to him in pilgrimage, named Mathona, sister of Benignus the successor of Patrick, and took the veil from Patrick and Rodanus; she was a nun to them and she went out across the mountain of the sons of Ailill and established a free church at Tawnagh, and she was honoured by God and men.

In the problematic Life of Monenna, a reading of the chapters identified by Esposito as being from the seventh century serves to add examples rather than counter-indications. Saint Monenna was highly peripatetic, and her first foundation was allegedly set up outside her region and by her own efforts, after several periods of study at the feet of holy bishops.[24]

Igitur Sancta Monenna veniens ad monticulum Focharde primum ibi habitare cepit. Congregatis simul multis Christi virginibus, habuit ut refertur in illo tempore secum centum quinquaginta.

So saint Monenna, coming to the hill of Fochard at first began to live there. Many virgins of Christ gathered together at one time, as is reported, one hundred and fifty of them.

Monenna however, after a time in this place, returned to Fochard to live there: *Sicque factum est ut reportata ad terram sibi a Domina destinatam in parte aquilonis Hibernie sitam ubi sancta Monenna . . . cognationem propriam quasi ad oves domus Isreal que perierant.*[25] Later Lives continue this kind of portrayal of foundation: the Salmanticensis Life of Darerca, the twelfth-century Life of Monenna, the Life of Samthann, the Life of Ita, and the ninth-century Life of Brigit (all of which will be encountered later) follow the pattern established here.

---

[23] Tírechán, Memoirs, ch. 24.

[24] Conchubranus, Life of Monenna, book 1, ch. 6. See also foundation at Murthemene, book 2, ch. 1, refoundation at another site, book 2, ch. 6, and Brignam's foundation, book 3, ch. 7.

[25] 'Thus it happened that she was brought back to the land destined for her by the Lord, the land situated in the northern part of Ireland, where saint Monenna came to her own kin, to the lost sheep of the house of Israel' (book 2, ch. 6). Similarly she sent her pupil Brignam back to her homeland to set up a monastery there (book 3, ch. 6).

Men Founding for Women

Many women's foundations in the fifth and sixth centuries appear to have commenced through the assistance of a male missionary saint. This method, too,
was characterized by travel. Male assistance in setting up women's places is
hardly surprising, for the laws tell us that Irish women did have less access to kin
land, and a lower legal position than men in native Irish society, and could not
achieve clerical status in the Church. Tírechán shows Patrick and other male
saints founding places for the women they had consecrated, placing them in
churches and leaving them behind to run them. For example, he says Patrick set
up at Fochloth a place for two unnamed nuns he had consecrated, then left it to
them to lead it. Similarly, he placed a holy maiden (*sancta filia*) in a church in Ard
Senlis, left the sisters of Bishop Failart in a large church, and placed two maidens in a church in Temenrige.[26] He also consecrated the virgin St Adrochta,
whose place was to become the women's monastery of Killaracht near Lough
Key in Co. Sligo (Ir. Cell Adrochta); although the claim that Patrick founded it
is not explicit, his patronage at least is implied by the assertion that he left with
her one of his own chalices and patens.[27]

Men's role in establishing women's settlements is greater in Tírechán than in
two Lives of Brigit, but such a difference might be explained by the respective
sexes of the saints and the documents' aim to aggrandize their own patron.
Tírechán described Patrick as founding many places that he doubtless did not.
Likewise he may not have placed many nuns in charge of churches. The Memoirs do, however, demonstrate that in seventh-century Ireland there were places
which were thought to have been headed by women in the fifth and sixth, and
that one of Ireland's most powerful male saints had endorsed this. The text also
strongly suggests that in the seventh century there were numerous church sites at
which the revered (dead) saint was a female, a woman who was thought to have
been the place's original leader or foundress. At such sites one can imagine a central grave shrine or other relics which constituted a focal centre of local devotion.

Later Lives from the Middle Irish period continued to mention male saints
founding monasteries and churches for women they had consecrated, often for
their mothers and blood-sisters who were nuns: indeed from the seventh century onward Irish hagiography asserts that men helped set up churches and
nunneries which were then headed by women.

HAGIOGRAPHIC MODELS FOR WOMEN'S COMMUNITIES AND THEIR FOUNDRESS SAINTS

The seventh-century hagiography claims to describe not only the foundation of
women's communities but life within them. In this material, the amount of

---

[26] Chs. 27, 35, 47.   [27] Chs. 11, 31, 43.

description is uneven. The Life of Brigit by Cogitosus, for example, gives very little on the life of Brigit's nuns, and Tírechán, concentrating as he does on Patrick's foundation activities, also says little about the nature of nuns' communities. By far the richest early source on this subject is Brigit's *Vita I*. It is the only text indubitably pre-dating the ninth century that gives extensive incidental information on the female community; it concentrates on the activities of Brigit in the world, and frequently mentions the band of religious who made up the saint's *familia*. In it is described a loose group of dedicated people engaged mainly in strengthening Christianity in a country still largely pagan. The group, as portrayed in this Life, was made up of the saint, her dedicated virgins, a charioteer, and sundry foster-daughters and girl students. Bishops and clerics were sent for, to come to the virgins and preach the word of God and perform the eucharist.[28] At some point the community did gain a permanent resident priest and then a bishop.[29] Life in the nunnery as described by the *Vita I*, and by Cogitosus for that matter, doubtless resembles more the time of writing than this early phase, but the basic idea is unlikely to be far wrong in broad outline.

The amount of travel is extraordinary, as was mentioned at the opening of this chapter. It is relevant because the hagiography gives the impression that being a holy Christian woman in these early days consisted essentially of leading an itinerant Life, studying under male saints, and then founding one or more monasteries. Altogether in the *Vita I* Brigit moved no less eighteen times, and covered all five provinces. Some of her stays were at existing churches, as in chapter 56 when she received pilgrims at 'a certain church'—*cum autem esset Brigita in aecclesia quadam et cum sedisset iuxta ianuam loci illius* . . . Other examples include mention of 'the church where she was' (*aeclesia in qua illa erat*);[30] and the phrases such as 'after this holy Brigit came Mag Breg'; 'when Brigit lived in another place;[31] elsewhere the reader is informed 'after this Brigit came with her maidens to Campum Clioch and she lived there in some place' (*post haec venit sancta Brigita cum puellis suis in campum Clioch et habitavit ibi in quodam loco*).[32] The hagiographer did clearly consider that holy women other than Brigit could have churches of their own, as in chapter 44 where Brigit visited St Lassair at her church.[33]

Tírechán's scanty coverage of female monasticism is nevertheless consistent with the portrait found in the *Vita I*.[34] According to the memoirs, holy virgins lived at churches, groups of virgins seem to have been small and *ad hoc*, men and women might be resident at churches together, travel was permitted to women as it was to men, and it seemed to have a missionary purpose; and finally, women

---

[28] e.g. chs. 63, 82.

[29] He is found as a member of the community also in ch. 28 of Cogitosus's Life.

[30] Ch. 25.   [31] Ch. 64.   [32] Ch. 75.

[33] *Eodem tempore hospitabatur sancta Brigita in aeclesia Sanctae Lasrae.* Lassar donated (*obtulit*) herself and her place to Brigit in this anecdote.

[34] See esp. Tírechán, Memoirs, chs. 24, 27, 30, 31, 35, 37, 43, 47, and its Additamenta, chs. 8, 9.

were perfectly capable of being the spiritual leaders of foundations which the author calls churches, *aeclesiae*.

WOMEN AS APOSTLES: THE MODELS

The elements of travel and of female foundation in Irish hagiography must be noted particularly because patristic texts often discouraged female travel. The question then arises: were the female apostolic activities and travels modelled on the known models, or other exemplars, or were they Irish innovations? Irish Lives were not formed out of whole cloth, though they are less formulaic than many written elsewhere. The texts circulating at this time which influenced Western European hagiographers included Sulpicius Severus's hagiography of Martin (the Life and Dialogues), Cassian's *Institutes* and *Conferences*, Athanasius's Life of St Antony, and Jerome's Lives of saints Hilarion, Paulus, and Malchus. These were known in Ireland by the seventh century. In Muirchú, for example, one finds a distinctive metaphor traceable to Cassian.[35]

No thorough analysis of Cogitosus's or the *Vita I*'s sources has ever appeared in print, but some observations should narrow the field in some respects. The cures effected by Brigit in these two early Lives are comparable to those in the above-mentioned sources, and may be borrowed from them either directly or indirectly. The Life of Antony is a likely source for some episodes, but not for Brigit's travel or for female evangelizing: in it sainthood is non-peripatetic, and Antony committed his sister to a convent. The life of Malchus offers an interesting parallel in that he spent some time as a slave (as was Brigit's mother) tending sheep (as did Brigit). Like Brigit Malchus was forced to marry, but unlike Brigit he consented to do so. Only a distant similarity may be seen in that Malchus and his wife supported each other's chastity and assisted each other in finding a band of Christians to join, much as Brigit and male Christians had cordial, mutually supportive relations. Hilarion's Life offers likewise tenuous similarities: both Hilarion and Brigit were born of Christian parents but were 'natural Christians' in childhood; and the multitudes flocking to the male saint's establishment could just about be seen to resemble the crowds flocking to Kildare in Cogitosus's preface. Paulus's Life tells of the saint travelling across the desert, but his aim was not to convert or found churches and nothing is made of adventures on the way; he had a sister but almost nothing is said of her.

In Sulpicius's Life of Martin the resemblances to Brigit's legends are equally scant, even though Martin has rightly been identified as an important influence on Irish hagiography. Sulpicius offers a cloak story for Martin, and so did Brigit's hagiographers give one to her: he divided his in two, she hung hers on a sunbeam. But Martin was not a founder, really, and any wandering he may

---

[35] Bieler, 'The Celtic Hagiographer', 244–5.

have done is not prominent in the text of the Life. It must be wondered why, if Martin was a model for Brigit, the author did not make her a missionary like him. The anecdotes of her interactions with pagans are strikingly different from those of Sulpicius's Martin. The Dialogues too have some possible contributions to Brigidine material: locked doors open magically in the palaces of hostile kings, both saints have converse with heavenly beings whilst in their cells, dropped vessels do not break, church buildings identify sinners in the saint's presence, food miracles are performed, adversarial kings are confronted. As for travel, the Dialogues have Martin travelling to the Holy Land, tales are recounted of holy wandering anchorites in the desert, and Martin himself visits monasteries in a peripatetic manner resembling what we find in the Brigidine Lives and in Tírechán. But on the sexes, the portrayal is mixed. Martin has female devotees in the village of Claudiomagnus, but he firmly insisted that a man living the eremitical life should send his wife to a nunnery, and another part of the text cites Jerome in advocating strict separation of virgins from monks and clerics. Martin also praised a virgin who was so strict about shielding herself from the male gaze that she turned even him from her door. In the Dialogues Martin's travels, like those of Brigit, do involve preaching to pagans, interacting with authorities, and spreading the teaching of the holy life, but there are no mixed-sex prayer meetings or extended visits, and there is no account of friendship between the saint and any women.

Cassian, an acknowledged important source for the regulation of the religious life in Ireland, may also have contributed to the Brigidine material, but he is far from providing a model. A short tale of shoes brought into the monastery by a newcomer in book 4 of the Institutes looks very much like one in Brigit's *Vita I*. On travelling around Cassian is distinctly disapproving, and there is no hint of an idea of founding churches through wandering. On male–female contact, he lectures at several points against monks and clerics subjecting themselves to sexual temptation; for all that, he is careful not to advocate the shunning of the opposite sex: in the tale of Abbot Paul the abbot did so and was punished by God with complete paralysis, to be nursed 'in all things' by holy virgins.[36] One suspects that Cassian's main contribution to the Irish church's attitude on gender was his message of monastic self-examination rather than condemnation of the opposite sex, and his failure to advocate the enclosure of religious women.

To sum up, the Irish did not get their blueprint of female sainthood from any of the popular models just described. There is simply too much apostolic travel, missionary work, leadership, and inter-sex collaboration. It was instead another genre that provided the model for that distinctive combination of activities which characterize Irish female saintly behaviour. The Apocryphal Acts and martyr stories showed holy Christian women as wandering and travelling in

---

[36] Institutes, book 7, ch. 26 (*PL* 49. 54–476).

their religious life; as learning their religion from a peripatetic male apostle; as being themselves teachers and witnesses for a wider pagan community; and as melodramatically avoiding the marriage bed. These texts, which purported to relate the acts of the apostles but whose contents failed to be deemed canonical and thus officially approved by church authorities, were in wide circulation across the West from even before Patrick's era. As was seen in the last chapter, they influenced him. They travelled as individual tracts and even more piecemeal too, as individual stories in a range of manuscripts, including books of religious miscellanea and *florilegia*. The stories have long been known to have been in Ireland by the seventh century if not before: their traces are found in male Lives as much as women's ones, including Muirchú and Tírechán; the fact that they were about apostles spreading Christianity into a pagan world made them attractive to the Irish, who viewed their missionaries in apostolic terms.[37]

Devout Christian women travelling and wandering are central themes in many of them, most prominently in the Acts of Paul and Thecla, the Acts of Peter, the Martyrdom of Agapetae and her Companions, and the Romance of Xanthippe and Polyxena; it is an attendant feature in the Acts of John and the Acts of Peter. Related to this is the stock 'plot feature' of the woman learning her religious vocation from a male apostle who was also a dear friend, a feature in stories of Brigit, Monenna, and in fact all the Irish foundress saints, whether written in the seventh century or the twelfth. In the apocrypha, Maximilla learned from Andrew in his Acts, Drusiana from John in his, and Perpetua from Paul in Perpetua's Story. Xanthippe, like Brigit, visited a number of apostles, Paul, Philip, and Andrew. Thomas's and Peter's Acts both report that they were visited by numerous women and virgins for guidance and teaching. Thecla was renowned for her devotion to Paul, and Polyxena also followed him for some time.

The Apocryphal Acts created and popularized the *topoi* of 'the reluctant bride' and the 'reluctant wife'—in which fianceés and wives shun the marriage-bed with extreme and sometimes histrionic gestures. Holy martyrs and female paragons of this sort are reported in the Acts of Andrew, of John, of Thomas, of Paul and Thecla, of Peter, and in the Romance of Xanthippe and Polyxena. In Ireland Brigit is the most famous such bride, for her two earliest Lives (Cogitosus and the *Vita I*) relate that she destroyed one of her eyes to put off a suitor. The Acts promote an image of an independent chaste woman saint in another way as well, as an inspiration to conversion to the as yet unconverted pagans. Those who were martyred inspired conversion through their brave deaths; but a few others, such as Thecla, were evangelizers: Paul told Thecla to go and teach the word of God, which she did, and by the time she died naturally in old age, she had enlightened many with the Christian message. Thecla is in this way (as well

[37] On the Continent, interestingly, these same models were also present but did not lead to peripatetic female saints in the Lives of the Merovingians and Carolingians (J. Smith, 'The Problem of Female Sanctity in Carolingian Europe, *c.*780–920', *Past and Present* 146 (1995), 1–37).

as others) an apparently direct exemplar for Brigit's two earliest hagiographers, who in turn set the tone for later Lives of her. The debt to the apocrypha and romances continues through later Lives as well.

The argument in favour of an Irish debt to this genre lies mostly in similarities of structure, admittedly. At a few points, though, it becomes even more close. Here is how St Monenna met Patrick, in her anonymous Life which was written in the twelfth century, but possibly followed closely a seventh-century exemplar:

Some years after her birth it came to pass that saint Patrick arrived in the province in which she had been born. There, when a number of people had been brought to him through the good offices of devout men, to be washed at the baptismal font and confirmed in the faith by the imposition of hands, one of the gathering crowd was saint Darerca [i.e. Monenna], who came and made herself known to the bishop. The saintly pontiff was filled with the holy spirit: he observed her closely and understood her fervent desire to serve God.[38]

Readers familiar with the Apocryphal Acts and romances will recognize this distinctive plot feature, in which a good maiden hears the travelling holy man when he comes to speak to a crowd in her community, and subsequently becomes personally devoted to him. Two examples suffice:

The blessed Paul, the preacher and teacher and illuminator of the world, left Rome and came even into Spain . . . The report of his presence ran through the whole city and the country round about, for some of that city having been at Rome had seen the signs and wonders. [Xanthippe went to him and] the great Paul straightway taking her hand, went into the house of Philotheus, and baptized her.[39]

In the opening chapters of the Acts of Paul and Thecla we learn that Paul was speaking in the midst of a crowded church and the woman Thecla nearby—

saw many women going in beside Paul [and] she also had an eager desire to be deemed worthy to stand in the presence of Paul, and to hear the word of Christ . . . And Thecla by night having taken off her bracelets, gave them to the gatekeeper; and the door having been opened to her, she went . . . in beside Paul, and, sitting at his feet, she heard the great things of God.[40]

Other Acts and romances also open with this plot feature: The Acts of Peter, the Acts of Thomas, the Acts of Andrew and Maximilla, and the Acts of John and Drusiana. The Irish female saints' Lives (both early and late) have other distinctive details in common with the romances, too. They feature anecdotes in which prison doors miraculously open, as they do in the Acts of Andrew. Brigit has an eye disfigurement, as does the virgin martyr Perpetua. Beams which are the wrong length miraculously change length to fit perfectly, as they do in the Pseudo-Matthew Gospel. Food multiplies, as it does in the Gospels of Thomas

---

[38] Latin Life of Darerca, ch. 1.   [39] Acts of Xanthippe, Polyxena, and Rebecca, chs. 5–15.
[40] Acts of Paul and Thecla, ch. 4.

and Pseudo-Matthew. The *Vita I* of Brigit recounts the misadventures of some monks whilst sailing to Rome, a story with striking similarities to the story in the Acts, in which the apostles attempted to sail to Rome.

None of this explains why the Irish were more attracted to the kind of Christian heroine found in the Acts than found in Jerome or Caesarius. The answer may lie in the actual situation in Ireland at the time when the events in these Lives allegedly took place. They are set in Ireland's own apostolic era, when it was of central importance for Christians to convert and baptize pagans, increase the number of churches, and enlarge the community of clergy and dedicated religious. Force of circumstance may have made Irish Christian authorities frame important females as a valuable resource in conversion and missionary activity rather than encouraging them to the patristic ideal of enclosed perfection. This pattern of activity must have been effective in gaining converts, which indirectly reflects on the *mores* of Irish pagan society: evidently it was deemed by the architects of the new church there that the pagans would be more impressed with Christianity by seeing its women active than by knowing they were enclosed behind walls.

THE PROBLEMATIC CASE OF SAINT BRIGIT AND KILDARE

The above discussion places the imagery surrounding the foundress of Kildare, saint Brigit, in the wider Christian tradition of the Apocryphal Acts. It is much more common for historians to frame her in native Irish terms, as a Christianized goddess, and her church, Kildare, is even seen by some as owing features to this background. Among non-specialists her pagan origins are expressed with even more certainty. To understand why the equation has been so frequently made between the pagan goddess and Christian saint, and why Kildare has looked to so many like a thinly-disguised temple of priestesses, requires a consideration of the various pieces of evidence in turn. A full exposition of the evidence and its interpretations could fill a monograph in itself, so it is here merely summarized.

As was mentioned in the previous chapter, we know very little about the pagan goddess of the name Bríg or Brigit in Ireland, owing to a lack of evidence, written and archaeological. Because no one has ever dug underneath Kildare to see if there is a pre-Christian temple site, even the presumed cult centre, if there was one, is not known to exist. The earliest evidence for the goddess is in the Irish vernacular law tracts, written down *c*.700, which contain a few little legal stories in which Bríg is the daughter, wife, or mother of the legendary judge Sencha of the distant Irish past. According to these she sat by Sencha's side as he made pronouncements on law, and on occasion intervened to correct or contradict him.[41] Nowhere in this material is she equated with the saint of the

---

[41] *Di Chetharslicht Athgabála* ['On the Four Divisions of Distraint'], *CIH* 352.25–422.36; 1438.36–1465.27; 1723.11–1755.16; also, with trans., *ALI* i. 65–305; ii. 3–118. *Din Techtugad* ['On Legal Entry'], *CIH* 205.22–213.37; also, with trans., *ALI* iv. 3–33.

almost-identical name. Then in the tenth century the compilers of *Sanas Cormaic* (Cormac's Glossary) included an entry on Brigit calling her the goddess worshipped by poets, adding that she had two sisters of the same name who were patronesses of smithcraft and healing respectively, and that her name was derived from *bri-sagit*, 'fiery arrow'.[42] It is uncertain whether they equated the deity Brigit with the saint Brigit, but it is impossible that the saint was unknown to them; for some reason they chose not to make explicit their understanding of the relationship between the two. It is with *Sanas Cormaic* that we find the first explicit link made between this goddess and the element of fire, in the word *bri*. McCone has convincingly shown that the three arts it claims Brigit supervised—healing, smithcraft, and poetry—were in early Ireland all associated with fire.[43]

The authors of the saints' Lives of Brigit seem to have been aware of the same-named goddess, though they never say so explicitly: all of her Lives give Brigit a druid father figure, so she is made into a member of the druid class, the same class as poets and judges. The hagiographers do not carry through the parallels, though, for the saint is not portrayed as a judge, nor a law-maker, nor a poet; she has no noticeable interest in smithcraft, and her healing miracles are not very physician-like. The only significant overlap is the motif of fire and light, but the references can all be attributed to common motifs and have equivalents in male Irish Lives. Another association between Saint Brigit and fire would in the twelfth century be reiterated by Gerald of Wales, but that too was not specific to her.

McCone has pointed out that another saint, the virgin Lassair, also has a fire name, from *lassar*, flame. In his view Brigit, like Lassair, was a goddess who became a saint in Christian times; both succeeded in the new religions because their attributes could be harmonized with those of the Christian God, for the Bible is filled with light and fire imagery.[44] The fire element in the name, then, betokens a goddess origin, for him, in spite of the insignificance of fire and its attendant crafts in the early texts from Brigit's cult. While one may reserve judgement on McCone's conclusions, it is more important to recognize that his argument has gone back to first principles, where other writers have generally just repeated the Victorian truism.[45]

Where there is overlap between goddess Brigit and saint Brigit, however, is in the patronage of women, an association evident not only in these centuries but also as late as the twelfth. In the early eighth century Brigit the goddess was

[42] *Sanas Cormaic* ['Cormac's Glossary'], ed. K. Meyer, *Sanas Cormaic. An old Irish glossary, compiled by Cormac Úa Cuilennáin . . . Edited from the copy in the Yellow Book of Lecan* (Halle, 1912).

[43] K. McCone, *Pagan Past and Christian Present in Early Irish Literature* (Maynooth, 1990), 162–74.

[44] Ibid., 170–8. See also id., 'An Introduction to Early Irish Saints' Lives', *The Maynooth Review* 11 (1984), 26–59 at 46.

[45] For contemporary examples of the solar-cult approach combined with the Frazerian method, applied to Brigit, see Condren, *Serpent and Goddess*, 56–73; J. De Vries, *Keltische Religion* (*La religion des Celtes*, trans. L. Jospin (Paris, 1977), 78–80; P. Berresford Ellis, *Celtic Women: Women in Celtic Society and Literature* (London, 1995), 145–7.

associated in the law tracts with women's rights, and later, in the tale *Cath Maige Tuired* (The Battle of Moytura) and the prose *Dinnshenchas* (Lore of Places), the goddess Bríg was named as the originator of certain types of women's outcry and of keening, a particularly female type of mourning cry. The saint's feast day fell in Imbolc, the official start of spring in the native Irish calendar. Cormac's Glossary has an entry on *imbolc*, defining it as 'the time the sheep's milk comes', but does not identify the festival with Brigit.[46] Care of sheep was a specifically women's activity in early Ireland, and there are stories of Saint Brigit shepherding and making dairy products, but it must be remembered that the girl, as the daughter of a slavewoman, is portrayed doing what non-noble girls would do normally.[47] Nowhere, in fact, is Imbolc said to be the festival of the goddess Brigit, and beyond that, the goddess's attributes do not include sheep care. It is only the connection to women that is marked.

Finally, in Brigit's pagan origins one must mention her parentage: in the Lives the druid father is sometimes cited as proof that she was a transformed goddess. Admittedly he was treated rather sympathetically even in the versions where he failed to convert to Christianity. For all this, though, the greatness of Brigit lay largely in her success in persuading people to abandon their religion and join Christ's, and she had little to do with either druids or their arts.

The popular belief in Kildare having been a pagan centre depends upon saint Brigit being either a Christianized version of that goddess or an eponymous high-priestess of her cult, and that, as discussed above, is far from established. It also depends, less directly, upon the existence in pagan times of female druidic enclaves—a point treated in the previous chapter and shown to be equally tenuous. The reports of Kildare's vestal flame and the question of its allegedly pagan antecents have a bearing on how one approaches the Christianity practised there in its first centuries. If one believes that it was a transmogrified druidic centre it is reasonable to ask, were the devotions practised semi-druidical? Were the nuns more like priestesses than orthodox Christian *devotae*? For this reason the key piece of evidence for this model must be addressed, i.e. the supposed perpetual flame at Kildare, the alleged sign of surviving fire worship or vestal devotion. There is no mention of it in any of the three early Lives of Brigit, namely the *Vita I*, Cogitosus, or the ninth-century *Bethu Brigte*. It is hard to imagine that it could be overlooked in all three Lives. It is, in fact, absent from all other Lives, from annals, from the martyrologies and their glosses—all sources, in fact, until Gerald of Wales, a visitor in the twelfh century, almost 700 years after the alleged pagan-Christian transition took place. There is no doubt that Gerald was referring to a genuine, existent perpetual flame, for it is confirmed in other sources, in particular in a twelfth- or thirteenth-century gloss on a Middle Irish

[46] E. Hamp, '*Imbolc, oimelc*', *Studia Celtica* 14 (1979), 106–13.
[47] e.g. L. De Paor, *Ireland and Early Europe* (Dublin, 1997), 94.

tale, and in Anglo-Norman documents for the year 1220. Today at Kildare there are the ruins of a smallish stone building called the 'fire-house', in which the fire was known to be kept through the fourteenth century at least, for a 'fyre house' is mentioned in a 1397 close roll.[48] The fire-house itself may not be very ancient, certainly not dating to the pre-Christian era; it may have been built as late as the tenth century, or, if it was built in earlier centuries, it may have previously had a different use. That the fire was a 'vestal' one also needs considering. Gerald did say that only nuns were allowed to tend the fire, and this may have been the case, but Kildare did have monks and clerics on its premises in his day as in earlier centuries. Nor was the presence of a perpetual fire unique to Kildare: in the twelfth and thirteenth centuries seven others are mentioned in the hagiography, all of them at male monasteries.[49] The inescapable conclusion is that such flames in Ireland were not especially associated with women and appear rather late in the historical record. The reasons for their existence were probably Christo-theological: the luminary imagery of Christian deity was as ubiquitous in Ireland as it was elsewhere in the West. Why they appeared suddenly in the twelfth century is a question not ventured here.

A third piece of evidence some cite for pagan survivals at Kildare is its great oak tree, first encountered in the late twelfth or early thirteenth century when it was added to Brigit's *Vita I* by the redactor identified by Richard Sharpe as 'D' as he wrote out what was to become the *Vita IV*.[50] The tree is not mentioned in any earlier source, but appears to have really existed in D's day, for he saw it as explaining the origin of the name of Kildare, 'Cell Dara'.[51] For nineteenth-century scholars such as Healy, the implication of the oak tree, the druidic cult, and the Kildare legend was obvious. Kildare was built in a druidic oak grove and the great tree was venerated even in Christian times.[52] This assertion, resting on this same constellation of evidence, is found in the late twentieth century, too, though not in academic writing.[53] The true origins of the name of Kildare are almost certainly the building material of the church, i.e. 'oaken church', suggested by both annal entries and archaeology.[54]

---

[48] Close Roll, Dublin, 28 Jan. 1397: orders a grant of royal protection to the *priorissa et conventus de Fyre-house de Kildaria*.

[49] The following are listed in *PVSH* vol. 1, cxl: Ciarán of Clonmacnois, D text, ch. 30; Ciarán of Saigir, D text, ch. 32; Irish Life of Moling, ch. 31; Latin Life of Berach, ch. 4; Latin Life of Maedóc, ch. 57.

[50] This Life of Brigit, the *Vita IV*, is edited in Sharpe, *Saints' Lives*, 139–208, with the redactor's alterations in italics. On the redactor and the identification of his alterations, ibid. 121–6.

[51] *Vita IV*, book 2, ch. 3: 'For there was a very tall oak tree there which Brigit loved very much, and blessed, of which the trunk still remains. No one dares cut it with a weapon, but whoever can break off a part of it with his hands deems it a great advantage, hoping for the help of God by its means; because through St Brigit's blessing many miracles have been performed by that wood.'

[52] J. Healy, *Insula Sanctorum et Doctorum: Ireland's Ancient Schools and Scholars* (Dublin, 1893), 131.

[53] Condren, *Serpent and Goddess*, 66.

[54] On the sacred trees, see D. Binchy, 'An Archaic Legal Poem', *Celtica* 9 (1971), 152–68; A. T. Lucas, 'The Sacred Trees of Ireland', *JCHAS: Journal of the Cork Archaeological and Celtic Society* 68 (1963), 16–54; A. Watson, 'The King, the Poet and the Sacred Tree', *Études Celtiques* 18 (1981), 165–80.

The community at Kildare was clearly neither semi-pagan in its Christianity, nor even sympathetic to native druidic religion. It was, in fact, anti-pagan. Its hostility in the seventh and eighth centuries is epitomized by the verses left by one Kildare clerical poet who saw in the comparative fortunes of his monastery and its neighbouring pagan religious fortress a cause for gloating. Brigit's church went from strength to strength, he crowed, but druidic Dun Ailline ('Alenn') was now an abandoned, empty ruin.[55]

> Adrad lítha ní fíu clúas,
> solud ná sén síabras bás;
> is bréc uile iarna thúr
> indid Alend is dún fás.
>
> Foglas a ngen tibes duitt
> a maig réid túaith Críchaib Cuirc,
> di cach lín ron alt a úair,
> do-rigni lúaith Life Luirc.
>
> . . . . .
>
> A Brigit 'sa tír ad-chíu,
> is cách a úair immud-rá,
> ro gab do chlú for a chlú
> in ríg, is tú forda-tá.
>
> Táthut bithfhlaith lasin Ríg
> cen a tír i fil do rúaim;
> a uë Bresail maic Déin,
> slán seiss, a Brigit co mbúaid.[56]

It is not worth listening to the worship of auguries, or of spells or prophecy that predict death for, when tried, they are all falsehood, since Alenn is a deserted fort. Bright is the smile that shines on you from the plain north of Corc's land; Liffey of Lorc has made ashes of every generation it has reared. . . . Brigit, in the land I behold, where each king has lived in turn, your fame has proved greater than that of the king, you are superior to them. You have an eternal domain with the King, as well as the land where your sanctuary lies. Granddaughter of Bresal mac Dian, sit safely, Brigit, in triumph.

Brigit may have started out as a pagan goddess, and may live in the twenty-first century as one again, but in the early middle ages she was a very Christian, very determined crusader for Christ. She sat safely, indeed, in a very Christian and very orthodox, triumph.

---

[55] B. Wailes, 'Dun Ailinne: An Interim Report' in D. Harding (ed.), *Hillforts: Later Prehistoric Earthworks in Britain and Ireland* (New York, 1976); B. Wailes, 'Irish Royal Sites in History and Archaeology', *Cambridge Medieval Celtic Studies* 3 (1982), 1–29.

[56] *Slán seiss, a Brigit* ['Sit Safely, Brigit', or 'To St. Brigit'], final stanzas (D. Greene and F. O'Connor (eds. and trans.), *A Golden Treasury of Irish Poetry, AD 600 to 1200* (London, 1967), 67–71). Originally ed., with commentary, by K. Meyer, *Hail Brigit: An Old-Irish Poem on the Hill of Alenn* (Halle, 1912).

CONCLUSIONS

The Irish hagiographers of the seventh and eighth centuries, in their portrayal of the earliest Christian female communties, perpetuate a trend encountered in the previous chapter, in that they silently rejected notions that God's virgins should be enclosed, non-travelling, and subservient to the male clerics. For their models they looked more to the Apocryphal Acts, and were probably influenced by native values and ideas of gender roles, though these are indeterminable. For the Irish, the consecrated virgin was considered able to participate in the apostolic work of spreading Christianity and of founding churches and monasteries. When the texts refer to places which had a female founder, the founding was done either by a woman acting on her own with male backing (usually a bishop, male kin, or magnate) or else by a male ecclesiastic on the woman's behalf. Textual evidence suggests that the earliest churches sometimes developed into cult centres and cemeteries after the death of the leader, whether male or female. As for the idea that female saints were modelled on pagan Irish goddesses, an examination of the apparently most likely case, that of Brigit, is inconclusive.

The hagiographical texts which give us the impressions described in this chapter are, of course, retrospective. They contain a variety of distorting features, of which the most significant are those created by the genre itself and those prompted by ecclesiastic rivalry of the authors. It would be unwise to rely upon these sources for accuracy of detail; nonetheless, they are unlikely to be very wide of the mark on the broad outline of social relations and behaviour. In the next chapters, which deal with the seventh to ninth centuries, these hagiographical sources become contemporary evidence—evidence for the attitudes and general organization of women's monasticism in their authors' own day.

PART TWO

The Seventh, Eighth, and Ninth Centuries

PART TWO

The Seventh, Eighth, and Ninth Centuries

Introduction

The general context of the seventh to ninth centuries is straightforward enough. Irish women who took up a dedicated religious life in this period entered a better-established Church than had their predecessors in the fifth and sixth centuries. There were now a number of large established women's monasteries, canon and secular law was being written down and further defined, theological writing was taking off, the cult of saints was growing, and noble patronage was becoming more widespread and deep-rooted.

The female religious profession, too, was becoming more complex and better defined. It is clear that the ideas of what constituted a nun were more articulated, and one can begin to speak meaningfully of 'nuns' in the coenobitic sense from the seventh century. Furthermore, it is in this period that we find increasing references in the texts to different types of nuns—virgin, holy widow, ex-laywoman, *peregrina*, and the enigmatic *mac-caillech* ('young nun'). And of course there is seen a development of the gradations of status within the profession: abbesses and certain other holy women have special legal rights according to some eighth-century law tracts; also, we read of the *banairchinnech* (female abbot usually in charge of business affairs), the *priorissa* (prioress), and the *tanist* (the 'second').

The body of evidence shows these changes very clearly, and in general they follow a normal Western pattern. The succeeding chapters, however, focus upon two of the most characteristic features of Irish female monasticism. The first is that nuns in Irish nunneries in the seventh to ninth centuries were not strictly enclosed. For all its development and the emergence of a few large nunneries, the female profession remained very open-ended, subject to personal initiative or inclination. The parameters for living a dedicated religious life were quite wide: for example, a nun could live outside a monastic setting, at a local church and possibly even with a priest in some sort of household arrangement. Even within the monastic setting the options of living arrangements are startlingly broad—in addition to the large formal nunneries, there existed women's communities at some male monasteries, and nuns' residences at or near small laity-serving churches. The second outstanding feature is that the women of the Church could enjoy a high regard in the eyes of the Church and laity, a remarkable freedom from the misogyny which is so often attributed to the 'ascetic' Irish church. One sees collegiality between bishops and abbesses, mutual relations and support between nunneries and monasteries, and highly regarded houses of women. According to the material on St Samthann (obit AD 739), a woman of this era could revive and bring to prominence a nearly defunct house and in so doing achieve sainthood.

These topics all raise questions concerning the connections between Ireland and elsewhere in the West at the same time. For instance, can the according of legal status to abbesses and holy women be traced to non-Irish sources? Were there precedents in non-Irish Christian texts for the variety of female professions? The question of Continental and patristic influence thought on Irish ideas of female sanctity remains important in this era as it was in the preceding centuries. Scholarship of recent years has taught historians to guard against automatically attributing 'unusual' social features to Irish nativism. Between Ireland and Britain, and Ireland and the Continent, the flow of ideas was greater than used to be thought. Imports certainly included texts on female sanctity, female religious profession, and female sexuality. However, it looks very much as though the Irish continued to be selective in adopting patristic, English, and Continental notions, especially those which treated holy women.

The popular notions of Ireland in the seventh, eighth, and ninth centuries have many significant differences from those of modern academe. Generally, Ireland is framed as a place where a romantic, holistic Celtic Christianity held on in spite of external Romanizing pressures coming from England—a conflict of spiritual cultures epitomized in the meeting on church practice at the Synod of Whitby held in 664. Though for scholars the significance of Whitby is now seen in a very different light, the old interpretation hangs on in popular belief. In this schema, the British church lost its Celtic distinctiveness as a result of the synod, but the Irish one did not; the latter flourished until the English arrived in the twelfth century. The Celt is classed as a romantic, the Anglo-Saxon and Roman a rationalist, and, as an extension of this (an inheritance from the old evolutionary school) the Celt is said to be more imaginative, intuitive, and thus 'feminine-positive', whereas the Englishman and the Roman, being more logical and concrete, is more oppressive. The linking of gender to these values has the effect of reinforcing the evolutionistic presumption that the Irish and other Celtic Churches must have valued women more highly. Numerous proponents of Celtic Christianity see in Augustine of Hippo's tormented psyche the commencement of a Roman Christian misogyny, one which was promoted in the British Isles by Augustine of Canterbury and his successors.[1] H. J. Massingham spoke for many of this school when he wrote, 'it is possible that the fissure between Christianity and nature, widening through the centuries, would not have cracked the unity of western man's attitude to the universe'.[2] The implication is, as well, that this applies also to the fissure between the male and female sexes and, by extension, to the masculine and feminine parts of the Jungian-styled psyche. The Celtic Christian vision of the early Irish church has other elements, too: it is seen as being profoundly peaceful and uncompromised by secular

---

[1] A. Duncan, *Elements of Celtic Christianity* (Shaftesbury, 1992), 49–55; Bradley, *Celtic Way*, 22–30.

[2] C. Bamford and W. Marsh, eds., *Celtic Christianity: Ecology and Wholeness* (Lindisfarne, 1982) 10, quoting from Massingham's *The Tree of Life*.

entanglements. Its monasteries were 'little pools of gentleness and enlightenment, oases of compassion and charity'.[3] It must be recalled, however, that the
academic studies of the past seventy years have determined without a doubt that
the Irish church was a male-dominated institution which evolved within a wider
society that had been patriarchal long into the pagan past. Female eminence,
therefore, is hardly a foregone conclusion; nor indeed were its values archetyp-
ally 'feminine' for far from being peace-loving and unworldly it was deeply
involved in politics and, at times, warfare.

For the modern pagans, the church of the seventh to ninth centuries is of
interest primarily as a preserver of information about Irish paganism. The texts
which record information about it, the law tracts, saints' Lives and sagas, are
combed thoroughly for snippets which are extracted and combined with other
evidence, mostly classical accounts, in the project of reconstructing the theology
and structure of the old Celtic religion. The Irish tales were recorded from
about the eighth century onwards, until about the twelfth, and they do indeed
record much about Irish paganism, as portrayed by legend if nothing else. For
this audience, the sagas are very important as a window on the Iron Age, however much scholars now agree they are not. Not only is there nature-reverence,
divination, and visionary activity in them; there is also something that looks
very much like goddess-worship. The accounts of the goddess Brigit were written for the most part after AD 900, but those of the Christian Brigit, as we have
encountered, start much earlier. Though most pagans believe that the saint was
a thinly-veiled goddess, Brigit is hardly appealing to this group: in the surviving
texts she is simply insufficiently goddess-like. Nor is there much interest in her
nuns, the erstwhile priestesses (so generally deemed).

Sources

Despite the fragmentary and scanty research tradition on Irish nuns, analysis is
made possible thanks to the many decades of work on male monasticism,
church organization, ecclesiastical authority, and pastoral care. So too is the
task made feasible by the work of the historians who have edited, analysed, and
dated many of the texts containing key evidence for women.

Sources for this period are relatively abundant—it is easier to gain a sense of
the Irish Church in the seventh to ninth centuries than in the centuries either
before or after, and so, unsurprisingly, women in the Irish Church are most
abundantly attested in these centuries too. A fair number of extant texts illumin-
ate numerous aspects of female piety. Among the relevant texts from the seventh century are the two early Lives of Saint Brigit, Muirchú's Life of Patrick,
Tírechán's memoirs of Patrick, the *Liber Angeli* from Armagh, several theological tracts, glosses, verses from Bangor, and contemporary annals. From the

---

[3] Bradley, *Celtic Way*, 119.

eighth century are annals, copious legal texts in Irish, the Hiberno-Latin law text *Collectio Canonum Hibernensis*, a handful of Latin Lives of male Irish saints, some religious poetry, and an abundance of hymns (a number of which are dedicated to female Irish saints). From the ninth century we have the story of Liadain and Curithir, the customs and rule of Tallaght, a metrical rule from Bangor, the Triads, the martyrologies of Oengus and Tallaght, and an Irish Life of Brigit (*Bethu Brigte*). However, as is to be expected, there is less on nuns than on monks and clerics, and less evidence on female houses than for male monasteries and churches. The evidence is made more difficult to use because some of the material contains terminological ambiguities. Furthermore, that evidence which is not shrouded in ambiguity often appears to contradict commonly-held notions about female monasticism, and some sources appear to contradict others about even general matters on the life of consecrated women. But the contradictions can be approached, and often resolved, by understanding that both gender relations and ecclesiastical relations were complex in this period; the evidence defies facile generalization.

3

Nuns in the Large Women's Monasteries

A visit to the monastic ruins of Glendalough or Clonmacnois must be the most vivid introduction to the early Irish monastery, for the geography and layout are themselves enlightening. A mid-size or large monastery comprised a rather large area whose boundary marker, a *termonn*, enclosed some open space, grazing area, many small huts including 'beehive huts' (named for their appearance), and numerous church buildings. The huts were for monks' dwellings, one for a school, another for a scriptorium, and another for a kitchen. Churches were generally of stone, though some were of wood, the material more common earlier in the period. What strikes visitors most vividly is the small size of even the 'large church', which hardly contains fifty or sixty people standing; the small oratories barely fit four or five. Outdoor stone altars were to be found, presumably where mass was celebrated for groups too large to fit into the churches, and numerous stone crosses were positioned at the boundary walls or inside them. There was also a cemetery, or two, centred round the grave of a saint: the Irish word for cemetery is *reilic*, from *reliquus*, highlighting the importance of saint's remains in burial grounds—many saints claimed to offer direct entry into heaven for all buried in their cemeteries.[1] In short, the early Irish monastery resembled nothing so much as a slightly miniaturized village.

By the seventh century there were many places resembling this general description, so successful had Christian evangelism been. A handful were women's monasteries, and one at least was a double house. Though the sources on large female monasteries are patchy, a good deal can be gleaned: the rules, daily activities, ministry to the laity, as well as attitudes on nuns' chastity. The contours of these practices and attitudes can be explored in some depth, but unanswered questions remain. It is probably most useful to preface the examination of life within the large female establishments with a thumbnail sketch of each, since for most readers, lay and academic alike, they are little more than names, there being no in-depth studies of any of them.

Kildare

Kildare, it hardly needs to be said, is Ireland's most famous female house and it would be a boon to scholars if the remains of this illustrious and large monastery

---

[1] See M. Herity, 'The Layout of Early Christian Monasteries', in Ní Chatháin and Richter, *Irland und Europa*, 105–16; Edwards, *Archaeology*, 104–14.

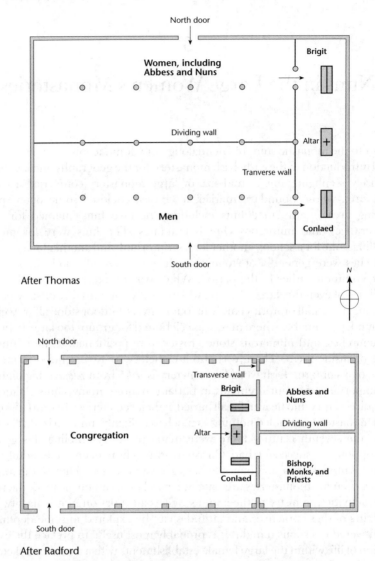

FIG. I   Kildare's Great Oak Church in the Seventh Century

Two interpretations of Cogitosus's description of the great church as it was in his own day. In it, he says, men and women worshipped together. On either side of the altar were the bodies of the foundress Brigit and her colleague Bishop Conlaed, in tombs encrusted with gold, silver, and jewels. Over them hung chandeliers of precious metals. Cogitosus speaks of a dividing board wall separating the abbess and her nuns from the monks; ambiguous language allows for two interpretations: either it separated the male and female congregations (Thomas's view) or it just came between the people in orders, who were in separate chapels, and the rest of the congregation (Radford's view). Thomas's plan fits the description much more comfortably and is preferred.

had survived. Sadly, no trace of the early medieval church survives and the foundations lie under the modern cathedral. Today's tourist can see in the grounds a few stone high crosses, a round tower, and the sunken foundations of a stone building called the 'fire-house'. The present remains give little sense of what Kildare must have been like in the early middle ages. In those centuries it would have looked much as Clonmacnois or Glendalough still do: a town of huts, oratories, and other small buildings surrounded by an enclosure, beyond which were fields and tenants' dwellings. One seventh-century resident, Brigit's hagiographer Cogitosus, described it as it was in his own day: a thriving townlike settlement with many inhabitants and boasting pilgrims flocking in from all over Ireland.[2] The *termonn* of a monastery represented a boundary within which fugitives could claim sanctuary, and Kildare was no different in considering its boundary a dividing line between the realms of secular authority and ecclesiastical jurisdiction. Because of this fact, some people came to Kildare to avoid violence, retribution, or court summonses, just as they went to other churches for the same purpose.[3] Kildare was organized around its large oak church building which supposedly had been built in Brigit's day. For masses, the women and men would come together in this great edifice.[4] This was different from the practice at the monastery of Armagh in the same period, which also had both male and female residents; there, men and women worshipped in separate churches within the *termonn*.[5] The church at Kildare had from the beginning been an oaken structure, giving the name to the community—Cell Dara, 'church of oak', and it continued as such, since the annals' entries continue to speak of the church building as the *derthaig* (oak-house).[6] It cannot be known whether the nuns shared a single dormitory or had separate huts. Since there was a population of monks, they too must have had living quarters of some sort but these too escape the view of the historian. The abbess, we presume, lived in her own little house, as this would be normal for abbatial heads. For a while at least Kildare had a 'house of the elders/scholars' which was headed in the eighth century by a female religious.[7]

Politically, Kildare has a special place in Irish history. Certainly it was powerful, for its abbesses were recorded in the annals for over a six-hundred-year span and it was an episcopal centre from as early as the sixth. But it is in the seventh-century that it entered the national arena, for it was then that it undertook to try to become the archiepiscopal church of all Ireland, that is to say, the head of all Irish churches.[8] In making national claims, Kildare joined in the highest levels

[2] Cogitosus, Life of Brigit, ch. 32.
[3] Ibid., Introduction and ch. 25; *Vita I* of Brigit, ch. 75. On ecclesiastical boundaries and sanctuary, see W. Davies, 'Protected Space in Britain and Ireland in the Middle Ages', in B. Crawford (ed.), *Scotland in Dark Age Britain* (Aberdeen, 1996), 1–19.
[4] Cogitosus, Life of Brigit, ch. 32.
[5] On Armagh, *Liber Angeli*, ch. 14. The *Liber Angeli* ['Book of the Angel'], ed. and trans. in Bieler, *Patrician Texts*, 185–91; also in Hughes, *Church*, 275–81.
[6] AU 762.   [7] AU 797.   [8] Brigit died AU 524 or 526.

of Church politics and economic power, and it became one of what Richard Sharpe has called the 'great churches', those not necessarily the oldest, which achieved power and wealth and which made extensive claims over the traditional churches of local and distant regions. Their networks are the so-called 'monastic-type *paruchiae* of the textbooks'.[9] It is in this context that Cogitosus's Life of Brigit was written. Kildare had wide responsibilities and privileges. In the 630s the predominant figure was Áed Dub, son of Colmán king of the Leinstermen (the Laigin); as bishop of Kildare he claimed jurisdiction over all the Leinstermen, while the monastery itself, under its abbess, was laying claim to a wide network of around thirty churches. It was in direct rivalry with Armagh for supra-episcopal status for most of the seventh century.[10] The resolution of the competition has been dated variously to the seventh or earlier eighth century, but whatever its date, it was a compromise in which Kildare was conceded supremacy in her *paruchia* (whose exact boundaries or constituents are uncertain), and Armagh was ceded authority over other areas.[11] In fact, neither church enjoyed the power of an archbishopric, and the issue fell by the wayside until the twelfth century. The mutual concessions were very much part of the writing of the period *c*.700, though: they were expressed in a typically Irish way, that is to say, by framing the agreement in pseudo-historical conversations between the personages involved, here Patrick and Brigit. One example, from the final paragraph of the Armagh tract *Liber Angeli*, relates the following:

Inter sanctum Patricium Hibernensium Brigitamque columpnas amicitia caritatis inerat tanta, ut unum cor consiliumque haberent unum. Christus per illum illamque virtutes multas peregit. Vir ergo sanctus Christianae virgini ait: 'O mea Brigita, paruchia tua in provincia tua apud reputabitur monarchiam tuam, in parte autem orientali et occidentali dominatu in meo erit.[12]

Between saint Patrick and Brigit, the pillars of the Irish church, there existed such friendship of charity that they were of one heart and one mind. Christ performed many miracles through him and her. The holy man therefore said to the Christian virgin, 'O my Brigit, your *paruchia* will be deemed to be in your province in your dominion, but in the eastern and western part it will be in my dominion.'

An eighth-century prayer praising Brigit, presumably composed at Kildare,

---

[9] R. Sharpe, 'Churches and Communities in Early Medieval Ireland: Towards a Pastoral Model', in J. Blair and R. Sharpe (eds.), *Pastoral Care Before the Parish* (Leicester, 1992), 81–109, at 106–7.

[10] Armagh's aggrandizement and rivalry with Kildare: L. de Paor, 'The Aggrandisement of Armagh', *Historical Studies* 8 (1971), 95–110; McCone, 'Brigit'; Sharpe, '*Vitae S. Brigitae*', with references on the dating of the *Vita I*; R. Sharpe, 'Armagh and Rome in the Seventh Century', in Ní Chatháin and Richter, *Irland und Europa*, 58–72.

[11] Proposed date of the resolution: mid-7th cent. (de Paor); end of the 7th (Bieler and Sharpe); earlier part of the 8th (McCone).

[12] *Liber Angeli*, ch. 32. This paragraph is not necessarily part of the *Liber Angeli* itself, and both the content and the manuscript would suggest that it is later, either an addition or a free-standing note. I am indebted to Herold Pettiau who cautions that the presentation of the text in Bieler's edition differs significantly from that of the original manuscript.

gives a similar portrayal of the resolution: Brigit is 'one of the columns of the Kingdom with Patrick the Pre-eminent', and calls her 'the saint of Leinster'.[13] The *Vita I*, a Kildare document, shows a good friendship between the two saints but one in which Patrick is acknowledged as an elder by Brigit; she goes to see him as a great man of the church, but she does perform miracles before him, and assists him in clearing the name of one of his clerics.[14] It is on the strength of the portrayal of this relationship that the text has been dated to either before the rivalry with Armagh began, or after the settlement. It is deemed impossible that Kildare could have produced such a 'happy' picture of cooperation at the time when it was trying to show that Brigit had supremacy over the whole of Ireland but Patrick did not. One very late witness to the division of power decided between Kildare and Armagh may be found in the eleventh-century commentaries added to the poem *Brigit Bé Bithmaith*, which claim that 'Brigit and Patrick divided out the kingship of Ireland between them, so that it is she who is the head of the women of Ireland and he who is head of the men.'[15]

Kildare was always involved in secular politics. Brigit had been a member of the leading Leinster kindred of her day, the Fothairt, and they had close ties to Kildare both early on and also even after they lost their hegemony of the region. Though they were replaced in regional predominance by the Uí Dúnlainge dynasty by the seventh century, one Fothairt branch, the Fothairt Airbrech, supplied the abbess Sebdann (obit 732) and her relative Duirc (obit 750); it is highly likely that many of the other clerics of Kildare, whose origins are unprovable, also belonged to the Fothairt.[16] The Uí Dúnlainge took over control of Kildare as part of their wider hegemonization of Leinster. They infiltrated and then came to dominate the offices of the monastery; they were fully in control by the seventh century, and in fact a member of that dynasty was probably abbot in Cogitosus's day. This kindred remained in power for the next five centuries, and in the ninth century, Kildare effectively was their dynastic capital of Leinster.[17]

Kildare's relics, so important for its secular claims, consisted of the bodies of saint Brigit and her fellow, Bishop Conlaed, which were entombed in the main church. After the early eighth century Kildare is less abundantly attested. We cannot, for example, know to what extent there may have been a loss of monastic life there during the eighth to tenth centuries. Signs of secularization include battles, killings, and burnings of the community; its abbot and bishop holding an abbacy elsewhere as well; and a possible father–son succession of the abbacy.[18] On the other hand, the composition of praise poems in the eighth

---

[13] *Brigit Bé Bithmaith* ['Brigit Ever-Excellent Woman'] (*Thes. Pal.* ii. 323–6). On its dating to the eighth century on linguistic grounds, see McCone, 'Brigit', 107.
[14] *Vita I* of Brigit, ch. 39.   [15] *Thes. Pal.* ii. 189.
[16] M. O'Brien (ed.), *Corpus Genealogiarum Hiberniae* (Dublin, 1962), 80–6; D. Ó Corráin, 'Early Irish Churches: Some Aspects of Organization', in id. (ed.), *Irish Antiquity: Essays and Studies Presented to Professor M. J. O'Kelly* (Cork, 1981), 327–41, at 329.
[17] O'Corráin, 'Churches', 327.
[18] Attacks: e.g. AU 710, 762, and 833. Dual abbacy: AU 866 reports that Cellach son of Ailill was

century, of Brigit's Irish Life in the ninth century, and the annal obits of scribes and scholars, makes it evident that Kildare's scriptorium remained active at a high level.[19] It also continued to have all three offices, bishops, abbots, and abbesses, and the eminence of all of them was was sufficiently high to warrant their deaths being reported in the annals.

Whether because of religious eminence in the monastic life, or because of political power, Kildare appears confident in the eighth and ninth centuries. Brigit's cult spread to the Continent.[20] Triumphal poems and hymns to the saint were composed in Ireland, most notably the eighth-century poems *Christus in Nostra Insula*, *Slán Seiss*, and the ninth-century *Ní Car Brigit*. Kildare's prominence is also evidenced by Brigit's recurring presence in the Lives of other saints, both male and female.[21] The place survived repeated Viking raids and attacks, and remained a major power into the later period.

Killeedy

The Munster monastery of Killeedy (Ir. Cell Íte or Cluain Credail) is another of the well-known women's monasteries with a long life. Today few remains can be seen at this southern hamlet, some forty-five miles south-west of Limerick in the countryside at the foot of the Mullagharick mountains. The most detailed portrait of the monastery and its nuns is the late Life of Ita, which purports to describe the church in her own day, but clearly may refer more to the place as it was in the author's own era, or may indeed not apply to reality at all except to witness the historical fantasies of a twelfth-century writer.[22] What is under no dispute, however, is the place's political connections; it was continuously associated with the Uí Conaill Gabra, the people of saint Ita, the foundress and first abbess.[23]

In the ninth-century Martyrology of Oengus, though, Ita is present: it calls her 'the white sun of Munster's women, Ita the devout of Cluain Credail'

---

abbot of Kildare and Iona; AU for 874 called Lechtnan son of Mochtigern, bishop of Kildare and princeps of Ferns. Father–son succession: possibly in AU 690 reporting the obit of abbot Forannán, and AU 752 reporting the obit of abbot Cathal son of Forannán. On dual abbacy of Cellach, cf. M. Herbert, *Iona, Kells and Derry: the History and Hagiography of the Monastic* Familia *of Columba* (Oxford, 1988), 73.

[19] e.g. AU 730.

[20] e.g. 9th-cent. metrical life of Brigit, D. N. Kissane, '*Vita Metrica Sanctae Brigidae*: A Critical Edition', *PRIA* 77C (1977). On date and authorship see Sharpe, *Saints' Lives*, 120, who argues, with Wade and Colgan but against Kissane, that it was composed by Donatus of Fiesole. For Brigidine material copied and composed in the Carolingian empire in the 9th cent., see Sharpe, 'Vitae S. Brigitae', 96–9. Also, D. Ó Riain-Raedel, 'Aspects of the Promotion of Irish Saints' Cults in Medieval Germany', *ZCP* 39 (1982), 220–4.

[21] In the Latin Lives of the 7th or 8th cent. (Sharpe's Φ collection in the *Codex Salmanticensis*) she appears in the Lives of Ailbe, Φ text, chs. 23–4, and of Áed mac Bricc, Φ text, ch. 17.

[22] Life of Ita, ch. 29 (*PVSH* ii. 116–30). On the date of Ita's Life, Sharpe is of the opinion that the redactor D, working in the 13th cent., used a 12th-cent. examplar (*Saints' Lives*, 394).

[23] AU 570.

(*in grían bán ban Muman / Ita Chluana credal*), which suggests that Killeedy had a regional importance at that time.[24] The ninth-century Martyrology of Tallaght also mentions her among its saints.

Three brief textual mentions suggest that monks joined the community at Killeedy some time before the tenth century—possibly long before then. There is a legend that male abbots had headed the place since Ita's death: in the notes of the Martyrology of Oengus dated to the tenth or eleventh century, Ita became angry with her nuns and declared that no nun (*caillech*) would ever take her succession.[25] In the Annals of the Four Masters for the years 810 and 833 one finds obits of two abbots of Killeedy, namely Cathasach and Finnachta, and no abbesses are recorded in any of the annal collections. Since the word for abbot used in these two entries is *abb Cill Ite*, one could argue that these were actually monastic heads, but in fact the term is known to have been used occasionally for monastic managers. John Ryan in his history of Irish monasticism took these two entries to mean that the place had become a monastery of men and had no more nuns there, i.e. that it had shifted from being a women's place to being one for men.[26] This is almost certainly not the case, because there is a ninth-century or later hymn written in which the nuns in the choir are addressed directly, and there is no known dependent house, to which we could attribute it:

> Canaid cóir, a ingena, d'fiur dliges for císucán;
> attá na purt túasacán, cía beith im ucht Ísucán.[27]

Sing a fitting harmony, maidens, to the legal recipient of your tribute.
'Little Jesus' is at home on high, even though he be in my bosom.

It seems most likely that at time the hymn was composed either both sexes were present at the monastery headed by an abbot, or there were only nuns but they were supervised by an abbot. Dagmar Scheider's study of Anglo-Saxon houses in this same period shows how a women's monastery could come to have a male abbot without there being a change in the composition of the inmates. Citing the case of Lyminge in the *Dialogi Ecgberti*, she notes that if a particular family dynasty controlled the church and always provided the head of a community (a mixed one, in the case of Lyminge), it was possible for the family give the headship to a male rather than a female.[28] Perhaps this is what happened in the case of Killeedy.

---

[24] Martyrology of Oengus, 15 Jan. (W. Stokes, *Félire Oengusso Céli Dé: The Martyrology of Oengus the Culdee* (Henry Bradshaw Society 29; London, 1905).
[25] Martyrology of Oengus, notes on 15 Jan.   [26] Ryan, *Irish Monasticism*, 140.
[27] '*Ísucán*', final stanza. Irish text from E. Quin, 'The Early Medieval Irish Poem *Ísucán*', *Cambridge Medieval Celtic Studies* 1 (1981), 43, 50. Quin notes that the language is substantially Old Irish (p. 41). Murphy dated the text to about 900 (*Early Irish Lyrics: Eighth to Twelfth Century* (Oxford, 1956), 26–9, at 26) but David Greene and Frank O'Connor put it at *c.*1000 (*A Golden Treasury of Irish Poetry, A.D. 600 to 1600* (London, 1967), 102–3).
[28] Schneider, 'Anglo-Saxon Women', 24.

Killevy

In the north-east of Ireland near Carlingford Lough and the modern town of Newry was another of the long-lived important women's monasteries Killevy, (Ir. Cell Shléibe Cuilinn, lit. 'Church of Slieve Gullion'). Saint Monenna (obit 519) founded the place at the northern foot of the mountain after first establishing a place named Faughart a little way to the south. Today at the very picturesque site there are the remains of two adjacent rectangular church buildings; the western one is was built before the twelfth century, the eastern one is possibly from the thirteenth. Formerly there was a round tower, but now its ruins are imperceptible. The territory, northern Louth and southern Armagh, was that of Monenna's people, the Conaille Muirthemne, and her sites were on kindred land, in the broader sense at least. The political connections with the dynasty at least into the seventh century are evident from the known names of its first fifteen abbesses and its links in the early eleventh century from the annals; those in the twelfth are implied in the saint's Life by Conchubranus (Ir. Conchobar).

The early references to Killevy are patchy. It is not mentioned in those Lives we know were early, but there do survive a couple of seventh- or eighth-century Killevy hymns praising the foundress and, with it in the manuscript, a list of the first fourteen abbesses.[29] Annal entries mention the death of abbess Conainge in 656/653. In the ninth century it was alluded to in the Martyrology of Oengus which sites Monenna, 'a pillar of the Church' at Slieve Gullion.[30]

Were there just women at Killevy, or men too? Monks may have been present in the seventh century: a mysterious reference in one of the two hymns to Monenna opens with the phrase, *Audite Fratres*. Who were the brothers being called to listen? Apparently brothers of the monastery of Killevy, for it is that house which produced the texts. No later material suggests the presence of brothers at the place, but this single reference appears to indicate them.

The monastery of Killevy itself is not described in any meaningful way until the twelfth century.[31] The absence of a surviving early Life, however, does not necessarily mean that we have no seventh-century hagiography. The twelfth-century Life by Conchubranus is a crudely assembled jumble of chapters and it may have a seventh-century strand.[32] Jane Stevenson in the 1980s followed

---

[29] The two hymns are *Audite sancta studia* and *Audite fratres*, in the BM Cotton Cleopatra Aii. Kenney considered that they were from the 8th, or possibly 7th cent., and were probably composed at Killevy (*Kenney*, no. 162. Esposito, '*Conchubrani Vita*', apps. A and B, 239–42, 242–4). The two hymns are followed in the manuscript by the 'List of Abbesses of Clonbroney, ibid., app. C, 244. The martyrology of Oengus (6 July) refers to her place on 'the mountain of Cuilenn'.

[30] Martyrology of Oengus, 6 July.

[31] The anonymous Life in the Codex Salmanticensis is edited in *Heist*, 83–95. There is a third Life of Monenna, compiled by Geoffrey, abbot of Burton-on-Trent from 1114 to 1151. For brief discussion of the various versions, see *Kenney*, no. 160, and Sharpe, *Saints' Lives*, 396–7.

[32] Esposito, 'Sources'. My disagreements with Esposito concern some chapters which appear to be from something like the 9th cent., not as late as others which look very 11th-cent. in nature. Like Esposito

Esposito in principle at least and added the supposition that the two early hymns and abbess-list (which appear together with it in the manuscript) were associated textually with a now-lost early exemplar.[33] In the allegedly seventh-century chapters, Killevy has links with Kildare in Leinster, Armagh in Ulster, and Bishop Ibar's Beggary Island in Wexford Harbour in the south-east.[34] No monks are mentioned as part of Monenna's *familia* except her brother Ronán.

The anonymous Life (the 'Darerca' Life') looks to at least one scholar to have undergone little change in its twelfth-century rewriting and is not directly derived from Conchubranus's text.[35] Monenna's first establishment, Faughart, is there portrayed as a great church attracting crowds.[36] Killevy, however, is described much as it is in the Conchubranus Life.[37] Again there is no reference to monks, but nothing actually saying they were not present. In terms of ecclesiastical networks, it too asserts links with Kildare and Beggary but also mentions Moville (through saint Finnian).

Clonbroney

The nunnery of Clonbroney (Ir. Cluain Brónaig) was in north-central Ireland in what is now Co. Longford, a few miles east of the modern town of that name. According to one source it had been founded in the fifth or sixth century by two sisters named Emer, but in others this achievement was attributed to a virgin named Funech or Fainche/Fuinche.[38] Despite its early origins it achieved prominence only in the eighth century under abbess Samthann. In her later Life stories of building and expansion at the church are prominent, and she comes across as a powerful force in the physical expansion of the settlement.[39] We know that Samthann left Clonbroney a legacy of eminence because the Irish annals (which record only the deaths of 'important' people) register not only her own death but those of her successors, whereas before her, annalists did not

---

I think that chapters were cut and pasted together without internal alteration, as is evidenced by lapses in continuity and sense between chapters and the variances in terminology and style between chapters which are nevertheless consistent within themselves.

[33] J. Stevenson, 'Irish Hymns, Venantius Fortunatus and Poitiers', in J.-M. Picard, *Ireland and Aquitaine* (Dublin, 1995) 81–110, at 84, where she also confirms the dating of the two hymns to the 7th cent. on linguistic grounds.

[34] Conchubranus, Life of Monenna, book 1, chs. 2–4; book 1, ch. 3. Beggary is Ir. 'Béc Ériu', lit. 'Little Ireland'.

[35] Sharpe thinks it may either share a common ancestor or be derived from it through an intermediary (*Saints' Lives*, 396–7).

[36] Life of Darerca, ch. 9.

[37] Chs. 27–32.

[38] Emer as foundress: Tripartite Life of Patrick (W. Stokes (ed. and trans.), *The Tripartite Life of Patrick, with Other Documents Relating to that Saint*, 2 vols. (Rolls Series 88; London 1887), i. 91. The text is not organized by chapter headings, so citations follow page numbers of this edition. Funech/Fainche as foundress: Life of Samthann, ch. 5.

[39] AU 780 reports the death of its abbess Forblaith daughter of Connla, *dominatrix Cluain Brónaig*; for 785 it relates the death of Ellbrig, *abatissa Cluain Brónaig*.

bother with the place. The earliest mention of the place is in a hagiographic anecdote which probably was initially recorded before Samthann's lifetime. The Latin Life of St Cainnech shows connections between Clonbroney and Cainnech's Aghaboe (Ir. Achad Bó): Cainnech and some followers stayed for a time at Clonbroney which is described as being a place without buildings or shelter in the saint's day; later in the Life he performs a miracle for one of the monks of Clonbroney.[40] It comes across in this as a small place, poor, with monks as well as nuns, and no mention is made of an abbess. Samthann achieved something like national eminence in her own lifetime, or very nearly thereafter. She was celebrated in a poem attributed to Áed Allán which appears in an annal entry of the year 734.[41] The first substantial appearance of Clonbroney is in the Customs of Tallaght, a ninth-century *céle Dé* document which contains an anecdote praising Samthann as a great soul-friend (i.e. spiritual confessor) of leading churchmen. This suggests there was a friendly relationship between Clonbroney and Tallaght, though it hints at an earlier period of trouble between the two houses.[42] Not only did the annal entries continue to appear for centuries after Samthann's lifetime, in the tenth and twelfth centuries, but other signs abound of the place's continued importance.[43] From the Middle Irish period the monastery of Kilbarry (Ir. Cluain Coirpthe) claimed links to Samthann: in the founder Berach's Life she attended an ecclesiastical council important to his career, and the two cooperated to perform a miracle for the king of Brefne, Áed Dub son of Fergna. Kilbarry's hagiographer made the association between Samthann and that king exceptionally close, for Áed says 'O Samthann, let me put my head on your breast, O nun, that I may sleep'.[44] Her Latin Life is the only detailed source on Clonbroney, but unfortunately it is late. It does not mention monks as part of the community but neither does it specify that there were none, though the monastery is called a 'monastery of virgins'.[45] Politically the Life links Clonbroney with a host of male institutions across Ireland through stories of visits between inmates in the saint's time—Aghaboe, Iona, Granard, Devenish—as well as associating it with local secular authorities. Also a connection with a nunnery called 'Ernaide' is asserted.[46] The Martyrology of Gorman (also from the twelfth century) calls for the commemoration of Funech as the church's foundress and of Samthann as its celebrated virgin. For all its apparent

---

[40] Latin Life of Cainnech, Φ text, chs. 35, 59 (*Heist*, 182–98). It is unclear whether the *monach* was meant to be a regular monk or a monastic tenant: Irish terminology is ambiguous.

[41] ATig, AFM 734; Martyrology of Tallaght, notes on 19 Dec. (R. I. Best and H. J. Lawlor, *The Martyrology of Tallaght, from the Book of Leinster and MS 5100–4 in the Royal Library, Brussels* (Henry Bradshaw Society 68; London, 1931)).

[42] Customs of Tallaght, ch. 61 (E. Gwynn and W. Purton, 'The Monastery of Tallaght', *PRIA* 29C (1911), 115–79).

[43] A. Gwynn, and R. Hadcock, *Medieval Religious Houses, Ireland* (London, 1970), 314–15.

[44] Irish Life of Berach, chs. 62, 65 (*BNE* i. 23–43; Eng. trans. ii. 22–43).

[45] Life of Samthann, ch. 11, *monasterium virginum*.

[46] Ir. 'Ernaide' is used for (at least) three women's houses: Gobnat's Ballyvourney in Munster, Urney in Eastern Donegal near the Mourne River, and Slieve Gorey in modern Co. Cavan (see *Onomasticon*).

prominence in the twelfth century, annal entries for the place die out after this save for occasional, ambiguous, late sixteenth-century references, which suggest that endowed hereditary courtships continued there until at least that date.[47]

Saint Lassair and 'Cell Lasrae' or Killesher

Saint Lassair and her community of virgins first appear in Brigit's *Vita I*; when Brigit visited her place 'Cell Lasrae' the grateful nun donated it to Kildare; thus one may assume that in the seventh century this place was part of the Kildare federation. As for its nature, it is described as a monastery of virgins.[48] What is evidently the same place (deduced from geography) next appears in the claims of Lynally (Ir. Land Élo), which claims its founder once went to Lassair's church and was rudely treated by two of its nuns. For this Lassair sent the two to be tried for their sin by the saint himself, and his judgement prompted their self-abasing apology. The nuns' self-recrimination is sufficiently grovelling to imply a political background to the story, perhaps attempted Lynally domination.[49] The foundress does not appear in the ninth-century Martyrology of Oengus but is mentioned in that century's Life of Brigit, *Bethu Brigte*, repeating the story of donation to Kildare. It appears in a list of churches which Kildare claimed owed it tribute.[50]

No mention is found in any of the Middle Irish Lives, however, and it may be significant that the Lynally story dropped out of that place's later Lives. It may have dropped out of existence by the twelfth century, for Lassair's Life, composed at that time, scarcely mentions this place (if at all) and concentrates on other places unattested in this period. The one late mention of what may be this early church is in a passage of the Life. The saint blessed and named after herself a church in 'Gailenga', which just might be the region of that name just north and west of Dublin, and thus feasibly the location of the church in the Kildare federation. There were, however, a number of territories going by the name. It may be that the early and later materials on churches called 'Cell Lasrae' are unrelated.

Cloonburren

The important and long-lived nunnery at Cloonburren (Ir. Cluain Bairenn) in Co. Roscommon lay on the west bank of the Shannon opposite the large monastery of Clonmacnois. It almost wholly eludes the scrutiny of the historian. Virtually nothing is known about the monastery or its nuns as there is no

---

[47] Gwynn and Hadcock, *Religious Houses*, 314–15.   [48] *Vita I* of Brigit, ch. 44.
[49] Latin Life of Colmán of Lynally, Φ text, ch. 12 (*Heist*, 209–24).
[50] 'List of Nuns Subject to St Brigit' (in O'Sullivan, *Book of Leinster*, vi., at 1580).

extant Life of its foundress, Cairech Dergan. None of the Lives of other saints (early or late) mention either the place or the foundress. The traces, though, are there. It is mentioned a few times in the Annals of Ulster: in 753 to report the death of 'Scannlaige of Cloonburren', in 779 to tell of its burning, and in 794 at the death of its abbess Lerben. The ninth-century Martyrology of Oengus includes its foundress's feast day and that of one of her virgins, Mugain, whose affiliation with the place is established by a gloss on her entry.[51]

In the tenth century, another clue appears: Cloonburren's abbess was recorded as also having been the abbess of Clonbroney. This link may tell us a bit about the place's wider political relations: it is possible that it had an affiliation with Clonbroney during this period, but this is hardly certain.[52] It is evident that Cloonburren survived into the eleventh century, when the obit of an erenagh (managerial abbot) named Fiagha is reported. These small pieces of evidence may signify a decrease in the size or rigour of the monastic life there, but they are too fragmentary to support such a conclusion. The place may not have lasted through the twelfth century: Gwynn thought it had ceased to exist before 1167.[53] The twelfth-century Martyrology of Gorman calls for the remembrance of three of its members: the foundress Cairech Dergan, the virgin Mugain, and one mysterious Gubsech.[54] None of these, nor the place itself, figures in any of the late Latin Lives, which makes one suspect that Cloonburren was a non-competitor, if indeed still present, in the game of ecclesiastical politics by the end of the twelfth century.

WOMEN'S LIVES AT LARGE WOMEN'S MONASTERIES

The Rule and Discipline at Large Irish Nunneries

At the turn of the eighth century, Irish jurists dealing with the means by which people were bound to duties pronounced the following:

Co astaidter túatha i mbescna adragar cach fria techta clerig 7 caillecha fri heclais fo reir anmcarat co racht 7 riagail co tarngaire co brud gell iar mbrud fri corus rachtge ecalsa fo reir abbad 7 anmcarat techta.[55]

Nuns, like clerics, are bound by their special rules; these two types are constrained by the Church, subject to the judgment of soul-friends; constrained too by law and rule; they are also constrained by their promises unless they break them.

The 'special rules' of the ecclesiastics, then, were recognized in secular law courts, and their promises were held to be binding, their surety, as it were, being

---

[51] Martyrology of Oengus, 9 Feb., 15 Dec. Scannlaige probably 'Scandal Cluaina' commemorated 27 June, and also in the Martyrology of Gorman on the same day.
[52] AFM 933.   [53] AFM 1066.   [54] Martyrology of Gorman, 9 Feb., 20 June, 15 Dec.
[55] *Córus Béscnai* ['The Regulation of Proper Behaviour'], ed. in *CIH* 520.1–536.27; 903.37–905.9; 1812.33–1821.27; also ed. and trans. in *ALI* iii. 3–79. This passage is in *CIH* at 523; in *ALI*, at iii. 14–15.

the Church itself in the form of its confessors or soul-friends. What were these 'special rules'? As was usual across Europe in this era, Irish monastics lived, not under the Benedictine rule, but under rules devised by their founders or other leading figures. Whilst several of these survive, none is from a female house. The rules under which nuns in these large monasteries lived, then, cannot be examined but only inferred. A glance through those that do survive is instructive only in a general way, because practices varied from place to place, and because they were written for men.

Two female Lives specifically refer to their nuns' rules, though sadly without detailing their contents. The first story, in a supposedly early chapter in Conchubranus's Life of Monenna, makes it clear that the rule was guarded by the saint, who was the house's foundress and first abbess. It is also probable that the nuns of Killevy believed the saint had formulated the house's rule, as this was normal in early Ireland. After saint Monenna died, the story goes, the nuns carried on without her, but she returned to them in a vision and chastised them for letting their discipline slip: 'Do you forget the fixed rule?'[56]

The second story, from the *Vita I* of Brigit, is somewhat different, for it tells instead of the origin of the monastery's rule. In this tale, Brigit had a vision of what was happening in Rome: she saw and heard masses being performed before the relics of Peter and liked their form so much she sent wise men to travel there to bring back the *ordo missae* and the *universa regula*, so she could implement them at Kildare.[57] This they did, and the abbess then instructed Kildare to follow the Roman example. The story indicates that Kildare at that time was closely allying itself with Roman practice and may even have followed a rule which came from there. Such a stance was a political one at this time, for the Irish Church was divided as to how far it would follow Rome in such matters as monastic tonsure, episcopal ordination rites, and Easter dating. The family of Iona, famously, took the regionalist or *Hibernensis* position and represented it at the Synod of Whitby in 664. There is no explicit evidence about which side Kildare took in the controversy, so this little tale may be the strongest hint we have on the matter. Clearly the Kildare *familia* was announcing to the world that it looked to Rome for explicit guidance on how monks should live and how ecclesiastical rites should be carried out. Though this is significant for our understanding of Kildare's politics, it is the content of the *ordo missae* and *universa regula* of Rome

---

[56] Conchubranus, Life of Monenna, book 3, ch. 10, where it is referred to as *statuta regula*.

[57] *Vita I* of Brigit, ch. 91. The story about the origin of Kildare's *ordo* and *regula* is absent from Cogitosus's Life and *Bethu Brigte*, but reappears in a variant form in the 11th or 12th century. In the later versions the story has changed: the messengers failed to retain Rome's rule of Peter and Paul but stopped off on the way home at 'Plea', a submarine place in the Otherworld. There they got Plea's rule and a beautiful bell, both of which they *did* bring back to Brigit. The bell, writes the glossator, is still at Kildare and the rule is the one Kildare follows, i.e. the Placentine rule, *not* the Roman. Late versions of the story: glosses on stanza 2 of the hymn *Ní Car Brigit* (*Thes. Pal.* ii. 327–49, at 328–9; also in J. Bernard, and R. Atkinson (eds. and trans.), *The Irish Liber Hymnorum* (Henry Bradshaw Society 14; London, 1898), ii. 189–205, at 191–2). Another version is in the glosses of Martyrology of Oengus for 2 Feb.

which would allow us to better understand its monastic practices. But unfortunately in the seventh and eighth centuries there was no monastic rule in Rome commonly called 'universal'. It is just possible that the author of the *Vita I* meant the Benedictine rule, but it is much more likely he meant *regula* in the more general sense, to refer to the 'ways of doing things' in Rome; those were certainly being promoted as universal in the eighth century if not in the seventh.

The office or *opus Dei* is the heart of monastic religious life. Day and night a community gathers to sing a set round of psalms, hymns, and prayers. If the offices at the large women's houses were anything like those at Ireland's male monasteries, and they most probably were, they followed the same sort of schedule. Jane Stevenson has teased out from fragmentary evidence that the offices themselves were largely typical of the West, but in Ireland *ad matutinam* was the longest and most important, and there was some variation in the *cursus psalmorum*.[58] A monastic rule or a *cursus psalmorum* from a nunnery would be immensely valuable, but as none survives we can only note the incidental mentions.[59] The fullest such mention, which may be early, relates a miracle which occurred once in the oratory (*oratorium*) at Killevy after the sisters had said matins: at the end of the prayers, the abbess signalled for silence with a knock, then announced that one of the sisters who had lapsed had to confess.[60] It would seem from this and other stories that it was in the oratory that a community's head would address the nuns on matters of communal importance, including discipline, and that a normal time to do so was (as in this story) at the end of the office after the final prayers.

The disciplines of the religiously enthusiastic are a favourite theme in saints' Lives everywhere, and the Irish were no different. We hear that Brigit used to pray all night standing in a cold pond, for example, and that Ita 'loved many severe fasts.'[61] Of course chastity was enjoined on every woman vowed to God, and there were abundant techniques to help those struggling with lust. One slightly unusual method is reported in Brigit's *Vita I*, where one nun who suffered greatly with lust burnt her feet severely to stop its torments.[62] More normal was the prescription of fasting to reduce blood-flow. The Irish believed in a correlation between the amount of blood in a person's veins and the degree of lust they experienced. Thus the ninth-century Customs of Tallaght relate the instructive story of the virgin Copar who was prescribed fasting for her lust problem. She abstained until 'until no blood came out' when she was pricked.[63]

---

[58] The Irish hours were *ad secundam* (mod. Prime), 6 a.m.; *ad tertiam* (Terce), 9 a.m.; *ad sextam* (Sext), 12 noon; *ad nonam* (None), 3 p.m.; *ad vesperitam* (Vespers), 6 p.m.; *ad initium noctis* (1 Nocturn), 9 p.m.; *ad medium noctis* (2 Nocturn), 12 midnight; *ad matutinam* (Lauds/Matins), 3 a.m. (Stevenson, 'Introduction', pp. xliv–xlviii, at p. xliv).

[59] Adomnán, Life of Columba, book 2, ch. 5.

[60] Conchubranus, Life of Monenna, book 3, ch. 5, a 7th-cent. chapter according to Esposito.

[61] *Vita I* of Brigit, ch. 96; Martyrology of Oengus, 15 Jan.

[62] *Vita I* of Brigit, ch. 99, relating the lust of the prioress Darlugdatha.

[63] Customs of Tallaght, ch. 60.

Nuns were told, via the Lives and probably in their oral teaching too, that great saints were naturally low on blood: Samthann proved her pure motive in offering to be a man's soul-friend by jabbing her cheek and showing that no blood would come out of the pin-prick wound, no matter how hard it was squeezed.[64]

Some sisters, however, succumbed to carnal temptation. According to the penitentials, sexual lapses were to be dealt with by penance. The Old Irish Penitential (a ninth-century tract) prescribed one year on bread and water for clerics and nuns who lost their virginity, with the duration raised to four years if a child was produced. This penitential also made it clear that homosexual lapses in the monastery might also occur, both men with men and, significantly, women with women. For this sin it prescribed two years of penance.[65] The penance which had been prescribed in the earlier Penitential of Cummean was similar: clerics and virgins were expiated from a single episode of fornication by a year on bread and water; if the act produced a child by a seven-year exile.[66]

The saints' Lives, too, attest to the problem of sexual lapses. In these sources this sin was dealt with by the abbess, as were all infractions of the rule. In all the extant Lives, the errant nun was given the opportunity to expiate her sin through penance within the community. Importantly, veiled women were not driven out on account of their lapses. In fact, when they showed contrition the saints were known to magically remove the offending foetuses. This was the happy reward for the pregnant nun who presented herself to Brigit in Cogitosus's Life, just as it was for the lapsed virgin who made her way to the great abbot Cainnech.[67] Patrick's followers were not immune to the problem: according to saint Ailbe's seventh- or eighth-century hagiographer one of Patrick's virgins became pregnant and it was Ailbe who stepped in to help identify the father. This story bears some resemblance to the slightly earlier one which emanated from Kildare. In that version, it was Brigit who stepped in to help Patrick: she cleared from blame one of Patrick's clerics who had been accused by a nun (*quadam virgo*) of being the father of the woman's baby.[68]

One discordant voice in this portrait of tolerance speaks out from the Life of Ailbe. Once when the saint was travelling a couple made the mistake of getting caught copulating in his proximity and, as was the custom of that place, they were condemned to death and executed, but Ailbe mercifully revived them.[69]

---

[64] Ibid., ch. 61. *Cf. Vita I* of Brigit, ch. 27.

[65] Old Irish Penitential, ch. 2, item 11, the terms used for the cleric and nun *mac-cleirich* and *mac-caillech*, which I take to mean those who were virgins at the time they took their vows, and item 25. Cf. *Riagail Phatraic* on the monk sinning with a nun.

[66] Penitenital of Cummean, ch. 2, item 17 (Bieler, *Irish Penitentials*, 108–35).

[67] Cogitosus, Life of Brigit, ch. 9; Latin Life of Cainnech, Φ text, ch. 31 (*Heist*, 182–98).

[68] Latin Life of Ailbe, Φ text, ch. 30 (*Heist*, 118–31). Cf. *Vita I* of Brigit, ch. 39. Perhaps the scribes of these two texts used these stories as a way of slyly insulting Armagh whilst appearing to pay it a compliment. At the times of writing, relations between the monasteries may have been tense but friendly on the surface.

[69] Latin Life of Ailbe, Φ text, ch. 20.

This is just the sort of story which is quoted in generalist books as proof that the early Irish Church was characterized by a ruthless asceticism. Given its unique-ness, this little episode deserves closer examination. The transgressors were re-ligious people, but it does emphasize that they were *near the saint*. Written probably in the latter half of the eighth century, this text was composed in a world of increased ecclesiastical secularity, when some abbots were married, when plunderers sometimes raided churches, when pilgrims flocked to see relics in large numbers, and when relics themselves were carried around the country-side on revenue-collecting circuits of mother churches. It seems to me that this anecdote is a warning to the laity to respect the relics of the saint, when visiting it at its shrine or when brought to their region on circuit—an interpretation which looks even more feasible when one recalls Ailbe's more moderate reaction to his Life's account of the sinning nun in saint Patrick's retinue.

The most daring modern interpretation of nuns' sexual habits, however, is that recently put forward by the popular historian Peter Berresford Ellis, writing about Kildare:

We seem to be left in little doubt that Brigid had a lesbian relationship with another member of her community. She certainly shared her bed with Darlughdacha, whose name means 'daughter of the sun-god Lugh'. It is recorded once that Darlughdacha had the temerity to look appraisingly at a passing young warrior. As a punishment, Brigid made her walk in shoes filled with hot coals. As Darlughdacha became Brigid's succes-sor as abbess at Kildare, one presumes that, after this penance, she dutifully returned to Brigid's bed. One could also argue that Brigid's sexual inclinations become clear in that she maimed herself rather than marry a male but was content to share her bed with a fe-male over whom she displayed signs of intense jealousy.[70]

This story, from the *Vita I,* is badly misconstrued by Ellis. To paraphrase the Latin, Darlugdacha greatly desired a man, and he her, and they arranged to meet. On the night of the assignation she was 'in one bed' with Brigit but rose secretly once the saint was asleep; on the way she desperately prayed to God for help to stop her; inspired, she stilled her lust by burning her feet in coals. She returned to her bed, and next day Brigit praised her fortitude.[71] The jealousy and the punishment which Ellis sees are clearly not part of the story. The only contentious passage is the one saying the two women spent the night 'in one bed' (*in uno lectulo*). Quite apart from the fact that the Life from which this passage

---

[70] Ellis, *Celtic Women,* p. 149.

[71] *Vita I* of Brigit, ch. 99: *Sancta Brigita habebat quandam alumnam nomine Darlugdacha quae alio die non bene custodiens oculos suos vidit alium virum et concupivit eum et ipse similiter amavit eam. Tunc ergo haec virgo in quadam nocte conduxit illum virum et illa nocte erat ipsa virgo in uno lectulo cum sancta Brigita. Cum autem paulisper dormiret sancta Brigita, surrexit virgo et cum processit de lectulo inruit in eam mira perturbatio cogitationum et magnum inenarrabileque cer-tamen habebat in corde, id est inter timorem et amorem; timebat enim Deum et Brigitam et vehementissimo igne amoris viri urebatur. Oravit ergo Dominum ut adiuvaret eam in magna angustia. Tunc inveniens a Deo bonum consilium, implevuit duos ficones suos carbonibus ignis et intinxit duos pedes in eos, et sic factum est ut ignis ignem extingueret, dolor dolorem vin-ceret atque retro in suum lectulum reversa est. Haec autem omnia sensit Brigita sed tamen tacuit, ut puella paulisper temptaretur et ut probaretur.*

is taken was written at least a century after Brigit's death, there is a *topos* in Irish literature in which a favourite shares, or longs to share, a bed with the king, without any apparent sexual implications involved: it was a sign of favouritism, and this would appear to be an echo of that, especially as the *Vita I* repeatedly praises not only Brigit's chastity but also her non-sexual nature. Most condemning of all to Ellis's interpretation, the Irish church knew well about homosexual activity in monasteries, including among women, and explicitly outlawed it as fornication, as has already been noted. In light of all the evidence, it is not possible to accept Ellis's claim that Kildare was a place of openly-admitted lesbian liaisons, though it certainly would be noteworthy if such an interpretation could be sustained.

Ceremonials in Large Irish Nunneries

The most important ceremony in any monastery, nunneries included, was the mass. In early medieval Ireland, mass was normally celebrated at dawn, on Sundays and feast days, including saint's days. Sometimes at least, hymns were part of the eucharistic service, which was unusual in Europe at this time.[72] Hymns to specific saints, some of which have already been encountered, were almost certainly used on their feast days, either in the office or in the mass.[73]

The way it and other rites were performed was determined by a house's *ordo*. *Ordines* were manuscripts describing the liturgical actions which accompanied the words of the mass. They were a 'stage script' for celebrants and their ministers: the arrangement of the entire ritual was laid out, with full directions on procedures and gestures.[74] Stevenson's analysis of the performance of the mass in Ireland led to her suggesting possible liturgical variations between houses, but also that Irish masses did have some distinctive 'Hibernian' features. She cites two known places that did *not* have these Hibernicisms, and one was Kildare. Just as Kildare boasted of getting its rule from Rome, it said explicitly that the mass as said at Kildare was identical to that said in the holy city.[75]

In the anonymous *Vita I*, Brigit miraculously became aware of the change to the *ordo* in Rome, so she sent messengers to collect for her the new, altered version. Whilst the Life attributes the shift to the fifth century it actually occurred at the end of the seventh. Supposing genuine contact between Kildare and Rome, Stevenson suggested that the *Vita I* was written as Rome was undergoing changes in its *ordines* and that the hagiographer was projecting those changes back to the foundress's day. Stevenson is surely right that Kildare were aware of, and must have had, the new version of the *ordo* at the time the Life was written. It makes sense if they claimed their mass was the Roman one and had been since

[72] Stevenson, 'Introduction', pp. lx–lxii.   [73] Ibid., pp. lxxxiii–lxxxix.
[74] C. Vogel, *Medieval Liturgy: An Introduction to the Sources* (Spoleto, 1981), 135–8.
[75] The other is the community of Ailbe (Latin Life of Ailbe, Φ text, ch. 45). This anecdote bears a strong resemblance to that in Brigit's *Vita I*—a possible borrowing?

early days.[76] This has implications for the date of the *Vita I*. In Rome the *ordines* of the grand stational masses were changed in the late seventh century, *c.*700, and the changes were made in Gaul in the early eighth. This would place the *Vita I* in the eighth century. Such a date looks increasingly likely when one factors in the account of Rome's universal Rule: Rome was pushing for the universalization of its practices at this time.[77] Whenever it was written, however, the story does imply relatively good communications between Kildare and the Holy See. On the subject of masses at Kildare, it is worth noting that the annals note a change in custom there in the mid-eighth century. On account of a bishop's murder in 762 at the altar of the great church at the hand of a priest, from that time forward no priest performed a mass there in the presence of a bishop.[78]

Like all women, nuns were able to receive the host except when menstruating. This stipulation, normal in the West, is found in three normative texts of our period, the fullest of which is in the Rule of the *Céli Dé*:

Galar mistae bis for ingenaib eclasa, saire a figle doib oiret bis foraib, maiten acas fescor, acas brochán do denam doib amtheirt, secip aimsir, fobith dlegar airmitiu in galair sin. Nis tiagat din do laim ind ar omande [read: immundae] sunt in illo tempore.[79]

During their monthly illness which is upon virgins of the church, they are free from their vigils while it is on them morning and evening; and let gruel be made for them at tierce. Whatever time it happens, that illness is to be attended to. They shall not go to the hand [i.e. receive communion] then, because they are unclean during that time.

In Frankia in the ninth century, not only could women not take communion, they could not even enter a church during their monthly periods. Looking at England, Schneider noted that the early Anglo-Saxon church did not have a horror of menstruation, but she observes a trend towards increased harshness over time, caused, she asserts, by the Carolingian reforms. According to Bede, Gregory had stipulated that women during their periods could enter churches, and so far as it is possible to tell, the Irish, at least those at Tallaght, took his position rather than that of the Franks.[80]

[76] Stevenson, 'Introduction', pp. lviii–lxx.

[77] Vogel, *Medieval Liturgy*, nos. 1–10 and 17. M. Andrieu, *Les 'Ordines Romani'*, 6 vols (Louvain, 1931–61), ii, pp. xxix–xxxvi.

[78] Recounted in AU, with fuller version in ATig 759 and 761.

[79] Rule of the Céli Dé in the *Leabhar Breac* (W. Reeves, 'On the Culdees'. *Transactions of the Royal Irish Academy* 24 (1873), here at p. 211); text discussed in *Kenney*, no. 266. It is also found in another version of the Rule, ch. 50, worded almost identically (Rule of the Céli Dé in a Franciscan, Dublin MS, ed. and trans. E. Gwynn, 'The Rule of Tallaght', *Hermathena* 44, 2nd supplemental vol. (1927), 64–87, here at p. 78). Old Irish Penitential, ch. 2, unnumbered item at the end of the chapter: *Banscala intan bis a ngalar mistae foraib ni tiagat do sacarbaic* ('women do not go to the sacrament when their monthly illness is upon them').

[80] Gregory as reported in Bede, *Historia Ecclesiastica*, book 1, ch. 28. Frankia: Hodgson 'Frankish Church', 373–8; England: Schneider, 'Anglo-Saxon Women', 180–2, with comments on the authenticity of the ruling attributed to Gregory. But note pregnant women's impurity in Ireland, such that at least some felt they should not enter churches: Latin Life of Ailbe, Φ text, ch. 21.

Another issue for a nunnery was that of mass in the absence of a priest. There was in the West the known practice of reserving the host, whereby a priest would leave consecrated bread and wine with nuns, so that they could celebrate a mass without his presence. This would have been a boon to small female communities served only by visiting clerics, and it would permit nuns, whose priest might perform a consecration only on Sundays, to take communion daily as part of their devotions. In Anglo-Saxon England it appears that some nunneries made use of the practice, but no Irish sources mention it, whether to acknowledge, attest, or condemn it.[81]

Much as one would like them to, no Irish sources permit us to make comparisons with many contemporary Frankish and Anglo-Saxon practices.[82] With regard to women touching altar items, elsewhere there was a prohibition of women washing the altar cloths, but the only Irish evidence is from the Irish Lives, in which female saints handle such things as chalices, chrismals, and patens. Whether this extended to mortal nuns of the seventh to ninth centuries is a matter of speculation. In the masses, Irish women did not take a deaconal or subdeaconal role. One seventh-century Irish gloss explained a biblical reference to deaconesses (*diaconissa*) as 'a foreign ancient custom'; nor are they indicated in any surviving texts. The well-known case of Lavocat and Catihern, Breton priests assisted in the mass by women, was evidently not typical of practice in Ireland, at least not one visible to the modern scholar.[83]

Fostering and Schooling at Larger Irish Nunneries

Several of the large women's monasteries were known in this period as centres of fostering and schooling, as were male houses. But large houses were by no means unique in this regard, for we find children being raised and taught by religious people in a host of environments. Most of the extant evidence for education at nunneries in this period comes from hagiographical sources, which is hardly ideal but is nevertheless taken as indicative of general practice at the time the material was composed. Even the Lives are not as helpful as one would hope on this subject. Brigit's *Vita I* mentions a female disciple she fostered and another who came to be her student—both girls were accepted into, and lived at, the saint's monastery.[84] The eminence of Brigit as a teacher is implied by Cogitosus's praise: 'she merited to acquire such great authority in divine worship . . . above all the virgins of her time'.[85] Given the fantastic claims made for Brigit

[81] Schneider, 'Anglo-Saxon Women', 185–7, with references.

[82] For Frankia, Hodgson 'Frankish Church', 373–8, with references. For England, practices before and after the importation of strictures of the Carolingian reform, Schneider 'Anglo-Saxon Women', 180–94, with references.

[83] Würzburg Glosses on the Pauline Epistles, on 1 Tim. 3: 11, following Pelagius's gloss, *quas adhuc hodie in Oriente diaconissas appelant* (*Thes Pal.* i. 683). Contrast with Anglo-Saxon England where women could act as deaconesses in the mass, Schneider, 'Anglo-Saxon Women', 188.

[84] *Vita I* of Brigit chs. 47, 75, 126.   [85] Cogitosus, Life of Brigit, ch. 12.

one must look beyond the Brigidine material in any attempt to glimpse actual practice. The Annals of Ulster in 797 noted a female religious who headed the house of the most venerable or holy of Kildare: Condal daughter of Murchad, 'abbess of the elders' house' (*abatissa tighe sruithe*). The eighth-century Life of Ailbe appears to provide some further confirmation, for one anecdote in that Life centres on an unruly male student (*alumpnus*) being raised and instructed by a group of religious virgins—the virgins are anonymous, the boy is likewise un-named, and the fact he is with women goes unremarked—all of which would suggest that such a situation was hardly unusual.[86] Later Lives, dating from the tenth to twelfth centuries, contain numerous claims that male saints had been taught in their childhood by famed holy virgins: in these, boys are fostered and taught their basic schooling by the virgins, but are sent to a male teacher as they reach puberty.[87] The compilers of the *Collectio Canonum Hibernensis*, working *c*.700, must only have been trying to stop nuns teaching grown men when they reiterated the Pauline injunctions against women speaking in church and teach-ing religious matters.[88] The fostering tradition was to remain strong for a long time yet.

Claustration?

Claustration, the practice of enclosing nuns and separating them from contact with men, had an important role in the theory, if not the practice of female sanc-tity from Jerome's day and before. In the course of the Middle Ages it came to be a predominant indicator of nunhood, distinguished in the later medieval period from the unenclosed women in tertiary orders. But in the early Middle Ages such a notion was often unenforced, or even unstressed among writers, as a range of writers on early medieval religious women, particularly those of the Wemple school, have noted. At its simplest we can summarize the Irish position by saying that to have enclosed God's brides away from the world seems not to have crossed their minds in this period any more than it had in the fifth and sixth centuries. This was so in spite of the existence of Continental, late antique, and patristic textual exhortations to do so, whose presence in Ireland by the seventh century is well attested and whose wide dispersion by the ninth is undoubted.[89] Apparently the only group to advocate strict enclosure was the Roman party in the Irish church. This faction, in existence from the sixth to the eighth centuries, is largely imperceptible, but generally speaking it preferred the Roman ways of

---

[86] Latin Life of Ailbe, Φ text, ch. 36.

[87] e.g. Brendan, fostered by Ita, then sent to Erc of Slane.

[88] *Hibernensis*, book 45, chs. 18–19.

[89] The participation of nuns in pastoral care can at least partially explain many unusual and enig-matic features concerning nuns, for example the legal equivalency between nuns and clerics (not just monastics) in many law texts, and the residence of nuns at local churches. These phenomena will be treated in depth in subsequent chapters.

doing things when Irish custom differed. The *Romani* are most famous for arguing against the *Hibernenses* (the opposing, pro-regionalism faction) on the date of
the Irish Easter. On the issue of women religious no great controversy arose and
their position is preserved only in a canonical collection assembled *c.*700:

Romani dicunt: Decet mulieres, sicut fragilitatis sexum acceperunt, districte semper vivere sub manu pastoralis regiminis; virgines habitu virginitatis ornatae sine omnium vi-
rorum conspectibus segregentur, et sic vivant usque ad mortem; penitentes vero
obedientiae subditae sint, et quanto expertae sunt fragilitatem, tanto fieri cautiores
debent.[90]

The *Romani* say: it behoves women, as they accepted the fragility of their sex, to live engaged under the hand of a pastoral regime; virgins adorned with the clothing of virgins
are to be segregated from the view of men, and to live thus until death; penitents are to
be subjected to obedience, and the more they have experienced weakness, the more
they should be kept secure.

The *Romani* position was articulated in the face of a widespread reality which
was considerably different. In fact, this one is the only such exhortation to claustration in Ireland before the eleventh century.

The *Vita I* of Brigit shows the nunnery to be more like a quasi-pastoral mission centre staffed in large part by women. For example, Brigit provided beer for
the eighteen churches of her area (*in circuitu oppidorum Medi*).[91] At holy feasts the
people were accustomed to come to the church.[92] Brigit was rightly accused of
regional/familial favouritism by two British invalids, who complained that she
healed only people of her own *genus*. Significantly, she corrected this shortcoming
of hers and henceforth helped all comers, regardless of their regional or family
background.[93] The people of Leinster called her back from Connaught to Leinster
when she had been away for too long.[94] Brigit had dealings with local rulers: one
king came to celebrate Pentecost with her[95] and another came to be blessed by
her.[96] There is also general involvement by the nuns in the concerns of lay
people in ways not specific to the region or diocese. The foundress arranged
baptisms,[97] bargained for the release of hostages, and supervised penance.[98]
Guests were welcomed to the *hospicium*, and for the ill there was the *hospitalium*

---

[90] *Hibernensis*, book 45, ch. 14 (H. Wasserschleben, *Die irische Kanonensammlung* (Leipzig, 1885)). This injunction is of especial interest because in hagiography the nun is hardly shut away from the view of men
but rather is often portrayed as working side by side with men of the Church.

[91] *Vita I* of Brigit, ch. 21. These passages refer not to Kildare, however, but to the Fothairt–
Airbrech–Mag Telach axis; Kildare comes in only in the last section of the Life.

[92] Ibid., ch. 49. Sharpe noted that in this early version the people came customarily, but in the later,
13th-cent. D redaction, they were invited to attend, a change implying that in the 7th cent. such a custom
was current and needed no explanation, whereas later it would have not made sense so required change.
Such changes, according to Sharpe, are typical of the D redactor (Sharpe, *Saints' Lives*, p. 167).

[93] *Vita I* of Brigit, ch. 25.

[94] *Orta est magna questio apud Laginenses de absentia sanctae Brigitae, miseruntque nuntios ad eam in regiones Connachtorum ut ad suam gentem rediret* (ibid., ch. 97).

[95] Ibid., ch. 55.   [96] ibid., ch. 70.   [97] Ibid., ch. 41.

[98] Ibid., chs. 68, 74. For receiving confession and supervising penance, see chs. 25, 56.

(to which, amazingly enough, Brigit sent one barren couple to have sex to con-
ceive a child).[99] Brigit even appears to have helped out the local farmers: she
rode her chariot around their field to bless it, presumably for a good crop.[100]
There is some hint that nuns were especially given to looking after the ill and
dying: nuns of another region went to the homes of the sick to sit by their beds,
praying and keeping vigil. Elsewhere it is related that Brigit and her virgins did
the same at Easter time, visiting the homes of the ill to pray for them there. The
Old Irish Penitential treats the matter of nuns who attend the dying and keen
over them, and the *céle Dé* teachings of the eighth-century Saint Maelruain
speak of a special recitation of the Song of Solomon over the dying and
just-dead, in which the part of the male was seen to be the Christian soul and the
part of the woman to be the spirit of the Holy Church, Lady Ecclesia. If women
were ever performers of these readings over male clerics, it would constitute an
enactment of the metaphor in a very vivid way.[101]

In providing services to the laity of the region the nuns had regular contact
with men. They are found engaging with both laymen as mentioned above and
also with ecclesiastics and other males in the monastic *familia*. In the *Vita I* there
is no suggestion that regular monks (as distinct from monastic tenants, called
manaig) lived at Kildare, but the *familia* did include other sorts of males: a *sacerdos*
who also served as chariot-driver, married lay dependents,[102] a slave who gave
himself and his family in perpetuity to her,[103] and mowers of the agricultural
land.[104] There was a resident bishop, Conlaed, but he was not considered a sexual threat to either the abbess or the nuns. By the end of the Life, Conlaed had
actually become a member of the household and thus made Kildare an 'episcopal church'.[105] Earlier the nuns had relied for preaching and the mass upon
Bishop Mel, *episcopus noster*, who lived at his own place,[106] and also upon
Patrick.[107] In none of the anecdotes of the *Vita I* is there any concern with keeping the nuns away from these men. There was no concern about temptation
arising from contact between the sexes, nor was there any suggestion that such
contact might impede the nuns' spiritual vocations. On the contrary, they are
shown interacting in amicable and relaxed ease. Visits by groups of monks or
clerics from other places are recounted with enthusiasm, and are reported as
lasting for three days and nights or up to a week. During these visits the word of
God was preached and there was much celebration. Hospitality was of course
to be provided by the hosting house, a difficult feat in times of poverty, but one

---

[99] *Vita I* of Brigit, chs. 56, 111, 112.   [100] Ibid., ch. 80.

[101] Ibid., chs. 95, 35. The Old Irish Penitential, ch. 3, item 17, set penances for the penitent nun (*caillech aithrigi*) or chief wife (*cétmuintir*) who lamented for those she tended, if they died (D. Binchy, 'The Old Irish Penitential', in Bieler, *Irish Penitentials*, 258–76; also E. Gwynn (ed.), 'An Irish Penitential'. *Ériu* 7 (1914), 121–95). For the suggestion that women had a special role in tending the dying, see also the Life of Ita, ch. 13, where Coemgen asked Ita to be the one who, at his death, would close his eyes and mouth. On the passage in the teachings of Maelruain, see McCone, *Pagan Past*, p. 81.

[102] *Vita I* of Brigit, ch. 73.   [103] Ibid., ch. 90.   [104] Ibid., ch. 100.

[105] Ibid., ch. 114.   [106] Ibid., ch. 26.   [107] Ibid., ch. 63.

essential to the event. Thus in chapter 51, Bishop Cellán stayed with Brigit 'for some days' *aliquantis diebus*, and upon leaving asked her to bless his chariot. In chapter 63, Brigit sent for Patrick to come and preach the word of God, whereupon 'he with his disciples and she with her maidens came together as one' (*ille cum suis discipulis et illa cum suis puellis in unum convenerunt*). Then Patrick preached for three days and nights. Even more striking is the fact that the nuns travelled extensively, the author showing no apparent concern to reassure the reader that they were keeping their vow to avoid the world. In the *Vita I* the theme is absolutely pervasive and more than half the life appears to take place during wanderings of the saint and her virgins to Limerick, Connaught, Meath, and Armagh. One passage illustrates it particularly well.

Alio post tempore sancta Brigita iter agebat per campum Tethbe sedens in curru. Tunc illa vidit quendam maritum cum sua uxore et tota familia et cum multis pecoribus laborantes et portantes onera gravia [qui] in ardore solis lassi fuerunt. Tunc Brigita miserta erat illis deditque eis equos currus sui ad onera portanda. Illa autem remansit iuxta viam sedens cum puellis suis, dixitque illis Brigita, 'Fodite sub cespite propinquo, ut erumpat aqua foras. Venient enim aliqui qui habent escas et sine potu sitiunt.' Tunc foderunt et erumpit fluvius. Post paululum per eandem viam venit alius dux cum multa turba peditum et equitum et ille audiens quod sancta Brigita de equis fecit, obtulit duos equos ei indomitos, sed statim domiti facti sunt quasi semper essent sub curru. Post haec venerunt per eandem viam discipuli et famila sancti Patricii episcopi dixeruntque ad sanctam Brigitam, 'Nos in via laboramus; cibum habemus sed potum deest.' Tunc comites Brigitae dixerunt, 'Nos vobis preparavimus potum fluminis aquae; predixit enim sancta Brigita vos futuros esse.' Tunc omnes comederunt et biberunt in commune, gratiam agentes Deo et Brigitam glorificantes.[108]

Another time Saint Brigit travelled through the plain of Tethbae sitting in her chariot. Then she saw a married man with his wife and family, along with many flocks, working and carrying heavy burdens; in the heat of the sun they were exhausted. Then Brigit pitied them and gave them her chariot's horses to carry their burdens. She stayed by the side of the road sitting with her girls, and they said to Brigit, 'Dig under this nearby hillock, so that water will gush out. Then some people will come who have food and will be without drink.' Then they dug and there burst forth a spring. After a little while along the road came a ruler with a great crowd of soldiers and horses and he, hearing what holy Brigit did with the horses, gave two unbroken horses to her, but they were quickly made tame almost as soon as they were under the chariot. After this there came along this road the disciples and household of holy bishop Patrick and they said to Saint Brigit, 'We shall labour in the road; we have food, but we lack drink'. Then Brigit's companions said, 'We have prepared for you a drink of spring water; Brigit predicted your arrival'. Then they all ate and drank together, giving thanks to God and glorifying Brigit.

Cogitosus's Life is the other seventh-century source treating Kildare in depth. He confirms the portrait outlined in the *Vita I*, in relation to both the pastoral mission and the involvement with male ecclesiastics. In fact, he addressed even

---

[108] Ibid., ch. 32.

more explicitly the relationship between the two sexes. He wrote that Brigit had called upon Bishop Conlaed 'in order that he might govern the church with her in the office of bishop and that her Churches might lack nothing as regards priestly orders'.[109] It was necessary, he wrote, for the abbess to have male clerics to hand so that she could better and more easily provide for the needs of the lay people nearby, as well as the needs of her own nuns. He portrayed Brigit and her community as offering quasi-pastoral services: the poor and needy, he related, used to come to her in droves on account of her famed generosity towards the poor.[110] She also interceded before a king on behalf of a layman at his trial for theft, preached to heathens to convert them to Christianity, and chastised and received the confession of a wicked layman who subsequently repented of his evil ways.[111] The normalcy of this state of affairs for Cogitosus is in itself worthy of mention. It was not strange to him that a woman's community might take in such a bishop, or that a bishop would willingly join such a place. Nor was it strange for him that a women's house should take an active role in organizing religious life in its region.

The closeness of the sexes at Kildare is evidenced by Cogitosus's description of its main church in his own day. He gave a detailed picture of the building at which the monks and nuns both worshipped, and at which gathered the many other people of both sexes who together made up the *familia*. Seating in the church building was organized in sections. Each grade of believer had its particular place. The church, he wrote, was of an awesome height and adorned with paintings. The interior was divided by board walls into three chapels, with one wall stretching width-wise in the east of the church, pierced by two doors, one at either end. These led into the sanctuary, where the altar was located and in which the eucharist was celebrated. Through one door to the sanctuary proceeded the high bishop, the monastic chapter, and 'those appointed to the sacred mysteries' (*summus pontifex cum sua regulari scola et his qui sacris deputati sunt misteriis*). Through another proceeded the abbess with her nuns and faithful widows (*abatissa cum suis puellis et viduis fidelibus*) to partake of the eucharist. Another interior wall ran along the length of the church and met the crossing wall. The church had two portals, the one on the right being that for the priests and other males (*sacerdotes et populus fidelis masculini generis sexus*); the door on the left was for the nuns and the women faithful (*virgines et feminarum fidelium congregatio*). Two reconstructions of the church have been attempted by modern scholars, both of which are equally possible given the ambiguities in Cogitosus's description.[112] 'And so', Cogitosus tells us, 'in one vast basilica, a large congregation of people of varying status, rank, sex and local origin, with partitions placed between

[109] Cogitosus, Life of Brigit, Preface.   [110] Ibid., chs. 10, 15, 28.
[111] Ibid., chs. 3, 8, 20, 22, 25, 27.
[112] C. Radford, 'The Earliest Irish Churches', *UJA* 40 (1977), 1–40, and Thomas, *Early Christian Archaeology*, 145, 206–11.

them, prays to the omnipotent Master, differing in status, but one in spirit.'[113] The significance of both sexes worshipping together in a single church can hardly be overemphasized in any examination of attitudes to gender in this era. The nuns of Kildare by the time of Cogitosus probably represented a numerical minority in the overall Kildare population. One wonders how separated they were from the monks and other males in daily life, for although we know they worshipped jointly in the same church as the men (albeit in separate sections), this does not tell us how members of the opposite sex interacted in other contexts or in daily dealings. But even though we do not know this, we can note that Cogitosus was not threatened by female sexuality, for he stressed not the separation of the sexes but their coming together.

There is a ninth-century Life of Brigit, *Bethu Brigte* which, though it does not make any references to Kildare at the time of the text's composition, does suggest that a relaxed attitude to female claustration continued. It follows the *Vita I* in portraying active, non-enclosed nuns engaged in the care of the lay community and (as in both the *Vita I* and Cogitosus) strongly linked to the male ecclesiastical establishment. If Kildare had experienced a dramatic increase in claustration between the seventh and the ninth centuries, one would see some shift in the portrayal of nuns travelling and their reception of visitors; *Bethu Brigte* implies that this had not occurred.

Killevy's nuns, as portrayed in the 'early' sections of Monenna's Life were portrayed in similar terms: they were providers of care to the laity, and were well-travelled and much-visited. Throughout the Life, the foundress and her maidens are often travelling, and Monenna visits neighbours to be fed by them, receiving hospitality and in return providing miracles; likewise the laity are shown as visiting the monastery and there admitting sins and receiving penances. Other Lives of this early period, such as those in Sharpe's O'Donoghue group in the *Codex Salmenticensis*, show much the same thing.

Given that we see no evidence of nuns being shut away from either male ecclesiastics or laymen in these centuries, the Irish nunnery can look un-monastic. As has been hinted, a similar claim has been made about Irish male monasteries in Ireland for the same period. Significantly, there was no terminological distinction between places for those dedicated to the regular or devotional life and places established to provide for pastoral needs. Nor did the terms for an ecclesiastical establishment convey its wealth, size, regularity of observance, or degree of pastoral care provided; equally there is no linguistic distinction indicating male, female, or mixed houses.[114] The Irish seem not to have

---

[113] Cogitosus, Life of Brigit, ch. 32: *Et sic in una basilica maxima populus grandis in ordine et gradibus et sexu et locis diversus interiectis inter se parietibus diverso ordine et uno animo omnipotentem orat dominatorem.*

[114] That is not to say other information cannot be gleaned from the terms describing ecclesiastical places; see A. MacDonald: 'Notes on Terminology in the Annals of Ulster, 650–1050', *Peritia* 1 (1982), 329–33, and his 'Notes on Monastic Archaeology and the Annals of Ulster, 650–1050' in D. Ó Corráin (ed.), *Irish Antiquity: Essays and Studies Presented to Professor M. J. O'Kelly* (Cork, 1981), 304–19. Similar

separated, even mentally, the places where a monastic life was lived from those responsible for providing pastoral care. As Thomas Charles-Edwards has observed, 'It is extremely difficult, and perhaps wrong in principle, to try to draw a sharp line between monastic and non-monastic churches.'[115]

If the pastoral focus accounts for some if not all of the un-monastic quality of male houses, then we may have the key to understanding the ethos behind the non-enclosure and the high level of contact with the male sex at nunneries. If the nuns' house, like the male monastery, played an important role in local care, then their participation in the effort would mean they had to be involved with men of the church and laity, and their *raison d'être* was not impeded by such contact.

'Open' Nunneries in the Seventh to Ninth Centuries: Was Ireland Unique?

Two comparisons may be broached with places elsewhere in Europe. For Frankia *c.*600 to *c.*900, one finds a good number of women's houses and double houses: the well-known ones were royal, well-endowed, and integral to secular politics. These communities were treated by Wemple in her *Women in Frankish Society*, where she argued that they (and their abbesses) were autonomously active in public life until the ninth century when, under the Carolingian reforms, they were constrained and reduced, and nuns' themselves increasingly strictly cloistered. Schulenberg followed Wemple, noting among other things the shifts in hagiographical portrayals of abbesses: those of earlier centuries are shown as great builders of churches whereas later ones are good at needlework, for example.[116] Like Wemple, she saw these changes as representing a shift in Frankish mores: namely, an acceptance of public female authority gave way to a refusal to have women in public roles. The limitations of this model have been pointed out, with critics noting that public and private were not distinct domains in early medieval Frankia, and also demonstrating that pre-Carolingian women were not as powerful as these two claimed, and post-Carolingian women were not as oppressed.[117] That there was some shift in female hagiographic portrayal, however, has not been disputed: the abbess saints of the

problems are faced by scholars of the Anglo-Saxon Church (S. Foot, 'Parochial Ministry in Early Anglo-Saxon England: the Role of Monastic Communities', in W. Shiels and D. Wood (eds.), *The Ministry: Clerical and Lay* (Studies in Church History 26; Oxford, 1989), esp. 45).

[115] Sharpe, 'Churches'; T. Charles-Edwards, 'The Pastoral Role of the Church in the Early Irish Laws', in Blair and Sharpe, *Pastoral Care*, 63–80; C. Etchingham, 'The Early Irish Church: Some Observations on Pastoral Care and Dues', *Ériu* 42 (1991), 99–118.

[116] J. Schulenberg, 'Female Sanctity, Public and Private, 500–1100', in M. Erler and M. Kowaleski (eds.), *Women and Power in the Middle Ages* (Athens, Ga., 1988), 102–25; J. Schulenberg, 'Strict Active Enclosure and its Effects on the Female Monastic Experience (ca 500–1100)', in J. Nicholls and L. Shank, *Medieval Religious Women I: Distant Echoes* (Kalamazoo, Mich., 1984), 51–86.

[117] Nelson, 'Women and the Word'; Hodgson, 'Frankish Church', esp. 97, 114–23, 145–56; G. Halsall, 'Female Status and Power in Early Merovingian Central Austrasia: the Burial Evidence', *Early Medieval Europe* 5 (1996), 1–24.

earlier Lives are significantly less domestic in their activities, and this may well be due to the needs of a society on the edge of conversion, where an 'all hands on deck' attitude prevailed. Little work has been done on the extent to which nunneries tended the laity beyond the nuns' personal families, but it certainly warrants further study. Small snippets in the Frankish sources may be significant. Regino of Prüm recommended that unwanted babies be left at churches, presumably to be raised in monastic environments.[118] Monasteries, including nunneries, served as boarding schools, and oblation was well-known. As for enclosure, according to the *Regula Cuiusdam Patris ad Virgines*, a seventh-century rule, nuns would work outside the monastery in teams of three or four for full days at a time.[119] For all this, though, there are signs of difference from Ireland, in some cases at least. Firstly, late Merovingian and earlier Carolingian hagiography does not show the patterns of nuns' travel and male–female interaction that we see in the Irish material of the same period.[120] Secondly, there is a sense of retreat from the world, even before the Carolingian reforms, in such a Life as that of Balthild, where the abbess saint was preparing to enter her newly-built monastery of Chelles but was delayed by the Neustrians who were loathe to lose her, so great was their love for her.[121] It seems too, that even a saint such as Fursey who had an active partnership with the woman Gertrude lived in a world where monks and nuns did not worship together, even on great occasions: when Fursey died his body, on its way to the graveyard, was taken through the nuns' church to give the nuns an opportunity to see it.[122] It is probably still too early for generalizations about female sanctity in Frankia, because for such a large area there were certainly regional and temporal variations; detailed small-scale studies must precede such a work if it is to rest on secure footing, and such studies are as yet few in number.[123] Though the Frankish material is very different from the contemporary Irish, it may be that behind the veil of the sources, some parts of the Frankish reality were not dissimilar to the Irish with regard to nuns in large houses and their community relations.

In England at this period, parallels with Ireland are much more apparent. English monasteries, including double houses, have long been recognized as having been centres of pastoral care.[124] Sarah Foot writes, 'a number of those living in monasteries were in clerical orders, but there is no evidence that pastoral

---

[118] Hodgson, 'Frankish Church', 358.

[119] Cited in Wemple, *Women*, 160.

[120] For patterns in Merovingian and Carolingian female hagiography, see Smith, 'Problem', with references. For discussion and translations of late Merovingian Lives, see P. Fouracre and R. Gerberding, *Late Merovingian France: History and Historiography 640–720* (Manchester, 1996).

[121] Life of Balthild, ch. 10.

[122] *Additamenta Nivalense de Fuilano*, in Fouracre and Gerberding, *Merovingian France*, 327.

[123] e.g. Martindale, 'The Nun Immena', in Shiels and Wood (eds.), *Women and the Church*, 27–42.

[124] Though it is thought that some were places of retreat from the world. The 'minster thesis' is a large, on-going subject in Anglo-Saxon ecclesiastical history, and understanding is developing continually.

work was restricted to priests and deacons.'[125] In other words, their nuns have been found providing services to the laity beyond their families and the royal court. Monastics of both sexes prayed for the souls of the king and his people, and both male and female saints were expected to intercede for particular individuals; the neighbouring community would come to the church, Foot thinks, on feast days and at burials. Schneider went further on the latter point, envisioning the laity as present to receive healing, to visit shrines, to visit nuns on their deathbeds, to seek sanctuary as fugitives, to seek spiritual advice, and to visit friends. Some houses, if not all, had a visitors' hospice where such people would stay.[126] This is generally the view of Nicholson, too, who wrote that for women in Bede's day, 'it was no use entering a monastery to get away from men and doubtful whether anyone really wanted to.'[127] Though the English Lives do not have the peripatetic quality so characteristic of Irish ones, nuns do go out from their houses, Schneider demonstrated: like monks they sometimes absented themselves for indeterminate periods to travel and undertake visits, though (unlike Ireland) there was some pressure for *stabilitas*. In addition, she says, nuns were known to teach outside the institution, something not evidenced in Ireland.[128] Schneider postulated that the double house, wherein men and women live in proximity to each other, resulted in the almost total absence of gynophobic writing among churchmen in early Anglo-Saxon England. Nicholson, like her and like Foot, saw the origins of female prominence in the early Church as lying in native secular society: 'Men and women worked together in the secular world and proceeded to do likewise in the cloister.'[129] In the study of English nunneries there is a perceived watershed, with changes, as in Frankia, attributed to ecclesiastical reform. Schneider's periodization is the most articulated version of a model generally accepted. She formulated an early period (*c*.AD 649–796) in which 'double monasteries were the most important political and cultural centres in their respective kingdoms', followed by a scarcely-sourced transitional period (*c*.AD 796–970), in which few new nunneries were founded and many disappeared; from the mid-eighth century, double houses seem to her to have lost their independence from bishops. During the second period, she thinks, there was a coexistence of various living arrangements for nuns, without one taking precedence over another, including religious women living on their own and women attached to male houses.[130] Foot, like Schneider,

[125] Foot, 'Parochial Ministry', 45.   [126] Schneider, 'Anglo-Saxon Women', 64–80.

[127] J. Nicholson, '*Feminae Gloriosae*: Women in the Age of Bede', in D. Baker (ed.), *Medieval Women* (Studies in Church History, Subsidia 1; Oxford, 1978), 15–29, at 19.

[128] Schneider, 'Anglo-Saxon Women', 66–8.

[129] Nicholson, '*Feminae Gloriosae*', 19; Schneider, 'Anglo-Saxon Women' generally but esp. 195–212; S. Foot, *Veiled Women* (forthcoming, 2001) in which it is a general thesis.

[130] Schneider, 'Anglo-Saxon Women', throughout, but for a clear, abbreviated summary see 302–5. She has a third, late period, which she dates from AD 970 onward, when Benedictinism prevailed; she sees in this a loss of power for nunneries (and their inmates), believing reformation came from without rather than from within as some have suggested.

has placed the cause of this watershed not with the Benedictine or Cluniac reforms (as others have), but with the earlier Carolingian reforms.[131] After the changes, whenever and however they occurred, Anglo-Saxonists agree that nunneries were neither as pastoral, nor as open, as they had been in the earlier centuries.[132]

The Irish situation, then, though sharing numerous similarities with England if not so evidently with Frankia, is hardly peculiar in the openness of its female communities. As will become evident in the following chapter, Irish holy women were not confined to these large institutions, so any attempt at comparison with other Western societies must take into account the full range of milieux in which they lived.

---

[131] Foot, *Veiled Women*.

[132] Interestingly, Schneider claims that even into the 11th cent. there were women's houses in England which were not Benedictine, so the changes were apparently not universally applied (Schneider, 'Anglo-Saxon Women', 83–5).

4

Nuns in Other Settings

The women's establishments discussed in the previous chapter do not account for all the hundreds of Irish nuns we hear of in the early medieval sources. As Kathleen Hughes observed, 'There were many women in early Ireland follow-ing a monastic life, for a calendar written about 800 names scores of them who are to be remembered. Yet we only hear of four women's foundations which survived as major monasteries over a long period, Kildare, Killeedy, Killevy, and Clonbroney.'[1] It is not just the martyrologies (calendars) in which the myriad names of holy nuns appear; they are also found in hundreds in the cor-pus of so-called genealogical texts of the saints. Though the texts are most likely to date from little earlier than the eleventh century, they give some sense of the sheer volume of holy women who had lived and were remembered.[2] Four large lists are dedicated solely to women, though women appear in other lists as well. Within the list *Comainmnigud Noem Herenn so sís* ('the Same-Named Saints of Ire-land') is *Comanmand Naebúag Herend so sís* (a list of Same-Named Holy Virgins of Ireland), which names 151 Irish holy women.[3] A second list of holy nuns is *Ingen-rada Noeb Herenn* which contains 109 entries.[4] A third is of the mothers of Irish saints, with 102 entries.[5] Another, a list of the female saints whose houses were governed by Kildare, names some sixty nuns.[6] For many of the names on these lists and calendars, a place name is given. But in what sort of monasteries, dwellings, churches, or hermitages did these nuns live? According to the sources, they lived in a range of environments, under a remarkable variety of arrangements.

---

[1] K. Hughes and A. Hamlin, *The Modern Traveller to the Early Irish Church* (London, 1977), 8.

[2] Ed. Ó Riain, *Corpus Genealogiarum*. The manuscripts in which these appear include the Book of Leinster, Bodl. Rawl. B502, the Book of Ballymote, the Great Book of Lecan, and BM Addit. 30512. Ó Riain's dating, pp. xvi–xviii.

[3] Ó Riain, *Corpus Genealogiarum*, 153–6. For an earlier edition see Brosnan, *Archivium Hibernicum*, 353–60. Text discussed in *Kenney*, no. 278.

[4] Ó Riain, *Corpus Genealogiarum*, 159–60. The version in the Book of Leinster is in R. Best *et al.*, *The Book of Leinster*, 6 vols. (Dublin, 1983) vi. 1678–81.

[5] Ó Riain, *Corpus Genealogiarum*, 169–81. Book of Leinster version in *Book of Leinster*, vi. 1692–97.

[6] 'List of Nuns Subject to Saint Brigit', Ó Riain, *Corpus Genealogiarum*, 112–18. Also in *Book of Leinster*, vi. 1580–1. Discussed in *Kenney*, no. 150: 'this document gives a list of nuns subject to Brigit, and of their churches'.

NUNS AT MEN'S MONASTERIES

Virtually unmentioned in the voluminous scholarly literature of Irish monasticism is the fact that many male monasteries had nuns in their *familiae*. As a result, the researcher comes upon the many documentary references to this effect with no small amount of surprise. Perhaps the older generation of Irish historians failed to take up these references in part because they fly in the face of the traditional image of the early Irish church as an ascetic 'Celtic' church, whose monks were so holy (so the stereotype goes) that they avoided contact with females. Gwynn and Hadcock, writing *Monastic Houses* in 1970, clearly knew of the phenomenon, for they mapped and indexed the male monasteries which had nuns and, according to their reckonings, very many fell into this category. These two authors, however, offered no analysis, explanation, or comment on their findings.[7] Lisa Bitel in 'Women's Monastic Enclosures' briefly remarked on the phenomenon of nuns at male houses as part of an observation that many women's enclosures were dependencies of male houses, a point she made in support of her argument that female foundations were economically weak as the early Irish church was generally misogynist, a view largely unaltered in *Land of Women*.

The evidence on the subject is substantial enough to reward study, and what emerges from the material is extremely interesting. The most noteworthy feature is the writers' lack of preoccupation with gender. Whilst the nuns who lived at male monasteries were doubtless housed separately, they were not demonized nor was their sexuality a topic on which ecclesiastical writers focused. Women and men are described as living together at Armagh 'almost inseparably'; Tallaght's monks were encouraged to go to speak to the monastery's nuns even though the monks might suffer lust in doing so. The evidence for this period simply does not support Bitel's claim that nuns outside nunneries 'became a threat to society, and male monastic society in particular'.[8]

In the seventh- to ninth-century period, there are approximately fifty references to nuns who were residents of male monasteries. 'Residence' requires some explanation. In some cases, a female church had its own name but was 'at' the male monastery; in such cases there can be problems in determining the degree of affiliation between the nuns' community and the monastery to which it was attached, especially in those cases where the holy women lived at some distance from the men. In such cases it is not always possible to determine whether the nuns' community was integral to the monastery's administrative structure and ruled by its abbot, or was simply within its jurisdiction or monastic federation. Of course there were differing levels and types of affiliation. And just as

---

[7] The vast majority of all such references are in the chapter on women's establishments, though the map enclosed in the jacket of the book lists many more places as having adherents of both sexes. For this no explanation is offered.

[8] Bitel, 'Women's Enclosures', 31.

there were various sorts of affiliation, so too do the texts show that the degree of contact between monk and nun also varied from place to place. In identifying a group of nuns as being 'at' a men's monastery, I include those which were within the administrative structure and which were physically within its bounds or locale. Included in the discussion below are monasteries at which women were reported only as temporary members, that is to say, students. This is because there would have been a constant female presence, transient though it may have been.[9]

Nuns at Armagh

Armagh (Ir. Ard Macha) in Ulster south of Lough Neagh was allegedly founded by saint Patrick, though this is by no means certain, and it achieved island-wide fame only in the seventh century when its leaders attempted make it into the archiepiscopal church for the whole of Ireland. It was wealthy and powerful, and remained so, and thus is unsurprisingly the best-attested of the monasteries which had nuns, though its function as an episcopal see means that to call it simply a monastery is somewhat misleading. A seventh-century text, the *Liber Angeli*, says that at Armagh, from its founding up to the author's day, Christians of both sexes lived together in religion, almost inseparably, but worshipping in different churches; the women included holy virgins.[10] Although the nuns attended church with the penitents and married people rather with the clerics and anchorites, it is of central importance that the author emphasized that the sexes lived 'almost inseparably'. The nuns and other devout women belong to (*adherent*) Armagh. It would be most normal, based on what is known of sanctuary boundary-setting, to presume that the church of the northern area (the women's church) lay within the monastery's boundary or *termonn*. Noting the language, which appears actually to boast of the closeness of the male and female communities, it might just be that the author was attempting to compete in this regard with Kildare, which was Ireland's foremost, if not its *only* double monastery. The two houses were in competition for archiepiscopal status during this period, and the text is part of Armagh's propaganda for that position, so perhaps serving both men and women was a selling-point of which Kildare boasted, and the author wished to offer Armagh as an equal in that respect. Such a suggestion is, admittedly, is no more than speculation.

In the seventh or eighth century another writer, the hagiographer of St Ailbe, imagined that in the fifth century nuns had been part of Patrick's community, telling the story of an *ancilla* in Patrick's retinue who became pregnant by one of his chariot-drivers.[11] Later texts report two specifically women's churches at Armagh, Temple Brigid and Tempul-na-ferta ('church of the graves'), the latter

---

[9] The Lives of Monenna and Finnian show this educational role of nuns quite strongly.
[10] *Liber Angeli*, ch. 14.   [11] Latin Life of Ailbe, Φ text, ch. 125.

claiming to have the relics of Patrick's sister Lupait.[12] The notes on the Martyrology of Oengus, dating to the tenth or eleventh century, say that actually
within the precinct boundary of Armagh was a Cell-na-Noebingen, 'church of
the holy virgins',[13] and to the east of Armagh a place called Cell-na-nIngen,
'church of the virgins'. The Tripartite Life of Patrick, written some time in the
tenth- to twelfth-century period, also mentions the Cell-na-nIngen in the east of
Armagh, which apparently boasted the relics of two female *peregrinae*.[14] It also
tells of a virgin (*ingen*) who set up at a place called Cengoba which must have
been adjacent to the monastery as a monk came every night from Patrick's place
to bring her ration of food.[15]

   In the latter churches, it can hardly have been known what sort of inhabitants
there were during the seventh, eighth, and ninth centuries because the 'virgins'
might be old relics rather than living inhabitants: that is to say, the *ingena* of
Cell-na-nIngen might be the remains in the graveyard. Given the thaumatur-
gical importance of the relics, even those buried in a grave, this is a possibility. At
many other places, however, a 'church of virgins' did refer to living nuns, and so
it may well be that it was so at Armagh as well.

Nuns at other Men's Monasteries

Tallaght (Ir. Tamlachta) was a large monastery located at the foot of Dublin
mountains, in a place that is now a south Dublin suburb. It was founded in the
late eighth century by saint Maelruain as a reform monastery of the *céli Dé* or
Culdees, a native movement whose aim was a return to monastic simplicity.
This new house, despite its reform agenda, included a group of nuns in its community. Like Armagh, it boasted an oratory named 'Cell-na-nIngen', but in this
case the witness is from the ninth century and is almost contemporary; beyond
that, it makes it clear that, at Tallaght at least, the *cell* was the church around
which a living female community at the monastery was based.[16] From *c.*AD 840,
only about fifty years later than the time it purports to describe, the Customs of
Tallaght show the *céli Dé*—though aiming to revitalize monastic life—reconcil-
ing pastoral duty with ascetic sex-separation: the monks would visit the nuns,
but a chaperone had to be present. Such visits were considered good and necessary, and if the mind wandered unbidden to lustful thought during such visits, it
was not a sin.

Maccaildecha craibdecha id serc lais daul doa hacaldaim 7 do nertad irsi doib 7 i nem-
fecsiu inda gnuis 7 senoir it coimitecht 7 anacaldaim iarum for aulaid oc cros ind dorus
lis no isind disirt imbíatt 7 ind senoir dano teiti latsa 7 senoir caildidi bis a comaitecht na

---

[12] Gwynn and Hadcock, *Religious Houses*, 312–13.
[13] Martyrology of Oengus, notes on 8 Oct.
[14] Tripartite Life of Patrick (Stokes, *Tripartite Life*, i. 232–3). Appears in the text as 'Coll-na-nIngen'.
[15] Ibid.   [16] Martyrology of Oengus, notes on 26 Oct.

maccaildidi do bith hi farrad 7 ni cian huaib imbíat. Andand donetarrat míaccobar nó míimradad tre faicsin no ac acaldaim mbanscál ma atrocuil am menme nad cometesta dó ceith folam deit ni fil bríg laisiom hisind accobar sin. Is fochric immurgu ma gabthair tairis andand mbis a foindel inda menmain commór fri mimradud a timtasad for caúlae feib dorrontar 7 tuidecht légind nó a scrutain fris 7 menme isind aurnaigti. Nicon aorsusa laisiom commas pende ara faoendel sin indda menman. Fobithin nícomór imbisom ifus eitir.[17]

Devout young nuns he thinks it right to go and converse with and to confirm their faith, but without looking upon their faces, and taking an elder in your company: and it is right to converse with them standing on the slab by the cross in front of the hostel, or in the retreat where they live. And the elder who goes with you, and the senior nun who lives in the company of the young nuns, should be present and not far from you, where they are. When ill desires or ill thoughts overtake you, through seeing women or in converse with them, it is not to be indulged by you even as an idle thought, then he considers that such desire is not great matter; it is meritorious, however, if a man gets clear of it.

Thus, contact was good, but care had to be taken by the monks to minimize the chances of an attack of lust. The monks were not to look at the nuns, but this advice is clearly given for the men's own sakes and not because the nuns were believed to be temptresses. The nuns of Tallaght were considered part of the overall community, for there are stipulations concerning them in the rule for monks, such as that, mentioned above, stipulating that during their monthly periods nuns were free from some vigils and got a special gruel at tierce. That notice, incidentally, not only informs us of their inclusion in the membership of Tallaght *familia*, but also shows that nuns were sympathetically accommodated.[18]

The martyrologies also show evidence of women there: they commemorate two holy women Cóemsa and Cróna, virgins of Tallaght, on 25 February, and the anniversary of the translation of the virgin Scíath of Fert Scéthe's relics there from Munster, 6 September, was a feast.[19]

At the same time, the other *céli Dé* monastery, Finglas (on the site of what is now another Dublin suburb) also had a nun's residence. The Customs of Tallaght relate the story of a nun (*caillech*) who approached Finglas's abbot, Dublitir, to ask if she could stay in its nuns' enclosure (*les callech*).[20] He rudely refused, and his confessor bishop, standing nearby, intervened to order him to give her the requested permission, plus a cow and a cloak in recompense for his

---

[17] Customs of Tallaght, ch. 62.

[18] Rule of the *Céli Dé* in the *Leabhar Breac* (in Reeves, at 211. As the chapters are not numbered, references are by page number of this edition).

[19] For the former two: Martyrology of Gorman. For the last: martyrologies of Tallaght, Oengus, Gorman, and Donegal, with Martyrology of Tallaght, *adventus reliquiarum Scethi filiae Mechi ad Tamlachtain*. Fert Scéithe in the 'Muscraige tri Maige' has been identified with mod. Ardskeagh, Co. Cork (*Onomasticon*).

[20] Customs of Tallaght, ch. 7. Gwynn and Purton give *les* as 'hostel', but it is better translated, with *Dictionary*, as 'the space about a dwelling-house enclosed by a bank or rampart' or 'enclosure' in the sense of a defined area in the monastic settlement.

unkind words. Since the nun had waited to speak to Dublitir in a field that was 'over the stile on the other side of the monks' garden' (*asind gurt . . . tarsa ceim isind faichti*), it suggests that nuns were not permitted inside one of Finglas's inner enclosures.

According to several authors the monastic church of Kells (Ir. Caenannus) in Meath also had resident nuns. Little is known about its foundation, but it was flourishing in the seventh century when Tírechán located the nun Comgella at a church next to it. In 807 it was taken over by the monastic community of Saint Columba, which moved there from Iona on account of Viking attacks. It was a Columban foundation when the later writer of Patrick's Tripartite Life repeated the story.[21] A tenth- or eleventh-century writer stated that a church called within the Kells precinct, Tech-na-mBretan, or 'the church of the Britons', might have been the home of four female saints.[22] Another writer of roughly the same era stated categorically that a holy nun named Lúachair had lived at 'Elgraige chapel' within the precinct of Kells (*i Termon Cenansa*).[23]

In Ossory, in what is modern Co. Laois, was the monastery of Aghaboe (Ir. Achad Bó), founded by saint Cainnech (obit *c.*560). A seventh- or eighth-century Latin Life says it had a nun living nearby who came to the abbot when she found herself in difficulty.[24] Another Life says Cainnech ministered to (*ministrabat*) a religious woman who once hit one of his boy students whilst he accompanied her on her milking chores. What does this mean? That she lived nearby? That she lived at his church? We cannot know more than that the writer imagined the nun to be near enough to Cainnech for his boys to tag along at her daily work.[25]

One ninth-century love story portrays a broken-hearted poetess as living out her days at the midlands monastery of Clonfert on the River Shannon as a nun under its famously ascetic abbot Cummean Fota (obit 661).[26]

For some places the only evidence of female presence, or female relics, is from the tenth century or later. Late male saints' Lives report affiliated nuns communities at Clones, Seirkieran, Monasterboice, Daig's Inishkeen, Edergole, and Lismore.[27] Of course, it would be immensely helpful to know whether there really were women at these places before the tenth century, but until such time as untrammelled texts or archaeology fill in the gaps in the evidential record, further conclusions cannot be drawn.

[21] Tírechán, Memoirs, ch. 27; Stokes, *Tripartite Life*, i. 105. On the site of Kells, see A. Simms with K. Simms, *Kells* (Irish Historic Towns Atlas 4; Dublin, 1990), and H. Roe, *The High Crosses of Kells* (Kildalkey, 1959).

[22] Martyrology of Oengus, notes on 26 Oct.

[23] Martyrology of Tallaght, notes on 5 Apr.

[24] Latin Life of Cainnech, Φ text, ch. 56. A version of the episode, also placing the nun, now a small group of nuns, next to Aghaboe, is in the Life of Samthann, ch. 18.

[25] Latin Life of Colmán of Lynally, Φ text, ch. 2.

[26] 'Liadain and Curithir', ed. and trans. K. Meyer, *Liadain and Curithir: An Irish Love Story from the Ninth Century* (London, 1902), paras. 1–2.

[27] See below, Ch. 8.

Some of the nuns' communities had more uncertain affiliations to male houses. Where a source is unclear the nunnery in question may have been autonomous, though not necessarily so. Attached to Seirkieran in north-west Leinster, for example, the founding saint Ciarán's mother Liadain was said to have headed a group of consecrated virgins who lived at some distance from her son's monastery.[28] At 'Cell Ailbe' (lit. Ailbe's church) in eastern Meath there were nuns who had been supervised by a virgin Segnith under the care of Saint Abbán.[29] Ruadán founded a place for his sister Daroi: that place, says Tírechán, was given (*oblatus*) to eternity to the people (*plebilibus*) of Ruadán.[30] These and other references are from saints' Lives, and as such may represent spurious origination stories to justify jurisdictional claims; on the other hand, they might be indications that at the time of writing there were women religious attached to the places.

In all of these cases, though, the nuns lived on land which was part of an established monastery, not kin land which was 'private' in the sense that the possessors could return it to secular use. Nor were they living under the aegis of a male family member, unless it was one who was the abbot. Thus we can assert with confidence that nuns who did not join the few large nunneries were not necessarily pawns of their relatives, and had options other than to try to convert kin land to a religious residence for the duration of their lifetime.

NUNS AT EPISCOPAL CHURCHES/MONASTERIES

The mid-sized monastery or church with a resident bishop is a type which Richard Sharpe calls a 'mother-church' (likening it to an Anglo-Saxon minster church), though this is a term I would eschew in favour of 'episcopal church'. Sharpe imagines that such places would typically have supplied priests and financial support to local chapels, would have overseen the pastoral care of an area, *túath* or province, and would have had a cemetery. They 'were often established at an early date, and served wide communities which looked to them as patronal churches for generations.'[31] In addition, they would take in payments from families with proprietary interests for the provision of that care. Tenants, clients, or *mánaig* worked the church's lands. Of the non-tenant monks, i.e. those who were technically clerical or monastic, a majority might not follow a regular life. At some places it was a only sub-group of the residents that followed a more strict regular observance.[32]

[28] Life of Ciarán of Seirkieran, D text, chs. 4, 8–9, 24 (*PVSH*, i. 217–33).
[29] Life of Abbán, D text, ch. 32 (*PVSH*, i. 3–33).
[30] Latin Life of Ruadán, Φ text, ch. 7 (*Heist*, 160–7).
[31] Sharpe, 'Churches', 106.   [32] Ibid. 100–2.

The mother-churches were surely communities of priests and other clergy, some of whom may have been monks living under vows; the communal life may well have included the regular singing of the office, but it did not exclude priests from pastoral activity. In recognizing that such churches were communities (Lat. *familia* or *populus*, Ir. *muintir*), it is all too easy to lapse into the phrase 'monastic community' and so to 'monastery', but we must avoid exaggerating the distinction between regular and secular communities.[33]

Sharpe did not address the situation of an episcopal church which was also a female community, but it is evident that a few female communities claimed to have had a bishop as a member in their earliest days, as was seen in the above, and at least one of the churches included by Sharpe in this category was founded by a nun: the free church of Tawnagh on the eastern shore of the Unshin River south of Sligo on the site of the modern village of Riverstown.[34] Whatever the extent of the pastoral care it provided, we know that it could boast free status and a bishop. According to Tírechán its foundress was a nun, a woman named Mathona who had been a nun to Patrick and Ruadán before she left them to found the place; the two saints then placed bishops at the church. Mathona made a solemn compact with the successors of Ruadán. This compact probably did not put the church in Ruadán's *paruchia*, at least as far as Armagh was concerned, for it was claiming it by including it in the Memoirs. At the time Tírechán was writing the church was held by Clonmacnois (*familia Cluain*).[35] The Additamenta to Tírechán outline how three nuns acquired property at Tawnagh (presumably the same place), then alienated to Armagh. Using a marital portion and the proceeds of the sale of a hand-made cloak (significantly a piece of movable property that had not been inherited) the nun acquired some land and with her companions gave (*immransat*) to the *paruchia* of Armagh the lands of Tawnagh, Tír Gimmae, and Muine Búachaile.[36] An unidentified Tawnagh, possibly this one, was remembered at the turn of the twelfth century for its virgins Ascla and Lucán, commemorated in the Martyrology of Gorman.[37]

The episcopal church of Aghagower (Ir. Achad Fobuir) in rocky western Connaught was initially inhabited by a brother and sister in religion named Senachus and Mathona, according to Tírechán. Patrick, he alleged, consecrated the place for Mathona and said to the pair, 'There will be good bishops here, and from their seed blessed people will come forth forever in this see.'[38] Finally, at Glentogher (in Inishowen) there was a church in the seventh century

---

[33] Ibid. 101–2.
[34] Ibid. 92–3. The place has been identified as mod. Riverstown, ten miles south of the town of Sligo.
[35] Tírechán, Memoirs, ch. 24.
[36] In 'The Cowherd's Brake', the latter three places are identified as being adjacent: Muinae Buachaele is *iuxta Tir Gemmae et Tamlach* (Bieler, *Patrician Texts*, 262).
[37] Martyrology of Gorman for 23 Jan. Lucán is also commemorated in the notes of the same day in the Martyrology of Oengus.
[38] Tírechán, Memoirs, ch. 37.

which was believed to have been first inhabited by a man and woman together: a bishop and his sister of the Corcu Theimne people.[39] This church may have been small in Tírechán's day, but it was sufficiently rich or important for him to claim it formally as part of the *paruchia* of Armagh.

A few *domnach* churches, those which originally were episcopal and often carried on as such, were known to be associated with women; these churches, according to such ideals as those posited in *Riagail Phátraic*, were charged with the provision of pastoral care. Donaghmore in Morett appears in the eighth- or ninth-century Notulae in the Book of Armagh. It was given, the text indicates, to Mugain and Fedelm, two virgins identified in the Martyrology of Oengus as the daughters of Ailill.[40] Another, Maynooth, appears in the Notulae with the name Erc who, according also to slightly later material, had been a holy woman of that place.[41] Finally, the martyrologies commemorate the virgins Segnat of Donoughkerny and Bí of Donnybrook, two otherwise unknown holy women whose dwellings, or final resting places, were at *domnach* churches.[42]

The presence of nuns at the communities inhabiting 'episcopal churches' as defined by Sharpe, and at *domnach* churches would locate them at known, longstanding centres of pastoral care. It is uncertain if the holy women named above represent more of a female presence than a burial in the churchyard, but it may be that vowed women continued in service at these places, and evidence may come to light of a more determining nature. More than this we cannot say, apart from adding that in late hagiography a number of bishops were said to live with virgins.[43]

NUNS AT SMALL CHURCHES

The process of understanding the small local church in early Ireland is in its early stages, and to consider nuns in this context one must first take a short historiographical detour. Ireland's early small churches, of which there were hundreds if not thousands, are attested in martyrologies, Lives, and lists; about most of them nothing more than a name, and possibly a location, is known. Traditionally they have been seen through one of two lenses. The first, the product of

---

[39]   Tírechán, Memoirs, ch. 47, where the place is called Mag Tochui or Tochuir.

[40]   Notulae in the Book of Armagh, no. 44, where it appears as Domnach Mór Maige Réto; the present location is Morett in the eastern midlands.

[41]   Notulae in the Book of Armagh, no. 39; Martyrology of Oengus, 27 Oct., also commemorates 'Erc of Domnach Mór', glossed as 'Mag [L]uadat'. Mag Luadat is the same as Mag Nuadat, hence 'Maynooth' (the place-name is treated in some depth in *Onomasticon*).

[42]   Segnat, 18 Dec.; Bí, 30 Sept. Domnach Ceirne is located on the east coast, either just north of Dublin or at the mouth of the Boyne, according to *Onomasticon*. Domnach Brocc is Donnybrook, Dublin.

[43]   There is a genre in poetry and hagiography relating to the earliest phase of the Irish Church, of the virgin who dwells with the sainted bishop. Most of these stories are from the 11 and 12th cents., but there is earlier material on sexually active bishops. See below, Ch. 6.

the decades of intensive monastic studies, creates an image of them as eremitic retreats and/or small monastic communities.[44] The other 'lens', more prevalent in this generation, is that of early medieval history of the West generally; it is ground of the glass of Bede's famous complaint that people in England in his day were designating their homes as churches simply in order to pay lower taxes, because 'church land' was taxed more lightly, but in doing so they did not actually adopt the religious life, nor did they dedicate their buildings to religious purpose. This trend was noted on the Continent as well as in England, as the *eigenkirche*, or 'proprietary church', phenomenon. It characteristically featured a landowning family retaining control over the buildings, staffing, revenue, and property of the church. It could also, presumably, return it to secular status if and when it needed to do so, providing it was willing to forego the benefits. Donnchadh Ó Corráin applied this analysis to Ireland, arguing that local churches were treated as inheritances, i.e. that a majority of local churches were private chapels on private land, owned and controlled by the landowning families.[45] There are corollary assumptions, too. Ó Corráin thought it followed logically that ministry in small Irish churches was probably 'haphazard and occasionally non-existent' and that such places could be put out of 'church' use.[46] This position assumes that the landowning families controlled small churches on kin lands *to the extent that* they could discontinue their use on the death of the heir or heiress who had endowed the church.

Kathleen Hughes took the idea of the private church and extrapolated that landowning families would often discontinue the religious use of those churches in which they had proprietary interests, and she applied this model, tailored to take account of female inheritance law, to small female communities. She noted that the martyrologies and the saint lists show that many nuns lived at small sites, because in hundreds of cases a place-name is given along with the saint's name. She saw these as short-lived places run by heiresses on land belonging to their kindred.

The enormous discrepancy between the minute number of women's houses and the very large number of pious women must be due to the Irish law of inheritance. For a woman could not acquire more than a life interest in the land she inherited: on her death it passed back to her kin. Only if she acquired land for services rendered or by gift could she transmit it to her heirs. I think that many monasteries were set up on family lands; there is some good evidence for this, and it explains many of the peculiar features of Irish monasticism. The pious women who appear in the martyrologies probably supported a few like-minded friends during their lives, but their households must have broken up

[44] e.g. Ryan, *Irish Monasticism*.

[45] 'Indeed, one may suspect that some churches were merely family estates which were turned into church establishments with little change either in function or appearance apart from a little church or graveyard and the ministrations of a priest if he were available' (Ó Corráin, 'Early Irish Churches', 338–9).

[46] Ibid. 334.

with their deaths. Only in the few cases where a substantial grant of land was obtained by some gift could a perpetual monastic community have been founded.[47]

The model, in slightly different form, is presented elsewhere as well.[48] The thesis meets some opposition from the evidence in Ireland. As the following discussion shows, many small holy women's sites served the wider laity, had collegial connections to church officials, and survived for centuries in ecclesiastical use. A solution to the problem can be found in an alternative understanding of the small church, namely that put forward by Sharpe in 'Churches and Communities'. To him it seemed more likely that small local churches were used for ecclesiastical purposes over the long term, rather than being returned to secular use by their proprietors. Secular families could have hereditary interests in, or control over, the property of the churches, but the bishop held control over the church itself. Bishops had considerable control over small foundations (whatever their origins), and *Riagail Phátraic* is cited as a central piece of evidence for this.[49] The bishop was responsible for making sure that the churches were properly staffed with clergy and financed by the landowning family, so that pastoral care would reach the laity through them. Church authorities could force the proprietary family to make contributions to the church's upkeep and through the bishop, the Church ensured that small churches did not cease being used for religious purposes. Thus a proprietary church may well have served the laity of a community, and may well have been regarded as a sort of parish church.

The significance of private control of churches has been emphasised by Professor Ó Corráin, who has drawn attention to the many churches mentioned in association with particular families by the secular genealogies. This pattern . . . is in no way peculiar. Nor should one assume that private ownership prevented a wider pastoral ministry: the church which a lord regarded as his *eclais dúthaig* 'hereditary church' may well have been perceived as the proper church of his kinsmen and all their clients; in other words, it served the local community.[50]

Women's situations can be fitted easily into this scenario. The proprietary church at which the heiress was established could become a feature in the local landscape; the people of the area might become accustomed to visiting it either for masses arranged by the local bishop, or simply to ask for prayers and spiritual assistance from the nuns. If this did indeed occur, it resolves the apparent conflict of model: we can see such places, then, in both their proprietary context and in the role of providers of spiritual care. There was no clear distinction between monastery and church, and it is plausible to think that the Irish would

---

[47] Hughes, *Sources*, 234–5.

[48] 'The Irish law of inheritance probably explains the discrepancies between the large number of holy women and the tiny number of women's houses. We should imagine a lot of small establishments for women at any one time, but they must have broken up on the death of the woman who had provided the endowment' (Hughes and Hamlin, *Modern Traveller*, 8).

[49] Sharpe, 'Churches', 101; see also Etchingham, 'Bishops'.   [50] Sharpe, 'Churches', 106.

tolerate holy women as concierges and/or residents of those small churches which had a laity-serving function. This would be consistent with the attitudes seen in the seventh-century evidence on outward-looking Kildare.

Hughes was right to point out that Irish law distinguished between inherited land and acquired land, and to point out that women inherited only a lifetime's use of property, so that a family might set up for a woman a place for her which, after her death, might revert to secular use. But that need not have been desirable, for if the woman achieved some fame for her holiness and was buried at her church, the cemetery thus became a *reilic*, a relic-cemetery. This would make the cemetery appealing to the nearby laity, since burial next to a holy person was most advantageous on Judgement Day. In Ireland there was a common belief that a holy person would ensure the entry into heaven of those buried in his or her cemetery, and it is known that many wished to be buried in the graveyards of saints.[51] When people made an arrangement to be buried with a saint they incurred certain obligations to that church; they in some way were entering the saint's *familia*.[52] This meant that a woman, becoming a virgin at a local church with a *reilic* attached, would thus become a head of a place that could, with any luck, become a centre for burial and thus income and honour from other noble kindreds of the region. Burials brought payments to the family owners. A graveyard would attract people for other purposes too, for graveyards with a holy grave were sites of oaths, treaties, business contracts, penitential acts, goods storage, meetings, and other community events.[53] If regular masses were said in the Irish countryside (and this is a point of debate), then these little churches would be an obvious place to host them, likewise baptisms, and the latter also incurred a fee. If a nun or two continued at the place, they could earn additional money from fostering and teaching, the fees for which are spelt out in the law tracts. Thus, the fact that a family retained ultimate control of a nun's land and may have reallocated it to another family member after the woman's death need hardly have meant the end of its ecclesiastical use. This would be the case even if it no longer served a female residential community, and possibly even if the next custodian was male, if the English examples are anything to go by.

A closer look at the inheritance law regarding land use reveals a loophole, too. If woman received land as a gift, or as payment for services rendered, she could sometimes bequeath it in perpetuity it to a monastic federation or to her female successors.[54] So holy women who had substantial acquired, rather than inherited, lands, could establish churches that would out-live them. Though the evidence is sparse, there may have been many such places. Regardless of how often this was done, it is evident that religious women had the potential to create and sustain long-lasting, monastic and laity-serving small-scale churches.

[51] On burial and cemeteries, see S. Fry, *Burial in Medieval Ireland, 900–1500* (Dublin, 1999); Edwards, *Archaeology*, 110–21.

[52] T. Charles-Edwards, *Early Irish and Welsh Kinship* (Oxford, 1993), 260–4.

[53] Fry, *Burial*, 47–56.   [54] Such a case is evidenced in the Additamenta to Tírechán, ch. 11.

Nuns at Local Churches: the Evidence

This model, too, most satisfactorily fits several important pieces of Irish evidence that demonstrate the presence of nuns at small local churches. Given the diversity of the sources, they are best discussed each in turn before the conclusions are stated.

The Old Irish Penitential, an eighth-century text, explicitly asserts that nuns, like clerics, might belong to a church of the *túath*.[55] A nun, like a cleric, would be based at the church, and moreover, the obligations of both were the same:

Cleirich nó caillech bís ind eclais oentath lasambí ní for a leortu sechib ret taibreth di bochtaib 7 adilcnib dond eclais imbíi. Mani denai escomnaigther oen eclais imbíi. Ma dogne aithrigi pennid sechtair airet rombói for a chubus cen forngaire senora air is ansu do eclais oentath imbí lóg ndirnai di sainchrund nó dichmairc oldas bith tene dia loscud ar met imefolngai di fodurd 7 formut 7 aninni indi lasambi amail dondrim eóin casian.[56]

Any cleric or nun who lives in a communal church [a church of the *túath*] and who has somewhat more than suffices him, whatever it be, let him give it to the poor and needy of the church where he lives. If he does not, let him be excommunicated from the church where he lives. If he repents, he is to do penance apart for as long as the sin has been on his conscience without express command of the superior: for it is worse for a communal church in which there is the value of a *dirna* of private property or stolen goods than if a fire were in it, by reason of the amount of murmuring and ill feeling of the man that owns it, as John Cassian stated.

This passage implies a number of things. The first is that the nun was responsible for the local church's work among the laity. The second is that she was attached to that church and could be excommunicated from it by a higher ecclesiastical authority. The third is that she was attached to the church of the *túath*, not just to an eremitical or monastic place.

Another piece of evidence is the legal tract *Bretha Nemed Toísech* from the early eighth century. It lists twenty-four indicators of debased practice which cause a church to lose its status, and the list includes being without baptism, without communion, without mass, without praying for the dead, without preaching, and without penitents; it concludes by mentioning misappropriation and private property. Some entries concern inappropriate people holding office: an ex-layman tending it, a young boy in its stewardship, and the last, of interest here: 'a nun announcing its canonical hours' (*caillech do fócru a tráth*).[57] That phrase indicates that when a church was neglected by proper clergy, nuns might take to tending to such needs as announcing the hours. In order for nuns to step in and assist with such things, it is reasonable to assume that they lived at (or adjacent to) the church site.

---

[55] Dating of the text: Binchy, 'Old Irish Penitential', 258.

[56] Old Irish Penitential, ch. 3, item 10 (Irish follows Gwynn, Eng. trans. follows Binchy).

[57] *Bretha Nemed Toísech*, ch. 6 (L. Breatnach, 'The First Third of *Bretha Nemed Toísech*', *Ériu* 40 (1989), 1–40, at 10–11).

Another regulation of a similar sort, also apparently directed at the small church in danger of neglect, is found amongst the ninth-century corpus of aphorisms called the Triads. Triad 66 gives three things forbidden of a church: a nun serving as bell ringer (*caillech fri clocc*), a veteran in the abbotship, and a drop (of wine?) upon the altar.[58] Again, such a regulation makes sense only if nuns lived on or by the premises of a church, and if they sometimes filled such roles when male clerics and monastics were in short supply.

The saints' Lives also provide relevant evidence. The solo nun living at a small church in the Irish countryside appears early on and continues as a stand-ard character throughout the early medieval period. A good example is in Brigit's *Vita I*: there was a *virgo religiosa* so poor she had but one calf, and she was in a terrible state when she had to kill it to prepare a meal of hospitality for a vis-iting saint.[59] Clearly this figure is a solitary woman, and one who was not an heiress. The Life also relates that the *nutrix* or fosterer of Brigit was a nun. As no community is mentioned, and she seems to be on her own, the suggestion is that solitary holy women might perform such services to the laity as fostering. Else-where the same Life mentions a religious widow who lived near the girl's family, seemingly on her own: *religiosa quaedam vidua in proximo vico habitans postulavit a patre eius ut sancta Brigita secum exiret ad sinodum.*[60]

Tírechán attests to several churches in the Wood of Fochloch (*Silva Foclutis*) in his day: 'Patrick's great church' containing the relics of bishop Cethiacus, a church containing the relics of a bishop Mucnoe, another those of the bishop Mac Ercce, and another consecrated (allegedly) by Patrick for two unnamed vir-gins.[61] The latter's wealth was sufficient for it to be claimed for Armagh.

Other examples are provided by the Latin Lives of the O'Donoghue group, written in the seventh or eighth century.[62] These mention small communities of outward-looking holy women, some named, others unnamed; they even indi-cate that some lived on their own with no recourse to family resources.[63] Áed helped a small group of poor nuns at an un-named location.[64] There was a com-munity of nuns at a place called Drumard (Ir. Druim Ard) now unknown and probably quite small.[65] In the Life of Ailbe we hear of the virgin Bithe and her companion, whose name and place would seem to have meant something to the intended audience, but who leaves no other trace.[66] In the Life of Cainnech, the

---

[58] In K. Meyer, *The Triads of Ireland* (Royal Irish Academy Todd Lecture Series 13; Dublin, 1906), at 8–9.

[59] *Vita I* of Brigit, ch. 113.   [60] Ibid., chs. 10, 14.   [61] Tírechán, Memoirs, chs. 42–3, 14.

[62] The process by which Sharpe dated the body of Lives (the O'Donoghue group texts, abbreviated Φ) to this 100-year span is laid out at length in his *Medieval Irish Saints Lives*, with conclusions on 329.

[63] Latin Life of Áed mac Bricc, Φ text (*Heist*, 167–81): unnamed female communities, chs. 12, 20, 22, and women's community at Druimm Ard, chs. 15, 16.

[64] Ibid., chs. 12, 16.

[65] Ibid., ch. 15. Plummer noted that there are many Drum Ards but this one might be mod. Drumard in Banagh, Donegal.

[66] Latin Life of Ailbe, Φ text, ch. 47.

saint fasted against a king on behalf of his religious sister (*soror religiosa*) resulting in the king leaving her a *locus*.[67] In the Life of Colmán, the virgin Camna gained the help of the saint in freeing her people from a wicked king, and when this was achieved they found a small church prepared for Camna (*invenerunt cellulam quamdam paratam apud sanctam Camnam*).[68] One Life at least speaks to the outward-looking ethos which could propel women: in Monenna's Life (in a part of uncertain date) the saint sends off one of her maidens to return to her native land to 'build hermitages and find the lost multitude'.[69]

The majority of incidents in the Lives involving nuns explicitly mention their communities or speak of them as a group, so it is exceptional for a nun to be mentioned without reference to her *familia*. Given that in all these tales the lack of resources is an issue speaks of an inability of the woman to rely upon her germane family. This militates against an image of women being supported by the wealth of their families whilst indulging in religion as a lifetime hobby. Rather, it suggests that at the time that these stories were written some religious women lived on their own or in very small groups at churches, and that their economic ties and personal identities were not taken primarily from their families but from their ecclesiastical status.

As a note to the consideration of small, now-unknown churches, it must be pointed out that they were not a particularly 'female' phenomenon—contrary to what might be inferred from Hughes's summary. The martyrologies and their glosses are filled with names of places of male saints about which nothing remains other than the name and, presumably, some long-buried ruins. So too the Lives of the eighth and ninth centuries, where we hear, for example, of a religious man named Mo-celloc, who lived in some *locus*, having with him just two *vacas* and *uno vitulo*.[70] Another mentions the place of the sons of Garbe, where there was a holy man who loved God.[71] It is important to remember that the insignificant small place housing a few followers of the religious life is not, *pace* Hughes, a gender-specific institution.

Elsewhere in Europe there are signs of similar situations. In England, though, the work of Sarah Foot suggests that very many religious women lived on land not designated as 'ecclesiastical' and thus invisible in charters; it is evident that religious women were often very much involved in land disputes. In Frankia, religious women are also to be found on family land, in informal, short-term occupations of property for religious purposes. It is hoped that in future more research will permit more meaningful comparisons between Ireland and elsewhere on the subject, but at present there is insufficient groundwork to allow it.

---

[67] Latin Life of Cainnech, Φ text, ch. 32.
[68] Latin Life of Colmán of Lynally, Φ text, ch. 45.
[69] Conchubranus, Life of Monenna, book 1, ch. 6.
[70] Latin Life of Finán, Φ text, ch. 32 (*Heist*, 153–60).
[71] Ibid., ch. 13.

Small Churches with Women's Relics: the Martyrology of Oengus as a Case Study

The Martyrology of Oengus, composed in a *céle Dé* context in the early ninth century, commemorates some 630 holy people on the various days of the year; about half are saints of late antiquity; half are Irish, and two are Anglo-Saxon. Of the total, just over ten per cent (about 65) are women, thirty of them Irish. These thirty Irish females, then, were sufficiently important to the author to warrant formal commemoration in the liturgical calendar.

Who were they? Frustratingly, but significantly, half are identified by just their first names. Some are famous, associated with either a monastery or a well-known Patrician legend: such are Brigit, Monenna, Fainche, Gobnat, Bríg, and Cairech Dergan. But who were Muirgen, Scíre, Ercnait, Curufin, Fled, and Ernach? That Oengus entered their names, and did so without so much as an adjective to help identify them, implies that *c.*830 his audience knew very well who they were and, more importantly, that he cared more about them as relics and cemetery-church sites than as female relatives of powerful men of Irish society.

One of the identifiable saints is Cíar daughter of Duib-re, who in the martyrology's main text is given two whole lines to herself as 'a fair sun, a fresh champion' (*cain grían, greit nua*), and glossed as being of the Muscraige Tire, and of Conaire's race (*síl Conairi*) in Mag Escat. The Muscraige Tire were the most important tribe in North Munster, and were located in the rich lands east of Lough Derg.[72] Cíar does appear in hagiography, in the O'Donoghue Life of Fintán (a seventh- or eighth-century text), where he gives her his church Tech Taille meic Segeni.[73]

The second saint identified by her parentage is 'the daughter of Feradach'. The glossators, who usually made a guess if not a positive identification, did not attempt to make one here: quite probably between the ninth and the tenth century knowledge about this holy woman and her burial site died out completely.

In the case of 'Mac Iair's four daughters', the glossators' evident uncertainty produced more rather than less comment.[74] Three of their names are given: Nassan, Beoan, and Mellan; or else they are Dairblinn, Dairmil, Cóel, and Comgall. Locating them was an even greater challenge. The father, Mac Iair, was either British or Irish; the girls were at one of the two Tallaghts, or they were at Kells; either they were at a church named Tech-na-mBretan, or at one of those called Cell-na-nIngen. Evidently, the glossators were trying to lay out all the possibilities provided by a handful of legends about at least two groups of maidens and their father. It would appear that the 'four daughters' with their association with Tallaght may have belonged to the eighth century; the fact that by the tenth century scribes struggled to firmly identify them further suggests

---

[72] Stokes did not identify Mag Escat. On the Muscraige Tire, see Ó Corráin, *Ireland*, 8.
[73] Latin Life of Fintán *alias* Munnu, Φ text, ch. 13 (*Heist*, 198–209). Tech Taille, mod. Tihelly, is just south of the monastery of Durrow, and both are under five miles north of Tullamore, Co. Offaly.
[74] Martyrology of Oengus, 26 Oct.

that their influence was powerful for a short time—in their lifetimes and shortly thereafter—but that in the long term they were essentially insignificant.

The daughters of Ailill, who were 'east of the Liffey', posed the later glossators problems as well.[75] They identified them as Mugain and Fedelm, the daughters of Ailill mac Dunlaing, king of Leinster. These two appear in the Patrician Notulae in the Book of Armagh as belonging to a different church altogether.[76] The Oengus glossators authoritatively placed them at Cell-Ingen-Ailella in the east of the Leinster plain of Mag Lifi.

'Sinech, daughter of Fergna', who was a 'fragment of the stone' (*blog don lig*), is the fifth of Oengus's maiden saints identified by her patronym, but helpfully he also mentioned that she was of the place 'Cruachan Maige Abna'.[77] The glossators agreed that this place was Cruachan Maige Abna in Eogangacht of Cashel, identified by Best and Lawlor as the modern Crohane in Slievardagh in Co. Tipperary.[78] Her father, though, was a mystery to the glossators, and they suggested Oengus may have meant that Sinech was not 'daughter of Fergna' (*ingen Fergna*) but rather simply a 'good maiden', *ingen [f]Ergna*.[79]

Thus it appears that these women, in spite of being identified by a patronym, were remembered more for their burial places—their churches—than for their genealogies or natal kindred connections. The latter point can be tested further by looking at the other entries of female Irish saints in the Martyrology of Oengus, those identified in the main text by their church rather than patronym. After all, if a woman was identified by her location in the main body of the martyrology, perhaps the glossator would concentrate on her geneaology to complement the total available information. Five women are in this group. Taking the cases in turn the answer becomes evident, and it again points toward a primary identification with church site, not family.

Monenna of Killevy has a number of glossator's comments: her church's location, her former name, the origin of her nickname, a poem about her and then, finally, her genealogy.[80] Saint Ita is glossed with a similar list of information: her church's location, the origin of her name, a poem about her, and then her genealogy.[81] Samthann's entry is glossed similarly, with a church location and a genealogy, given last. In the whole of the glosses, these three and Brigit are the only women who are given a genealogy. Only Brigit's genealogy comes first rather than last in the gloss.[82] The other, minor saints identified by Oengus by

[75] Martyrology of Oengus, 9 Dec.

[76] Notulae in the Book of Armagh, item 44, where Mogain and Fedelm, identified by Bieler as daughters of Ailill, are said to be in Domnach Mór, Maige Reto.

[77] Martyrology of Oengus, 5 Oct.

[78] Best and Lawlor, *Martyrology of Tallaght*, 220.

[79] She is one of the two little-known ones (the other is Scíath) among five female saints mentioned in a litany in the Stowe Missal, suggesting that Cruachan Maige Abna had a connection with Tallaght and/or the other *céle Dé* churches. (Stowe Missal, folio 30v; ed. G. Warner, *The Stowe Missal*, 2 vols. (Henry Bradshaw Society 32; London, 1906), here at 14).

[80] Martyrology of Oengus, 6 July.   [81] Ibid., 15 Jan.   [82] Ibid., 1 Feb.

patronym are the small handful discussed earlier: in these the glossators evidently did not know who even the fathers were. There were only two other female saints whom Oengus mentioned with their churches. One was Sinchell of Killeigh (Ir. Cell Achid Drumfota), who may have been a male but the glossators thought female, and he/she is glossed with a location of the church in Offaly, and a little poem saying 'she' lived to age 330; nothing is said about her kindred.[83]

And finally, what of the fifteen other Irish women saints remembered by Oengus the Culdee, those whom he identified simply by their forenames? Did the glossators identify their kindreds and genealogies? For what were they remembered in the long term? Were they eminent as heads of communities, or as individuals? Fainche (alternatively Fuinche or Funech), was the foundress of Clonbroney, but the glossators presented two possibilities for her identity: Fainche 'the Rough' from Lough Erne, who was in Toorah (Túath Ratha in Uí Echach Ulad); this was the daughter of Carell, who was from Ross Airthir. Stokes identified Ross Airthir as modern Rossorry in Co. Fermanagh, and Túath Ratha as Tooraah, also in that county.[84] The place, if it did house other religious women or men, did not produce any others of sufficient eminence to be mentioned in any martyrologies. Its near-anonymity suggests that this Fainche may have been either on her own or in a small group, though the church she left behind did remain known at least until the glossators' time. The other identity proposed was Fainche of Clonkeen in Eoganacht of Cashel, now Clonkeen in Tipperary.

The glossators knew of two women who might have been the next holy woman Oengus commemorated, Muirgen.[85] One was a daughter of Aidán who was in Leinster near the River Barow (Ir. Belach Gabráin, now Gowran Pass near Kilkenny) a place which also boasted the relics of saints Enda and Lochan.[86] But they also thought she might be the legendary Murgein who was drawn from Ulster's Lough Neagh and baptized by saint Comgall.

Oengus's virgin Ernech left the glossators with two possible identities, too: a Connaught woman or an Ulster maiden of the name: the former was known at 'Dún in Cíarrage Ae', the latter at Duneane (Dún dá én in Dalríada). As for the maiden Scíre, she left a church known to the glossators and identified by them,[87] but her parentage was either unknown or unimportant to them, for it goes unmentioned. The place, however, had been the head of at least a small monastic federation in the seventh century.[88]

---

[83] Ibid., 26 March. Killeigh was very near the male monastery of Lynally; the modern hamlet of Killeigh is four miles south of Tullamore.

[84] Stokes, *Félire*, 397.   [85] Martyrology of Oengus, 27 Jan.

[86] Ibid., notes on 31 Dec. The relics were said to be in a church there called 'Cell maic Cathail'. But the church of the virgin is not identified, so may have been this one or another.

[87] Martyrologies of Oengus and Gorman, 24 Mar.; Stokes, *Félire*, 218. There are two churches called Cell Scíre: one in Meath, at the present village of Kilskeery, and another, seeming the less eminent just west of the large church of Clogher; it is in present-day Kilskirry a few miles east of Lough Erne.

[88] Tírechán, Memoirs, ch. 16. According to the text her *familia* owned the church Cell Bile in

Similarly Oengus's virgin Fled was glossed as the virgin of 'Tech Fleide' (lit. 'Fled's church') located in the lands of the Uí Garchon tribe in the Wicklow region of Leinster, and Fled herself was allegedly the daughter of a Leinster king. In spite of her alleged royalty, however, the glossators had nothing to say about her parentage beyond this. In these two cases, there was an eponymous church. Neither of these made a big mark on the ecclesiastical world, for no other known saints or eminent figures emanated from them. What were they in Oengus's day: functioning local churches, or ruins on private land?

Was the legacy of these women ongoing small communities, laity-serving chapels, or merely tiny cemeteries with a miracle-working grave? These are the imponderables which beset the search for information not only on Fled and Scíre, but also on the others whose places were neither large nor famous. But there are implications to be drawn from these entries on the holy women as a whole. Firstly, that in the ninth century it was not simply abbesses and early foundresses of large monasteries who were considered important enough to re- member as 'saints'. Furthermore, we cannot know when these women lived, but the indication from the daughters of Mac Iair and Samthann is that a few whom Oengus considered important lived as late as the eighth century. Thirdly, they were remembered more for their burial places—their churches—than for their genealogies or natal kindred connections. From the point of view of the martyr- ologist, what really mattered about these women (and men) was where their churches were, or where they had lived. Given that Irish society as a whole was deeply obsessed by genealogy and kinship, this is somewhat surprising. The an- swer lies, I think, in the predominance, in this situation, of the burial site of the saint, which was also their main relic: in Irish, after all, the single term *reilic* con- tains the two meanings, both of 'cemetery' and of 'relic' in the modern sense. It is evident that what survived in the collective memory about holy virgins was not their family connections but the place in which they had lived and died. In their own day the property of their dwelling may have been proprietary (either their kindred's or their own), but in the centuries afterward people of the wider community knew of the site—church, house or cemetery—as a holy one. It was not just for her family, for example, for whom the fields on which Fled had lived were called Tech Fleide. It was 'Tech Fleide' for everyone, including the glossators of the martyrologies.

Nuns at 'Parish Churches' as 'Wives' of Priests

There is also contemporary evidence from the eighth and later centuries which suggests that nuns sometimes lived on the same small church site as clerics.[89] *Hibernensis*, the canonical collection from the early eighth century, reiterated the

Mag Taidcni, possibly mod. Rathvilly (Bieler, *Patrician Texts*, 253); it does not appear in the Lives or martyrologies.

   [89] Archaeological excavations show this; see Edwards, *Archaeology*, 114–21.

Council of Nicaea's stipulation that a woman might not live with a priest unless she was a close female relative, a rule evidently rarely heeded in the Christian West generally, including Ireland.[90] *Berrad Airechta*, a law tract from the early eighth century, implies this when it asserts that the fees of a priest for baptism or communion are immune from claim . . . unless the priest has given them to his nun (*caillech*) or to a son born after he entered the priesthood.[91]

Similarly, a short legalistic poem in the notes to the martyrology of Oengus says that a baptism is worthless if performed by a priest who has just come from the bed of his nun. The scholia themselves were written in the tenth or eleventh century, but the language of this ditty may be slightly earlier:

> Sacart ic denam comna · ic baisded, bec a tarba
> ni con tic baisted de · iar taistel a cailligi.[92]

> A priest, practising coition, small is his profit in baptizing;
> baptism comes not from him, after visiting his nun.

Whether these 'veiled ones' (as *caillech* literally means) were consecrated virgins, or priests' wives, or both simultaneously, is uncertain. These 'partners', indeed, may have sometimes been the *caillecha* ringing the bell or announcing the canonical hours, mentioned in the earlier section above. But the fact that the word *caillech* is used is significant; it makes it quite clear that one type of female religious life consisted of being a priest's live-in companion, or resident colleague, at a church. It is possible that the nun-companion to the local priest mentioned in these three texts is the later successor to the priest's companion of the earlier penitentials, which refer to the priest's *uxor* and *clentella*.[93] In this I am in agreement with Ní Dhonnchadha, who reached the same conclusion, using other texts, including *Berrad Airechta* and a poem on saint Cuchuimne.[94]

Solitary Religious Women

Those who sought a solitary religious life could achieve it by being affiliated to a monastery; indeed it was shown earlier that some women were to be found adjacent to men's houses, but same-sex arrangements were certainly available to both male and female hermits.[95] There were also genuine solitaries. These are

---

[90] *Hibernensis*, book 10, item b, of the text says: *Clericus cum extraneis mulieribus non habitet.*

[91] *Berrad Airechta*, ch. 8, corresponding to *CIH* 591.30 (trans. R. Stacey, '*Berrad Airechta*: An Old Irish Tract on Suretyship', in T. Charles-Edwards, M. Owen, and D. Walters (eds.), *Lawyers and Laymen: Studies in the History of Law* (Cardiff, 1986), 210–33, at 211). This text is also cited as part of Ní Dhonnchadha's demonstration that *caillech* also meant cleric's spouse, '*Caillech*', 77–8.

[92] Martyrology of Oengus, notes on Oct. 27.

[93] For *uxor* see Pа1, ch. 6, and for *clentella* see Penitential of Finnian, ch. 27 (both in Bieler, *Irish Penitentials*, at 54–5 and 82–3 respectively).

[94] Ní Dhonnchadha, '*Caillech*', 77–80.

[95] Female hermit: Conchubranus, Life of Monenna, book 2, ch. 12. British male anchorite: lived in the extremes of Fintán's monastery, making carts for the brothers (Latin Life of Fintán, Φ text, ch. 31).

even more intriguing than the priests' companions, because they lived outside the protective sphere provided by a community of other women, however few, by a male clerical partner, or by a houseold of blood relatives. Such women admittedly appear almost exclusively in the Lives, so perhaps the 'poor solitary nun' is no more than an Irish hagiographical *topos*, but if it is, that in itself is instructive as to ecclesiastical mores and to the perception of the place of religious women in the wider landscape.

In an early Life of Brigit, a virgin who lived on her own had trouble providing a sufficient feast for the visiting saint. Sharpe notes that the redactor 'D', when copying the Life in the late twelfth or early thirteenth century, changed the original so that the woman was living in a small group—presumably customs had changed. Sharpe imagined that the woman in Brigit's *Vita I* lived her own home, as she had only one calf; and this is clearly the case. But beyond this, it implied she was genuinely isolated. Her one animal was all the food the nun could procure. I would argue that had the hagiographer envisioned her living at a relative's homestead or *ráth*, he would not have been able to write the anecdote as he did, for it was unthinkable that the nun's lay family would not lay on a feast for Brigit.[96]

Then there is the tale of the virgin Scíath of Ardskeah (Ir. Fert Scéthe). She asked St Ailbe for two beasts for her agricultural work and for a set of gospels for her devotions, and was also evidently on her own. Her need for beasts should prevent us from thinking the author imagined her in a familial setting with access to family resources.[97] She did not after her death have a *reilic* or relic-burial at her own place, for we know Oengus's *céle Dé* church celebrated the translation of her relics from her place in Munster to Tallaght, and her inclusion in the Tallaght *familia* is confirmed by the fact that as early as the eighth or ninth century she was one of only two minor female saints remembered in its Litany of the Saints.[98] Another example is the virgin Columba, related in the Life of her brother, Cainnech. She too evidently lived on her own, with a young boy *alumpnus*, for once the boy died there was no one to do the little chores associated with greeting guests.[99] An unnamed *sancta femina* who lived by the sea is reported in Áed's Life; when falsely accused by the local king she turned to the saint for help; no family came to her aid and the hagiographer portrays her as being on her own.[100]

Though there has been little study of them there were religious women elsewhere, in Frankia, who lived alone—but the role of their families in supporting them may have been considerable. Such were the women mentioned by the Council of Friouli (AD 796–7), and they continued to exist through the ninth

[96] *Vita I* of Brigit, ch. 113; cf. *Vita IV*, book 2, ch. 79; Sharpe, *Saints' Lives*, 201.

[97] Latin Life of Ailbe, Φ text, ch. 38.

[98] The other saints mentioned are Brigit, Ita, Samthann, and the little-known Sinech (Stowe Missal, folio 30v).

[99] Latin Life of Cainnech, Φ text, ch. 31.   [100] Latin Life of Áed, Φ text, ch. 33.

century. They lived under a binding vow of chastity, dressed in a black vestment, but without having been veiled. At the turn of the tenth century religious widows were added to their number, so legislation applied to them also.[101]

RELIGIOUS WOMEN ON FAMILY PROPERTY

If Hughes was right and the majority of women lived on lands ceded to them for but a lifetime or who, in the *eigenkirche* model, were living within the economy of their secular families, we should expect to find some sources locating them there. Though it seems absolutely reasonable that many would have lived in such a manner, accounts of this are very thin on the ground. When historians of England or the Continent have considered this issue in their own areas of study, they have relied upon charters, a particularly useful type of source for this matter. Ireland in this period, however, produced no real body of charters, so one must rely upon other sources, with their attendant imperfections. The Lives are, of necessity, the first port of call, for they are at least abundant. Incredibly, those of this period yield only three possibly useful anecdotes.

The first is from the Life of Columba, written by Adomnán of Iona. The little story concerns the virgin Mogain, daughter of Daiméne (obit 565) who lived at Clochar macc nDaiméni, 'the stony place of the sons of Daiméne'. This royal Ulster site at modern Clogher, Co. Tyrone, was a ring fort in use from prehistoric times through the ninth century. The well-known church of Clogher, of unknown foundation date, was about half a mile north of it. Adomnán tells that Mogain used to walk to and from the church, presumably Clogher, to perform the *opus Dei* or monastic office. Mogain's house is not described. Was it within the enclosure of her brothers' cashel, or outside it? Did she perform the office in a small oratory on the site, alone or with a single priest? Alternatively, was she associated with the church up the road which, we know, had a male monastic community? The answers, as Sharpe notes, are imponderables. Mogain was imagined either as a home-dwelling virgin, or else as one attached to a male community.[102]

In Colmán's Life, written in the seventh or eighth century, the virgin Camna was envisioned as living in her family region, for she came to the saint for his help in liberating her tribe (*gens*), which had been taken into servitude by king Brendan mac Cairbri. We cannot speculate, given the lack of other detail in the anecdote whether the writer imagined her within a family economic unit, or as self-supporting.[103] She was, however, involved with the welfare of her natal kindred.

[101] Hodgson, 'Frankish Church', 100–1, with references.
[102] Adomnán, Life of Columba, book 2, ch. 5 (A. and M. Anderson, *Adomnán's Life of Columba* (Edinburgh, 1961)). Comments in R. Sharpe, *Life of Columba* (New York, 1995), 320–1.
[103] Latin Life of Colmán of Lynally, Φ text, ch. 44.

The third anecdote, the richest, is from Conchubranus' long and often amusing Life of Monenna. The Life is in general too late to be of use, but this story is located in two chapters which Esposito (perhaps rightly) claimed were wholesale blocks of seventh-century material. After Monenna received the veil from Patrick, it says, her religious education was to continue: 'With the blessing of Bishop Patrick she returned to her parent's home with whom she stayed, but apart from them—because the house plunges people into destruction.'[104] However, until Esposito's thesis has been confirmed, this anecdote, rich though it is, cannot be used with safety as seventh-century evidence.

The Irish virgin who lived on family territory must remain, for the forseeable future, an unknowable figure. There is no comparing these fragments with the much more abundant material from England. For there, sufficient evidence exists to make a very strong case that a vast majority of vowed religious women lived on land, or in properties, which were not alienated from private family or individual ownership, that is to say, not designated officially as 'church land': this is the thesis of Sarah Foot's study, *Veiled Women*. Moreover, the charters show nuns wrangling over, receiving, and transmitting property. It has been speculated, doubtless correctly, that in such an environment a small religious community would be somewhat insecure, though its actual existence would be threatened only if the new owner acquired the land on which the house or church stood, and was able to close it down as an ecclesiastical centre. In England it appears that that was the case. Even losing other holdings would jeapardize a small community's viability, as it would deprive the nuns of the income.[105] The charter sources make this scenario much more visible than it is in Ireland, but it seems undoubted that to some extent this kind of instability did bedevil small female communities there as well, though perhaps the situation was not as extreme, nor the treatment of religious life so offhand, as in England. Frankia too, had small female communities in this period, which legislation tried with scant success to put under episcopal authority. There, too, the diversity of living situations is said to be similar to what is found in Ireland, particularly for canonesses.[106]

MALE-ONLY ESTABLISHMENTS

The portrayal of the Irish monastic landscape outlined in this chapter appears to fly in the face of the received stereotype of Ireland as an ascetic 'Isle of Saints', a place where the monks were so holy they never looked upon womankind. This notion appears both in the popular literature on early Ireland and even swayed Lisa Bitel, one of very few contemporary historians to consider gender issues in

---

[104]   Conchubranus, Life of Monenna, book 1, ch. 3.
[105]   See Schneider, 'Anglo-Saxon Women', 253–64 with references; also Foot, *Veiled Women*.
[106]   Hodgson, 'Frankish Church', 97–9, with references.

the early medieval church.[107] Succeeding chapters treat attitudes to religious women—virgins and widows in particular. At this juncture, however, it is appropriate to take up the challenge of the evidence for men-only monasteries and hermitages.

The Lives of the seventh to ninth centuries very occasionally mention *anchoritae* as holy men who undertook the avoidance of the female sex as an heroically ascetic practice. In no seventh-, eighth-, or ninth-century text is the single-sex arrangement, which strictly excludes contact with women, enjoined or even described as the norm. In all the texts of this era, the ascetic practice of avoiding women is portrayed as exceptional. In fact, one is hard pressed to find examples, of which only three have been found. The first is from the seventh or eighth century, in Brigit's *Vita I.*[108] Brigit and her nuns, we are told, when in Munster lived not far from an anchorite who avoided women (*facies mulierum videre vitabat, totus Deo deditus et perfectus*). The anchorite decided to move from his previous place to an island, and on the journey to it he and his band passed by where Brigit lived. Some men in the group suggested they stop to visit, but he vetoed the idea saying, *Scitis votum meum quod nullam feminam volo videre.* The band carried on, but that night their luggage disappeared and they were forced to go the nunnery for help. Miraculously, they found the baggage sitting in the central area of the nuns' sanctuary. The anchorite and his band stayed three days and nights with the nuns, praising the Lord and preaching the word of God. Brigit blessed them when they left. Subsequently, the anchorite settled on an island. He wished to have it to himself, but faced conflict with a married couple living there who did not wish to leave. They refused even after he explained he wished to avoid looking upon womankind (*vero devitans videre mulierem*). Brigit was brought to the scene to help, and she miraculously drove off the man and wife, thus permitting the anchorite to fulfil his ascetic vow. Through this story the hagiographer implied a good but conditional relationship between the church of Brigit and female-shunning anchorites. Brigit would support the community which renounced women, so long as it was not *her* nuns that the men treated as a threat.

Lugaid *alias* Molua, the founder of Clonfertmulloe or Kyle, is portrayed as a great avoider of women in his earliest Life, which is in the O'Donoghue group in the Codex Salmanticensis and is thus datable to the seventh or eighth century.[109] He refused to establish his monastery on the site recommended by an angel: *Lugidus in illo loco, temptatione mulierum valde gravatus, habitare non potuit.*[110] Another place was also rejected because he heard sheep bleating there: *ubi enim fuerit ovis, ibi erit mulier, et ubi fuit mulier, ibi peccatum; ubi vero peccatum, ibi erit dyabolus, et ubi dyabolus, ibi infernus erit.*[111] One could get the impression that Molua's redactor was a woman-hater. It is a strong statement to make that where women

[107]   See Bitel, 'Women's Monastic Enclosures'.   [108]   *Vita I* of Brigit, ch. 73.
[109]   Sharpe, *Saints' Lives*, 329, 334–6.
[110]   Life of Lugaid *alias* Molua, Φ text, ch. 32 (*Heist*, 131–45).   [111]   Ibid., ch. 27.

are, there one finds the devil. But in this same Life Molua also assists women, and sexually active women at that: on his travels he helps a queen in a painful childbirth safely deliver her child. Molua's hagiographer was not necessarily contradicting himself in this tale, for the saint may not have had face-to-face contact with the woman; nevertheless, the presence of the story shows that the author was comfortable portraying his saint performing a 'midwifery miracle', one which aids women giving birth to the fruit of their sexuality.[112] Perhaps there is something in the fact that the hagiographer attributed Molua's rabid separatism to the saint's struggle with lust; after all, the writer could have said that it was caused by the evil nature of women, and he (only just) stops short of that. What is strongest about this message, though, is not the nature of the female sex but rather the promotion of the single-sex community. The message from the hagiographer relates less to monks meeting women in the world than it does to the proper set-up of a monastery. A monastery, it implies, should be a place free of sexuality, even from the temptation of sexual sin. A holy man of God might come face to face with a queen in distress, but he should not face temptation in the place where his monks live. It may be recalled that in the era this was written men's monasteries were not always headed by celibate abbots. At Clonfertmulloe, though, this hagiographer emphasized, asceticism and celibacy were a priority. In putting across his message he did something unusual for an Irish cleric of this time, but which foreshadowed future trends: he projected the sexual sin onto the female sex.

One version of the ninth-century 'Rule of the *Céli Dé*' contains the same saying, attributing it instead to Coemgen.[113] The *Céli Dé* did not in practice actually avoid contact with women, and there was a women's hostel and a women's church at Tallaght. As mentioned earlier, the Customs of Tallaght encouraged monks to undertake collegial visits with the nuns, though guarding their eyes while they did so. Tallaght's nuns were central enough to the community to be mentioned in the Rule, as was seen above, and to stress that they ought to be visited.

MARRIED COUPLES AT MONASTERIES

Equally fixed in the general imagination is the idea that people who had active sex lives, however licit they might be, were not to be found within the precincts of early Irish monasteries, yet we find occasional references to lay couples living temporarily at monasteries while they undertook a period of intensive religious instruction. The most memorable illustration is in the ninth-century love story 'Liadain and Curithir', a story which has caused scholars no little perplexity.

---

[112] Life of Lugaid *alias* Molua, Φ text, ch. 60.
[113] 'Rule of the *Céli Dé*' in a Franciscan, Dublin MS (ed. Gwynn, at 79).

Set in the early seventh century, it relates the fate of a pair of lovers, poets by pro-fession, who decided to go to Clonfert to submit to the spiritual direction of St Cummean Fota (obit 661). The saint housed both the man and the women within his monastery's bounds, in an arrangement whereby they could speak to each other but not see each another. The author seems to have envisioned the lovers in adjacent huts, for he says that when Curithir went walking around the gravestones, Liadain would be shut in her cell, and whenever she went out he would be closed in his.[114] It initially seems unlikely that a man and a woman, even temporarily in the religious life, were in the ninth century housed in adja-cent cells, unless it was in guest-house premises. Nonetheless, the ninth-century writer imagined such a set-up existing. More significantly and more generally, he implied that dual-sex residence at male houses was a time-honoured practice going back to the days of great ascetic saints like Cummean. In fact one can go a step further and say that the author could tell the story he did precisely be-cause in his own day, too, both men and women could join a predominantly male house like Clonfert.

Tallaght in the same century had married couples under what looks like a very similar weekly regime. Its Customs specify three points during the week when they may have sexual intercourse, and they stay (and sleep) in what is evi-dently some part of the monastery, for the times of joining and separating are governed by the monastic office. 'The course prescribed for a wedded couple under spiritual directions' is as follows: from *prime* on Monday until *matins* on Wednesday they may have sexual intercourse and meals; then for the next twenty-four hours they must abstain and fast; they again have licence to indulge from Thursday *matins* until Friday *matins*; then they are to live separately for the next three days and nights over the Sabbath period. On Sunday and Sunday evening they may have a meal but not have sex.[115] Cummean's regime is by far the harsher, making the reform Culdee house look mild by comparison.

CONCLUSIONS

To imagine that the majority of nuns lived secluded lives in large all-female nun-neries is to ignore the weight of evidence which places many nuns in other set-tings. The distinction between monastery and church in early medieval Ireland is not a clear one, and perhaps not a useful one. There were residential churches serving the laity, at which ascetics sometimes lived; and there were 'monasteries' at which only a minority of the residents followed a regular, monastic life. Nuns are clearly present in many of the establishments in this diverse and eclectic ec-clesiastical environment. All indications are that they were not walled up, either proverbially or literally. Although in the eighth- and ninth-century texts we see

[114] Paras. 1–4.   [115] Customs of Tallaght, ch. 50.

beginnings of concern for scandal, Lives do not begin to promote strict female claustration, nor do most of them make a point of mentioning strict sex separation as a virtue. Given that nuns were located in, among other places, laity-serving churches and nunneries serving outlying populations, one may conclude that the ease between the sexes in the Church related in part at least to Irish monasticism's pastoral outlook, in the female as well as the male sphere.

Lisa Bitel attempted to prove that misogyny and distrust of women were characteristic of the early medieval Irish church. Using the exceptional anecdotes of Molua and Coemgen, but mostly later hagiographic tales, she generalized that male saints and their weaker brothers 'feared' nuns, tolerating them only so long as they remained 'inside their enclosures'.[116] This was evidently not the case, especially for the seventh, eighth, and ninth centuries. The contemporary evidence suggests by contrast that the Irish church was at this time largely unconcerned about consecrated women, and was not focused on their sexuality. This would change noticeably around the tenth century. Molua's ditty about women, sheep, and the devil is a proverbial cloud on the horizon. More such clouds come rolling across the skies of this landscape as the centuries progress, and we shall return to them in a later chapter.

Because nuns were apparently in such a wide variety of locales, one must conclude that the small, private, and short-lived communities Hughes envisioned cannot be called the only, or even the main, alternative to the large nunneries. The sources make it clear that smaller establishments housing nuns were not always marginal or transient, nor were they necessarily sheltered from the lay populace any more than large places might be. Nuns were eminently visible in society by virtue of living in a wide variety of places which were at the centre of Church activity: not only at laity-serving nunneries, but also at male monasteries, important churches, hermitages, and those local churches providing the eucharist for the local populace.

[116]   Bitel, 'Women's Monastic Enclosures', 30–1.

5

Women of God in the Seventh to Ninth Centuries

If the living situations of Irish religious women were diverse, so too were the grades and varieties of their profession. There were two, possibly three, grades of female monastic: the virgin, the widow/penitent, and the priest's 'wife', in addition to the *peregrina* or religious pilgrim. Some religious women acquired a special status in law, achieving a high degree of law-worthiness, and were deemed as equivalents to bishops and presbyters. Their high legal and ecclesiastical status is understandable in the context of the theological ideas which lay behind the idea of their offices. The virgin and penitent widow in particular carried a complex of symbolisms which, though grounded in the Western tradition, reflected a particularly Irish 'take' on them.

Before turning to discussions of each of the grades of nunhood in early Ireland, though, it is as well to digress to consider the means by which women would decide to enter the church, and the reasons why they might do so. Such decisions, in Ireland, were taken not by women alone but rather by their male guardians with the input of other men in the kindred—just as in decisions on contractual marriage. The fact that nuns were highly regarded and could command great respect would make such an option attractive for not only a woman but also her family, of course, but there were pragmatic aspects to consider.

HIGH STATUS FAMILIES AND THE VIRGINAL PROFESSION: CONSIDERATIONS

In early medieval Ireland, women were an integral part of their kindreds and an important tool in their strategies for economic well-being.[1] The matter of taking up the religious life thus had serious implications for the immediate family and wider relatives. It was of particular relevance for the *derb-fine* ('certain kindred'), which was all those descended from a common great-grandfather, and more technically, was the body of men who administered and handled the property and affairs of the group. Men inherited property from the kin land, and could pass it on to their heirs but could not alienate it. In contrast, women could not

---

[1] As explored most fully by Charles-Edwards, *Kinship*.

inherit kin land, but only movable goods, unless their father had produced no sons. In such a circumstance the heiress, as she was called, did get a portion of kin land but only for her use during her lifetime, and after her death it returned to the common stock of the *derb-fine*. Heiresses were probably no more than one in five women, given the roughly twenty per cent occurrence of nuclear families with only daughters. Women who married in a formal contract, however, passed out of the responsibility of the kindred, and became largely the responsibility of their husband's. Those women who did not marry, or who had less formal marriages, remained largely or exclusively the responsibility of their natal kin, making them somewhat of a burden on its collective resources.

One question which must be asked, given the power of the kindred in shaping and guiding a noble woman's life, was why she would be allowed to forego marriage and take up life as a holy virgin. Several things would appear to militate against it, most importantly the fact that women were so useful in cementing family alliances. As Thomas Charles-Edwards has put it, 'a woman's expected role in kinship was that of a principal bonding agent'.[2] Another was more the monetary consideration, for a bridegroom 'purchased' his bride from her family with a bride-price. There appears to have been no equivalent payment by monasteries to families of incoming nuns, so a woman's male relatives forfeited the bride-wealth windfall if she took a heavenly rather than a worldly spouse. In the case of Brigit, as told by her hagiographers, this was a major reason the saint had so much objection to her vocation. Her brothers, angrily disappointed at the prospect of losing out on the bride-price if she became a virgin, tried to force her to marry a noble suitor. As is well known, she thwarted them by plucking out her eye or, in other versions, getting a horrible eye disease, thus making herself undesirable to mortal men. Not all women were as strong-willed as Brigit, and the vast majority were, like most early medieval people in the West, identified strongly with their family and its interests, so widespread teenage rebellion cannot account for the flowering of Irish female monasticism.

The advantages to kindreds in having some of their women as 'brides of Christ' are nowhere made explicit, so any answers must be deduced tentatively from surviving material on other, related topics and from cautious comparisons with elsewhere. The question could easily be the subject of an entire monograph, so a few suggestions are simply offered here. Firstly, there is the matter of alliances. At times it would certainly have proved advantageous for a kindred to strengthen its links with local church hierarchies, given their political and economic power. To insert a woman into an ecclesiastical *familia* could best be done, in many instances, by making her a religious—she could then be co-opted into the church *familia* whilst at the same time bringing honour, prestige, and 'protection' of a sort to her natal kindred, much as if she had married into it. If the family was ambitious, as were the Uí Dúnlainge in Leinster who succeeding

---

[2]   Charles-Edwards, *Kinship*, 87.

in taking over Kildare, they could use women in their strategies to infiltrate a monastery's leading offices and subsequently share in the wealth of the place's income from tributes and renders. If a family was going to place a woman in an extant institution, the ideal would be for her to become its abbess, by hook or by crook, though it could prove very difficult if the place was run by an unrelated family group.

Then there were economic considerations. Though it was customary for bridegrooms to provide bride-wealth, Charles-Edwards has identified a trend among the nobility towards payments going the other way, namely dowries, where the flow of wealth went from the bride's family to the new husband.[3] Thus as time went on during this period, the loss of income to a woman's kindred resulting from her entering a monastery possibly diminished, and in some cases her failing to marry could have produced a saving. When entering a monastery, though a woman doubtless brought some wealth with her, there is no evidence to suggest that a dowry was required, though one cannot of course argue from silence. It may have been a cheaper option than marrying her. In the absence of charters it is impossible to trace the transfers and negotiations over property by secular and ecclesiastical families, but from what we know of Irish maneouvring for status and wealth, these few observations seem secure enough.

Demographics may have played a role in why families allowed some of their women not to marry; if there were more women than men of marriageable age, then there would have been too many women for too few husbands. Whether this was the case seems impossible to determine, though it is feasible that a good number of adult males were unavailable for marriage, either because they were vowed to celibacy, or because they were simply absent through having been killed in battle. Given that from the eighth century many of the men in the church were married, not only most priests but some bishops and abbots, and given that the number of celibate monks and anchorites (*anchoritae*) is unknown, it is impossible to guess even the proportion of unmarried churchmen. Ireland did have another way to deal with any imbalance in the sexes. This was a form of polygamy, which was not only legal but apparently widespread: in addition to a principal wife (*cétmuinter*) a man might take a 'concubine' spouse (*adaltrach*) or two. Thus, if a *derb-fine* had an excess of women compared to the number of suitable husbands, it could encourage the 'surplus' female relatives to try to become a rich man's *adaltrach* rather than join the church. Why they might not do this, though, is that in becoming an *adaltrach* a woman would consign herself for life to having a quite low status, probably lower than if she became a nun, and her status would reflect at least indirectly upon her family.

Certainly families must have considered the religious life for women with more interest given the range of options, the varieties of profession, and flexibility in living arrangements, which they could work with. If a woman was entered

---

[3] Ibid. 463–6.

as a member of an established community, the father and/or the other members of the *derb-fine* could consider which would be most advantageous for her to join—like a choice of husband. The relative relations of dynasties, kindreds, and the issues of honour and tribute would have been, one presumes, the subject of some consideration, for these had an impact not just on the woman herself but on the kindred as a whole.

Another option, the sources hint, was to set up the woman at a small local church. This could be done in one of several ways. The kindred could set aside some of its land and build a church on it for her, which would not require its alienation from the collective patrimony (as it would be a proprietary establishment), nor loss of control of the staffing of its offices. The kindred could also place her in an existing small church, situated on kin land or on lands acquired by purchase. If the woman could perform miracles or do other things to make herself something of a major character in the region, this would only add to the likelihood of the church turning into a revenue-producing centre. This strategy had another advantage: if at the death of the virgin the church was successful in these mercenary terms, the kindred could place into her shoes a successor of either sex—there are numerous examples of churches having leaders of first one sex then the other. Or, of course, the woman could presumably continue to live off her family's wealth on family land which remained essentially dedicated to secular use. The kindred had many options.

WOMEN'S RELIGIOUS PROFESSIONS: VIRGINS

An essential key to understanding the female profession in Ireland, and indeed much of the willingness of families to encourage female members to join it, lies in the symbolic status associated with the holy virgin. The seventh century saw the rise of the literature of sanctity, and it is from this time onward that the writings provide material for such an understanding. The virgin was the highest grade of nun, as we have seen, and for the Irish, as for Christians elsewhere, the holy virgin epitomized the ideal of womanhood transformed through dedication to God. She captured the poetic imagination of the Irish as she did writers in churches across Christendom, and she was clothed with epithets, symbolic attributes, and exalted metaphors. She dwelt at the pinnacle of the hierarchy of believers, was the especial daughter of the Virgin Mary, a bride of Christ, a mother of Jesus, a warrior against Satan, and a possessor of the hardiness of men. The particular package of symbolic qualities attributed to the holy virgin is in some ways general to the Christian West, and in other ways particular to Ireland.

The threefold schema of Christians, discussed in the context of earlier centuries, remains centrally important during the seventh to ninth centuries, staying popular perhaps because it appealed to the Irish legalistic sense of hierarchy in social structure.[4] The seventh-century anonymous exegetical tract *Expositio Quattuor Evangeliorum* states that the thirtieth fruit—

ostendit ordinem coniugatorum, sequentium mandatum Dei; fructus sexagisimis ordinem viduarum, perseverantium in Domino; fructus centesimus, hoc sunt ordines martyrum, monachorum, vel virginum.[5]

shows the order of the married, following the mandate of God; the sixtyfold fruit is the order of widows, persevering in the Lord; the hundredfold fruit, these are the orders of martyrs, monks and virgins.

Here the virgin is not only placed at the top of level of the threefold schema, she shares this spot with two other types of believer, the martyrs and the monks. The virgin is, in the *Expositio* author's eyes, their spiritual equal. The virgins, too, are an order (*ordo*) just as are the monks and martyrs. There is no sense here that the female is placed below the male in that grade.

According to another text, not only are virgins the best type of Christian, their patron is the queen of heaven herself. The eighth-century litany *Ateoch Frit* gives patrons to each 'order' in the threefold schema:

Ateoch frit hule noeb-inghena ógha in uile domuin, im Muire óig, imot noeb-máthair uadhessin; Ateoch frit na huile fhedbai aithrigecha im Muire Magdalena; Ateoch frit huile lochta in chomamais dligtheig, im Iob nimnedach, forsa tarta faichide.[6]

I entreat Thee by all holy virgins, with virgin Mary, Thine own holy mother; I entreat Thee by all penitent widows with Mary Magdalene; I entreat Thee by all folk of lawful marriage, with Job the suffering, on whom came [many] trials.

Mary was generally known in the West as the patroness of holy female virgins, for she embodied the highest virginal ideal. In other words, she was all that religious women were told to aspire to. In the twelfth-century litany *A Muire Mór*, for example, she is called 'head of virgins' (*chend na nóg*).[7] The Irish likened their female saints to Mary, for such women had, as it were, achieved the goal of becoming like their patroness. In two seventh- or eighth-century hymns, Monenna is said to be *sancte Marie imitatrix, una cum sancta Maria*, and *Marie matris imago mirabilis*.[8] Brigit is *Mariae sanctae similis* in another of the same period.[9] Irish hymn writers and ecclesiastical authors were unafraid to put their female saints on a par with Mary. The concluding lines of the ninth-century hymn

[4] The Irish use of the threefold schema has also been observed by Ní Dhonnchadha, '*Caillech*', 72–3.

[5] *PL* 30. 531–90, at 552.

[6] Plummer, *Irish Litanies*, 31–2; discussion and dating in *Kenney*, 725–6.

[7] *A Muire Mór*, in Plummer, *Irish Litanies*, 48–51 at 48–9 (there titled 'Litany of the Virgin'). Dating according to Stokes; discussion in *Kenney*, no. 592.

[8] *Audite Sancta Studia*, stanzas 15 and 22; *Audite Fratres Facta*, stanza 12. Both hymns dated to 7th or 8th cent. Discussion of texts in *Kenney*, no. 162.

[9] *Christus in Nostra Insula*, stanza 2 (J. Bernard and R. Atkinson (eds. and trans.), *The Irish Liber Hymnorum*, i (Henry Bradshaw Society 13; London 1898), 14–15). Dated to 7th or 8th cent. Discussion of text in *Kenney*, no. 98.

Ní Car Brigit run, 'I have found not [Brigit's] like save Mary' (*ni far a set ached Maire*). And elsewhere in the same hymn the writer says

> Fail dí chaillig i rrichid · nícosnágur dom díchill,
> Maire ocus sanctBrigit · for fóessam dún díb linaib[10]

> There are two nuns in heaven, who I do not fear will neglect me,
> Mary and Saint Brigit: may we be under the protection of them both.

Possibly inspired by the deep importance of kinship in Irish society, the likening to, and pairing with, the Virgin Mary could be expressed in explicitly familial language. In the Martyrology of Oengus, Monenna is called 'sister of great Mary'.[11] The placing of virgins at the pinnacle of a spiritual hierarchy, with Mary as their patroness, was reflected also in their dress and veil, which, unlike elsewhere in the West, was white in colour. It recalled to mind the white garb of heavenly beings and angels who presided in heaven with Christ and who might deign to visit the living in visions, and to give guidance or prophecy. Not only do the sources report angels dressed in white, but so too the virgins when they appear in visions. To cite but two examples, in the *Vita I* Brigit apppeared thus to a magus, and a hymn to Monenna says she *fulget in albis / stolis claris candidis*.[12]

Virgins were also the brides of Christ, the king of heaven. Conjoined to the celestial *ard-rí* or high king, they had the honour of being spouses of the most powerful ruler of Creation. In Ireland, the idea that the dedicated virgin was the bride of Christ was widespread. Of course, Mary is the first and foremost virgin bride of Christ, and she is described as such in a seventh-century poem from Bangor as *nuptiis quoque parata regi domino sponsa*.[13] That *all* dedicated virgins were Christ's brides is seen first in the seventh century, in Tírechán's memoirs. Patrick says to two pagan princesses: *ego vero volo vos regi caelisti coniungere dum filiae regis terreni*.[14] In Brigit's *Vita I* the consecration of an unnamed aspiring nun is described in marital terms: *filia liberata a carnali sponso colligata est Christo, sicut vovit in corde suo*.[15] The bridal motif is found also in a seventh- or eighth-century hymn in praise of Monenna, *Audite Sancta Studia*, likely to have been composed at Killevy. It opens with a praise of God: *Deum deorum dominum / autorem vite omnium / regem et sponsum virginum*. It calls Monenna very dignified spouse of God, *sponsa Deo dignissima*, and later states that *sponsum sequitur ubique*.[16] Another poem to her contains the stanza *Celestis virgo / intrans cum melodia / obviam sponso / cum electo oleo*.[17]

---

[10] Discussion and dating of the poem to the 9th cent. in *Kenney*, no. 148.

[11] Martyrology of Oengus, 6 July.

[12] *Hibernensis*, book 45, ch. 10, *pallium a palliditate dictum*; *Vita I* of Brigit, ch. 123; *Audite Fratres Facta*, stanza 10.

[13] From the *Versiculi Familiae Benchuir*, stanza 3, in P. O'Dwyer, *Mary: A History of Devotion in Ireland* (Dublin, 1988), 35–43. See also *Kenney*, no. 92, who dated it to the 7th cent. Carney dated it to *c*.AD 600 (*PRIA* 73C, 335). The poem is actually describing the rule of Bangor, but uses Marian imagery throughout making a metaphorical point.

[14] Tírechán, Memoirs, ch. 26.   [15] *Vita I*, ch. 120.   [16] Stanzas 1, 4, and 19.

[17] *Audite Fratres Facta*, stanza 3. For other examples see Ní Donnchadha, 'Caillech', 81–3.

The Irish picked up on the marital theme from normal Western ideas. Legrand, who studied the doctrine of virginity in depth, wrote 'it is the allegory of marriage . . . which accounts best for the Pauline and Christian doctrine of virginity'.[18] The association between virginity and marriage to God was taken up by other Christian writers very early on. Precedents for the analogy were set by the Old Testament, in which Israel was frequently called the bride of Yahweh; New Testament authors, following this tradition, came to call the new Church, Ecclesia, the bride of Christ.[19] In the New Testament Matthew and Paul show the beginnings of a bridal analogy for the individual in relation to Christ, thus introducing the virginity/marriage image to individuals. It is Paul who most explicitly formulated a Christian linkage between virginity and marriage to Christ:[20]

For I am jealous of you with the jealousy of God. For I have espoused you to one husband, that I may present you as a chaste virgin to Christ. But I fear lest, as the serpent seduced Eve by his subtlety, so your minds should be corrupted and fall from the simplicity that is in Christ.[21]

The marital theme as a spiritual metaphor was taken up avidly both within and without canonical circles in the early church. Among canonical writers, Tertullian in the third century is the first known author to designate the Christian virgin as the bride of Christ: he portrayed Christ specifically as the bridegroom of virgins and holy women dedicated to chastity. In the fourth century, Athanasius asserted that virgins were customarily called brides of Christ, while Ambrose stated that a virgin was one who 'gives her hand in marriage to God'.[22] Cyprian applied the bridal idea almost exclusively to female virgins in his *De habitu virginum*, warning them to avoid dressing so as to attract mortal men.[23] Jerome, too, used the bridal imagery for Christian virgins in his letter to Eustochium, for example where he says 'Let the seclusion of your chamber ever guard you; ever let the bridegroom sport with you within. If you pray you are speaking with your spouse.'[24] Thus, the conclusion to be drawn is that the Irish were indeed citers of patristic orthodoxy at times, but selectively: as a rule, they quote the exhortations which are positive and affirming of the nun rather than those restrictive ones demanding her enclosure.

The virgin was also spiritually fertile, in contrast to the sexually active woman who was physically fertile.[25] The three-grade schema contains these implications,

[18] Legrand, *Biblical Doctrine*, 104.

[19] OT references: Hosea 2: 21; Joel 1: 8; Isaiah 54: 5; Jeremiah 3: 1; Ezekiel 16: 6–43. Discussion of Old and New Testament parallels in Legrand, *Biblical Doctrine*, 102–4.

[20] Legrand, *Biblical Doctrine*, 102–4.

[21] 2 Cor. 11: 2. In the Book of Armagh this passage is underlined and the word 'Brigit' is added in the top margin of the page, folio 125v.

[22] Bugge, *Virginitas*, 59. Tertullian, *De oratione*, ch. 22 (ed. G. Diercks, *CCSL* 22. 255–74); Athanasius, *Apologia ad Constantium*, ch. 33 (*PG* 25. 593–642); Ambrose, *De virginibus* I, ch. 8.

[23] Cyprian, *De habitu virginum*. [24] Jerome, *Epistola* 22, ch. 25 (*PL* 22. 394–425).

[25] Discussed in depth in Legrand, *Biblical Doctrine*, ch. 7.

for in it the virgin bears the most fruit, the 'hundredfold'. So too was Mary the archetype of virginal fertility, having given birth to God in the person of Christ. As one seventh-century Irish poem expressed it, Mary was 'virgin most fruitful, and yet an inviolate mother' (*virgo valde fecunda; haec, et mater intacta*).[26] In Irish sources altogether the idea that exemplary virgins were, like Mary, spiritually fruitful was held both directly and indirectly. The indirect association is expressed in the *topos* of the Irish saint who suckles the infant Christ as would a mother, most famously expressed in the (probably) early tenth-century poem *Ísucán*, written in the voice of St Ita.[27]

The above demonstrates that the Irish believed that dedicated virgins could transcend female weakness—those who did might be female saints, their successors the abbesses, or female ascetics. This conviction is evidenced not solely through the symbolic language of poetry, however. It manifested in the 'real world'. It is in the legal texts that it is most apparent that consecrated women, or some of them, were considered so different from laywomen that they had an authority in law usually reserved for men. It was the virginal nuns who held the highest status, not only in the theologian's threefold schema, but also in Irish law. It was these who enjoyed some legal autonomy. This of course reinforced the nun's identification with the Virgin Mary. But holy women shared in Mary's position as mother of Christ even more explicitly than this. Brigit, in *Ní Car Brigit* is called 'mother of my great king' (*mathair mo rurech*) and 'unique mother of the Son of the Great King' (*óenmathair Maicc Ríg máir*).[28] An Irish exegetical note suggests that it may have been an interpretation of a biblical passage which lay at the root of this rather literal expression of the idea; the seventh-century *Expositio Quattuor Evangeliorum* glosses Luke 1: 42 ('blessed art thou among women and blessed is the fruit of thy womb') with the comment *dum non sola Maria mater Christi est.*

Some Irish virgins were fruitful like Mary in a literal way. These were the alleged holy-virgin mothers. Reported in hagiographic texts, their conceptions are usually described in the context of the life story of the child produced, who was invariably a male who grew up to become a great monk or cleric. There are, unsurprisingly, only a few. Beccnat, mother of saint Fínán, was one such; when she was bathing in Loch Lein a salmon of red-gold swam up against her 'so that it became her husband' and as a result 'like the Son of the Virgin was Fínán Camm born to her'.[29] Another was Cred (also called Trea), mother of the male saint Báithíne; she was unwittingly impregnated by eating some cress she had picked which, unbeknownst to her, had upon it the fresh semen of a Peeping Tom who had been spying on her from a tree. We know that Cred was a holy virgin (not just a secular virgin) from two references in the anecdote: first, the

[26] *Versiculi Familiae Benchuir* (O'Dwyer, *Mary*, 35).

[27] An excellent discussion, with bibliography of the scholarly literature and main debates, is that in E. Quin, 'The Early Irish Poem *Ísucán*', *Cambridge Medieval Celtic Studies* 1 (1981), 39–52.

[28] Lines 4, 63.   [29] Martyrology of Oengus, notes on 7 Apr.

well was within the walled bounds of a church, and secondly, a poem is quoted which describes Cred 'with her dear church' (*cona caimcill*).[30]

The Irish also exalted the woman of God for her ability to transcend the limitations of her sex, according her epithets associated with military heroes, for they were seen as people who were engaged in combat with evil forces. The hymn *Brigit Bé Bithmaith* (dated to the seventh century) contains actual military elements: 'May Brigit deliver us past throngs of devils: may she break before us the battles of every plague. May she destroy within us the taxes of our flesh' (*ronsóira Brigit sech drungu demne: roróina reunn cathu cach thedme. Dirodba indiunn ar colno císu*).[31] Another says Brigit achieved victory over her adversaries when tempted by the sons of Satan and furthermore *donavit illi maximam Deus virtutum gratiam*.[32] *Ní Car Brigit* shows Brigit not as a soldier of Christ *per se*, but as a military-spiritual ally:

Donfair co claidiub thened don chath fri íalla cíara. Ronsnádat a nnóebitge hi flaith nime sech píana. Ria ndul la haingliu don chath recam in neclais for rith.[33]

May she help us with a fiery sword for the battle against dark flocks. May her holy prayers protect us into heaven's kingdom past pains. Before going with the angels to the battle let us come to the Church speedily.

Brigit is not exceptional in being cast in this way. The Martyrology of Oengus is particularly rich in military imagery, applying it to numerous virgins: 'a fresh champion was Cíar', 'crucified was the body of Agatha, pure champion', 'ten shapely holy virgins with the passion of a manly host'.[34] Other women in the Martyrology of Oengus are also described as being with a host (*slóg*), a word which has the ambiguous implications of both military hosts and angelic hosts.[35] This dual meaning of course mirrors the late antique association between military spirituality and the *vita angelica*. Like other early medieval writers, these Irish authors found no inconsistency in giving military descriptions of virgins in the same texts which also call the same women 'brides of Christ'; the readers were able, we presume, to absorb the multiplicity of metaphors without difficulty, although the modern reader can find the juxtapositions somewhat jarring. Bugge observed that in both male and female monasticism, 'monastic virginity takes on a profound metaphysical significance: it becomes far more than bodily integrity, but a symbol, in some way, of the invincibility of the soul which renounces contact with matter' and that 'monasticism drew its picture of the perfect Christian life along martial lines in imitation of the angels' military prowess'.[36]

---

[30] Ibid., notes on 22 May.
[31] Quote from *Thes. Pal.* ii. 325. Discussion and dating in *Kenney*, no. 95.
[32] *Audite Sancta Studia.*   [33] *Ní Car Brigit*, lines 91–4.
[34] Martyrology of Oengus: 5 Jan., 1 Feb., 28 Feb.
[35] e.g. ibid., 23 Mar. For use of *slóg* for a host of angels, see the Preface, verse 129.
[36] Bugge, *Virginitas*, 54, 49.

Elva Johnston has suggested that laudatory ascription of martial qualities to exalted women was unusual, and when it did appear it was focused on Brigit in the context of Laigin politics; also, she takes the view that 'Brigit's participation in battle is an essentially "unfemale" thing'. Of course she is right that in Ireland mortal women were not supposed to engage in military activity, but Brigit is not in fact exceptional in being a martially-imaged female saint, and we have to see both her and other saints' ascriptions as coming out of a widespread and long-standing Christian tradition.[37]

The virgin who successfully defeated temptations had *virtus*. Thus, for ex-ample, the *Vita I* praises Brigit's *divina virtute*[38] and a seventh- or eighth-century hymn says the same saint *fulsit virtute*.[39] Even the Virgin Mary, epitome of meek-ness and mildness, was given by the Irish the muscular attribute of *virtus*: an eighth-century hymn includes the line: *Per mulierem et lignum mundus prius periit, per mulieris virtutem ad salutem rediit*.[40] Some Irish texts went further than attributing *virtus* to their holy women and actually likened them explicitly to men. In Brigit's *Vita I*, a virgin student of Brigit's countered an attack of lust by burning her feet, and was praised for fighting lust *viriliter*.[41] Making the gender point even more explicitly, another hymn likens Monenna to a man in a woman's body (*virum gerens proposito in corpore femineo*).[42] Only a little less explicit is the eighth-century hymn, *Christus in Nostra Insula* which says of Brigit not only: *Ymnus iste angelicae summaeque sanctae Brigitae fari non valet omnia virtutum mirabilia*, but also *perfectionem quam promisit viriliter implevit*.[43]

The dress of nuns, like that of monks, included a belt or *zona*, integral to the religious identity. The *zonae* of saints served as wonderworking objects and much was made of them in the Lives; Brigit's belt accomplished at least one miracle, and Coemgen's (according to a late Life anyhow), was said to be made of gold.[44] Presumedly it is a saint's *zona* which was formerly contained in the famous Moylough belt shrine, for we know they could be preserved as relics, as was Monenna's. The *zona* was symbolic as well as practical, and was linked in the early Irish mind with the Biblical injunction to harsh austerity, 'Gird up thy loins', which is cited for women in particular in the very famous Epistle 22 of Jerome.[45] In the twelfth century at least one writer thought that this holy command was unsuited to women, but in these earlier centuries the *zona* was treated almost like

---

[37] E. Johnston, 'Transforming Women in Irish Hagiography', *Peritia* 9 (1995), 197–220, at 218–19.

[38] *Vita I* of Brigit, ch. 107.   [39] *Audite Fratres Facta*, stanza 13.

[40] *Cantemus in Omni Die* (Bernard and Atkinson (eds.), *Liber Hymnorum*, i. 32–4). Text discussed in O'Dwyer, *Mary*, 54–6, and *Kenney*, no. 98.

[41] *Vita I* of Brigit, ch. 99.

[42] *Audite Sancta Studia*.   [43] *Christus in Nostra Insula*, stanzas 1 and 2.

[44] *Vita I* of Brigit, ch. 46; Latin Life of Coemgen, D text, ch. 26 (*PVSH* i. 234–57).

[45] Jerome invokes the commandment with regard to chastity rather than fasting, but notably juxta-poses with the reference to the wearing of a leather girdle, the material of the Irish *zonae*. *Ep.* 22, ch. 11: 'God says to Job: "Gird up thy loins as a man." John wears a leather girdle. The apostles must gird their loins to carry the lamps of the Gospel.'

a warrior's buckler, but recalling the discipline of fasting. Of Monenna, whose supreme virtue was her great fasting, and who was likened to John the Baptist in a number of ways, her nuns sang a hymn with the line, 'the hard belt of Christ surrounded the holy body' (*zona Christi durissima percinxit sancta viscera*), a reference to John's leather belt. Monenna, also like John, was said to have worn rough animal skins—both were warriors against the temptations of softness. Brigit's followers, too, sang of the belt of their holy warrioress, which encircled that saint's holy loins: *zona sanctae militiae sanctos lumbos praecingere consuevit diurno nocturno*.[46]

When a woman, by her holiness, transcended the weakness associated with the female gender in the male authors' eyes, she did not lose any of her positive female qualities. She gained a strength beyond that considered normally possible for those of her sex, but the texts also continue to praise them for such feminine attributes as humility, beauty, and bridal status. Nor should this be seen as evidence that the Irish were prone to loathe women, for they did not. Rather it shows that the Irish partook of a typical Western patriarchy reinforced by Christian doctrine, but they put a slant on it which, paradoxically, could pave the way for certain women to be regarded as being more capable of responsibility and autonomy.

Consecration Rites

Virgins were consecrated in rites performed by bishops, and three accounts from early Ireland survive. The earliest of these is in Brigit's *Vita I*, probably from the seventh century.[47] In this account several virgins were presented to the bishop, the priest Maccaille announcing, *Ecce sanctae virgines foris sunt quae volunt velamen virginitatis de manu tua accipere*. The text relates that the bishop consecrated Brigit first, placing a veil on her head with speeches and readings; then, with her head bent in submission, she touched the wooden base of the altar (*lectis orationibus Brigida capite submisso pedem altaris ligneum in manu sua tenuit*). The other virgins then received the veil in the same manner. It is unclear whether the touching of the base of the altar was part of the ceremony or a chance action on Brigit's part. Her parents seem to have been present, because after the ceremony they offered her some land, though in Cogitosus's shorter account of the same event there is no mention of parental permission or presence. The attitude of the woman is also given: the girl was to be kneeling humbly and offering her virginal crown to almighty God (*genua humiliter flectens et suam virginalem coronam Domino omnipotenti offerens*).[48] In the ninth-century *Bethu Brigte*, Brigit's consecration ceremony was performed by a bishop, but here there is mention of another person, a minister, one of whose tasks in the ceremony was to hold the veils.[49]

---

[46] Irish Life of Adomnán, ch. 1; *Audite Sancta Studia*, stanza 24; *Christus in Nostra Insula*, stanza 3.
[47] *Vita I* of Brigit, ch. 18.   [48] Cogitosus, Life of Brigit, ch. 2.
[49] Ch. 18. There are similar descriptions from later Lives. Ita's late Life mentions who performed the

From these sparse indications, it would seem that the Irish consecration of virgins was roughly standard in relation to other parts of Western Christendom in the same period. This impression is corroborated by the one other known source directly relating to the consecration rite, a ninth-century St Gall manuscript fragment found in 1874 by a Dr Keller of Zürich. Kenney dated the fragment to 'the tenth century or earlier' and Keller himself dated it, on the basis of the manuscript, to the early ninth.

Permaneat ad prudentibus qui . . . virginibus vigilantia. . . . adferte copuletur . . . per dominum nostrum Jesu Christum . . .
Oremus, fratres carissimi, misericordiam, ut euntum bonum tribuere dignetur huic puellae N. quae.
Deo votum candidam vestem perferre cum integritate coronae in resurrectione vitae aeternae quam facturus est; orantibus nobis, prestet Deus . . .
Conserva, domine, istius devotae pudorem castitatis dilectionem continentiae in factis, in dictis, in cogitationibus; per Christe Jesu, qui cum patre vivis . . .
Accipe, puella, pallium candidum quod perferas ante tribunal Domini.[50]

As in Cogitosus, there is both a white veil and a white garment. The term *pallium* was used, from the fifth century in the West, to refer to a holy virgin's veil; it remained the normal term until around the time of the *Missale Francorum*, so in this respect the Irish terminology is standard.[51] What is unusual, however, is what the virgin received in the rite. In Frankia holy virgins received a veil, a ring, and a *torques* or crown; in England they were given a veil and ring: the Irish virgin received a dress but no ring.[52] The formal presentation of the dress, furthermore, is not found in the Roman pontificals. As mentioned previously, the colour the Irish virgin wore was distinctive, too, in comparison with other parts of the West, where veil and dress were normally black rather than white.[53] Cogitosus is among the several sources who specified the colour of the veil as also being white.[54]

In the Zürich fragment there have been noted similarities to the consecration in the Gallican use, but the wording of all but the last few lines is different. In this text, as in the Gallican and unlike the Roman, the officiant's speech is addressed to the others present, identified as *fratres*. The Gallican version begins *Faventes*,

ceremony and the fact that its central act was the acceptance of the veil: *ab ecclesiasticis viris consecrata est, et velamen virginitatis accepit.*

[50] Untitled entry, *Archaeological Journal* 31 (1874), 85–6. Printed in F. Warren, *The Liturgy and Ritual of the Celtic Church* (2nd edn., with introduction and bibliography by J. Stephenson; Woodbridge, 1987), 23. Discussed in *Kenney*, no. 565, under 'The Zürich Fragments'.

[51] Hodgson, 'Frankish Church', 224.

[52] Ibid., 101–2, 226–8; Schneider, 'Anglo-Saxon Women', 57–9.

[53] Hodgson, 'Frankish Church', 165, with references. At the Irish monastery of Bobbio in northern Italy, however, the virgin received a white dress with her veil (E. Lowe (ed.), *The Bobbio Missal* (London, 1920), at 547).

[54] Cogitosus, Life of Brigit, ch. 2: *caeleste intuens desiderium et pudicitiam et tantum castitatis amorem in tali virgine, pallium album et vestem candidam super ipsius venerabile caput inposuit.*

dilectissimi Fratres; in the Roman rite the equivalent speech is addressed to God (*Respice, Domine, propitius super has famulas tuas*).[55] Mohlberg found that three of the four prayers have counterparts in Continental texts, and as for the fourth, Sims-Williams has determined that it uses a peculiarly Irish phraseology.[56]

In Irish texts, both in this fragment and in the numerous hagiographical accounts, the person who performs nuns' consecrations is always male and, where identified, is of episcopal grade. There is no suggestion here, as there is elsewhere, that abbesses, perform the rite, though it cannot be ruled out as a possibility.[57]

NUNS IN THE ECCLESIASTICAL STRUCTURE AND AT LAW

An anomaly to be noted in both the Latin and Irish legal texts is the sheer paucity of references to nuns, which is striking, in contract with the coverage given to every other conceivable type of person or entity; the laws cover all sorts of women, even rare ones (e.g. female druids), and there are thousands of references to clerics and monks.[58] One possible explanation is that nuns were so few in number that mention in legal texts was not felt to be warranted, but this idea can be eliminated in the light of the very large number of nuns mentioned in such texts as the Lives and martyrologies. Another is that nuns were so segregated that their rules were not sufficiently 'mainstream' to warrant inclusion in the laws; but since nuns were clearly not enclosed and had much interaction with both ecclesiastics and laypeople, this too seems extremely unlikely. The most plausible explanation for this curious lacuna (though by no means a satisfactory one) is that nuns were governed by a combination of the normal rules for either Church members and those for women generally.

---

[55] M. Duchesne, *Christian Worship: Its Origin and Evolution* (London, 1927), 424–7.

[56] P. Sims-Williams, 'Thought, Word and Deed: An Irish Triad', *Ériu* 29 (1978), 78–111.

[57] e.g. in Frankia, *Admonitio Generalis* (789); in England, an 11th-cent. fragmentary Life (Schneider, 'Anglo-Saxon Women', 191).

[58] On the usefulness of these texts for ecclesiastical matters, see Sharpe, 'Some Problems'; L. Breatnach, 'Canon Law and Secular Law in Early Ireland: the Significance of *Bretha Nemed*', *Peritia* 3 (1984), 439–59; G. Mac Niocaill, 'Christian Influences in Early Irish Law', in Ní Chatháin and Richter, *Irland und Europa*, 151–6; D. Ó Corráin, 'Irish Law and Canon Law', ibid. 157–66; D. Ó Corráin, L. Breatnach, and A. Breen, 'The Laws of the Irish', *Peritia* 3 (1984), 382–438.

The laws have long been used in studies of the social position of Irish *lay* women, e.g. in *SEIL*: Power, 'Classes of Women', 81–108; D. Binchy 'Family Membership of Women', 180–6; D. Binchy, 'The Legal Capacity of Women with Regard to Contracts', 207–34; M. Dillon, 'The Relationship of Mother and Son, of Father and Daughter, and the Law of Inheritance with regard to Women', 129–79. More recently: D. Ó Corráin, 'Women in Early Irish Society', in M. MacCurtain and D. Ó Corráin (eds.), *Women in Irish Society: the Historical Dimension* (Dublin, 1978) 1–13; C. McAll, 'The Normal Paradigms of a Woman's Life in the Irish and Welsh Law Texts', in D. Jenkins and M. Owen (eds.), *The Welsh Law of Women: Studies Presented to Professor Daniel A. Binchy on his Eightieth Birthday* (Cardiff, 1980), 7–22. On married women specifically, D. Ó Corráin, 'Marriage in Early Ireland', in A. Cosgrove (ed.), *Marriage in Ireland* (Dublin, 1985), 5–24; Kelly, *Guide*, 70–5; D. Ó Corráin, 'Women and the Law in Early Ireland', in M. O'Dowd and S. Wichert (eds.), *Chattel, Servant or Citizen: Women's Status in Church, State and Society* (Historical Studies 19; Belfast, 1995), 45–57; B. Jaski, 'Marriage Laws in Ireland and on the Continent in the Early Middle Ages', in C. Meek and K. Simms, *The Fragility of her Sex?* (Dublin, 1996), 16–42; Charles-Edwards, *Kinship, passim*.

For the ecclesiastical and theological status of nuns as reflected in social prerogative and identity, the early eighth-century *Collectio Canonum Hibernensis* is an
important text. It is admittedly problematic, because it is difficult to assess its relevance to its own time. For the most part it imports material from earlier, often
foreign, sources without alteration; thus, as Sharpe observed, 'one must naturally pause before accepting any statement as directly relevant to the Irish
church at the beginning of the eighth century'. But equally 'one ought not reject
any section as irrelevant or inconsistent without showing why it was included'.
Inconsistencies are not, however, due to the text being of antiquarian nature
and containing legislation at least in part redundant (as Hughes had suggested),
but because it was a living text compiled in an environment in which some diversity prevailed, even on important issues.[59] The *Hibernensis* gives a definition
of the nun, the *caillech* or *palliata*:

> Pallium a palliditate dictum, hinc et palliata sive Pallas Dea, quae et Minerva, cuius tem-
> plum pallidum est, cuius sacerdotes virgines erant palliatae, hoc est velatae; hinc mutata
> specie eodem nomine perseverante, licet in novo ad palliatas, hoc est velatas censeri
> permissum est.[60]

> *Pallium* [veil] is named from paleness, this and *palliata* or 'Goddess Pallas' who is Min-
> erva, whose temple is white, whose priests and virgins are *palliatae*, that is, veiled; this, in
> mutated form perseveres with the same name, [thus] it is permitted nowadays that the
> pallium-wearers, that is to say, the veiled women, may be esteemed.

The authors also state explicitly that nuns are to be greatly honoured because
they have transcended the fragility of their gender:

> Palliatae, hoc est velatae, magno honore habeantur, quia sexum, hoc est fragilitatem
> vincunt, et se mundi actibus abdicant.[61]

> Pallium-wearers, that is the veiled women, are to have much honour, because they con-
> quer their sex, that is to say, their fragility, and they withdraw from the world through
> their actions.

This conquest has more to do with the spirit than the body: *Hibernensis* follows
Jerome in asserting that a nun remained pure if she had been raped against her
will—her purity was a spiritual state which physical violation could not mar;
as the chapter headed *De eo, quod non inficiat sanctaemoniales vi obprimi* states, the
bodies of holy women are not soiled, except by will.[62]

---

[59] Sharpe, 'Some Problems', 236–7. *Hibernensis* is now used as a living text by scholars examining ecclesiastical structure and offices, e.g. Charles-Edwards, 'Pastoral Role of the Church'.

[60] *Hibernensis*, book 45, ch. 10, citing *Sinodus Hibernensis* as its source. It is worth mentioning here that it
is from *palliatae* that the Irish derived their word *caillech*, which literally means 'veiled one'. Regarding
Hibernensis, see Hughes, *Church*, 123–42. Hughes felt it was antiquarian and could not be used as a living
text (*Church*, 124, cf. 132), but Sharpe successfully defends its currency in 'Some Problems', 236–7.

[61] *Hibernensis*, book 45, ch. 13, citing *Sinodus Romana* as its source.

[62] Ibid., book 45, ch. 17: *Corpus sanctarum mulierum non vis maculat, sed voluntas . . . non ita amittitur*

Hibernensis also links the status of nuns to the 'grades' of the Church, a concept normally associated with the Church's men, and clearly articulates the idea that in the female religious profession there were two grades, that of the virgin and that of the widow or penitent. It cites Augustine for a division into virgins and widows, Jerome for a division into virgins and penitents: 'the first is similar and comparable to bishops, the second to the grade of presbyters, i.e. seniors' (*primum genus episcopis simulatur et comparatur, II gradus presbiteris, hoc est senioribus*).[63] By stating that nuns were equivalent either to bishops or to presbyters, *Hibernensis* is rendering explicit a very important notion which is found obliquely in other material of the period. Furthermore, by specifying that the second type of nun had to be under the 'hand' of a pastor for her whole life, the text implies that the virginal nun did not. In other words, the virgin could enjoy a level of autonomy which, although not specified here, is in some way comparable to that of a bishop.

The application of grades to nuns is interesting because the grades, after all, are those of the clergy—bishops, presbyters, deacons, and so forth, as described at length in this text and others. Monastics might be laymen or holders of a grade (*fer gráid*), meaning that they were also clerics. Donnchadh Ó Corráin observed that the monastic who is a grade-holder is more closely identified with the Church than is the lay monastic; when an abbot parts from his church his separation arrangements vary depending on this factor; he takes less with him if he is also a *fer gráid*, a priest. In other words, those who hold a grade are more tightly bound or 'married' to the Church.[64] The same language is used for nuns, i.e. nuns are holders of a 'grade': some Middle Irish notes refer to a 'penitent grade' sought by a nun from a priest, for example.[65] Furthermore, the language of ceremonial inauguration is often the same: the Irish term 'ordain' is used for consecration of nuns as well as the inauguration of abbesses.[66]

There are other indications in the literature which suggest some ecclesiastical equivalence between nuns, monks, and clerics. *Hibernensis* tends to accord nuns the kind of privileges given to male clerics. Its burial regulations, governed by considerations of status and sanctity, permitted religious women to be buried with honour near the altar of a church. It cites Gregory on the rulings about the burial of nuns, stressing that the virginity of a nun is a more important consideration in the decision to bury her near the altar than even her *stultiloquium*.[67]

---

corporis sanctitas violata, animi puritate manente, etiam corpore oppresso; sicut amittitur corporis sanctitas violata animi puritate, etiam corpore intacto.

[63] Ibid., book 45, ch. 12.

[64] Ibid., book 43, ch. 6. Discussion in Hughes, *Church*, 158–60; see also Ó Corrain, 'Early Irish Churches', 333, who thinks the analogy of marriage is a very good one, as the separation rules are 'remarkably close to the secular rules governing divorce'.

[65] 10th- or 11th-cent. gloss on *Ní Car Brigit* (*Thes. Pal.* ii. 330).

[66] e.g. Gilla Easpuic, *De Statu Ecclesiae* on ordination of abbesses (*PL* 159. 995–1004, at 1002).

[67] *Hibernensis*, book 18, ch. 8, entitled *De eo, quod non prodest malis sepeliri in locis sanctis: Quedam femina sanctemonialis in ecclesia sepulta iuxta altare, pars eius una igni consumpta visa est, pars intacta permansit, id est inferior, quia ipsa mulier virgo fuit, tamen stultiloquium non vitavit.* Cf. Gregory, *Dialogi*.

Equivalence is not restricted even to the Latin material. One vernacular law tract specifies that the evidence of a nun may be accepted against that of a cleric, because both parties are in orders, are holders of 'grades'.[68] Another classes nuns, with clerics, among those who are governed by the Church: they are both bound by the Church subject to their soul-friends.[69]

In arguing that the Irish mentality included nuns into the corporate body of ecclesiastics, and that virgins were equivalent to male counterparts and might be so esteemed, we are not losing sight of the very real differences which the Irish specified between nun and cleric or monk. It is very clearly spelt out, for example, that women could not receive sacerdotal office. Citing Isidore, the chapter in *Hibernensis* reiterates the biblical injunction against women speaking or teaching in church, and against trespassing into areas of the sacerdotal office reserved for men.[70] So although sharing an equivalence of sorts, the nuns of Ireland were very clearly not clerics.

Status in Vernacular Law

The status of a person in Irish society was marked by such things as honour price, the mode of compensation for injury, and the ability to give testimony. Thus these laws are a natural place to turn in looking for the social and legal position of nuns. Unfortunately there is too little on nuns *per se* in the material to allow certain or comprehensive conclusions, but there is enough evidence to warrant consideration in light of the ideas raised so far.

With regard to the honour price of nuns, the evidence indicates that nuns were not actually above the highest laywomen, but rather were classed with them. Thus when raped, a *mac-caillech* (usually translated as 'young nun') who has not renounced her veil (*i-mmaccaillig na diulta cailli*) was entitled to the maximum fine, the same as that which a daughter of childhood age or a first wife would receive.[71] The fine consists of 'the full *eric* fine', and the full honour price (*lóg n-enech*) of her superior is to be paid to that person. The fine went to a superior within the Church, not to a member of the nun's kin, according to the gloss.

We may digress here to ask: what exactly was a *mac-caillech*? A novice nun? More logical would perhaps be a 'virginal' nun, as distinguished from a widow or penitent nun. Although one cannot be sure, as there is nothing on the honour prices of other sorts of nuns in *Cáin Lánamna* ('the Law of Connections'), logic

---

[68] *Gúbretha Caratniad*, ch. 35 (*CIH* 2192–99, at 2197.5–6; German trans. in R. Thurneysen, 'Aus dem Irischen Recht III. Die falschen Urteilssprüche Caratnia's', *ZCP* 15 (1925), 302–70, at 345). See also Kelly, *Guide*, 78.

[69] *Córus Béscnai* (in *CIH* at 523; with trans. in *ALI* iii. 14).

[70] *Hibernensis*, book 45, ch. 20, entitled *De mulieribus vel feminis non accipientibus ullum virile vel sacerdotale officium*. It says: *Feminis in ecclesia loqui vel docere non permittitur; sed nec contingere vel conferre ullius virilis muneris aut sacerdotalis officii sortem sibi vindicare.*

[71] *Cain Lánamna*, ch. 8, entitled *Lánamnas Eicne* (*CIH* 502.29–519.35; also R. Thurneysen, 'Cáin Lánamná', in *SEIL*, 1–80, at 71–2; also *ALI* ii. 404, 406).

and the other extant references to *mac-caillech* suggest that it actually refers to a virginal nun—in this and other instances. The word prefix *mac*, meaning 'son' or 'boy', is seemingly illogical at first glance. There is, however, a parallel term for the male, *mac-clerich*, which appears somewhat more frequently in Irish material: it is normally treated as 'young cleric' or 'novice'; however if it is translated as a virginal cleric, one who was in orders before becoming sexually experienced, such passages are rendered more comprehensible.[72] This, I would suggest, is the basic term, from which the female one was formed—the *mac* prefix coming to connote virginity generally and thus being grafted unchanged onto the *caillech* term. The argument in favour of interpretating the *mac-caillech* in this way is strengthened by a passage an eighth-century penitential tract, *De Arreis*. In the section on the appropriate commutations for the cleric, monk, *mac-caillech*, and laywoman, the authors make a set of parallels, in which the layman is said to differ from the cleric in the same manner as the laywoman differs from the *mac-caillech*. Even more persuasive is the appearance of the word *ban-maicc*, used in a ninth-century text to refer to female holy virgins; when Oengus called Romula, Curufin, and Sabina *ban-maicc* he meant not 'woman-boys', the literal translation, but female virgins.[73] It is then, as virginal nuns, that one reads the setting of penances in the Old Irish tract on commutations:

Amal file tra deochair etir laechu 7 clerchu, etir maccaillecha 7 laechesa, imtha samlaid deochair etir a saethar 7 pennainn. Ata dano etir na harraib ata cora do denum doib. Arra na n-athlaech 7 na athlaiches cétumus, feis i n-uiscib, feis for nenaid, feis for blaescaib cnó, feis la marb i-ndeirc, uair nad bi coimtig laech nó laeiches nad bi cuit oc marbad duini. Ate immorro arra ata cóire do clerchib 7 do c[h]aillechaib acht anti dib marbas duine, mani dentar ar imt[h]ormach fochraice .i. feiss doib i n-ecailsib uaraib nó a cubachlaib deirritib oc figlib 7 oc ernaigthib cen cumsanud .i. cet suide, cet lige, cet cotulta . . .[74]

As there is a difference between laymen and clerics and between virgin-nuns and laywomen, so too there is a difference between the kind of mortifications due from them, as well as between the kind of commutations which may properly be performed by them. First, commutations proper for former laymen and women: spending the night in water or on nettles or on nutshells, or with a dead body . . . On the other hand there are commutations which are proper for clerics and nuns except such of them as have slain a man (who are required to perform the first kind) unless (a commutation of the first kind) be performed for the purpose of increasing one's reward: spending the night in cold churches or remote cells while keeping vigils and praying without respite, i.e. (without) leave to sit or lie down or sleep.[75]

---

[72]   There are many such references, but see e.g. the Stowe Missal (Warren, *Stowe Missal*, 28, 42) where the best and holiest kind of cleric is deemed the *mac-clerich*.

[73]   Martyrology of Oengus, 20 July.

[74]   *De Arreis*, chs. 7–8 (ed. K. Meyer, 'An Old-Irish Treatise *De Arreis*', *Revue Celtique* 15 (1894), 484 98, at 488).

[75]   *De Arreis*, chs. 7–8 (trans. D. A. Binchy, 'The Old-Irish Table of Commutations' in Bieler, *Irish Penitentials*, 277–83, at 278–9; Meyer, 'An Old Irish Treatise *De Arreis*', 484–98).

It follows that there was some semblance of equivalence perceived between the cleric on the male side and the *mac-caillech* on the female side. One notes that further down in the same passage the author has reverted to a looser term for nun, the simple *caillech*. The passage does not make much sense if we interpret *mac-caillech* as a novice nun, just as the above section of *Cáin Lánamna* is less comprehensible for doing so.

There is nothing to my knowledge in the edited legal corpus which comments on the nun *per se* as plaintiff, but presumably a nun would have needed a superior's backing to instigate a legal case, unless perhaps if she were of very high religious status—an abbess or an anchoritic holy woman with semi-saint status. Free women could be plaintiffs, and numerous rules survive about the notice they had to serve, the limitations on distraint they had to observe, and the situations in which they could stand surety. One hagiographic tale has a nun as a plaintiff. A tenth- or eleventh-century anecdote in the Martyrology of Tallaght tells of the nun (*caillech*) Lúachair of Kells bringing a complaint to a king when his son stole her special cow. The king condemned the prince to death.[76] The judge is here a king rather than a legal judge, but even so it is noteworthy that there is no mention of a male advocate for the nun, and the word of the nun was taken over the word of a prince. Whether or not nuns in reality usually brought cases or made testimony against laymen, at least one later hagiographer was happy to portray them doing so.

The validity of a person's testimony is another means of assessing status. One must note first that the norm in Irish law was for the testimony of women to be considered invalid, either outright or unless supported by a man. *Hibernensis* in one place denies the testimony of women altogether: *testimonium feminae non accipitur, sicut apostoli testimonium feminarum non acceperunt de resurrectione Christi.*[77] Elsewhere the text expresses the view that women can give testimony, but only with the approval of their (male) superior: *mulier si iurando se constrinxerit maritusque aut si pater eius una die tacuerit, voti rea erit.*[78] The ambiguity in law is evidenced elsewhere too; one vernacular tract says that a woman's evidence is always invalid; another says it is valid, providing her superior concurs.[79] A nun was not just a woman, but also a monastic: monastics too had limitations on their ability to give testimony. Monks needed the approval of their abbatial head when they were witnesses.[80] It is therefore safe to infer that most nuns would have needed

---

[76] Martyrology of Tallaght, notes on 5 Apr. Fergus Kelly discusses the material which deals with king's roles as law-enforcers (*Guide*, 22–3).

[77] *Hibernensis*, book 16, ch. 3, citing *Sinodus Hibernensis*.

[78] Ibid., book 35, ch. 6, entitled *De iuramento non solvendo*, citing *Lex*.

[79] Kelly points out that Heptad 49 places a total bar on female testimony, but notes that elsewhere one finds the view that women could bear witness in civil law in the context of their capacity to requisition land (*Din Techtugad*) and to take rent or fines (*Di Chetharslicht Athgabála*), at least from other women: (Kelly, *Guide*, 75, 207).

[80] Monastics also needed a superior in order to be witnesses, at least as a general rule. *Hibernensis*, book 35, ch. 5, citing *Sinodus Hibernensis*, says: *Iuramentum filii aut filiae nesciente patre, iuramentum monachi, nesciente abbate, iuramentum pueri et iuramentum servi non permittente domino irrita sunt.*

the concurrence of a superior in order to give testimony. As to the identity of the superior, perhaps it was the abbess or a male cleric: the *Díre* text says that when a woman is in the Church it is the Church who supervises her, but unfortunately it does not specify further. Another specifies that fines for a nun's rape went to the Church, as her superior.[81] The gender of the head is by no means a settled matter, as the next chapter, which deals with abbesses, will demonstrate.

One law tract does actually deal with a situation in which a woman gives evidence against a cleric. *Gúbretha Caratniad* ('The False Judgements of Caratnia') deals with exceptions to normal legal principles, and it asserts that the evidence of a woman is valid against that of a cleric when it is a case of one ordained person giving testimony against another. The relevant passage takes the form of a dialogue between the mythical judge Caratnia and a king about a specific case. In that instance Caratnia had decided, seemingly against custom, that a woman's witness against an ordained person (*rucus fiadnisse mná for fer ngráid*) was valid. Challenged by the king, Caratnia explains, 'I did it quite in order because an ordained person was opposed to another ordained person' (*Ba deithber, ar ba fer gráid for fer ngráid n-aile*).[82] Fergus Kelly saw this passage as applying to nuns, presumably taking *fer ngráid* as referring to a nun.[83] If interpreted this way, the tract suggests that judges should permit a nun to give testimony against a cleric on the basis of her ecclesiastical equivalency to a cleric. An alternative view of the passage, which takes account of the fact that a closer translation of *fer ngráid* would be 'a man in orders', could be that a woman could give such testimony providing she had a sponsor who was a man in orders. The women most likely to have such a sponsor were nuns, whose superiors were ecclesiastical.

Thurneysen thought that this law meant that women were allowed as witnesses at certain periods or in certain regions when there was a suit between ordained people, perhaps only because an ordained person was representing a woman. He also thought it meant that the glossator did not recognize the witness of women, though the glossator apparently knew two other cases where women could bear witness: when a lord exercised his office as judge over his vassals, and in commercial contracts. These cases were not mentioned explicitly, but as women were allowed to offer their own goods as guarantees and to engage in business with them (the goods) then presumably, Thurneysen ventured, they could appear as a witness in these matters.[84]

The hagiography does show nuns bringing legal complaints against clerics. A single story, appearing in two versions, *Bethu Brigte* and Brigit's *Vita I*, deals with exactly this. In both versions the nun brings a charge against a cleric, not to a

[81] *Díre* Text, ch. 38 (*SEIL* 213–14); *Cáin Lánamna*, ch. 8 (Thurneysen, '*Cáin Lánamná*', 71–2).

[82] Quotation follows R. Thurneysen's edition, '*Gúbretha Caratniad*', 345–6, corresponding to *CIH* 2197.5–6. The text itself discussed in Kelly, *Guide*, 24, 266.

[83] 'A nun has certain legal rights not possessed by laywomen. Hence the evidence of a nun may be accepted against that of a cleric, though a woman is not normally entitled to give evidence' (Kelly, *Guide*, 78).

[84] '*Gúbretha Caratniad*', 345–6.

secular judge but to a synod of church authorities.[85] In the *Vita I* version the nun complained she had been made pregnant by one of Patrick's bishops; in *Bethu Brigte*, the nun accused the bishop of having raped her. In both versions the bishop denied the accusation, and the synod did not know how to resolve the issue, as it was a case of her word against his. It is noteworthy that the nun's complaint is portrayed as being taken seriously, and her word is not dismissed as invalid on account of her being a woman. In the end Brigit miraculously revealed incontrovertible proof that the nun was lying, and she set the nun's penance.

The legal sources contain special stipulations for certain types of high-status nuns. For example, the sick-maintenance of holy women 'abundant in miracles' was handled differently from that of ordinary women. A woman's testimony was valid, according to *Hibernensis*, providing she was a *domina* and/or a *virgo sancta*. These cases are discussed in the following chapter as they may well be most relevant to abbesses or other nuns of very high office, in which cases the specific privileges can be better thought of as belonging not so much to their virginal status as to their position in a monastery, church, or community. Another angle on this must be mentioned as well. Irish law made special provision for women who were members of professions, giving them extra autonomy approaching that of men in some situations, as has been demonstrated in a study of the status of those in the secular sphere.[86] The ultimate origins of such an attitude, whereby those females who hold power and greater responsibility are entitled to a legal position accordingly higher than they would have otherwise, must lie in native Irish culture: it appears that the Irish allowed for, and recognized, the 'exceptional woman'.

The legal material, offering as it does a way into the social organization of Irish society in this period, demonstrates that as far as the lawyers were concerned there were numerous sorts of holy women, or nuns at least. It also makes it clear that nuns formed a segment of the female population who were governed by special considerations, though the texts are not always clear how these worked. What is evident, though, is the conviction that, sometimes at least, nuns could transcend the more normal female legal incompetence.

Holy Virgins and Sexual Lapses

In the last chapter it was shown that in the Lives of the seventh, eighth, and ninth centuries, the living arrangements and monastic environments were largely unconcerned by the proximity of nuns to monks or other members of the opposite sex. The Irish monks, in their turn, suffered little if at all from gynophobia and did not normally ban women from their places. This relaxed approach was not, according to the evidence, restricted to matters of accommodation. The

---

[85] *Vita I* of Brigit, ch. 39.

[86] T. Clancy, 'Women Poets in Early Medieval Ireland: Stating the Case', in Meek and Simms, *Fragility*, 43–72; see also Ó Corrain, 'Women and the Law'.

prescriptive material shows a similar outlook regarding nuns' sexuality generally. A virgin, it was acknowledged, might have a lapse. As the various stories indicate, there were women who did not live up to the glorious ideal of Christian virginity so exalted in the religious literature. The legal implications of lapses in Ireland, for both clerics and for virgins, are of especial interest.

An early penitential stated explicitly that a virgin might regain her virginity after losing it, after seven years' penance. In this period we have more relevant material; an eighth-century Irish penitential does assert quite clearly that, as far as ecclesiastical rules went, a fallen nun could make amends for sexual sin (at least if it was a one-off event) through penance: the penance, as in the earlier penitentials, is the same as that of a cleric:[87]

Maccleirech adella banscail fu oen bliadain pennite for usciu 7 bargin ma dufusme clann is a cethoir is samlaid dano pennit mac-cailligi cuilles a ccaillecht.[88]

A virgin-cleric who visits a woman but once does penance for one year on bread and water: if a child is born from it, four years. The same penance is for a young nun who pollutes her virginity [lit. nunhood].

This later penitential does not, however, say that the woman could regain her status as 'virgin'. It might be that by the time the Irish penitential was written, the transition back to being a 'virgin' was an informal one, occurring without ceremony after the nun had completed penance and was again admitted to communion. Alternatively, there may have remained a formal reinstatement which is simply not mentioned as such. A third possibility is that by the eighth century there was a wider variety of people in female communities, and the issue of being 'virgin' in a strict sense may have declined in social importance within the community; the eighth century saw a well-documented decline in celibacy in Irish church communities generally, and nuns' places had on their premises a whole host of different sorts of women.[89]

We do know that a cleric could regain his status after a lapse. The following entry is one of several dealing with general guidelines for sexual penances:

Asbert tra arre aili dinab ecnaib fri huaiti aesa graid consacratar inna huli grada-sa frisna timtherechta cetna iar pennind 7 aithrigi 7 tiagait fo laim nespscuip .i. epscuip túath 7 asrochoilet a mbith-manchai fu mam apad chraibdich.[90]

---

[87] This entry on nuns, like that of the earlier Latin penitential, essentially consists of an addendum which states that the penance for nuns is the same as that for the cleric. This raises the question as to whether this was a general rule, and whether the penances in entries following this one (which is first in a series of sexual penances for clerics and monks) were understood to apply to nuns as well, on the basis that they were to perform the same level of penance as clerics, if a cleric's penance was specified.

[88] Old Irish Penitential, ch. 2, item 11. A more accurate translation of the passage is in Bieler, *Irish Penitentials*, 263. I have translated *mac* as 'young', the traditional translation of the word, rather than 'virginal', although I suspect the latter might be more what is meant.

[89] The decline of asceticism in the Irish Church from the strict asceticism of the first two centuries is treated at length in Hughes, *Church*, and Ó Corráin, *Ireland Before the Normans*.

[90] Old Irish Penitential, ch. 2.10. The preceding clerical offices discussed did not include nuns or any female office, so when the author writes 'these orders' he is not directly (if at all) referring to female orders.

One of the wise said, on account of the fewness of persons in orders: All these orders are reconsecrated after doing penance, with the same functions; and they go under the hand of a bishop (meaning a bishop of the laity), and they vow perpetual monkhood under the yoke of a pious abbot.

Did the female side of ecclesiastical life suffer from 'the fewness of persons in orders'? The term used for 'orders' is *grád* and it was used also for women monastics, but as to a shortage, the question is open. It does seem unlikely, since it was a shortage of people able to perform pastoral duties like saying the mass, baptism, and so forth that concerned Church authorities at this time. But even if female monasticism did not suffer from low numbers, we may still wonder if in the eighth and ninth centuries fallen nuns might regain their position as 'virgins', as had been possible in the earlier penitentials. A vernacular law tract says that dedicated widows (and/or penitent nuns), i.e. nuns who had sexual experience, enjoyed the same honour price as virginal nuns, providing they kept to the religious life.[91] The hagiography certainly affirms the power of penance for redemption of the fallen virgin: the corpus of Lives contains a handful of anecdotes in which a young nun falls pregnant, either through rape or through calculated assignation. When a nun deliberately engages in sexual activity, the abbess saint always prophetically discovers the fact, and the girl always confesses. Usually fallen virgins agree to, and perform, the penance prescribed. The anecdote usually ends at this point, and we do not know what happened to the nun's status, legal standing, or social condition afterwards. But there seems to have been no further ado once the penance was accepted, and the stories treat penance as a real and complete solution to the problem, so it seems reasonable to infer that such nuns could be re-integrated back into the monastic mainstream with their non-lapsed colleagues, regardless of whether they held a title of 'virgin', if indeed such titles remained important. In most of these anecdotes, once the nuns have committed the sin they are no longer called *virgo* but are referred to by other terms: *filia, sponsa Dei, famula, monialis*, and the like, as well as by general female terms, like *mulier, bánscal*, and *femina*. While perhaps no longer 'virgins', they had definitely not lost their standing as nuns. Certainly there is no case of a nun being evicted from the monastery for such a sin, providing she expressed regret and was willing to perform penance. The generous attitude of lawyers towards nuns who fell pregnant is made more understandable in light of the open monastic living arrangements in Ireland at the time, discussed in the previous chapter. The temptation for sexual lapse was presumably greater, and perhaps more forgivable, than it was in those societies where strict enclosure was the rule.

One legal source in which one would expect to find material on nuns is in *Cáin Adomnáin*, promulgated in the late seventh century jointly between secular and

[91] *Di Astud Chirt 7 Dligid* (*CIH* 223.22–244.22; also *ALI* v. 426–93, at 448). For a superior translation see Power, 'Classes of Women', 108.

ecclesiastical authorities for the protection of innocents: women, clerics, and children.[92] But oddly, nuns are not mentioned in the law even though they were innocents on two out of three counts. The law portrays the Church as a protector of women and an elevator of their position in Irish society

quod grande peccatum qui matrem 7 sororem matris Christi 7 matrem Christi occidit 7 collum unumquemque portantem 7 omnem hominem vestimentem contrivit.[93]

for the sin is great when anyone slays the mother and the sister of Christ's mother and the mother of Christ, and her who carries the spindle and who clothes everyone.

Nuns did not need to be actually mentioned in order to be covered by the stipulations of the ruling, since the text prescribes an equal fine for the injury of all women regardless of class or profession, but their absence is none the less peculiar. It seems even more so in the extensive Irish accretions to the text, which do mention offences against different types of women, for example, rape of a maiden (*ingen*), the humiliation of a gentlewoman (*dagmná*) and women of other grades, including the wife of an *aire désa*, the most common grade of nobleman.[94] Perhaps nuns were not mentioned because this portion of the text stresses that the law was to be applied also to clerics and children, with exactly the same fines applying to injuries against these people as to injuries against women. Nuns, belonging to both the Church and the female sex, were clearly going to have the stipulated fines applied to them. And in the section on rape, where fines are prescribed for attacks on maidens, perhaps nuns were automatically understood to be 'maidens'—this is not unlikely considering that the word for maiden, *ingen*, is a common Irish term for a nun.

And yet the virtual absence of nuns in *Cáin Adomnáin* serves to highlight a more general silence in prescriptive texts, and in this case as in many others one is forced to fall back on classifying the nun as either a 'woman' or a 'monk' and presuming that the Irish used for them the regulations for one of the two. As mentioned above, there are no rules for nuns on many of the indicators of social status. As to which set of rules Irish judges used in any given case involving a nun, the example of Judge Caratnia suggests that it was not always clear. But it seems reasonable that the decision would be taken on a case-by-case basis, using the laws which could be deemed applicable, bearing in mind the nun's social background and family wealth.

The Irish virginal nun remains somewhat enigmatic, and yet her relationship to her sexuality, namely having transcended it and its attendant feminine weakness, helped to give her a special place in Irish law. So too did it inform her

[92] Discussed in M. Ní Dhonnchadha, 'The *Lex Innocentium*: Adamnan's Law for Women, Clerics and Youths, 697 AD', in O'Dowd and Wichert, *Chattel*, 58–69.

[93] Ch. 33, with the Latin of the original uncorrected (K. Meyer (ed. and trans.), *Cáin Adamnáin: An Old Irish Treatise on the Law of Adamnán* (Anecdota Oxoniensia 12; Oxford, 1905)).

[94] *Cáin Adomnáin*, chs. 50–1.

position within the ecclesiastical hierarchy, as equivalent in some way to the bishop's. Like the bishop, the virginal nun was 'ordained', and bound to the Church with vows likened to those of marriage, in a ceremony presided over by the bishop. In society and in the church, she was rewarded highly for having vanquished the debility normally afflicting her sex. It is possible that even if she lapsed, she might have been able to regain her position amongst the virgins after doing penance, and if this was indeed the case it must surely be one of most remarkable of all the equivalencies between virginal nuns and bishops in the clergy in early medieval Ireland.

HOLY WIDOWS AND PENITENT NUNS

To be a religious widow in Ireland in the early medieval period was to be part of the church's holy people, and to enjoy a paradoxical status which on the one hand placed her above the married laity in the eyes of God and yet might also place her in the ranks of the penitents, those who were atoning for former sin. The holy widow, for all the anomalies of her position, was nevertheless very clearly a member of a recognized and dedicated path within the Irish church, and her profession was formalized with a promise which was considered binding in the eyes of both ecclesiastical and secular law, as we shall see below.

In spite of the certainty that holy widowhood was a distinct and demarcated religious profession, it is none the less problematic for the historian. To begin, Ireland has left no treatises on widowhood, no homilies or epistles extolling its virtue, and no hagiographic stories centring on widows. Furthermore, identifying a religious widow is sometimes tricky, for unless a qualifying adjective or the context indicates religious context or profession, the historian is left guessing as to whether the woman was simply a bereaved wife of the ordinary laity. Sometimes a text helpfully discloses that a woman was a *religiosa vidua, sancta vidua*, or, in Irish, *fedb chráibdech*.[95] Other times the context itself indicates that a widow was religious; in other cases however, the context is of no help whatsoever. In my analysis, I use only widows actually specified as religious.

The Irish word for widow, *fedb*, was derived from the Latin *vidua*. Its primary meaning was the same as in late antiquity, namely a married woman whose husband had died. But in the Irish law tracts we meet a woman called a 'widow' who is a sworn-celibate woman whose sexual partner, not necessarily a formal husband, might still be alive. The compendious etymological *Dictionary of the Irish Language* notes that the term *fedbacht* ('widowhood') could refer to a committed continence by either a man or a woman after the loss of a spouse, and it cites a number of examples from the thirteenth to fifteenth centuries. One

---

[95]   e.g. *Vita I* of Brigit, ch. 14.

of these is in the Annals of Ulster for the year 1224, where there is a report of a man who after his wife's demise, 'observed the strictest continence (*feadhbhacht*) until the day of his own death'.[96] This secondary meaning is evidenced also in the late antique world, where *vidua* can also refer to a woman who has professed religious continence but who might not have been bereaved. Since the Irish were voracious readers of patristic literature, it is not too surprising that they should have taken it over. However, before we can understand the Irish widow's profession we must take into account the late antique Christian concepts which informed it.

Late Antique Background

By the seventh century there existed five hundred years of practice and writing affirming Christian holy widowhood as a vowed or sworn profession with a special place in the theological hierarchy of believers. It originated with the very beginnings of Christianity, from which it evolved into a multi-faceted and complex vocation. The Pauline epistles contain reference to religious widows in 1 Timothy 5: 3–20, where Paul writes of the election of widows to a religious order or to some position of responsibility within the Church.[97] Tertullian, writing in the early third century, bears witness in his essay on the veiling of virgins to an order of widows, but his language is unclear regarding what sorts of women actually belonged to it.[98] In the fourth century John Chrysostom's treatise 'Against Remarriage' shows the profession as having become more formalized: in his day, we learn, undertaking the widow's life involved a pledge not to remarry, something the profession had not involved, at least formally, in the second century— an inference we may draw from Paul's letter to Timothy. Elizabeth Clark emphasizes that by Chrysostom's time both widowhood and virginity were 'true religious "professions" for which a solemn pledge was taken'.[99] Widows often appear in the Apocryphal Acts, e.g. the Acts of Paul, Thomas, John, and Peter. These too date from around the fourth century.

The widows we may find in the Acts would include women who are virgins or widows or women who have separated from their husbands by choice. They would be somewhat different from the widows known to us from most other early Christian literature wherein women were encouraged (if not required) to maintain their marital ties.[100]

[96] This secondary use is evidenced as late as the 15th cent.

[97] See discussion in B. Witherington, *Women in the Earliest Churches* (Society for New Testament Studies 59; Cambridge, 1988), 201–3. Also discussed in S. Davies, *Revolt of the Widows: The Social World of the Apocryphal Acts* (Carbondale, 1980), 70–1. Also discussed in O. Stählin, 'Chéra', in G. Friedrich (ed.), *Theological Dictionary of the New Testament* (Grand Rapids, 1974), ix. 448–65, at 453.

[98] He speaks of a virgin of less than 20 years being enrolled with the widows, and mentions that apparently married women and even mothers and teachers of children were being elected to an order either of widows or virgins. See Stählin, 'Chéra', 462–5, and Davies, *Revolt*, 71–2.

[99] Clark, 'Introduction to John Chrysostom', 233.   [100] Davies, *Revolt*, 72.

Throughout these early centuries *vidua* could refer to any woman who had formally renounced sexual activity after having participated in connubial relations. To qualify as a widow one's spouse need not have died; he might be abandoned. Tertullian, for example, wrote of pagan priestesses who renounced their husbands and lived in strict *viduitas*. In late antique hagiography and in the Apocryphal Acts 'the technical term "widow" might often apply to a woman, virgin or widow, particularly dedicated to continence and Christian piety'.[101] Widowhood implied 'a pledge of continence, a resolution to be faithful to Christ rather than to a partner in an earthly marriage'.[102] Furthermore, the Apocryphal Acts obliquely encourage women to leave their husbands and become religious widows.

The widow's profession received a boost during the Church's debates on remarriage. Many Christian thinkers believed that marriage was literally forever, and at the resurrection couples would be reunited. In this view, people who remarried after the death of their spouse were perforce committing adultery. So bereaved wives were encouraged to take a vow not to remarry but instead to dedicate the remainder of their lives to God.[103] We should not be surprised, then, to find the chaste widow in the popular threefold schema of the faithful. In late antique texts the widow was the sixtyfold fruit, enjoying the sixtyfold reward of heaven, located as she was between the hundredfold virgin and the thirtyfold married Christian. Jerome said that the widows reap the sixtyfold reward 'because they are placed in a position of difficulty and distress', on account of their depression and 'the greater difficulty in resisting the allurements of pleasure once experienced'.[104] The heavenly reward for the widow was quite exalted: she 'will be honoured on earth by men and she will receive eternal glory from God in heaven' and those widows 'who have served uprightly will be magnified by the archangels'.[105]

Holy Widows in Ireland

The earliest appearance of the widow in Ireland is in this context, in Patrick's fifth-century *Epistola*. He refers to women of the three grades—virgin, widow, and celibate married—and says that in Ireland there was an increasing number of virgins, 'widows, and the self-denying'. If Patrick was not just writing formulaically, we could infer that he was recruiting women for dedicated widowhood, in which case it was a path open to Christian Irish women from as early as the fifth century. In any case Patrick is establishing that widows have an identity in Christianity *as widows*. Somewhat later Pa2, the Second Synod of St Patrick,

---

[101] Davies, *Revolt*, 72.   [102] Ibid.

[103] Tertullian, *De exhortatione castitatis*, ch. 9 (E. Kroymann, *CCSL* 2. 1013–36). Also, the Apostolic Constitutions, ch. 3, as cited in Stählin, 'Chéra', 462. See also Clark, 'Introduction to John Chrysostom', 233.

[104] Jerome, *Adversus Iovinianum*, book 1, ch. 3.

[105] *Didascalia* book 3, ch.1, as quoted in Stählin, 'Chéra', 465.

says that the sixtyfold are the clergy and widows who are continent: *clerici et viduae qui continentes sunt.*[106] Widows appear in the threefold schema also in the
seventh-century *Expositio quattuor evangeliorum*, which says that the sixtieth fruit
are the order of widows, who are persevering in the Lord (*fructus sexagisimus
ordinem viduarum, perseverantium in Domino*). It is worth noting that the author says
ordo viduarum, treating widows as an order. These two texts show familiarity with
the spiritual rewards offered the religious widow and with what was expected of
such a widow, namely continence and perseverance in a religious life.

In the seventh century the writings of Isidore of Seville were transmitted very
quickly to Ireland, and it may well be from Isidore that the Irish gained some of
their concepts of widowhood. In his *De ecclesiasticis officiis*, Isidore dedicated a
chapter to the widow (situated between chapters on virgins and married Christians) and discussed the biblical and patristic sources which treat the profession,
stressing the irreversibility of a widow's vow of continence:

Praedicat autem idem apostolus damnationem habere viduas quae post propositum
continentiae nubere cupiunt: cum enim, inquid, luxoriatae quia primam fidem irritam
fecerunt, id est quia in eo quod primo voverant non steterunt.[107]

This same apostle predicts to have damnation those widows who after their promise of
continence desire marriage; when, then, he says, they are harlots it is because they made
their first vows void, that is, because they did not stay in that state which they first vowed.

Thus by the time it arrives in Ireland, and at the time we first see evidence of it
there, the profession of widowhood was both theologically contextualized and
liturgically formalized. The late eighth-century litany *Ateoch Frit* asks for the protection of virgins, widows, and the lawfully wedded (in that order).[108] The late
eighth-century Stowe Missal, possibly from Tallaght, contains petitions for all the
officers of the Church, including one *pro integritate virginum et continentia viduarum.*[109]

It is known that women could separate from their living husbands in order to
enter religious life in monasteries, and in those circumstances they would have
had the widow's grade. Columba's Life recounts a story in which a woman so
hated the connubial act with her husband that she asked permission from the saint
to leave him and enter a monastery. In such cases it would be normal for the
spouse's permission to be sought. Indeed Irish biblical glosses do stress that both
women and men require their partner's agreement to abandon the marital bed.[110]

[106] Pa2, ch. 18. Bieler thought that the line must have had an extra *et* after *viduae*, rendering the meaning 'clerics and widows and those who are continent'; however, I have translated it without the insertion.
Expositio quattuor evangeliorum (*PL* 30. 531–90, here at 552).

[107] Ch. 19 (C. Lawson (ed.), *De ecclesiasticis officiis, CCSL* 113 (Turnhout, 1989), 89).

[108] The word used for widow is *fedb*; emphasis mine. *Nom Churim ar commairge* also called 'Litany of the
Virgins' (Plummer, *Irish Litanies*, 92–3). Textual discussion in *Kenney*, no. 590. *Ateoch Frit* (Plummer, *Irish
Litanies*, 30–45).

[109] From the section on the Mass (Warner, *Stowe Missal*, ii. 11).

[110] Adomnán, Life of Columba, book 2, ch. 46. Eighth-cent. Würzburg Glosses on the Pauline Epistles, 1 Cor. 7: 4: 'she cannot practice continence unless the husband pleases, i.e. unless it be agreeable to

The dedicated widow formed the second grade in some formulations of the two grades of holy women. *Hibernensis*, cited earlier, speaks of two levels of nuns, and says the lower must think of Anna, the traditional patroness of widows. Cogitosus's seventh-century Life of Brigit affirms this further, where the description of the church at Kildare mentions there is a door to the sanctuary reserved for 'the abbess and her nuns and faithful widows' (*abbatissa cum suis puellis et viduis fidelibus*).[111] Cogitosus's remark joins with others in other Lives to confirm the reality of the widow's profession. In the *Vita I* of Brigit, for example, Brigit was taken as a young girl to a religious synod by *religiosa quaedam vidua* with the permission of her father. The widow lived near to Brigit's father's house, we are told.[112] In the ninth-century *Bethu Brigte*, the same story is related, but with the widow now called a 'senior holy nun' (*senior caillige craibdigi*). These remarks certainly confirm that the Irish writers of this century were familiar enough with holy widows to include them without much ado into their hagiographic tales, and could, in the case of *Bethu Brigte*, imagine them attending a synod.

Widow as Penitent

On the theological level the widow presents numerous complexities. The glory of the religious widow, her exalted status on the heavenly plane and the Church's approval gained for her continence, were accompanied in Ireland by another, more dubious connotation. In Ireland, widows were seen to have links with, or in fact to be, penitents, people in especial need of God's forgiveness.

Máirín Ní Dhonnchadha has demonstrated this interchangeability, citing these and other examples. Legal and ecclesiastical writers were clearly working in a long tradition which made loose associations between widowhood and the renunciation of sexual activity, which was in turn associated with the notion of being a penitent.[113] The seventh-century *Liber Angeli*, for example, uses 'widows' and 'penitents' interchangeably. In the description of Armagh, the author mentions three categories of religious people who belong to it. In this place, it says, *tres ordinibus adherent: virgines et poenitentes [et] in matrimonio ligitimo aeclessiae servientes*.[114] Thus the middle grade, usually of widows, is here again made up of penitents. The *Hibernensis* passage on the two grades of nun, cited earlier, says the second grade, penitents comparable to presbyters, should take their inspiration from the biblical widow Anna and, presumably unlike virgins, must remain under the hand of a pastor for the whole of their lives.[115] Elsewhere it classifies the two explicitly as the *virgines habitu virginitatis ornatae* and the *penitentes*. In this

the husband, i.e. let the husband not boast this time in his power for he, too, cannot practice continence or copulate unless the woman pleases' (*Thes. Pal.* i. 556).

[111] Ch. 32.   [112] *Vita I* of Brigit, ch. 14.   [113] Ní Dhonnchadha, 'Caillech', 83–4, 89.

[114] Bieler, *Irish Penitentials*, 186. Here I agree with Bieler's interpolation of *et*, since the text goes on to refer to these as three orders. See also Ní Donnchadha, 'Caillech', 72.

[115] Book 45, ch. 12.

formulation, the penitent takes the second level of nunhood. To cite a final source, a gloss on the vernacular legal text *Córus Béscnai* says of the bonds binding members to the church, that penitent nuns and pilgrims (*o ailithrib ocus o caillecaib aitrige*) are bound by a promise (*tarngaire*) they have taken; this shows that penitent nuns belonged to an order of sorts, and had joined it by taking a formal oath.[116]

Why and how could the Irish have come to associate the dedicated holy widow with the reformed penitent harlot? Ní Dhonnchadha proposes that it was *because* many who took up the order of penitent were in fact widowed women, often elderly women, and thus the term evolved connotations of widowhood. In that case one should not overstress the penitential nature of the position. The penance implied by the term *caillech aithrige* should not be overplayed if the root of *aithrige* connotes departure from a former way of living more than it does penance for former sinfulness. *Caillech*, meaning 'veiled person', can have uxorial and marital connotations. So for her, these women are more to be seen as *conversae* from marital, i.e. lay life, who have adopted dedicated celibacy.[117] My own study of the texts leads me to agree strongly with much of this view. The nuns who are interchangeably called widows and penitents are best seen as gaining their designation from their departure from the life of the laity and the sexuality which, for the Irish, characterized it.

Certainly it is right that the grade of penitent did not always have connotations of former lasciviousness, and Ní Dhonnchadha astutely observed a passage supporting this in the notes on the Martyrology of Oengus, which date from the tenth or eleventh century. The gloss explains how Brigit was consecrated: seeking to have the order of penitence (*grada aithrige*) conferred upon her, Brigit went with seven other nuns in search of Bishop Mel. Finding him, she was introduced as the famous nun (*caillech arderc*) of Leinster, and he agreed to confer the orders of penitence upon her.[118] Although these notes are dated from beyond the period under consideration here, it is important to mention them because they show that at that time, if not earlier, people could imagine an already pious, chaste woman actively seeking out the formal conferring of an order of penitence. Because Brigit is definitely universally accepted to have been a virgin and someone who did not have a sinful life, we have to consider that taking the order of penitent nun was seen in the glossator's day as a pious undertaking rather than an imposed punishment.

The term widow was not, however, incorporated into the terminology of the order of penitents. Rather, I see it as being the other way around. *Viduitas* or *fedbacht* from the outset meant a state enjoyed by those who renounced the lay life. This is amply demonstrated in the late antique precedents. Furthermore,

---

[116] *Córus Béscnai* at CIH 523 and *ALI* iii. 14–15. For discussion of *ailithir* and *caillech aithrige*, see Ní Dhonnchadha, '*Caillech*', 88. *Hibernensis*, book 45, ch. 14.

[117] Ní Dhonnchadha, '*Caillech*', 83–5.

[118] Martyrology of Oengus, notes on 2 Feb. See also Ní Dhonnchadha, '*Caillech*', 88–92.

some texts allude to the particularly sexual cast of the previous life, and do so in strong, even condemnatory tones. The key text is a dramatic passage in the law tract *Di Astud Chirt 7 Dligid*, which dates from the seventh or eighth century. The tract itself is a long text containing a wide variety of legal material, and within the section on honour-prices of various sorts of women, widows are covered. The passage under consideration links the holy widow's profession to that of the converted, penitent harlot.

Fedb, aindir, be carnna, doranidar setaibh oige diarub la fo fuiristar, acht ro pennead a nilpeacta ciarob iar nilar comleachta.[119]

A widow, a 'non-virgin', a wanton, are paid *dire* [honour-price] in chattels of virginity (i.e. receive the same honour-price as a virgin), if they abide by goodness [virtue], even should it be after many cohabitations, provided that they have done penance for their many sins.

The widow here is defined as a formerly dishonourable woman who had given up her carnal ways and done penance for them. We may note parenthetically that an eleventh- or twelfth-century gloss on the above passage specifies that the penance was to be done 'according to the directions of a confessor', a phrase which emphasizes the involvement of ecclesiastical officers. Both the tract and its gloss use the term *bé carnna* to describe the woman; Power has translated it as 'wanton'. It is here glossed as 'a woman who sleeps with numerous men in one night'; in another text, the word is defined as meaning *merdrech* (Irish equivalent to the Latin *meretrix*, i.e. 'harlot'), and another says that the *bé carnna* is the worst type of woman there is.[120]

The idea of the widow as a woman reformed from a sexual, even harlotlike existence, is found elsewhere in Irish sources as well. The eighth-century Irish litany *Ateoch Frit* speaks of widows as penitents, whose patroness is Mary Magdalene: 'I entreat Thee by all holy virgins throughout the whole world, with the Virgin Mary thine own holy Mother; I entreat Thee by all penitent widows (*fhedbai aithrigecha*) with Mary Magdalene; I entreat Thee with all the people of lawful marriage, with Job the suffering, on whom came many trials.' As the sequence indicates a use of the threefold schema, it is notable, and unusual, that widows are specified here as *penitent* widows, as this is not seen in patristic formulations. It is significant that Mary Magdalene is given as their patroness in *Ateoch Frit*, and not the usual widow Anna. In Augustine's *De bono coniugali*, one reads of the married chastity of Susannah, the good of the widow Anna, and the excellence of the Virgin Mary. Isidore of Seville in *De ecclesiasticis officiis* specified that widows should think of Anna, and virgins of Mary.[121] Anna appears in the Bible in Luke 2: 36–8, speaking in the temple about Jesus to all who looked for

---

[119] *Di Astud Chirt 7 Dligid*, section on the *fedb*, as cited in Power, 'Classes of Women', 108; an older edition and translation is in *ALI* v. 448.

[120] Power, 'Classes of Women', 107–8.

[121] Augustine, *De bono coniugali*, ch. 8 (*PL* 40. 373–96); Isidore, *De ecclesiasticis officiis*, chs. 17, 18.

redemption. Mary Magdalene, in contrast, was by the seventh century named as the biblical prostitute who famously renounced her wicked ways for love of Christ. Gregory the Great's homilies, widely circulated across the West (and indeed reaching Ireland) had made the identification unequivocally. Beyond this, she was also conflated with the adulteress with five unlawful husbands whom Christ had met at the well (John 4: 17–18)—and she too became a devotee of Christ.[122] The Irish use of Mary Magdalene as the patroness of the middle grade has the same kinds of allusions to sexual promiscuity that we saw in *Di Astud Chirt*.

Whilst Ní Dhonnchadha is certainly right that many who took up the order of penitent/widow were older women whose husbands had died, one is inclined to think that many came to it from a type of sexual life about which the Church had a certain amount of disapproval, namely marriages which were perhaps looser in structure than the full-fledged lifelong monogamy defended by church fathers since Augustine. We would do well to remember that divorce and re-marriage were normal and legal in native Irish law, and are well-attested practices. There must have been many women who had had more than one, or even two, husbands. Patristic sources considered any woman who remarried after divorce a harlot (*meretrix* or similar). By patristic definition, therefore, Ireland was rife with women who were harlots, even though such women were behaving normally in terms of Irish secular custom. Added to this, patristic writers used *vidua* of a woman who voluntarily separated from a living husband in favour of religious continence. Thus, a woman married more than once (via divorce) who then renounced marital life for religious continence would be both a penitent harlot and a widow. Ireland doubtless had many such women. In addition, it must be remembered that marriage in Irish custom was not an either/or affair, with one being either married or single. Rather there were different types of union, some stronger than others. Some of the less strongly bonding types of union may not have been considered by ecclesiastically-minded law authorities as full marriages in the Christian sense—i.e. as eternally bonding in the eyes of God. And if they were not, then the sex between such partners perhaps lay on the border lines of fornication, and turning from this to a life of continence may have been seen as a renunciation of lasciviousness.

Overall, the Lives are unforthcoming on the marital or sexual backgrounds of the religious widows they do occasionally mention. Thus there is admittedly little in Irish hagiography to add confirmation to this theory, but neither do the texts provide evidence against it. Other sources are equally silent on that paradoxical interweave of harlotry, penance, and the order of widows. Nevertheless,

---

[122] On Anna: 'And there was one Anna, a prophetess . . . She was far advanced in years and she had lived with her husband seven years from her virginity. And she was a widow until fourscore and four years, who departed not from the temple, by fastings and prayer serving night and day.' On Magdalen as 'harlot' in Gregory the Great, and dissemination of the identification with prostitute and adulteress: S. Hoskyns, *Mary Magdalen: Myth and Metaphor* (New York, 1993), 16–26, 40, 95–6.

we can conclude with certainty that the Irish mentally associated widowhood with the repentance of sexual activity and even of sexual promiscuity.

The search for illumination of the religious widow leads inevitably to a study of other 'wanton' women who come to the religious life. The very famous and enigmatic poem in Irish, the 'Lament of the Caillech Béirre', deals with exactly that. This poem of uncertain date essentially consists of the lament in the voice of an old woman, who calls herself the *caillech Béirre*, the 'nun' or 'old woman' of Beare.[123] Controversy has raged over whether the old woman is meant to be understood as a nun, because there is no incontrovertibly monastic material in it; on the other hand, there are semi-religious references, and *caillech* means 'nun' so often in Irish texts of the period that a non-religious use of the word strikes one as odd. Ó hAodha thinks that the *caillech* is indeed a nun, but one who took up religion late in life, as does Ní Dhonnchadha.[124] If this is the case, and I think it is, then she is a woman who would qualify as a holy widow/penitent nun. Furthermore, the poem has even those veiled allusions to former sexuality which are also seen in *Di Astud Chirt*, namely the promiscuity.

The poem, long and descriptive, is quite rich in suggestive information. The *caillech* is a formerly beautiful woman of the secular world, now living in poverty in a church. She mourns the passing of her resplendent youth, remembering dressing in finery, embracing kings, and wearing 'coverings of many colours' upon her head. Now, her many years of beauty are gone 'because wantonness has spent itself'; she is too thin to wear even a ragged shift, covers her head with a white veil (*caille finn*), and drinks watery whey among withered old women (*eter sentainni crína*).[125] She is, she says, in the darkness of a wooden church (*dorchae derthaige*), a sad comparison with her former feasting by bright candlelight.

We should note that the *caillech* is nowhere in the poem described as a widow. Though she may not have been a religious *widow*, she does fit even more closely into a category of religious woman, the 'ex-laywomen' or *athlaeches*. This is the female equivalent of an *athlaech*, literally an 'ex-layman', but more fully it means a man who has become a cleric (presumably at an age later than normal).[126] The eighth-century tract on penance, *De Arreis*, is one of the few texts, if not the

---

[123] Donncha Ó hAodha dates the text to *c*.900, Murphy thought it was from the late 8th or early 9th cent., and Meyer thought it was from the 11th (ed. and trans. D. Ó hAodha, 'Lament of the Old Woman of Beare', in D. Ó Corráin, L. Breatnach, and K. McCone (eds.), *Saints, Sages and Storytellers: Studies in Honour of Professor James Carney* (Maynooth, 1989), 308–31).

[124] Ní Dhonnchadha, '*Caillech*', 92.

[125] The commentaries on *Cáin Adomnáin*, possibly somewhat later, state that penitent nuns wear white garments with black borders; the 8th- or 9th-cent. Stowe Missal, like the earlier penitential, attests to the penitent receiving a white garment at their rite of reconciliation (Warren, *Stowe Missal*, 31–2); so this white veil was probably typical.

[126] Royal Irish Academy, *Dictionary of the Irish Language* (compact edn.; Dublin, 1983) under *athlaech*. Textual citations as given there. For a related example, in the 9th-cent. story of Liadain and Curithir, a poet becomes a pupil of a saint, living in the monastery; he is referred to as an ex-poet (*athéces*), presumed by Greene and O'Connor to be a play on *athlaech*, 'ex-layman' (Greene and O'Connor, *Golden Treasury*, 75).

only, one, which deal specifically with the female version, the ex-laywoman. The text mentions appropriate commutations for the cleric, monk, *mac-caillech* (young-nun), and laywoman; it then goes on to those appropriate for ex-laymen and ex-laywomen.[127]

The ex-laywoman, having come to the Church later in life, was likely to have had less religious and ascetic training.[128] The Customs of Tallaght (dated to the ninth century) a story in which an *athlaech* tells a monk (*mac bethad*, lit. 'son of life') 'I do not understand your continual singing of the *Beati* and the Canticle of Mary'. From this one infers that such a person would often have little knowledge or understanding of religious practices, even though living in a monastic context.[129]

Other sources containing evidence on the *athlaech* link them with penitence. In one law tract there is a reference to 'ex-laymen who renounce their sins' (*athlaich fristongat dia pecthaib*).[130] Elsewhere, 'penitent' is equated to an ex-layman and *ailithrigh*.[131] Given all of this, it is not surprising that there is some suggestion that the *athlaech* was ineligible for some ecclesiastical offices.[132] If we apply this to the *caillech Béirre*, it is not difficult to imagine her as an ex-laywoman, living out a worldly life until, in her old age, she turned to the Church to support her in her final days, but harbouring no moral regrets about her sumptuous and sexual past.

It is perhaps in this context that we should consider the annal entries that praise kings and queens for dying 'in penance'. The Annals of Ulster tell, for example, of Eithne daughter of Bresal of Brega, queen of the kings of Tara (obit AD 768) who 'deserved to obtain the heavenly kingdom, having done penance'; Gormlaith daughter of Donnchad (obit AD 861) who 'died after repentance'; Flann daughter of Dungal, queen of the king of Tara (obit AD 891) who 'fell asleep in penance'; Eithne daughter of Áed (obit AD 917) who 'died truly penitent on the feast of Martin'; and Gormlaith daughter of Flann son of Mael Sechnaill (obit AD 948) who 'died in penitence'. Perhaps these queens ended their days attached to the church, like the *caillech* of Beare, guaranteed support, piety, and a place in heaven, having made a commitment such as is alluded to in *Córus Béscnai*, and supervised at least indirectly, as is suggested in *Hibernensis*.

Irish Nuns in the Context of the West

The Irish profession of holy women, having two main levels, has some similarities with that elsewhere. In Frankia, there were regular, virginal nuns (the *sacrae virgines*) in the top rank and canonesses in a lower position. There, liturgical

---

[127] Chs. 7–8.   [128] Ní Dhonnchadha, '*Caillech*', 84–5.   [129] Customs of Tallaght, ch. 1.

[130] *Bretha im Fuillema Gell* (*CIH* 462.19–477.30; also *ALI* v. 377–423), here from *ALI* v. 420.

[131] O'Donovan's law transcripts of the Royal Irish Academy, 3.17, *c*.654, cited in *Dictionary* under *athlaech*.

[132] *Dictionary* cites evidence suggesting that an *athlaech* was barred from certain ecclesiastical offices.

sources survive for both, unlike in Ireland, so much more can be said about the latter and the distinctions between the two. The canoness, for example, received at her consecration only a veil rather than the ring and crown which the virgin received, and there were in the ninth and tenth centuries both regular and canonical abbesses.[133] In England, Bede is a relatively early witness to the fact that in monasteries there the holy virgins were but one type, and that highest level, of females who lived under the vow. They were distinguished from those who entered religion in later life.[134] It is only in the post-970 period though, that English sources clearly show the distinct grades of nuns found earlier on the Continent, namely the virginal or regular nun and the canoness. In that later era, though, the English material refers to the vowed widow, not as a canoness but as a third type. Though the evidence on the last is indirect, Schneider found they could be found living at nunneries or in minster churches, as well as alone.[135]

For Ireland probably even more than England and Frankia, we shall never fully understand the conceptual boundaries distinguishing the professions of widows, penitents, and ex-laywomen. The sources suggest a certain amount of fluidity, and perhaps evolution over time. It is evident that the female profession was often thought to consist of two tiers, the upper being that of the virgin and the lower being this less clearly-defined grade of late-comers, old women or pious humble women. The upper tier, that of the virgin, seems to have been accorded a great deal of legal status and autonomy. The women of the lower tier, according to *Hibernensis*, were always under the direct guidance of a pastor, right up until death. They may have been bound by a different sort of vow than virgins, if we correctly understand *Córus Béscnai*. What is quite clear, however, is that being a penitent nun or a holy widow involved formal links to the ecclesiastical hierarchy and to Church authorities, having made a formal promise and undertaken to wear a veil as part of that new life.

Much more basically, however, these professions and the women who lived them were fully Christian. To scholars familiar with the early medieval period, this is a point so obvious it appears silly to make it, but it is worth stressing for the benefit of those whose background may lie in the more feminist or folkloristic school of thought. Yes, some were of special status if they were deemed miracle-workers and held in special esteem by their communities; yes, some did provide direct care to laypeople, including at their deaths; yes, some were treated as sufficiently exceptional to enjoy legal autonomy. For all this, though, just as Kildare was no vestal temple, these vowed holy women were not priestesses. There is the obvious fact that Irish pagan religion, almost imperceptible though it is, had not normally included women in its priesthood. But in the Christian era too, nuns

---

[133] Hodgson, 'Frankish Church', 204–11, 226–8.

[134] Schneider, 'Anglo-Saxon Women', 50, citing Bede, *Historia ecclesiastica*, book 4, chs. 9, 23, 25 (C. Plummer, *Historia Ecclesiastica Gentis Anglorum* (Oxford, 1896)).

[135] Schneider, 'Anglo-Saxon Women', 87, 93, 305.

were not even quasi-priests. They did not administer sacraments, or even appear to help doing so as deaconesses.[136] There were in these early Christian centuries Irish poetesses, female druids, and women in other post-druidic professions, but none of the associated activities—judging, satirizing, composing poetry, and suchlike—appear among nuns' duties. Only magic in the broadest sense did they have in common, but even this, among the nuns, is framed in such Christian-miraculous terms, and owes such great debts in the texts to patristic and Continental models, that it cannot be treated as evidence that the Irish nun was essentially a pagan priestess in a veil.

[136] Inspite of the well-known early case of two priests in Brittany, Lavocat and Catihern, who were chastised for using female assistants in the mass, this was not apparently a pan-Celtic practice, nor even necessarily one common in Brittany. For the classic discussion see L. Duchesne, 'Lavocat et Catiherne, prétres bretons du temps de Sta Merlaine', *Revue de Bretagne et de Vendée* 57 (1885), 5–21; J. Loth, 'Un Ancien Usage de L'Église Celtique', *Revue Celtique* 15 (1894), 92–3. Ellis has misinterpreted the original text as indicating that the women themselves performed the mass (*Celtic Women*, 142), whereas it actually states that they helped distribute the chalice.

6

Abbesses and other High-Ranking Holy Women

The highest level a nun could achieve in Ireland was the office of abbess and, like other female professions, it was imbued with symbols and metaphors. It is the understanding of this office which is the main subject of this chapter, but against its background must also be examined the other types of 'exceptional' nuns which the Irish acknowledged. These were women who, though we can perceive them but dimly, gained many of the honours—and even elements of the legal status—of abbesses, without being heads of monasteries. They seem to have earned their status through pilgrimage, holiness, miracle-working, or service to their wider communities. In the highest echelons of the female religious profession there was the same trend toward diversity and flexibility which have already been seen in the living arrangements and grades of nunhood.

The sources of material on Irish abbesses are extremely patchy, and the overall quantity of evidence quite slim. The Irish left no guiding or prescriptive texts on this office; there is no surviving correspondence such as is found in Anglo-Saxon England and which proves so illuminating for the abbess's position there. There is a small but important quantity of legal material in which are found occasional notes concerning abbesses' rights and privileges; there is a large amount of hagiography containing anecdotes about abbesses; and there are annal entries for abbesses of the most famous houses. These supply little in terms of genealogy, making it difficult to build up an understanding of the relationships between the office of the abbess and local ruling kindreds. They are nevertheless useful in studying dynastic politics and ecclesiastical office in specific establishments. This examination is not, however, dedicated to analysing specific families as they relate to churches but rather the perceived powers accorded to abbesses and the evidence for their realization. For this purpose, the bulk of useful references is to be found in the saints' Lives. These, considered in tandem with legal writings, yield sufficient clues about the understanding of the office to allow some observations to be made. In female saints' Lives, the characterization of the foundress serves repeatedly to restate the holy ideal not only for the ordinary nun, but also for the abbess, since in Ireland the major female saints were abbesses. As the spiritual heir of the foundress saint, the abbess was supposed to manifest at least in part her patron's virtues and be in her own lifetime a role model in the religious life. The Lives also offer insights into the practicalities of an abbess's duties, both to her own nuns and also to the outside world. Thus the foundress formed the prototype for the abbess's role, both spiritually and practically.

Abbess as Governor

Although there are no extant prescriptive texts instructing abbesses how to carry out their responsibilities, there do exist guidelines for abbots. *Hibernensis* tells abbots they should reject certain types from the monastery and details the sins warranting a monk's excommunication.[1] The abbot is the governor of the monastics: *non oportet monachos fieri sine gubernatione, nisi tantum una hora, ne ventus discordiae et dissensionis disperdat ecclesiam.* The abbot is to be obeyed, and harsh punishments are prescribed for disobedience. For the female side of monasticism, one presumes that either there were separate texts for abbesses which do not survive, or else such guidance was adapted from the instructions applying to the male monastic sphere. In her community of nuns, the abbess too was the supervisor and governor, *domina* and mother. In the female Lives, the abbess is the person who is directly responsible for ensuring the monastery's survival. She decides if the community is to move location. She procures food and beer in times of scarcity, and organizes help in fending off attackers in times of danger. It is she, for example, who asks for charitable help from clerics, monasteries, and other nunneries when her own community runs into difficulty. Cogitosus's Life of Brigit, of which several chapters take place after Brigit's death and in Cogitosus's own lifetime, shows that at the very large community of Kildare some of the worldly duties had devolved on to male officers. Thus, some time after Brigit had died, it was the male prior who organized the carving of a large millstone and the erection of a new church door.[2] It is not surprising that this should have evolved at larger places, especially those with political prominence, but at smaller places it is logical to presume that such things would have continued to be the concern of the abbess herself.

Decisions on who joined the *familia* were within the abbess's remit: it was she who approved the intake of novices and the adoption of fosterlings and abandoned babies. She was responsible for the maintenance of the moral standard and adherence to the rule. Then there were matters of discipline, and in the Lives the abbess appears as inspector, judge, and setter of punishments.[3] Her

---

[1] *Hibernensis*, book 39, chs. 9, 11.　　[2] Cogitosus, Life of Brigit, chs. 31, 32.
[3] For just two early examples of many which span the centuries of hagiography, see the *Vita I* of Brigit, ch. 30, and *Bethu Brigte*, ch. 31.

jurisdiction, however, was over not just her nuns but also the many males in the *familia*: boy fosterlings, household staff, male penitents, and men who farmed the land as clients or dependents.[4] The hagiography shows the founding abbess discovering misdemeanours, extracting confessions, and setting penances to these people as well as to the nuns. We must remember that the abbess, if she was also the controller of the temporalities, as she is in the Lives, was the *domina* of all these people.

Worldly and Unworldly

Like the foundress saint whose heir she was, the abbess had to strive to embody the seemingly contradictory qualities of world-renunciation and temporal dominion. She was to uphold the ascetic tradition whilst at the same time shoring up and even expanding her church's sphere of control. Traces of this thinking are found in the early medieval hymns. *Ní Car Brigit*, written in the ninth century and attributed to Broccán, begins 'Victorious Brigit loved not the world; she sat the seat of a bird on a cliff' (*Ní car Brigit búadach bith · síasair suide eóin i nailt*); it adds 'she was not greedy for treasures' (*ní pu for séotu santach*).[5] And yet another poet in the same era exalts her temporal dominion and triumph: 'Sit safely, Brigit, in triumph on Liffey's cheek to the strand of the sea; you are the princess with ranked host . . . though the shining Liffey be yours today, it was once another's land . . .' (*slán seiss, a Brigit co mbúaid, for grúaid Lifi lír co tráig; is tú banfhlaith buidnib slúaig . . . in-diu cid latt Life líg ropo thír cáich ala n-úair . . .*).[6] In her ninth-century Life, the infant Brigit prophesied that one day the lands surrounding her home in Connaught would be hers. *Meum erit hoc*, she said, *meum erit hoc*.[7] One of the abbess's most important tasks in the continued work of aggrandizing her church was the provision and reception of hospitality, which in early medieval Ireland formed one of the major currencies of social interchange, social cohesion, and assertion of power and status. Failing to provide hospitality to those whose rank warranted it brought dishonour upon the failed host; providing abundantly brought status, and fulfilled economic and/or ecclesiastical obligations. The Church was a major player in the political landscape, and those in abbatial office had duties and privileges. *Hibernensis* stipulated that hospitality was owed to ecclesiastical officials.[8] In the hagiog-raphy, a common motif centres on the unexpected arrival of a high-ranking ecclesiastic to a religious community (or individual living alone) when there is no food in the house, because of

---

[4] One especially interesting example of male dependents is the 9th-cent. hymn *Ní Car Brigit* which refers to a male 'vassal' of hers (*a hathig*) (*Thes. Pal.* ii. 348). Another clear example of a male dependent is Ita's brother-in-law, Life of Ita, ch. 18.

[5] *Ní Car Brigit*, stanzas 1, 4.   [6] *Slán Seiss, a Brigit*, stanzas 1, 12, 13.   [7] *Bethu Brigte*, ch. 4.

[8] Section 5, 'Of the Refusal of Hospitality to Persons of Ecclesiastical Rank' (Bieler, *Irish Penitentials*, 172–5); also found in *Hibernensis*, book 56. This is a sharp contrast with the rule of Caesarius of Arles for his nuns, ch. 39 of which expressly forbids extending hospitality to male ecclesiastics.

either poverty or famine; in the female Lives, the poor community is normally a female house. The abbess had somehow to feed the guests with meat, dairy products, and ale to drink. When the guests arrived, she ceremoniously washed their feet[9] and ordered the preparation of the feast and/or sleeping quarters. There was a often a mutual blessing between the abbess and the head ecclesiastic of the visiting party, and there was also what the hagiographers describe as 'rejoicing'.

The ideal abbess was a provider of abundance to all the religious superiors who came to her community. A poem attributed to St Brigit from the tenth or eleventh century, shows her as the giver of hospitality: the feast she provides is one of spiritual nourishment, and her overlord is none less than Christ and the hosts of heaven.[10] Hospitality was a Christian virtue and Brigit its exemplar, just as Monenna was treated as an exemplar of the discipline of fasting.[11] Lisa Bitel has maintained that 'women's houses were guesthouses for travelling bishops and abbots. Abbesses had to scurry to find food and drink for their important guests, for the lives often mention a community's lack of provisions for hospitality.'[12] Certainly the Lives do include many stories of impoverished nuns praying for a food or ale miracle in order to be able to provide the requisite hospitality for arriving bishops or abbots but the hagiography does not single out nuns in this respect.[13] In many anecdotes clerics give assistance to abbesses and their nuns, as in Brigit's *Vita I*, where during a food shortage the abbess went to a bishop to ask for bread for her *familia*, and the bishop gladly gave her some.[14] Nor was this assistance a one-way thing: Brigit's *Vita I*, for example, shows the abbess saint assisting a male hermit community with property difficulties.[15] It is misleading to 'gender' the structure of the ecclesiastical hospitality networks.

The Lives also repeatedly give examples of abbesses receiving hospitality, from laymen and clerics and nuns. Roughly speaking, they refer to the hospitality due to abbesses just about as frequently as that due to male ecclesiastics. And sometimes the people who had to feed the abbess had little food with which to do so. In the *Vita I*, for example, Brigit visited a poor religious woman who fed her with her last cow,[16] and in *Bethu Brigte* the nuns of St Lassair were unable to provide enough food to feed both Brigit and Patrick, who by unfortunate coincidence arrived at the same time, both requiring hospitality. Such stories

---

[9] For examples of ritualized foot-washing see *Bethu Brigte*, chs. 31, 36.

[10] *Ropadh maith lem* ['St. Brigit's Alefeast'], ed. and trans. D. Greene, 'St. Brigid's Alefeast', *Celtica* 2 (1952–4), 150–3. This poem is believed to exist in a sole manuscript, Brussels 5100, 33, written by Míchel O Cléirigh. Text discussed and dated by Greene in *Celtica*; see also *Kenney*, no. 153.

[11] There has been a tendency to see Brigit's hospitality miracles as remnants of a former existence as a pagan goddess in Ireland, but her hospitality is not in fact exceptional—most saints provide hospitality and perform food multiplication miracles. Brigit's reputation as excelling in this activity is found in a later poem which named the Irish saints and their specialities, *Nom Churim ar Comairge*, discussed in a later chapter.

[12] Bitel, 'Monastic Enclosures', 20–1, 26.   [13] e.g. *Vita I* of Brigit, chs. 44, 82.

[14] Ibid., ch. 54.   [15] Ibid., ch. 73.   [16] Ibid., ch. 99.

demonstrate not an oppression of female religious but rather their full membership in the web of hospitality provision and mutual assistance. This formed a
fabric of social cohesion and multiple relationships which, admittedly, could
place a heavy burden on the poorer households in Irish society, whether they
were religious or lay, male or female.

The Abbess as 'Head'

The extent of the authority and legal competence accorded to abbesses in the
social and ecclesiastical spheres, as evidenced in prescriptive texts, poses an interesting question. Abbesses were in a paradoxical position. On one hand they
were heiresses of their founding patron saints, with both spiritual authority and
temporal jurisdiction comprising the inheritance; on the other, they were
women, and most women were deemed legally incompetent. The resolution arrived at by the Irish is ultimately uncertain, but a key to at least partly unlocking
the problem lies in Irish notions of supervision.

An essential concept in the matter of personal autonomy was that of the *cenn*,
the head. This notion had two aspects, the spiritual and the practical. A confessor
was the spiritual head of those to whom he was the soul-friend, be they king, noble,
or abbot. A saint was a *cenn* through the connection to God achieved by grace and
virtue. Spiritually speaking, the Irish felt that to have a head was a spiritual necessity in order to link with God: they had a proverbial saying that 'a person without
a confessor is like a body without a head' (*uair colann gan ceann nech gan anmcharaid*).[17]

On the worldly side, there were those who oversaw legal incompetents, and
these too were thought of as 'heads'. Thus an abbot was *cenn* of his monks; a
father of his daughters. One text says that every woman must have one,
including women of the Church:

Messom cundrada cuir ban. Air ni tualaing ben roria ni sech oen a cenn. Adagair a
athair imbe ingen. Adagair a cetmuinter imbe be cetmuintere. Adagairet a mme[i]cc
imbi be clainne. Adagair fine imbi be fine. Adagair eclais imbi be eclaise. Ni tualain[g]
reicce na creice na cuir na cuinduruda sech oen a chenn acht tabairt bes techta d'oen a
cenn cocur cen dichill.[18]

The worst transactions are women's contracts. For a woman is not capable of alienating
anything without [the authorization of] one of her 'heads'. Her father has charge over
her when she is a girl, her husband when she is a wife, her sons when she is a [widowed]
woman, her kin when she is a woman of the kin [i.e. with no other guardian], the
Church when she is a woman of the Church. She is not capable of sale or purchase
or contract or transaction without the authorization of one of her superiors, with
agreement and without neglect.

---

[17] Martyrology of Oengus, notes on 2 Feb.
[18] The *Díre* Text, ch. 38 [corresponding to *CIH* 444]. It is partially edited in D. Binchy, 'The Legal
Capacity of Women in Regard to Contracts', *SEIL* 207–34, at 213–14. Discussion in Kelly, *Guide*, 76,
267. Here, the Irish follows *CIH* and the English follows Kelly, *Guide*, 76.

On the basis of this evidence, one might naturally come to the conclusion that even an abbess was thus legally incompetent. There are, however, some powerful counter-indications. Female patron saints were expressly believed to have been 'heads' themselves: Cogitosus, writing in the seventh century, said of Brigit, 'all things were permitted to her because she was a living and most blessed member attached to the supreme head' (*Nam cum ipsa esset vivum et felicissimum summi capitis membrum, potenter omnia, quae desiderabat, operabatur*).[19]

Acknowledging that Brigit was not always typical, we can also note the remarkable level of authority and autonomy attributed to other saint-abbesses in the Lives, discussed at length in earlier chapters. Firstly, the Irish understood the saint's power to continue as a living presence at a monastery. The saint's office was understood to be bequeathed as an inheritance to the current abbess or abbot, who was traditionally called *comarba* which means literally 'heir' or 'successor'.[20] The inheritance of this role can be thought of as a threefold one: spiritual, social-ecclesiastical, and legal. On the spiritual level, the abbess had a link with the foundress through visions, links whose immediacy was emphasized by the presence of relics of the foundress kept on the site and revered by residents and pilgrims. Ecclesiastically and socially she, like the foundress, was a *virgo sancta* (in theory at least) and had obligations such as that of providing hospitality. Her patroness's headship formed part of the body of privileges she inherited. *Hibernensis* gives two exceptions to the rule of female incompetence: the lady of authority (*domina*) and the holy virgin (*virgo sancta*).

Non est dignus fideiussor fieri servus, nec peregrinus, nec brutus, nec monachus, nisi imperante abbate, nec filius, nisi imperante patre, nec femina, nisi domina, virgo sancta.[21]

It is not proper that a surety should be a slave, nor pilgrim, nor imbecile, nor monk without his abbot's supervision, nor a son without the supervision of his father, nor a women unless she be a lady [or?] a holy virgin.

The phrasing here leaves the relationship between *domina* and *virgo sancta* ambiguous, but the other recension of the text reads *nec femina nisi domina, nec virgo Christiana* and so it seems most likely that the compilers were intending to enumerate two sorts of women.[22] The passage suggests that the *virgo sancta* is unlike the monk in that she is not obliged to gain the permission of a superior in order to stand surety. It also accords an indirect equivalency between the holy virgin and the *domina*, who is perhaps best understood as an heiress. Heiresses had a

---

[19] Ch. 28.

[20] Although from the 8th cent. this title was sometimes held by a lay abbot, i.e. the person controlling the church's temporalities.

[21] Kelly, *Guide*, 282. *Hibernensis*, book 34, ch. 3.

[22] Hatton MS 42 (folio 67r). Welsh Law, which had a source in common with *Hibernensis*, reads *neque femina, nisi domina fuerit principalis debitoris* (Lat. Red. A 125.8–11); Huw Pryce has written that the *Hibernensis* source 'may well have given *virgo* as a separate item rather than in apposition to the *femina nisi domina*' ('Early Irish Canons and Medieval Welsh Law', *Peritia* 5 (1986), 107–27, at 116).

strong position in law; for example, they had an equal or overriding say in financial and contractual matters within their marriages when they married men of equal or lesser means.[23] The sort of women to whom the compilers referred were certainly not the ordinary nuns, dedicated virgins though they might have been; the ordinary nun was the female equivalent of a *monachus*, who would have required the permission of an abbess or some other superior to stand surety. The holy virgin referred to in *Hibernensis* was much more likely to be an abbess. Heiress of a holy founding saint, she was in her own way a holy woman out of the ordinary, even if she was not herself a miracle-worker. *Domina* could be used for abbesses as well as secular women of authority: *domina* is a form of address for abbesses in the Lives, and in the *Vita I* Brigit is even called *domina ecclesiae*.[24] In addition, *dominatrix* through the eighth century was the term used in the Kildare and Clonguffin abbess obits of the annals of Ulster.[25] Though abbesses may have drawn their authority from the headship inherited from their patron saint, in many cases they may have possessed it by virtue of being heiresses in the worldly sense: many if not all came from noble families. Quite probably *Hibernensis*, by speaking of the autonomy of a *virgo sancta* rather than using a term linked to an office (such as *abatisa* or *comarba*), meant to give legal capacity to eminent female hermits, who will be discussed later.

The sources do show ordinary abbesses (i.e. ones who are not also founding saints) acting autonomously. The early *Vita I* of Brigit tells of a religious virgin who travelled outside her own region to collect donations, and with them purchased land (*emit agros*). The unnamed virgin is not the saint of the Life, so there was no need for the hagiographer to exaggerate her authority. In the charter-like Additamenta to Tírechán's Memoirs, religious women bequeath land to one another.[26] In the spiritual sphere too abbesses seem to be considered as heads: one may recall that, according to *Hibernensis*, as a *virgo* the abbess could be compared to a bishop (*episcopis simulatur et comparatur*).[27]

Also important to the argument that abbesses were 'heads' is the fact that they were confessors or soul-friends, those without whom people were deemed proverbially headless. Ryan noted this in the 1930s and gave this explanation:

In Ireland at all times the *anamchara* or spiritual guide who heard such confessions was probably a priest, empowered to give the penitent sacramental absolution, though confession to a distinguished *senior* who was not a priest might be practised on occasion as a penitential exercise. In monasteries for women, confession of the latter type to the abbess, for purposes of guidance, might be recommended or even exacted.[28]

[23] Binchy, 'Legal Capacity of Women', 207–34.
[24] *Vita I* of Brigit, ch. 35. On the term *domina* in Frankia, there used for abbesses and queens, see Hodgson, 'Frankish Church', 186.
[25] AU 731, 743, 758, 773, 780 (Kildare), and 771 (Clonguffin). The latter place (Ir. Cluain Cuifthin) is otherwise little known, though its site is identified with the modern village of that name directly across the river Boyne from Clonard in Meath.
[26] Additamenta to Tírechán, ch. 11.   [27] *Hibernensis*, book 45, ch. 12.
[28] Ryan, *Irish Monasticism*, 223.

Jonas's Latin Life of Columbanus, composed on the Continent in the seventh century, contains the story of a nun who in the end made her confession to a holy woman: *Quod mane per confessionem humilem matri patefecit, sacroque corpore reconciliata, religiosam postmodum vitam peregit.*[29] The abbess's authority to receive confession could extend beyond her own nuns. In the ninth-century *Bethu Brigte*, Brigit set the penance of a sinful virgin who was not one of her own community, and instructed two lepers to do penance.[30] In the *Vita I*, Brigit gave a suffering layman a penitential task which cured him.[31] Samthann was a great soul-friend, including of men.[32] In later Lives, too, there are numerous anecdotes of this type.

Local conditions would obviously have determined the extent to which an abbess wielded real power, and the extent of her ecclesiastical or spiritual autonomy. There were many small clusters of religious women whose abbesses were from a minor noble family and whose churches were dependent upon larger establishments; it seems most unlikely that these women in practice enjoyed much legal or ecclesiastical power. If the abbess was a member of the area's ruling family and the church was wealthy and independent, and had a prominent founding saint, it seems much more likely that she would be accorded the status of a 'head' and called *domina*. Many churches, however, were small and their leaders no more than local nobility, whose esteem in the neighbourhood might be quite high but who were unimportant in the wider ecclesiastical and secular polity.

Abbesses and Bachalls

The Irish bachall, or crozier, was an instrument not restricted to bishops but served as a symbol of ecclesiastical authority more generally. Missionaries were called 'bachall-bearers' and, by using a bachall much like a magic wand, a saint could work miracles over nature. In shape they were simple crook-headed staffs, and were so much a part of a holy person's identity that they often acquired names, rather like the swords of medieval knights. Also somewhat like the later medieval sword, solemn oaths were sometimes sworn upon them. Carried clockwise around a king at his inauguration, or an army before battle, they conferred blessing; carried anti-clockwise around a person, they invoked a curse.[33] After the death of the sainted owner, they became relics, and were enshrined in gold and silver: several survive to this day and are displayed in the National Museum of Ireland among other places. Female abbess saints had bachalls, according to the Lives. The earliest testament to this fact is Brigit's *Vita I*: she appeared in a vision to the king of Leinster as he was about to go into battle, with

---

[29] Jonas, Latin Life of Columbanus, book 2, ch. 13 (B. Krusch, *MGH, Scriptores rerum Merovingicarum*, iv (1902), 1–152).

[30] Chs. 40, 34.   [31] Ch. 56.   [32] Customs of Tallaght, ch. 61.

[33] For discussion of attributes, with references, see *PVSH* i., p. clxxvi.

her *baculus* in her right hand.[34] In a later (tenth- or eleventh-century) gloss she blessed a wood with it, to tame a wild boar.[35] It would appear that this was not a Brigidine peculiarity, or it did not remain one, for the holy abbess Samthann in her late Life was said to have had one also. In one episode she struck an unrepentant man with her bachall to try to talk some sense into him; in another she used it to encourage some branches blocking the road to grow away from the path; in a third the bachall, which had become misshapen, miraculously regained its original form whilst being ensconsed in gold and silver by a king with whom she had good relations.[36] Monenna, according to her hagiographer Conchubranus, had a bachall which she left as a relic, not to her community of Killevy in Ulster but to 'another land'.[37] If Irish abbesses used the bachalls as their actual staffs of office, and it seems probable that they did (male saints' bachalls were held by abbots), then the abbesses wielded a mark of authority which was the same in kind as their male counterparts'.[38]

Coarbs, Erenaghs, and Abbesses

In Ireland the matter of abbesses' office is intertwined with the wider changes that occurred in the seventh- to ninth-century period. During these centuries Ireland developed a handful of terms to designate monastic leadership to correspond with an increasingly complex network of authority. Before the eighth century the person in charge of a monastery's jurisdiction was the monastic head, the abbot in the normally understood sense of the term, but by the middle of the eighth century this person might be a married layman. In large churches or monasteries, this person was really a ruler of an ecclesiastical state, in which the monastics (be they male or female or both) were but a minority.[39] There was the rise of new terms. One is *princeps*, 'prince', ambiguously meaning the head of a church without indicating whether he was a monk. Another was *airchinnech* (anglicized as 'erenagh'), which meant a monastic manager or managerial abbot and implied that the office-holder was not a monk. Those who held the traditional title *ab*, 'abbot', were no longer necessarily monks, though they often were. Such a trend made sense, given the developments in monasteries: some of the greater churches were political units, hardly distinguishable from secular communities except in nucleated settlement pattern; the erenagh was their ruler, their prince. As Wendy Davies observed, *Hibernensis* called the ruler of the monastery *princeps* and treated him largely as a political figure.[40] On the female side, a term which began appearing in the

---

[34] *Vita I* of Brigit, ch. 89. The anecdote is repeated in the much later *Vita IV*, book 2, ch. 11.

[35] Gloss on the hymn, *Ní Car Brigit* (*Thes. Pal.* ii. 341).   [36] Life of Samthann, chs. 16, 17, 19.

[37] Life of Monenna, book 3, ch. 9.

[38] A bachall said to be of the female St Dympna is owned by the National Museum of Ireland.

[39] Sharpe, 'Some Problems', 259.

[40] W. Davies, 'Clerics as Rulers: Some Implications of Ecclesiastical Authority in Early Medieval Ireland' in N. P. Brooks, ed., *Latin and the Vernacular Languages in Early Medieval Britain* (Leicester, 1982), 81–97.

eighth century is *dominatrix*. That is how we hear described the Kildare abbesses of the eighth century: Sebdann daughter of Corc, Affraic, and Marthu daughter of Mac Dubain. After the eighth century we find *abatisa* again, or (after 900) *comarba*. We cannot know if it is meaningful that Kildare's male monastic heads are called *abbas* during the eighth, when the female title goes over to *domitissa*. At other monasteries there is a shift in terminology too, during the eighth century: *dominatrix* is the term applied to Conlaith of Clonguffin who died in 771; at Clonbroney we hear of abbess Forblaith, daughter of Connla (obit 780) who was called *dominatrix*; the leader who died five years later, Ellbríg, was called *abatissa*. Was Ellbríg (the *abatissa*) the successor of Forblaith (the *dominatrix*), or the holder of a different type of post? It seems most likely, given the absence of evidence to the contrary, that she was the successor, but taken with the other examples this suggests that *dominatrix* could be used in the eighth century as the female equivalent to the male term *princeps*. Collectively, these examples more than anything serve to illustrate the point that the fluidity and evolution of terminology for monastic rulership were as active in the female sphere as in the male. It may be more than coincidental that the abbess in England in this period was equivalent to a secular lord, according to Dagmar Schneider, who notes that they received from their dependents a sworn oath of allegiance like the one a lord received from a retainer, and that in office they fulfilled many of a secular lord's duties.[41]

The office of coarb (an anglicization of *comarba*) was one which underwent change over the eighth century in some areas. The term literally means 'heir' and applied to the heir of the patron saint. As discussed above, in the seventh century it was a synonym for the abbot or abbess, and that person had responsibility for both the spiritual and temporal facets of their 'inheritance'. This included the church's rights of property and jurisdiction, as well as overseeing the religious life of the place. With the changes evident from the eighth century, the term 'coarb' began to be used at some large churches for a person who held a new role: controller of the church's temporalities. Possibly the term moved over to this post because, conveniently, it was neutral in its ecclesiastical significance.

At some monasteries or churches the controller of temporalities (whatever their name) and/or the abbot might also be an ordained bishop, and in those instances the temporal powers were combined with the powers of episcopal jurisdiction. Bishops, though not normally powerful in themselves, did have certain privileges: they were the principal judges in ecclesiastical cases and exercised spiritual discipline within the *túath*, and according to *Ríagail Phátraic* (the Rule of Patrick) they were also the confessors of secular lords and heads of churches in their designated regions.[42] At women's houses this potent combination of authority could not come together in a single person, because an abbess, whatever

---

[41] Schneider, 'Anglo-Saxon Women', 264–72, 304.
[42] Charles-Edwards, 'Pastoral Care', 69–75.

else she could do, could not be a bishop—usually, at least. In one absolutely extra-ordinary circumstance the abbess did claim exactly this power and authority: in the tenth or eleventh century the abbesses of Kildare claimed episcopal powers through a retrospective claim that Brigit herself had been ordained as a bishop.[43] Only at Kildare could so audacious a claim be sustained. There had long been claims that Brigit had equal honour to Patrick, that she ruled the women of Ireland as he ruled the men; this new claim suggests that even bolder claims were felt necessary at this time.[44] One may speculate that perhaps the Kildare authorities were concerned about the strength of their leadership struc-ture. Maybe they felt that a strengthening could be achieved by fusing the epis-copal and coarbial authorities, as had long been common practice at male houses. Other women's churches had to make do with affiliated bishops or, even less desirably, to come under the care of one who was based elsewhere.

In those large churches where the managerial function had been separated from the office of abbot, the coarbships became more temporal over time; for example, at Armagh in the tenth and eleventh centuries the office was heredi-tary in a group of families and was negotiated and passed on in a fashion simi-lar to a royal office. Where these great coarbships existed, they functioned on the basis of property and political rights.[45] Monastics of such large churches were supervised by another person, one who would live in the holiest part of the *civitas* and who would often hold an alternative title.[46]

Some female houses acquired a male who controlled their temporalities. This person might be called 'coarb' but more usually was called an erenagh be-cause the female head was the saint's heiress and thus the traditional coarb. The records leave traces of a few male erenaghs at the large, traditionally female churches, but in two cases at least the development of the managerial position seems not to have involved any diminution of the abbess's authority. The first was Cloonburren on the Shannon which had a female erenagh, *a banairchin-nech,*in the lady Lerben (obit 793), according to the Annals of Ulster. The other was Kildare.

That complex and changing institution was clearly one in which the abbess was prominent over the long term. Supposedly at Kildare there was a bishop co-ruling with the abbess from Brigit's day: Cogitosus describes him as being in charge of the male side of things.[47] The seventh-century annals show abbots there too, such as Oengus and Áed Dub (obit 639, who was also a bishop). Erenaghs of Kildare itself are visible in the Annals of Ulster from the seventh

---

[43]   See discussion in Johnston, 'Transforming Women'.

[44]   The 7th-cent. Book of the Angel calls Brigit and Patrick 'the two pillars of the Irish' (Hughes, *Church*, 279); so too does a 7th-cent. hymn, *Brigit Bé Bithmaith*, which calls them 'the two pillars of sovereignty of the Irish church'. The 11th-cent. gloss on this line in the hymn says that as the pillars divide a house, the two have divided Ireland between them, so that Brigit is head of Ireland's women, and Patrick of its men (*Thes. Pal.* ii. 23–6).

[45]   Sharpe, 'Some Problems', 264.   [46]   Ibid. 265.   [47]   Cogitosus, Life of Brigit, Preface.

century to the late ninth. Muiredach, who died in 885, was *princeps* of Kildare and also king of Leinster, and the annals of the Four Masters relate the deaths in 923 and 968 of the abbot of Kildare and the *rioghdamhna* of Leinster (*abb Cille Dara 7 rigdamna Laigean*).[48] The relative power of the three offices—erenagh, abbess, and bishop—is impossible to discern, but in the seventh century Cogitosus had claimed that there was parity between the bishop and the abbess. Gwynn and Hadcock thought the bishops after Conlaed may have been subordinate to the jurisdiction of the abbess, noting that in some periods Kildare had more than one bishop.[49] The title of 'coarb of Brigit' remained with the abbess's office throughout the centuries up to the twelfth rather than going to the abbot, erenagh, or *princeps*; moreover, whereas the Annals of Ulster report obits of only seven bishops and one 'superior', they report fifteen Kildare abbesses.

Killeedy in the south-west merits special attention as an enigmatic example of male 'headship' at a successful female house, one thought to have been founded by a woman at that. In the notes to the Martyrology of Oengus and in one of her Lives, Ita is said to have decreed that no nun would ever succeed her, i.e. have her coarbship (*ni géba caillech tre bithu mo chomarbus*).[50] In the ninth century at least Killeedy was headed by an abbot, an *ab*.[51] If a male abbot did take over the rulership of the church and its property shortly after the foundress's lifetime, then its nuns were over centuries headed by a male superior, at least in regards overall rulership. Thomas Charles-Edwards has demonstrated that *ab* need not mean a spiritual supervisor of monastics but could signify an overall head of a monastery. This may be significant in view of the Martyrology notes' reference to Ita's coarbship going to a man. It could be that the woman who supervised Killeedy's nuns was called by another name and possessed little or none of the more worldly authority which abbesses might enjoy. The same or similar situation could well have been found at other communities of religious women. In those male monasteries which had nuns attached to them, the women were headed by a senior nun who, it seems, would not have possessed the title of abbess or coarb; at Tallaght in the ninth century, for example, the head of the nuns was called the *senoir caildidi*.[52]

Caution warns against presuming that the extent of 'secularization' was uniform in Ireland during the eighth and ninth centuries: even at large churches the influence of 'temporal' practice could vary widely. There was a significant difference in the level of 'degeneracy' between Slane and Iona in the eighth and ninth centuries, for example. When it came to smaller monastic communities, secular elements may not have taken root as deeply, or they may have tended to operate differently. These places were less likely, it seems, to have a secular

---

[48] AFM 920, 965; NB dates in this text are up to three years out.
[49] Gwynn and Hadcock, *Religious Houses*, 320.   [50] Martyrology of Oengus, notes on 4 Apr.
[51] AFM 810, 833. Ryan takes this to signify that Killeedy had become, by that time, a male monastery (*Irish Monasticism*, 140).
[52] Customs of Tallaght, ch. 62.

erenagh or coarbial officer controlling their temporal interests. Doubtless life at some nunneries carried on through the eighth, ninth, and tenth centuries in much the same manner as it had in the seventh, with an abbess who supervised the nuns, oversaw the economic well-being of the place, and was the *domina* of the monastic tenants. But many smaller places were subsumed in monastic federations or jurisdictional *paruchiae* of powerful churches. The saints' Lives contain many references to nuns donating their churches to male saints. This we glean not just from the seventh-century's Tírechán, but also from later Lives. One such is the Irish Life of Bairre of Cork, which gives the names of the twelve virgins who studied under him at his school and who subsequently donated their churches to him and to God 'in perpetuity'.[53] Understanding these and the many other similar stories as anachronistic expressions of ecclesiastical supremacy, one gains the impression that a vast number of abbesses must have had ecclesiastical overlords at large male monastic churches. Abbesses of such places had less external authority, less political and economic power, than the abbesses of independent nunneries.

As was mentioned in an earlier chapter, the lists and martyrologies speak of family monasteries or churches. Many of these places were recorded as being 'of' a man and his sisters, or 'of' a collection of sisters. In some of these, likely to have continued as family-run institutions, a sharing of power and authority among the male and female proprietors within the family may have been involved. These and other questions along such lines are imponderables, and it would be unwise to fall into unsupported speculation. The effect of the rise of lay coarbships and erenaghs can be seen sanguinely in terms of custodianship, or more pessimistically as domination and hegemony. If one draws the lines along boundaries of gender, one could envision the scenario as a male domination of female communities. But this is rather simplistic. Irish society was held together strongly by, amongst other things, ties to one's kin group, one's *fine*. Some noblewomen who gained leadership positions within the religious life during and after the eighth century very likely continued to identify very strongly with their family and its interests. When there were both an abbess and a male erenagh, it is entirely likely that the abbess and male coarbs were relatives, and that together they may have worked for the aggrandizement of their church, with a view to enhancing the wealth and status of their own family. It would be naïve to think otherwise in the face of the overwhelming evidence of a highly secularized Irish Church. Where male managers came into place, abbesses may have suffered a comparative loss of authority and power. One can easily imagine that as the abbess's male relatives and/or the local magnates took on more control over the nunnery's temporalities, her job became a more inward-looking one rather than what seems to have been normal before, in which she was an active part of her kindred's ambitions and schemes. As the trend for lay control grew, it may

---

[53] Irish Life of Bairre of Cork, ch. 22.

well have become a more frequent occurrence for abbesses to be placed into their positions by their families, regardless of whether they had a spiritual calling or administrative skill.

Selection and Consecration of Abbesses

In Irish vernacular law, an abbatial headship stayed in the family of the founder, and so was legally hereditary. The law tract *Córus Béscnai* is but one of the sources which make this explicit, and others allow for, and even encourage, the successor to be named before the demise of the incumbent, in order to achieve a smooth transition.[54] If a house was hegemonized by a royal family, as was Kildare, then the abbots were from the new, dominating dynasty. In a few houses at least, though, the abbots did not have obvious familial connections, which implies that successors were chosen according to ability and popularity within the monastic community itself.

The evidence on succession at nunneries is not as full as one might hope. In Brigit's *Vita I*, Brigit chose the nun Darlugthacha with the words *successor mea eris*. This, however, can hardly be used as grounds for generalizing to say that Irish abbesses always, or even normally, picked their own successors.[55] Nominated successors, however, are to be found. We read of a *tanist*-abbot at Armagh in the Annals of the Four Masters for the year 927, and there is mention of a *tanist*-abbess at Kildare in (probably) the eleventh century, in a legal gloss.[56] The term *tanist*, which literally means 'second', is a person designated to succeed before the death of the incumbent ruler, though it can also mean the person who is second in command. Use of the term *tanist* in relation to abbacies shows the ecclesiastical sphere reflecting secular kingship institutions. The question which remains open here is, of course, the identity of the person or persons who did the nominating. Given the depth of political involvement of the ruling dynasty in the leadership of such places as Armagh and Kildare, it seems highly unlikely that the abbess or abbot alone picked the tanist. It seems especially unlikely in the case of an abbess, for she was a woman. Unless she was able to wield genuine and extensive power over her family as well as over the nuns, it seems more likely that it was a group decision taken primarily by the dynasty's males.

In the case of Killevy we are able to see something of the practice of keeping the abbess-ship in the foundress's family. There the first fifteen abbesses were of the same family, the Uí Chonaill Muirthemne, a fact determinable from the earliest successor's names in the saint's Life and, more importantly, from a seventh-century abbess list which includes not only the forenames but also the

---

[54] D. Ó Cróinín, *Early Medieval Ireland, 400–1200* (London, 1995), 162–4.

[55] *Vita I* of Brigit, ch. 132.

[56] *Cáin Lánamna* gloss (in *SEIL* 73; also in *ALI* ii. 409). The gloss is in Middle Irish and was probably written after AD 1000.

patronyms of some fifteen abbesses in succession into the seventh century.[57] At Kildare, too, the practice may be seen as well, but with a twist. The earliest heads were of Brigit's kindred, the Fothairt, but by marrying into it the Uí Dúnlainge managed to infiltrate and then take over the monastery. Alfred Smyth's and F. J. Byrne's examinations of the Kildare evidence show the ruling Leinster dynasty providing not just abbesses but bishops, *seniores*, and the other top positions in their programme of hegemony.[58] The take-over of Kildare by the Uí Dúnlainge dynasty may have been initiated by one Fáelan, king of Leinster (floruit 628) through marriage to a Fothairt woman; for after the marriage we find his brother and nephew in the Kildare offices of abbot and bishop. The hegemony was cemented by the placement of his great-great-grand-daughter Condal (obit 797) into the abbesshood.[59] Right up until the twelfth century, dynasties fought to gain or keep control of the office of the coarbship, which had in theory at least to be filled by a woman who was of Brigit's family. Finally, at the synod of Kells-Mellifont in 1152, Kildare lost its status and the office was never again what it had been for so many centuries.[60]

Where abbesses' inauguration procedures and ceremonies are concerned, there is even less material from which to reconstruct Irish practice than there is for selection customs. From the few references that do exist, it is apparent that the inauguration was called an ordination, the same term as was used for the act of conferring, amongst other things, episcopal office.[61] This was the same as it was elsewhere, where the only female position entered by 'ordination' was that of the abbess.[62] There is some suggestion that in the eleventh or twelfth century at least, the ordination of an abbess might be performed by the head of the larger monastery in whose jurisdiction or federation the house lay. The *Vita Tripartita* says that because the founder of the church of Granard was the foster-brother of the two virgins who founded the Clonbroney 'it is the erenagh of Granard who always ordains the head of nuns in Clonbroney' (*airchindech Granaird ortness cenn caillech dogres iCluain Bronaig*).[63] These two midland establishments were only about eight miles apart, so we may infer that at this time the nunnery was subject to Granard and that the historical detail simply served to justify a current reality. Interestingly, it was an erenagh who performed the rite,

[57]   List of Abbesses of Killevy.

[58]   F. J. Byrne, '*Comarbai Brigte*', in T. W. Moody and F. J. Byrne (eds.), *A New History of Ireland*, ix. *Maps, Genealogies, Lists* (Oxford, 1984), 259–62; A. Smyth, *Celtic Leinster: Towards an Historical Geography of Early Irish Civilization AD 500–1600* (Blackrock, 1982).

[59]   The brother was Áed Dub (obit 639), abbot and bishop of Kildare; the nephew was Oengus (abbot of Kildare), son of Fáelan's other brother Áed Finn. Ó Cróinín thinks it began earlier than Fáelan, *Ireland*, 157. For the most current proposed genealogical trees of the Uí Dúnlainge, see Ó Cróinín, *Ireland*, 308–9.

[60]   Johnston, 'Transforming Women', 216–17.   [61]   e.g. Stokes, *Tripartite Life*, i. 90–1.

[62]   Hodgson, 'Frankish Church', 197–211, where she also suggests that in the 9th cent. abbesses and abbots were ordained with the same rite, and notes that there were two types of abbesses, the regular and the canonical, the latter being the head of canonesses rather than regular nuns.

[63]   Tripartite Life (in Stokes, *Tripartite Life*, i., at 90–1).

rather than a person designated as coarb or abbot (Ir. *ab*), but it is impossible to draw conclusions from this as the use of these terms was not standardized. In the earlier period, under discussion here, it would make sense to imagine that the abbess's ordination ceremonies would normally be performed by the nearest, or most closely related, bishop, who might well be located at an affiliated male house. Bishops in this period often lived at such establishments.

Kildare is a special case with regard to the ordination of its abbesses, for a longstanding legend had it that Brigit had been ordained as a bishop, and that her exceptional status was passed on to the later generations of abbesses.[64] It may be that this legend had an effect on the actual ceremony of inauguration at Kildare. A tenth- or eleventh-century glossator on a hymn wrote that because Brigit had been ordained a bishop 'her successor is always entitled to episcopal orders and the honour due a bishop' (*is dosen dliges comarba Brigte do gres grad n-epscuip fuirri 7 honoir epscuip*) and the abbess is clearly the person meant by 'coarb' or successor.[65] It was always applied to a female, a woman we presume was the abbess. If it is actually so that the abbess also gained episcopal status, in addition to the coarbial mantle, her inauguration ceremony must have been very interesting indeed.

Abbesses at Synods

Usually in the West only bishops attended synods, but in Ireland others were present, as evidenced in the letter of AD 640 from the pope-elect to a gathering made up of not only bishops but priests and *doctores* as well. In the 630s the Synod of Mag Leni was attended by non-bishops as had been, allegedly, the Synod of Tailtiu.[66] Although Brigit's Lives show consecrated women attending synods, the abbess of Kildare was not a guarantor of the document produced by the synod in AD 697 which promulgated 'the law of Adomnán', *Cáin Adomnáin*; it was the abbot.[67] This does not mean she was powerless, or even inactive at the assembly. The extant anecdotes of religious women at synods, both of which are admittedly from Brigit's *Vita I*, do have them present and active. Comparisons may be made with the synod of Whitby, where abbess Hild not only participated but led a party in the debate; abbesses also proved to have attended other synods in England though they almost never signed royal charters.[68]

Scholars looking at Frankish and English nuns have become well aware that abbesses who were prominent in ecclesiastical and secular politics owed their

---

[64] Discussed in Johnston, 'Transforming Women', 216–17.

[65] Gloss on the hymn *Ní Car Brigit* (*Thes. Pal.* ii. 330).

[66] T. Charles-Edwards, paper delivered to the Celtic Seminar, spring 1993.

[67] This was Forandán, who served as its abbot for the years 696–8. See M. Ní Donnchadha, 'The Guarantor List of Cáin Adomnáin', *Peritia* 1 (1982), 178–215.

[68] Schneider, 'Anglo-Saxon Women', 295–301.

eminence much more to their royal status than to their ecclesiastical grade. This was doubtless the case in Ireland, not only for the office of abbess but also for the high-status classification of other types of religious women whom vernacular law treated with esteem, who are discussed below. The Frankish and English abbesses are much better attested, in terms of their genealogies and social networks, than their Irish counterparts, so whilst this truth is demonstrable by example in those societies, for Ireland it is to be accepted by inference from wider political trends and from what we know about how Irish society worked in general. Abbesses as a group were unlikely to have had equal status in practice, if they even had it in theory. Their levels of actual power must have varied enormously, given that status in Ireland was linked not just to office but to wealth, and that there must have been hundreds of heads of proprietary churches of both sexes. The abbess of a small, poor place was much less likely to have been present at the promulgation of *cána* or other ecclesiastical gatherings than, say, the abbess of Kildare. In other words, the holding of abbatial office was likely to have been necessary but not sufficient, the other qualifications being wealth and royal birth. Such a model is presented as only the most likely option, but there may be more than fiction in the *Vita I*'s portrayals of holy women, including widows, attending synods as a matter of course.[69]

Abbess and Holy Woman: the Case of Samthann

In Carolingian Frankia, there were no known living saints; the era of saints was well and truly over, and Church authorities seem to have discouraged living sanctity.[70] It is clear that in Ireland in this era, by contrast, there were still women and men who were valued in both their religious communities and their lay communities (*túatha*) for their holiness and for a resultant ability to bring about divine favour from God. Samthann is fascinating because she was such a woman, and because she was at the same time the abbess of a nunnery.

Samthann, abbess of Clonbroney in the northern midlands, died in 739. She thus lived around the time of the composition of many law tracts and of the *Hibernensis*. The earliest record mentioning her is her obit in the Annals of Ulster, and shortly thereafter she is mentioned at greater length in three texts: the ninth-century Customs of Tallaght (the bulk of which were written shortly before 840), and the martyrologies of Oengus and of Tallaght, both composed near the turn of the ninth century.[71] From a later period, we have also have Samthann's Latin Life.[72]

The annals show Samthann the abbess rather than Samthann the miracle-worker. The pattern of annal obits suggests that she elevated Clonbroney from

[69] *Vita I* of Brigit, ch. 72.   [70] Smyth, 'Female Sanctity', esp. at 36.
[71] For the dating of the Customs of Tallaght, see *Kenney*, no. 264.
[72] *PVSH*, i., p. lxxxvii; *Kenney*, no. 253.

relative unimportance to considerable prominence. She was the first of its abbesses the annals mention, although she was not its foundress; the AU annalists went on to report the obits of Samthann's five successors, but there are none of her predecessors.[73] The changes wrought by this remarkable woman are not documented by any contemporary source, but her later Life suggests she was responsible for the physical expansion of Clonbroney: having taken up the guardianship of the rule (*suscepta autem cura regiminis*) Samthann arranged for the building of a new wooden oratory, and the enlargement of the space of the monastery; a new building, a *cenaculum*, was also constructed.[74] Building anecdotes feature more strongly in this Life than in other female Lives, so it is possible that the hagiographer, although writing centuries after the abbess's lifetime, was drawing on the collective memories of the community. As building implies a rise in population and/or disposable funds, it looks as though Samthann was responsible for the rise in fortunes. We may surmise that she enlisted the patronage of a powerful family, very possibly her own, a suggestion which is strengthened by the long genealogy attributed to her by the annotator of the Martyrology of Oengus.[75] Or perhaps she attracted attention and donations to the place through the strength of her personality. Alternatively it may have been a deep and compelling mystical spirituality, or an ability to perform what were believed to be miracles, which drew economic resources, followers, and patrons to Clonbroney. It seems reasonable to assume that it was a combination of at least some of these elements.

The sources closest in time to Samthann's lifetime speak of Samthann the saint. She appears under 19 December in the Martyrology of Tallaght (as simply *Samthand Clúana Bronaig*) and in the more poetic Martyrology of Oengus as a more evocatively described saintly being: 'Blithe unto my soul, with the vastness of her host, be the fair pure manna of Elemental God—Samthann of Clúain Brónaig' (*Frimm anmain rop fáilid co n-aidbli a slógaid, cain glanmann Dé dúilig, Samthann Clúana Brónaig*). The near-contemporary annal obit in the Annals of Tigernach hints at Samthann the politician when relating that she sang a rhyme at the slaying of Fergus mac Crimthain.[76]

But it is through the Customs of Tallaght, written about a century after she lived, that Samthann the saint really comes to life. Here we see her as a respected holy woman. The text relates a tale about her: at Clonbroney she used to stay in touch with the holy men of Munster through an itinerant pedlar (*negotiator*), to whom she would give messages and greetings to convey to the 'sons of life' (*maic bethad*), who were religious men. On one occasion she dispatched him

---

[73] Life of Samthann, ch. 5, names Funech as the foundress. The account in the Tripartite Life says it was founded by two princesses named Emer (Stokes, *Tripartite Life*, i. 90–1).

[74] Life of Samthann, chs. 6, 14, 15, 16.

[75] She is 'daughter of Dimrán, son of Ferdomnan, son of Díchu, son of Fiacc, son of Trichem, son of Fiacc, son of Imchad' (Martyrology of Oengus, notes on 19 Dec.).

[76] ATig 737.

to another part of the country, to take a very important message to a holy man she admired greatly—the author was uncertain whether this was Maelruain, the head of Tallaght, or alternatively Fer dá Chrích, abbot of Armagh.[77] Her message was this: he was her favourite amongst the clerics of the desert, and she wished to ask him whether he received the confession of women. If he did, would he be her soul-friend? The pedlar took the message. The holy man, on hearing that he was Samthann's favourite, gave thanks to God; but then hearing Samthann's question about soul-friendship to women 'he blushed down to his breast', made three genuflections, and remained silent for a long time. 'Tell her', he said finally, 'that I will seek counsel from her' (atbertsom apur siu friesi tra olsesem conimthisi comarli hude). The pedlar returned to Samthann and reported the cleric's reply. When she heard it, she pricked herself in the cheek with the needle of her brooch. Out of the wound came no blood, but only two filaments of milk. She squeezed harder, and after a time there came out a tiny droplet of water. After Samthann had managed to emit the drop onto her fingernail, she held it up and spoke. 'So long', she pronounced, 'as there is this much juice in his body, let him bestow no friendship nor confidence upon womankind' (asbertsí tra airet bés iarum olsí a cutrumesi do súg inda curpsom ni be mundteras indda taobatu dó fri banscala).[78]

As mentioned in an earlier chapter, the reduction of blood in the body of an ascetic symbolized the reduction of lust.[79] The author was making a point when he contrasted the deep blushing cheeks of the cleric against the pale cheek of Samthann who did not issue blood even when stabbed with a needle. She was spiritually superior, having transcended sexual desire and its physical manifestation (the rushing of blood in the body); the cleric, abbot though he may have been, acknowledged this when he replied that he would take her counsel. The story culminates with her judgement on him: he may not be a soul-friend of women. This judgement, and indeed the whole tale, does seem to be one which reflects particularly poorly on the male cleric but remarkably well upon the female saint. It was feasible, in the ninth century, for a holy woman to gain sufficiently high esteem for her decisions to be heeded in leading monasteries. Nor was Samthann the only one: the Customs of Tallaght also relate the pious example given by a certain unnamed nun (caillech) whose incessant repetition of the Lord's prayer inspired the reforming abbot Maelrúain to incorporate its frequent use into his own spiritual practice and into the liturgical practice of his céle Dé community.[80] But Samthann was exceptional even against a background where there were many women of holiness and eminence. It is perhaps unsurprising that later abbesses of Clonbroney were be described as Samthann's coarbs, in the light of the spiritual and temporal inheritance she left.[81]

---

[77] Fer dá Chrích, abbot of Armagh, obit 768 (Hughes, *Church*, 170).
[78] Customs of Tallaght, ch. 61.   [79] This is made explicit in ibid., ch. 60.
[80] Ibid., ch. 32.
[81] AU 1109, the obit of 'Cocrich, *comarba* of Samthann of Clonbroney'.

OTHER EXCEPTIONAL HOLY WOMEN

The example of Samthann is the most extensive piece of evidence proving that some of the hundreds of thousands of Irish nuns of the seventh to ninth centuries actually achieved the status of saint. Samthann is the most famous, and the only one whose identity we can name, locate, and date. But others, anonymous, emerge hazily from other texts, and their presence reminds us that in this era other nuns too could become esteemed holy women. Apart from the mention of the holy *caillech* who repeated the Paternoster so ceaselessly, there are few narrative accounts of women who were deemed eminent and sagagious but not heads of nunneries.

Prescriptive Texts

The prescriptive texts make provisions for such exceptional women, often calling them hermitess or pilgrim (*bandeorad Dé*, lit. female exile of God), or holy virgin *virgo sancta* or *banóg*). From the law tract *Bretha Crólige* we learn that holy women were so special that they received sick-maintenance in a manner reserved for people of indispensable importance to the community.[82] The text says these women had their payment assessed by a judge in proportion to their worth and their property, if they counted themselves not dependent on a husband.[83] Two sorts of women so categorized were holy women. The first was the woman 'who turns back the streams of war'. We know she was a religious, for she is glossed as 'the abbess of Kildare or the *aíbellteóir*, one who turns back the many sins of wars through her prayers' (*ut est bancomarba cille dara .i. in banaibellteoir .i. impodus imad peccad na cocad for cula trena hirnaigthi*).[84] Donnchadh Ó Corráin in 'Women in Early Irish Society' considered this claim possible, at least for abbesses of important monasteries like Kildare; he noted that the abbot of Armagh, for example, could act as an intermediary in negotiating peace between warring kingdoms.[85] But whether her intervention took place on the spiritual or the practical level, the holy woman's role was doubtless inspired by traditions regarding foundress saints: Brigit, for example, gets involved in military conflicts, mainly in their resolution and prevention, and later female Lives have many examples of this too.[86]

Bretha Crólige also makes special sick-maintenance provision for 'the woman abundant in miracles'. She too receives a payment for illegal injury, rather than being taken away to be nursed, and is glossed as 'the female virgin, i.e. the

---

[82] *Bretha Crólige: CIH* 2286.24–2305.3; also D. Binchy (ed. and trans.), '*Bretha Crólige*', Ériu 12 (1938), 1–77. Comments and partial trans. in Kelly, *Guide*, 77, 129–34, 271, 351.
[83] Binchy, '*Bretha Crólige*', 29.   [84] Ibid. 26; Kelly, *Guide*, 69.
[85] In Mac Curtain and Ó Corráin, *Women in Irish Society: the Historical Dimension* (Dublin 1978), 10–11.
[86] Also in later hagiography: Conchubranus, Life of Monenna, book 3, ch. 9; Latin Life of Enda, chs. 2–3.

female holy hermit' (*in banogh .i. in ban deorad de*).[87] Why is the virgin not to be nursed outside the *túath*? The section of *Bretha Crólige* which deals with the male hermit whose miracles are granted (*deorad de ernidter ferta*), answers the question. The glossator asks rhetorically, 'Whence is to be procured a holy hermit who works miracles?' (*can toagar deora[d] de dogni firta?*).[88] Holy hermits, then, regardless of sex, were not to be taken away for nursing on account of their irreplaceable rarity. Whilst the extent to which the provisions of sick-maintenance law were actually implemented is uncertain, what is significant here is the evidence provided by the text for the existence in this period of both male and female miracle-working hermits and for the high esteem they enjoyed.

As was already mentioned, the ability to stand surety without authorization was denied to legal incompetents: insane people, children, monastics, and females. The two exceptions in *Hibernensis*, the *virgo sancta* and the *domina*, imply strongly that there were holy women who, unlike ordinary monastics, were legally competent to act without authorization from a supervising head. Although the extent to which the text's provisions were actually applied is uncertain, it is a document designed for the present, and this rule is neither foreign nor obviously derivative. *Hibernensis* also accorded holy women special privileges regarding burial. A *femina sanctemonialis* might be buried within a church or with a holy man of equal rank, and St Benedict and his holy sister are cited as precedents for this, with the remark that in death they were rewarded with corporeal proximity and spiritual union, as they had been of one mind during their lifetimes.[89] Interestingly enough, Cogitosus reports that in his own day the bodies of Brigit and her contemporary, Bishop Conlaed, were both entombed by the altar in the church at Kildare.[90] With regard to property, too, autonomous action is evidenced in law and practice. *Hibernensis* supported women gaining control over land, doubtless in the context of their being able to dedicate it to ecclesiastical purposes, when it cited the Old Testament example of Caleb and his daughter Axa: Caleb gave his part to Axa, 'because she asked him for it'. It went on to cite the example of Jacob who gave a *hereditatem* to Dinah, who was a dedicated widow.[91] There may well have been some men, or kindreds, who did endow property inheritances on women, though these are imperceptible; there is, nevertheless, the intriguing reference in the ninth century to the king's daughter who allegedly bestowed land on St Fursey.[92] The nuns in the Additamenta to Tírechán dealt autonomously in property, it is remembered, but the lands they were transferring were clearly not inheritances but acquisitions which were theirs alone according to even vernacular law.[93]

To summarize, both vernacular law and canons provided for holy women

---

[87] Quoted and discussed in Kelly, *Guide*, 77. I follow Kelly's translation of *deorad Dé*, literally 'exile of God', as hermit whilst aware that it also means 'pilgrim'.

[88] '*Bretha Crólige*', ch. 32 (ed. D. Binchy).   [89] *Hibernensis*, book 18, chs. 8–9.

[90] Cogitosus, Life of Brigit, ch. 32.   [91] *Hibernensis*, book 32, ch. 17.

[92] Customs of Tallaght, ch. 19.   [93] Additamenta to Tírechán, ch. 11.

who, though not abbesses, were still largely legally autonomous and/or who received special treatment at law on account of an importance gained through means other than holding the abbatial office.

Peregrinae

The Lives of the seventh, eighth, and ninth centuries refer to women going on pilgrimage at numerous points, with little comment. The term *peregrinatio* is used almost synonymously in the *Vita I* of Brigit, for example, for going on a visit to another monastery or church in a different part of the country. Monenna, for her part, was called a *peregrina* in a seventh-century hymn.[94] Jonas of Bobbio's, Life of Columbanus, written on the Continent, contains the most vivid short episode involving female pilgrimage: it was allegedly an Irish *peregrina* who initially encouraged Columbanus to make his great journey to the Continent; but for the fact she was a women, she said, she would have gone abroad rather than confine her wanderings to Ireland.[95] There is no indication, however, that there was disapproval for women being *peregrinae*, whether going abroad, as some of the female saints allegedly did, or within Ireland itself. Most of the anecdotes on female pilgrimage are late, but these are as *laissez-faire* about the practice as those in the seventh- to ninth-century window under consideration here.[96] Certainly the Irish had plenty of positive examples from the early church: Egeria whose travels were written down and circulated; Palladius's *Historia Lausiaca* which related the extensive wanderings of the holy Melania the Elder, and even Jerome's beloved Paula, whose peregrinations were not inconsiderable. As has been discussed at length in an earlier section, Irish ecclesiastics differed from their English and Frankish counterparts in that they did not legislate against women going on pilgrimage, with the one implicit exception of the anomalous rule in *Hibernensis*.[97]

As *peregrinatio* became formalized, the 'exile for God' or *Deorad Dé* acquired high status on account of his sacrifice of homeland.[98] This formalization,

---

[94] *Audite Fratres*, stanza 15.

[95] Jonas, Life of Columbanus, book 1, ch. 3 (B. Krusch, MGH, *Scriptores rerum Merovingicarum*, iv (1902), 1–152).

[96] e.g. Second Irish Life of Ciarán of Seirkieran, ch. 25, where Brendan of Birr's mother, Mansenna, wished to go into exile to Oilén Doimle, probably mod. Inis Doimle or Little Island, in the Suir near Waterford. She was advised against it because the saint could perceive that the place designated for her resurrection (and thus her death) was at Tallaght (*BNE* i. 113–24; Eng. trans., ii. 109–20). The Third Irish Life of Coemgen, ch. 18, tells of the death and revival of two nuns who had come on pilgrimage to him (*BNE* i. 155–67; Eng. trans., ii. 151–62).

[97] *Hibernensis*, book 45, ch. 14, which instructs that they be kept cloistered and out of men's sight. Hodgson, 'Frankish Church', 104–14, with references; Schneider, 'Anglo-Saxon Women', 223–31, arguing for mixed views and citing, among others, Boniface and Alcuin.

[98] T. Charles-Edwards, 'The Social Background to Irish Peregrinatio', *Celtica* 11 (1976), 43–59. Also on *peregrinatio*, K. Hughes, 'The Changing Theory and Practice of Irish Pilgrimage', *Journal of Ecclesiastical History* 11 (1960), 143–51.

though not much evidenced in the Lives, is abundantly clear in the law tracts, both for men and for women, as is evidenced in the tract discussed above referring to the *ban-deorad Dé*. There are to my knowledge no narrative accounts of these formalized, high-status pilgrims, either for men or women, so the nature of their lives must remain opaque.

CONCLUSIONS

A few points will have become apparent. In the seventh- to ninth-century era there lived a number of women whose perceived holiness resulted in their being exalted to the point of achieving recognition as saints. Some were held in such high esteem by their local communities that Irish law made special provision for them. Abbesses continued to run many monasteries, and although the abbatial office underwent changes and was partially supplanted with lay abbacies and coarbships, it is clear that in a few cases at least the office of the abbess remained highly sought after, as in the case of Kildare. Considering the matter of high-status religious women from a broader perspective, that of wider attitudes to sanctity and gender, we may note the high regard with which female holy women could be held, a fact made apparent in some of the hagiographic texts of this era. It is surely of significance, for example, that some perceived Ireland to be spiritually held up by two pillar saints, one of whom was female. Likewise, we would be foolish to ignore the influence of female holy women upon male monastics and laypeople, as is evidenced by the textual material on Samthann who was held up as a paragon in her own lifetime to the monks in the *céle Dé* movement.

The warm treatment of exceptional holy women survived into the succeeding centuries. The eleventh and twelfth centuries brought some changes to Ireland's ecclesiastical and religious atmosphere, and at that time the beginnings of new, separatist, attitudes about female sanctity are evident in the hagiographic, apocryphal, and literary texts. Although the evidence suggests that a nun could still achieve a level of moral authority so high that her teachings might be thought worthy to serve as guides to clerics, new pressures and developments were soon to emerge.

PART THREE

The Tenth, Eleventh, and Twelfth Centuries

Introduction

The tenth to twelfth centuries were ones of great change for the Irish church. Through the ninth and tenth centuries, the Vikings made a notable impact on the church in general and on monasteries in particular. Many smaller places disappeared, for only the wealthiest and largest could withstand repeated attacks. The very strong lay influence, evidenced by such things as lay abbacies and hereditary clerical offices, began to come under criticism from reform efforts within Ireland, and then later from outside it.[1] During the twelfth century Continental orders came into Ireland to supersede the native Irish monasticism, and a territorial parish structure was instituted.[2] The end of the native Irish church is traditionally placed by scholars in the twelfth century, and with good reason this dating has remained unchanged over a century in which the historiography has overturned many older ideas.

Among the non-specialists with a keen interest in early Christian Ireland the twelfth century is the watershed, too, for this very reason. Modern Celtic Christians see the changes of the twelfth century as the end of their Golden Age, and can portray the arrival of such features as dioceses, Romanesque architecture, and Continental monastic orders as signs of mystical spirit giving way to the bureaucratic: 'With its massive stone cathedrals built to last centuries, the Norman church had a more settled and established feel than the essentially provisional Celtic Christian communities with their wattle and daub huts for worship, ever-itinerant monks and bishops who regularly retreated to hermits' cells.'[3]

The first time, to our knowledge, that the Irish church insisted upon the celibacy of men in orders was at the turn of the twelfth century, at the first synod of Cashel, held in 1101.[4] In spite of this, the Irish appear to have had little interest in the matter; the issue had nothing of the explosive power it did on the Continent, and there was little effort put into enforcing it. The abbacy of Armagh, for long a hereditary post, did as a result of this synod become one requiring celibacy,[5] but the surviving evidence suggests that married priesthood carried

---

[1] e.g. Herbert, *Iona*; also T. Ó Fiaich, 'The Church of Armagh Under Lay Control', *Seanchas Ard Mhacha* 5 (1969–70), 75–127. See also the accusations of St Bernard in his Life of St Malachy, ch. 10.19 (ed. and trans. H. Lawlor, *St Bernard's Life of St Malachy of Armagh* (London, 1920)).

[2] A. Gwynn, *The Twelfth-Century Reform* (Dublin, 1968); J. Watt, *The Church in Medieval Ireland* (Gill History of Ireland 5; Dublin, 1972); G. Carville, *The Occupation of Celtic Sites in Medieval Ireland by the Canons Regular of St Augustine and the Cistercians* (Kalamazoo, Mich., 1982).

[3] Bradley, *Celtic Way*, 27.

[4] A. Gwynn, 'The First Synod of Cashel', *IER* 66 (1945), 81–92; 67 (1946), 109–22. See also Hughes, 'Sanctity and Secularity', 35, and Flanagan, *Irish Society*, 21–2.

[5] Cellach son of Áed took holy orders when he assumed office in 1105, and in 1106 received orders as a 'noble bishop', *uasalespoic*, according to the Annals of the Four Masters (Flanagan, *Irish Society*, 21).

on without much ado in Ireland. Bernard of Clairvaux, writing the Life of St Malachy some years after the synod, regarded the Irish church as an institution of failed morals.[6] It should be borne in mind that many of the authors studied in the following chapters, certainly many of those writing in Middle Irish and probably a good number of those writing in Latin, had close personal relations with women—because they themselves were married, or their abbot was, or their father was an ecclesiastic and their mother a cleric's wife.[7] Ireland reformed late, very late. Scholars have traditionally said this was because the Irish church was essentially out of touch with England and the Continent until the twelfth century. But Irish sources from these centuries show less ignorance of the debates than at first appears, a fact which is only beginning to be appreciated.

Three interwoven changes are visible in Irish writing of the tenth to twelfth centuries, all of which can most readily be explained as responses to the sexual agendas of the foreign reforms. The first is an increase in anti-female remarks which, though neither extreme nor consistent, is marked. The cult of female saints remained strong, however: more female Lives survive from this era than from any earlier period, eulogizing a number of female saints—Ita, Monenna, Samthann, and Lassair, in addition to Brigit, showing the cult of the female saint in action. This period also saw a parallel and even greater increase in the number of male Lives. Written in Latin and Irish, these corroborate the suggestion of the female Lives that unease about women increased during this era; indeed they contain examples of what looks like extreme misogyny. It is such extracts that are usually quoted by historians making the generalization that the early Irish church was ascetic about sexuality. Examined in greater depth, however, the Lives reveal a more complex set of attitudes, which demonstrate instead that female saints remained important in the world of devotion, as indeed did nuns and other holy women.

The second trend is a new defensiveness about the Irish male saints' historic intimacy with the opposite sex, of which the most extreme expression was rise of the *topos* of the holy man's female consort. Called 'syneisactism', the phenomenon of chaste proto-marriage between a male cleric and a dedicated virgin is found in late antique texts and has been noted by historians of early Christianity, but in Ireland it first appears as a feature in hagiographical accounts in this period, in the tenth century.

The third is a tone of negotiation with the 'new order', in which there is an acknowledgement of changing times and a need for those in orders to avoid

---

[6] Bernard of Clairvaux, Life of St Malachy of Armagh, esp. books 1, 6.

[7] e.g. reference to the abbot of Kells' wife, Mor of Mag Sainb, in a poem attributed to Cormac mac Cuileannáin (O. Bergin, in D. Greene and F. Kelly (eds.), *Irish Bardic Poetry* (Dublin, 1970), 213–14, 314); also the hereditary anchorites of Clonmacnois, discussed in A. Kehnel, *Clonmacnois, the Church and Lands of St Ciarán: Change and Continuity in an Irish Monastic Foundation (6th–16th Century)* (Munster, 1995), 133–44; and the ecclesiastical parentage of St Malachy, Bernard of Clairvaux, Life of St Malachy, book 1, chs. 1–3.

situations which lay them open to suspicion of sexual scandal. Women *per se* are more of a topic than they ever were in preceding centuries, and one finds more explorations of such emblems of the female sex as Eve, the Virgin Mary, and Herod's women. Texts such as *Mé Eba Ben* (a poem in the voice of Adam's wife) and the *Saltair na Rann* (an account of Genesis) take up the issue of 'the female sex', but tend to betray a remarkable level of compassion for even that most culpable of women in the whole of the Christian tradition.

As the reforms dawned on the horizon, Ireland in large part continued to treat the female sex with a regard, bolstered theological and ecclesiastically, which was increasingly at odds with the general trends elsewhere in the West, a position which it evidently knew made it a target of criticism.

THE IRISH SOURCES

The Irish sources for this period are extremely uneven. The legal material consists of glosses on the classical eighth-century texts rather than main texts *per se*; there are few theological tracts and, importantly, virtually no contemporary texts describing in present-day terms such things as clerical issues or monastic life. Instead, a veritable mountain of more challenging texts presents itself to the historian. First to be mentioned is the hagiographic and devotional material; it consists of the very many Latin and Middle Irish saints' Lives (many of which were edited by Charles Plummer and W. Heist) and a fascinating Life of Patrick known as the Tripartite Life or the *Vita Tripartita*. On the poetry side, there are scores of litanies, hymns, lyrical verses, and other poems on religious themes. Glosses too are vast in number and include hagiographic notes, rhymes, and stories; some of the most interesting are those appended to the martyrologies of Oengus and Tallaght and to such earlier poems and hymns as *Ní Car Brigit*.

The shortcomings of the material are considerable, for all their volume. Little, for example, can be said about women's legal or canonical status, or about the monasteries and monastic life. The Lives are of little use as evidence for monastic practice at the time of their composition, as they purport to describe a world which existed half a millennium earlier. That said, it is possible to explore in considerable depth such topics as female sanctity, female sin, clerical celibacy, sex segregation, and the notion of ritual impurity. The remaining chapters, therefore, will concentrate on the areas about which the texts are most revealing, namely mentalities and attitudes.

The later saints' Lives are many, numbering approximately eighty, and are located in two main collections, the Kilkennensis and the Salmanticensis, both of which are described and analysed in depth by Richard Sharpe in his *Medieval Irish Saints' Lives*. The female Lives of this period contain the bulk of the evidence on nuns and female sanctity. So a few words on their composition and manuscript survival are warranted.

Beatha Lasrach, the Life of Lassair, is a late Middle Irish Life, most probably initially composed in the twelfth century. It is from the Stowe MS B IV I, fos. 97b to 103a, copied and the language modernized by David O'Duigenan in 1670. It is unfinished, and the scribe's note shows that the conclusion was missing in the manuscript.[8]

The Latin Life of Samthann exists in one form only, and was deemed by Kenney to be 'late and brief'; it probably dates from the twelfth or thirteenth century. It is in the Codex Insulensis collection, which exists in three manuscript forms; the earliest dates between the late thirteenth and early fourteenth centuries.[9] Plummer's edition, collated from all three, shows little variation amongst them and no major additions or omissions.[10] Dorothy Bray believes it is the work of a single author or redactor, citing the consistency of the style and language and the order in support of this assertion; furthermore, only once does the chronological progression seem to falter. She proposes that the Life was composed only shortly before the Codex Insulensis was compiled, and considers that possibly the original Life was redrafted expressly for inclusion in the collection.[11]

The Latin Life of Ita exists in three recensions. One manuscript (Bodl. Rawl. MS B505, fos. 169–72v) is Austrian, from the twelfth century, *c.*1127 × 1140. Plummer, for his edition, used a manuscript in the Dublin collection (Codex Kilkennensis, fos. 109v–112v), written probably around *c.*1220. The third manuscript (Bodl. MS 240) dates from the fourteenth century, and is a short epitome made by John of Tynemouth. Although Kenney believed that all versions went back to a seventh-century original, Sharpe finds this unlikely.[12] The Kilkennensis version contains a reference to an individual 'whose son still lives'; if this were true, noted Kenney, it would place the original text of the passage to not later than the mid-seventh century; so on this basis Kenney opted for dating some passages to the seventh century. It must be remembered, however, that such 'touches of verisimilitude' were on occasion manufactured out of whole cloth by hagiographers.[13]

The Life of Monenna by Conchubranus exists in a sole manuscript (BL MS Cotton Cleopatra A ii), which Esposito dated to the first half of the twelfth century; the Life itself he thought originally composed between 1000 and 1050. The author was an Irishman, possibly a cleric of Kildare, who had visited Killevy, had seen the relics of the saint, and had journeyed there several times on foot.[14]

[8] L. Gwynn (ed. and trans.), '*Beatha Lasrach*' *Ériu* 5 (1911), 73–109.

[9] The definitive in-depth study of the major collections of saints' Lives, including the Insulensis and Kilkennensis collections and the Codex Salmanticensis, is Sharpe, *Saints' Lives*.

[10] Plummer's own introduction to the text is in *PVSH* i., pp. lxxxvii–viii, and the edition itself is in ii. 253–61.

[11] D. Bray, 'Motival Derivations in the Life of St Samthann', *Studia Celtica* 20–1 (1985–6), 78–86, at 79–80.

[12] Sharpe, *Saints' Lives*, 16.   [13] *Kenney*, p. lxxiii.

[14] Edited first by Mario Esposito in *PRIA* 28C (1910), 197–251, and more recently by the Ulster Society for Medieval Latin Studies in *Seanchas Ard Mhacha* 9.2 (1979), 250–73; 10.1 (1980–1), 117–41; 10.2 (1982), 426–53. Her anonymous Life in the Codex Salmanticensis is edited in *Heist*, 83–95. For descriptions of the two texts, see *Kenney*, no. 160.

Esposito attempted to render the text usable to the historian, believing that the redactor interposed unaltered whole chapters of a seventh-century *vita*.[15]

The Latin Life of Darerca, also called Monenna. In this Latin Life Monenna is called by her original name, Darerca. It is in the well-known fourteenth-century manuscript, Codex Salmanticensis (Brussels no. 3179, fos. 79r–82v), which contains mostly male Lives. The text itself is of uncertain date; Zimmer placed it 'later than the tenth century'; Kenney considered that 'it is not older than the twelfth century, and quite possibly is not much older than the Codex'. Sharpe believed that the Lives in the codex, including this one, were essentially faithful to their older sources, and he was of the view that the exemplar for this was dated to the seventh century.[16]

The Burton-on-Trent Lives of Monenna/Modwenna. There are two other versions of the Life of Monenna, compiled by or under Geoffrey, abbot of the Benedictine Abbey of the Blessed Mary and Saint Modwen, Burton-upon-Trent, from 1114 to 1151; BL MS Lansdowne 436, fos. 126v–131v, and BL MS Cotton Tiberius E i, fos. 199v–204v. Both are English and deeply problematical, and so have not been used.

The Homily on the Life of Brigit in the Leabhar Breac. Not, strictly speaking a Life, but it very much resembles one. This Middle Irish homily appears with two others, on Patrick and Columcille, in the fifteenth-century codex, the Leabhar Breac. Like the other, it was collated in 1100 or later, but the date of actual composition is uncertain. Stokes, who edited this and the other two homilies in the manuscript, noted the frequent use of infixed pronouns and the many Old and Early Middle Irish verbal forms but did not propose a date, and Richard Sharpe has recently reiterated the uncertainty involved in any such attempt.[17]

The Homily on the Life of Brigit in the Book of Lismore has a great deal of similarity to that in the Leabhar Breac, but the overlap is not complete, for each has a anecdotes the other lacks.[18]

Brigit's *Vita IV*, largely copied from her *Vita I*, is the work of a redactor working *c.*1200 who has been studied by Richard Sharpe. It is a testament to the continued interest in Brigit, but its usefulness to the historian lies mostly in what can be learnt from it about the redactor, 'D'. Sharpe's work on 'D' has shown the latter to be a copyist who made few changes in his exemplars, apart from adding the occasional Biblical quote, clarifying sentence, or minimization of saints' sexual impropriety such as inducing miraculous abortions.

One male Life must be mentioned individually, namely the *Tripartite Life of Patrick*. This long text, written in a combination of Irish and Latin, is found in a

[15]   Esposito, 'Sources'.

[16]   Sharpe, *Saints' Lives*, 243–6, with references. Johnston, 'Transforming Women', 210.

[17]   In W. Stokes (ed. and trans.), *Three Middle Irish Homilies on the Lives of Saints Patrick, Brigit and Columba* (Calcutta, 1877), 50–89; linguistic forms, p. viii. On dating, see Sharpe, *Saints' Lives*, 23.

[18]   Homily on the Life of Brigit in the Book of Lismore, in W. Stokes (ed.), *Lives of the Saints from the Book of Lismore* (London, 1890), 34–53.

small number of fourteenth- to sixteenth-century manuscripts. It is of disputed date, attributed variously to the tenth, eleventh, and twelfth centuries. A detailed account of the history of the scholarly debates on its date has recently been rehearsed by David Dumville, so does not need to be repeated here.[19] It suffices to note that the confident placing of the text by its original editor, Kathleen Mulchrone, to the years 895 × 901 has been demolished, and Dumville considers that the field is wide open; he says that a date in the latter twelfth century has to be considered as a real possibility. Richard Sharpe, however, continues to place it in the tenth century.[20] Many others view it as essentially a tenth-century composition with later accreted layers.

Other sources are mainly glosses and scholia on earlier texts. Most important are those elaborating the Martyrology of Oengus, for these date from the tenth or eleventh centuries and are particularly rich, including hagiographical stories, place-lore, poems and place-lore. There are also glosses on earlier poems such as the voluminous notes on the Old Irish compositions *Ní Car Brigit* and *Brigit Bé Bithmaith*, and these are immensely useful. The law tracts too, are ornamented with interlinear and marginal commentaries from the tenth, eleventh, and twelfth centuries; these give clues as to the interpretation and application in this era of the previously-codified legal principles as Nerys Patterson has showed, rather than being worthless and confused antiquarian additions as had often been thought.[21] Later material of use includes the litanies and hymns whose date of composition can be narrowed down to what is called by linguists the 'Middle Irish' period, *c*.900–*c*.1200.

---

[19] D. Dumville, 'The Dating of the Tripartite Life of St Patrick' in Dumville, *Saint Patrick*, 255–8. The dating of the text hinges on linguistic forms. In the process by which proposed dates have been reached for this text 'the element of circularity is very considerable' (Dumville, 'Dating', 258).

[20] Sharpe, *Saints' Lives*, 20.

[21] N. Patterson, 'Brehon Law in Late Medieval Ireland: "Antiquarian and Obsolete" or "Traditional and Functional"?' *Cambridge Medieval Celtic Studies* 17 (1989), 43–63.

7

Nuns, Abbesses, Saints, and their Monasteries, c.900–1200

By all accounts much of female religious life was little affected by the changes of the tenth, eleventh, and early twelfth centuries. The structure of the professions, for example, seems unchanged. The two types of nun, the virgin and the penitent-widow, continued to exist. Two litanies from the earlier Middle Irish period compiled in the *Liber Hymnorum* attest to this, as one was for use by religious virgins, the other for holy widows. Virgins at their veiling continued to be enrobed in white, as late as *c.*1200, for redactor 'D', working on Brigit's Life, added to his exemplar (the *Vita I*) the specification that white had been the colour of Brigit's garment at her consecration.[1] The commentaries from (probably) the eleventh century on *Cáin Adomnáin* speak of the penitent nuns who wear a white garment with a black border. This comment on their dress is to my knowledge the only one in the Irish corpus and as such is quite notable—it seems reasonable to think that this had been the standard garb for them in earlier centuries as well.[2] The second tier of the nun's profession looks largely the same as well. Holy widows continued to appear in hagiography: one Irish Life, for example, specified that Ciarán's fostermother had been a holy widow, a *feadhbh craibtech*, and hagiographical glosses claimed that Brigit had originally sought the order of penitence (*grád aithrige*) from the bishops she visited as a maiden.[3] Hagiography also continued to portray religious women who were pilgrims and solitary hermits.[4] In England, during the reforms of the tenth and eleventh century, a new nun term appeared, *mynecena*, meaning a female monk and connoting holiness; the older general term, Pauline Stafford observes, was often used in a new way, denoting nuns of a status below that of the *mynecena*. According to Stafford's analysis, monks were ranked above priests as *mynecena* were ranked above *nunnas*.[5] This appears to have no parallel in Ireland.

---

[1] *Vita IV* of Brigit, book 2, ch. 77. Noted by Sharpe, *Saints' Lives*, 201.

[2] White veil (*caille finn*) of penitent widow in Lament of the Caillech Béirre; white veil with black border specified for penitent nuns in the (probably) 11th-cent. commentary on *Cáin Adomnáin*. For a possible patristic precedent on the use of a garment with a border stripe by not-quite virginal nuns, see Jerome, *Ep.* 22, ch. 13: 'their robes have but a narrow purple stripe, it is true'.

[3] Martyrology of Oengus, notes on 1 Feb.; glosses on the hymn *Ní Car Brigit*.

[4] Third Irish Life of Coemgen, ch. 18; Life of Darerca, ch. 24 (*Heist*, 83–95).

[5] P. Stafford, 'Gender, Religious Status and Reform in England', *Past and Present* 163 (2000), 1–35, at 11.

There is a small possibility that there were Benedictine nuns at Glendalough in the twelfth century. St Coemgen's Middle Irish Lives speak of a group of 'black nuns' who lived at the monastery, joined by two women he raised from the dead.[6] One Life says simply in prose that he 'made black nuns of them in his own church' (*doroine caillecha dubha dibh ina cill féin*). The other, not directly related to the first, contains the same anecdote in verse:

> Rucc Caoimghin beo don bhaile
> Na mná dar benadh a ccinn,
> 'S doróin dibh caillecha dubha
> Craibhtecha, cubdha, 'na chill.

> Coemgen brought home alive
> The women whose heads had been cut off,
> And made them black nuns
> Devout and proper in his church.

This term 'black nun' is a new one for Ireland, and the suggestion is that they were Benedictine, given what we know about the Irish use of white even for penitents' robes. Plummer, editing the text, thought so. It is hard to know what would have prompted such a distinctive enclave to evolve there. The contacts between England and Ireland were not inconsiderable in this period in the ecclesiastical sphere; Irishmen are found at monasteries and cathedral schools in the west of Britain, and 'Saxons' were active enough to have established a church in Mayo, and there is considerable evidence of mutual fertilization in religious texts. A British inspiration would thus appear more likely than a directly Continental one. A less likely possibility is that the author was using 'black nun' to mean penitent nuns, if at the time of writing garb of this grade had changed from white with a black border to a fully black garment: this hardly seems likely, though, since the women had been religious *caillecha* on holy pilgrimage. Because the dates of the Middle Irish Lives are uncertain, and because the Latin Life of Coemgen redacted by 'D' *c.*1200 does not contain any references to black nuns, it may be that the Lives, and the black nuns, both date to the thirteenth century.

The educational level of nuns in this period, as it may have been in the earlier centuries, appears to have been quite high. The Lives speak not only of the high level of erudition of the female saints, but of the nuns themselves reading, teaching students the psalms (the text on which most learned to read Latin), and lending manuscripts. Thus Monenna's virgins taught a converted king as well as a princess, and also read to themselves.[7] So great was Killevy's reputation, it claimed, that one girl travelled all the way from Britain to study there and she

---

[6] First Irish Life of Coemgen, ch. 18 (*BNE* i. 125–30; Eng trans., ii. 121–6); Second Irish Life of Coemgen, ch. 19 (*BNE* i. 131–54; Eng. trans., ii. 127–50). Textual discussion in Plummer, *BNE*, i., pp. xxvii–xxxii.

[7] Conchubranus, Life of Monenna, book 2, chs. 11, 15.

was so successful as a student that she eventually became an abbess herself in her native land.[8] Kildare's longstanding excellence as a centre of learning is attested by centuries of obits of scholars and, in this period, by Gerald of Wales's story about Kildare's beautiful Gospels which were said to have been written out during the foundress's lifetime at an angel's dictation, 'with Brigit praying, and the scribe imitating'.[9]

Direct evidence of female literacy is provided by two prayers for salvation in the twelfth-century collection known as the *Liber Hymnorum*. Though both are interesting, the first provides the stronger case for actual private reading. *A Sláinicidh* is a Middle Irish litany addressed to the saviour of the human race written in the first person singular, by a woman who ended her petition with the wish 'that I may merit a place of rest among the religious widows in the unity of the heavenly church in the presence of the Trinity' (*Gorro airillnigher sosad cumsantach etir na fedbaib iresachaib i noentaig na hecalsa nemdai, i frecnarcus na Trinoti*).[10] The nature of the prayer may reflect the status of the petitioner as a widow-penitent, for it is focused on seeking forgiveness from sins committed in the world. The widow praised Christ as physician of illness and misery, and outlined his incarnation through the Virgin Mary, his crucifixion and salvation of humanity from hell, his ascension into heaven and his future presiding at Judgement. She went on to seek forgiveness for her sins, and asked for the seven cardinal virtues to counteract the seven deadly sins, concluding this penultimate section by asking additional protection against lust. The Litany is found in four manuscripts: Bodleian Rawlinson MS B.512; Brussels MS 4190; BM Additional MS 30, 512; BM MS Egerton 92. There are some variations among the copies, in general a sign of individual use in private devotions, according to Plummer.[11] Without further work on the manuscripts, it is not possible even to guess as to provenance, though Clonmacnois was tentatively proposed by Plummer. This prayer was read, learnt, and used by at least a handful of Irish nuns of the widow-penitent grade—the actual reading and personal use by several distinct individuals being evidenced in the fact that the different copies all have slight personalizations. The other prayer, *Impide Maire*, appears immediately after *A Sláinicidh* in three of the same four manuscripts, which led some scholars to think it was a second part of it. Plummer thought not, for it is composed in the first person plural whereas *A Sláinicidh* is in a singular voice.[12] He was certainly correct, because it is evident

---

[8] Life of Darerca, ch. 25.   [9] Gerald of Wales, *Topographia*, book 2, ch. 72.

[10] Plummer translated *fedbaib iresachaib* as 'faithful widows', but I would argue for 'religious widows'; see *Dictionary* on *ires*, demonstrating that it connotes religion in an organized sense, and a person's rule or manner of life, as much as it does personal faith.

[11] *A Sláinicidh* ('O Saviour'): *Kenney*, no. 589, 'Litany to the Saviour and the Saints', part 1. Discussed in Plummer, *Irish Litanies*, pp. xvi–xvii; edition and trans. based on Rawlinson MS in Plummer, *Litanies*, 20–3, under the title 'Litany of the Saviour'; edition based on the Brussels MS by K. Meyer, *Otia Merseiana*, ii. 98–9.

[12] *Impide Maire*: *Kenney*, no. 589, 'Litany to the Saviour and the Saints', part 2: 'it seems to be complementary to part one, but may be separate.' MSS: Bodleian Rawlinson MS B.512; Brussels MS 4190;

that the collective prayer was written for nuns of the virginal grade. The nuns prayed not to forsake their marriage to their noble espoused bridegroom Jesus Christ so that in heaven 'we may sing the song that only virgins sing, that we merit the crown of eternal glory' (*coro canam an canntaic nád canat achd oigh, coro airillnigem coroin na glóire suthaine*). Like the widow's litany, this one addressed the problem of sexual urges in a significant location, in this case very near the outset: praying for purification of the senses it commenced with asking God 'to subdue our fleshly lusts and to check our unfitting thoughts' (*do troethad ar tol collaide, do cossc are nimraitiud nanairches*), but there was no suggestion of a worldly past. As with the private widow's litany, there are minor variations among the three MS versions, indicating its actual use, though perhaps not individual use.

As for nuns' legal and ecclesiastical status in these centuries little can be said, for there is almost nothing on them in the glosses on the vernacular law tracts, which would be the main source for such an investigation. One is reduced to such observations as the fact that Irish Lives portrayed female saints other than Brigit as delegates at early synods, such as the virgin Cainnle who attended a church council at which she had a vision which was of great help to the assembly.[13] Almost as unsatisfactory, for all that it is contemporary, is the mystifying remark by the *Cáin Adomnáin* commentator: 'Now, after the coming of Adomnán, no good woman is deprived of her testimony, if it be bound by righteous deeds' (*Iar tíachtain do Adamnán, hifecta ní gatar forgall ar domun degmná, mád i ngnímaib fíraib forsither*). Evidently the legal competence of at least some women was perceived to have improved. If women were in fact able to use 'good deeds' to establish their worthiness then the proportion of women able to give testimony would have increased since the day of the writing down of the classical vernacular tracts at the turn of the eighth century. However, in the absence of more on the subject, no conclusions may be drawn with safety.

The matter of enclosure appears not to change: in all the extant material holy women are evidently as peripatetic as they wish to be, and there are no perceptible pressures for them to stay within the confines of the convent. Not only are the later Lives of the major female saints as full of travel and wandering as the earlier ones, but equally incidental mentions in the other texts make it evident that for less exalted nuns the monastery or church was more a sanctified place at which to do God's work than a haven from the outside world.

In England in this era there was an upsurge of queenly involvement in monasteries, a subject on which Pauline Stafford has written in some depth.[14] The role of the queen in the English reforms was not paralleled in Ireland: there

---

BM Additional MS 30, 512. Edition based on Rawlinson MS, Plummer, *Litanies*, 26–7, as 'Litany of the Virgin and All Saints'; edition based on Brussels MS, Meyer, *Otia Merseiana*, ii. 99–100. Discussion in Plummer, *Litanies*, p. xvii.

[13] Irish Life of Carthach *alias* Mochuda 'The Expulsion of Mochuda', ch. 3.

[14] Most recently, 'Gender', with references, but see also her *Queen Emma and Queen Edith: Queenship and Women's Power in Eleventh-Century England* (Oxford, 1997), ch. 6.

was no contemporary reform movement, nor was kingship at a similar stage of development there. There are indications of queenly involvement in women's communities, but we cannot know how much this might represent a new trend because we cannot see how queens were involved in earlier centuries. One may, however, note that in the twelfth century the wife of an extremely powerful Irish king rebuilt the nun's church at Clonmacnois and was a donor to the new Cistercian house of Mellifont; and that queens, like kings, often chose to die and be buried at monasteries.[15]

ABBESSES IN THE TENTH TO TWELFTH CENTURIES

Abbess obits continue to be noted in the annals, mostly those of Kildare abbesses. This may have been as a result of a centralization of power on Kildare at the expense of other female houses, or may simply reflect scribal habits. The annals entries also tell us that the post of Brigit's coarb ceased to be held by a virgin: the abbesses Gormflaith (obit 1112) and Sadb (obit 1171), according to the annals, 'died in penitence'.[16] This phrase, applied to men as well as women in the annals, manifestly does not imply any stigma: the term most certainly refers to those who turned to the religious life as adults or in older age. Penitent nuns were the second tier of nuns and, it will be recalled, were often equated with widows. It is not clear whether the abbesses held their offices whilst still living secular lives, as many managerial abbots did, or whether they took the office after turning from the worldly life and taking the veil. A few facts point towards the latter. In both the 1041 and 1131 seizures of Kildare the abbess was dragged from her place. In both cases the takeover was established by raping her. In the 1131 entry the raped abbess is referred to as the *caillech*, the nun. *Caillech* may have been an alternative term for a nun abbess in these centuries: this is the most reasonable interpretation of the very enigmatic 1042 obit of the Nun of Finnian (*Caillech Finnéin*) who seems likely to have been the head of a female community at Clonard or Moville.[17]

The female monastic manager appears in this era too, for the annals attest a *banairchinnech* at the Columban church of Derry.[18] A homily on Brigit's life uses the term *banairchinnech* to refer to the abbess, clearly a traditionally monastic one, of a convent in Brigit's day, which points to a certain looseness in the use of the term in some quarters at least.

In the Lives of this later period, the abbess comes across as an independent actor in legal terms and within, it seems, the ecclesiastical structure. Like the earlier ones described in a preceding chapter, the later Lives also portray

---

[15] On Irish queenship, see A. Connon, 'The Banshenchas and the Uí Néill Queens of Tara', in Smyth, *Seanchas*, 98–108, and also M. Ní Dhonnchadha, 'On Gormfhlaith Daughter of Flann Sinna and the Lure of the Sovereignty Goddess', in ibid. 225–37.
[16] AFM 1112; AU 1171.   [17] ATig 1042.   [18] AFM 1134.

abbesses overseeing and vouching for their nuns. There is continuity in that they too show them acting as 'heads', i.e. in a manner similar to fathers to their daughters, or male relatives to women kin. In the Latin Life of Enda, for example, the abbess of Clonbroney is *cenn caillech*, 'head of nuns'. Abbesses in the saints' Lives also act like fathers in the arrangement of marriages: at the age of marriage, the laws assert, a 'head' could give a girl either to a husband or to the Church, and only a special category of girls were given the right to choose for themselves which life they would follow. The right to choose between marriage and a life in the Church is the prerogative of the 'woman of choice' or *bé togai*, who is allowed to decide herself whether to marry or be a nun (*tic di co aos togai na togai .i. in co fer theis fa inngaba chaille*).[19] In three relevant hagiographic anecdotes a sainted abbess arranges the marriage of one of her girls. In the Latin Life of Mochoemóg, the abbess involved is Ita. Her sister Ness wanted to be a nun, but Ita insisted on giving her to a man in marriage, comforting her with the assurance that a wonderful child would be born from the union. Here Ita acts like a 'head' and does not give her sister the choice of which husband she is to have:

Ipse honorificus artifex in lignis et lapidibus erat, audax in militia. Ipse amavit quendam pulcram feminam multum pudicam, ingenuam, de Mumenia, videlicet de gente na nDesi, que erat soror sanctissime virginis Ythe. Ipsa femina vocabatur Ness; que volebat vivere in castitate in evum, sicut sancte virgines que antea virum nesciebant. Set sancta virgo Yta, sua soror, eam dedit Beoano in uxorem, egregio artifici.[20]

This same honoured man was an architect in wood and stone, and brave in warfare. He loved a beautiful woman, very modest and refined, from Munster, of the Dési people, who was the sister of the very holy virgin Ita. This woman was called Ness, and she wished to live permanently in chastity like the holy virgins who never before knew a man. But the holy virgin Ita, her sister, gave her to Beoan, the eminent architect, as his wife.

The same principles are found in the story as it is related in the Latin Life of Ita. In this version, however, marriage is arranged by the abbess as part of a financial arrangement.

Quidam bonus artifex, qui erat homo honorabilis de provinchia Connachtorum, in exilio ad terram Mumenensium venit. Et audiens beata Yta famam artis eius, rogatus est ab ea, ut ageret sibi edificia. Ille vero artifex quesivit sibi uxorem a sancta Yta et agrum ad habitandum. Et beatissima Yta dedit ei sororem suam, et agrum in quo maneret. Et ille cum omni devotione edificia in monasterio sancte Yta agebat.[21]

A good architect, who was an honourable man from the province of Connaught, came in exile to the land of Munster. And Ita, hearing of the eminence of his work, asked him to make some buildings for her. This architect asked Ita for a wife and for fields on which to live. And the blessed Ita gave him her sister and land on which to stay. And he with all devotion constructed buildings at Ita's monastery.

---

[19] This was the *bé togai*, 'the woman of choice', discussed in Power, 'Classes of Women', 107–8.
[20] Latin Life of Mochoemóg, D text (*PVSH* ii. 164–83), ch. 1.   [21] Life of Ita, ch. 18.

In the Latin Life of Enda, a young nobleman came from battle to the monastery of his sister Faenche, the abbess of Rossory in Fermanagh near Lough Erne (Ir. Ross Airthir). He made a deal with her whereby he would do what she asked providing she gave him one of her girls to marry.[22] She went to one of her fosterlings and asked the girl which husband she preferred, God or the man, whereupon the girl chose God by dying on the spot. Faenche then proceeded to talk Enda out of marriage and sex altogether while showing him the girl's corpse.[23] By deciding which girl to select and making her choose between that particular suitor and lifelong chastity, the abbess acted like a 'head' in the laws. She did, however, treat the girl like a *bé togai*, a girl who could at least choose the Church if she wanted to.

The headship of abbesses was not always this extreme in its resemblance to the behaviour of a legal 'head', but the supervisory role is stressed very heavily in the later hagiography, as it was in the earlier. In the Lives of this period, an abbess's freedom to oversee her nuns as she saw fit is seemingly unhindered by any male authority. And what do they actually do? Responsible for practical upkeep of the nuns, they arrange the procurement of food and beer in times of shortage, and ask for assistance in the form of supplies from other monasteries and nunneries at such times. They supervise the physical structure of the monastery, arrange building and construction, and sometimes negotiate payment for the builders and architect. They also procure other, more ecclesiastical resources: the holy abbess Scíath of Ardskeagh sent for a scribe from a men's house, and the abbot dispatched the scribe to the nunnery to do what she requested: write out the text of the four evangelists for the nuns.[24] In another Life, an abbess sent a nun to take a holy book to another nunnery. Abbesses in these later Lives also supervised the taking on of fosterlings, accepted abandoned babies, and received children's parents when they visited. This is very much the sort of thing seen in earlier Lives. In the hagiography there were rumblings but no revolution in church authors' views of abbesses. Whatever was happening in practice for women of the church at this time, they still inhabited a *mundus* wherein female sanctity was believed to have the potential to wield significant power.

MONASTERIES

Political events and trends at monasteries are evidenced primarily by the annals, the entries of which are fuller in this era than before. In some cases, affiliations with particular dynasties or kin-groups are perceptible, but not always. The

---

[22] Martyrology of Oengus, 21 Jan.; Martyrology of Gorman 1 Jan.; AFM 1084, which must refer to a re-foundation.

[23] Latin Life of Enda, chs. 2–3.

[24] Latin Life of Ailbe, D text, ch. 32 (*PVSH* i. 46–64). Scíath is there misprinted as Scletha.

annals are not on their own a good indicator of a female establishment's success, because failure to register the deaths of abbesses may reflect scribal regionalism or other habits. For this reason it is worth noting also the presence of any remains at the site of the monastery and evidence of rebuilding during the twelfth century.

Relics, too, are worth noting. They had really started to come into their own in the eighth century in Ireland, and are prominent from that time onwards. Items belonging to a church's founding saint were kept in elaborate metal reliquaries and, like relics elsewhere in the West, Irish ones were used in political and social life. Oaths were sworn on them, they were taken on circuits for the collection of revenue, they were taken into battle, and they were brought to assemblies (*oenachs*).[25] They continued to be instruments of healing, blessing, and cursing: they might be carried around people, objects, or buildings—clockwise or *deosil* to bless, anti-clockwise to curse.[26] The relics which survive most, and which appear in the texts to have been most esteemed by later generations, were saints' bells and croziers (bachalls); significantly, neither of these were exclusively—or even particularly—associated with men. Female saints' items, including bells and bachalls, evidently survived, for the texts of this period refer to them being venerated, and furthermore venerated by both sexes. As for their use, no less than male saints' relics they were deemed effective in battle for defeating enemies. Lassair's hagiographer, for example, suggests indirectly that her handbell, which went by the name 'Ceolán Lasrach', was still in existence at the time he was writing—and the author of the extant text's exemplar lived in the twelfth century.[27] Female relics were considered as worth collecting as men's, and their power was in no way less than that of male saints. This is illustrated, for example, in the way in which the hagiographer describes Drumlane's great collection, allegedly bequeathed to it by Maedóc, in particular its large ornate reliquary:

Fáccbaim fos Clocc an deilcc, 7 clocc na ttrath i nDruim Lethan, 7 an mionn oirderc ilcumhachtach ele .i. mo minister maisech mó ir-fhertach, no bodh ar aistter i ngach ionad accam, ina bfiul ní do thasaibh na naomh 7 na nuasal-aithreach .i. taisi Steafain mairtir, 7 Laurint, 7 Clemint, 7 ina bfiul mudhorn Martan, 7 cuid d'folt Maire, maille le morán do thaisibh na naomh 7 na naomh-ogh archena, 'arna comhroinn 7 'arna comhbrecadh eter an Bric 7 an menister; óir as aire adberar an Bhrec fría, ó comhmbrecadh taisedh na naomh 7 na naomh-ogh a náoinfeacht.[28]

---

[25]   On relics, C. Doherty, 'The Use of Relics in Early Ireland', in Ní Chatháin and Richter, *Irland und Europa*, 89–101; A. T. Lucas, 'The Social Role of Relics and Reliquaries', *JRSAI* 116 (1986), 5–37.

[26]   Out of date in terms of interpretations, but rich in specific textual references is *PVSH* i., pp. clxxiii–clxxx; similarly S. Ferguson, 'On the Ceremonial Turn Called Desiul', *Proceedings of the Royal Irish Academy*, second series, 1 (1877). The clockwise circumambulation remained important in Celtic modern folk custom, and thence was adopted into the rites of revived paganism, adopting the Irish term *deosil* (G. Gardner, *Witchcraft Today* (London, 1954), 25; S. Farrar, *The Witches' Way* (London, 1984), 56–81, *passim*).

[27]   Irish Life of Lassair (Gwynn, 'Beatha Lasrach', 78–81, 100–1).

[28]   Second Irish Life of Maedóc, ch. 72 (*BNE* i. 191–290; Eng. trans., ii. 184–281).

I further leave 'The Bell of the Brooch' and 'The Bell of the Hours' to Drumlane, together with the other illustrious and potent relic, that is, my beautiful wonder-working reliquary, which travelled with me everywhere, in which are relics of the saints and patriarchs, i.e. relics of the martyr Stephen, Lawrence, and Clement, and the ankle of Martin, and some of the Virgin Mary's hair, and many other remains of saints and women-saints besides, which had been divided between the Brecc and the reliquary; and this is why the name Brecc was given to it, because of the variegated arrangement together of the relics of the saints and women-saints which had been united and made fast in it.

For this collector the relics of female saints were not different, distinct, or of less value than those of males. He twice used the phrase 'saints and women-saints' in the short passage as part of the boast of the reliquary's abundance of holy remains. At the monasteries of women as much as men, the relics of virgins were preserved, taken on circuit, and used to attract devotees and pilgrims.

Large, well-endowed nunneries in England appear to have suffered in the tenth and eleventh centuries, on account of the changes brought about by the Benedictine reforms there. Numerous Anglo-Saxonists point out the the the absence of records from female houses in this period, in contrast with the abundant evidence for the earlier centuries. In Ireland the sources show unbroken continuity, though Ireland's nunneries faced the challenge of Viking attacks rather than the likes of Aelfric and Dunstan. The cult of female saints remained equally strong, suffering no apparent waning such as has been noted in other parts of the West in this era.

Cloonburren

Though Cloonburren was very near two of Ireland's major ecclesiastical centres, Clonmacnoise and Clonfert on the River Shannon in the rich midlands, it is unmentioned in any annals. It may well have disappeared as a religious community, though there is a small chance it did carry on as such, given that the place is mentioned in 1226 as a site, where soldiers had been placed to defend it, of a battle between two dynasties.

Killevy and Monenna

Killevy remained important in this period, and so correspondingly did its foundress Monenna. In this period she of all the saints of Ireland was the one recalled for her fasting.[29] Her two extant Lives date from the later era, and the Conchubranus Life in particular attests to the spread of her cult to England and Scotland. She was included in the later martyrologies, those of Gorman

---

[29] *Carais Pattraic* ('Patrick Loved', or 'Cuimmín's Hymn') on the virtues of many Irish saints, ed. and trans. W. Stokes, 'Cuimmín's Poem on the Saints of Ireland', *ZCP* 1 (1897), 59–73.

and Donegal, and was given extensive glosses in the earlier ones of Oengus and Tallaght.

Killevy continued to exist long after the arrival of English settlers and was not dissolved until 1542.[30] Not only does the early church still stand, but it does so along with the medieval stone church which superseded it.[31] In the annals, we hear that it was attacked by Vikings in 923, and that in 1029 Donnchadh Ua Donncain, king of Fermoy, and Cinaeth mac in Geirrci, king of the Conaill, fell in a duel there.[32] In the twelfth and thirteenth centuries saint Enda's church claimed an ancient friendship with the foundress. The Martyrology of Oengus glosses claim links between Killevy and various male houses by calling Monenna the foster mother of Ciarán of Clonmacnois and of 'Laissrén the Happy' of Iona and 'Laissrén the Great' of Min. The first Laissrén, of Iona, might refer to the abbot of that name who died in 605. The second is unknown unless it means to refer to Laissrén of Devenish.[33] In the thirteenth century it is mentioned in the Latin Life of Enda of Aran, with the Life claiming a tie between the saints' two institutions.[34]

Monenna's relics, too, were evident in this period, for in her Life she bequeathed to the place her leather garment, hoe, and other tools, but specified that her body and bachall were to go elsewhere. The former relics are mentioned as early as the seventh century, in the two hymns to the saint, so perhaps they were genuine.[35]

Ballyvourney

Though there is no surviving Life of St Gobnat, her monastery deep in southern Munster has left remains and relics, indicating that worship at the site and devotion to the saint were continuous.[36] The remains, south-west of the village, consist of a round beehive hut with traces of early iron-working (now called

---

[30]   It attracted a bit of antiquarian attention in the 19th cent., with two articles on the foundress appearing in Irish journals. While of scant historical value, one of them provided some sketches of the ruins of the nunnery as they appeared in the 1860s: G. Reade, 'Cill-Sleibhe-Cuillinn', *Journal of the Historical Association of Ireland* (forerunner of *JRSAI*) 3rd ser., 1 (1868–9), 93–101.

[31]   Latin Life of Enda, ch. 9.   [32]   AU 923; ATig 1029.

[33]   Conchubranus, Life of Monenna, book 3, ch. 13. Martyrology of Oengus, notes on 9 Sept. The text is unclear whether the Molaisse at Iona is the same one as that of Min, but it appears not to be. The short poem making up the gloss runs: *Morthrecheng nád donae / maNinn núall cech gena / in Hí Laissrén sona / la Laissrén mor Mena.* If the writer intended the second Laissrén to be the founder of Devenish he was confused: *Min* is the river Main which enters Lough Neagh, whereas the island monastery of Devenish is in Lough Erne. Obit of Laissrén of Iona: AU 605.

[34]   Latin Life of Enda, ch. 9 (*PVSH* ii. 60–75).

[35]   Conchubranus, Life of Monenna, book 3, ch. 9; Life of Darerca, ch. 30; hymns *Audite Fratres* and *Audite Sancta Studia.*

[36]   Gobnat is said to have been patron saint of bee-keepers. Harbison, *Pilgrimage*, 133–6; D. Harris, 'Saint Gobnet, Abbess of Ballyvourney', *JRSAI* 68 (1938), 272–7, with map and site photos. In *Journal of the Cork Historical and Archaeological Society* 57 (1952) see D. Ó hEaluighthe, 'St Gobnat of Ballyvourney', 43–60; M. J. O'Kelly, 'St Gobnat's House', 18–40; and F. Henry, 'Decorated Stones at Ballyvourney, Cork', 18–61.

'Gobnat's church', *Tigh Gobnatan*), a medieval church with a sheela-na-gig, and a mound of rocks surmounted by a ballaun stone which is alleged to be Gobnat's grave; some distance away is a holy well. It is still a pilgrimage site, particularly popular on Gobnat's feast day and Whit Sunday.

Killeedy

Mentions of Killeedy are absent from the annals, but the evident abundance of anecdotes on the saint more than suggests its continued existence. There was enough of a church there for it to be rebuilt in the Romanesque period, and the latter building remained standing until burning down in the early nineteenth century.[37] No sources to my knowledge refer to Ita's relics, either in these centuries or earlier, but the present church, rebuilt over its Romanesque predecessor, contains a grave claiming to be the saint's.

Looking at the tenth and eleventh-century Middle Irish Lives of male saints, one finds that Ita and her monastery have really come to prominence in two of them. In one of the Lives of Brendan, such a close relationship between the two is so fulsomely asserted that there must have been extremely cordial relations between the houses of Clonfert and Killeedy.[38] In the Second Irish Life of Maedóc, the male saint performed a miracle for Ita whilst in the neighbourhood on a visit to his confessor Molua mac Oiche, an episode which may represent a claim by Maedóc's monastery (Ferns) for some sort of tax from Killeedy.[39] Other hagiographers were keen to claim that their patron had known Ita, the great fosterer: such claims were made as well, though in less depth, in Lives of Carthach, Móchoemóg, and Cummean.[40] In these Killeedy is noted for its fostering of both young boys and girls, though there is no mention of monks in the *familia*. There may be a connection between the introduction of male leaders (and possibly monks) to the monastery and the seeming rise of prominence of the *topos* of the place as a fostering centre for boys, but the evidence is far too imperfect to speculate on the matter. The fostering *topos* remains strong in the twelfth- and thirteenth-century Latin Lives of the Plummer collection and figures strongly in the relevant twelfth-century glosses on the Martyrology of Oengus.[41] A poem on the characteristic virtues of the saints indicates that Ita

[37] Lord Killanin and M. Duignan, *The Shell Guide to Ireland* (London, 1962), 187; Hamlin and Hughes, *Modern Traveller*, 68.

[38] First Irish Life of Brendan, chs. 9, 10, 19, 92, 165 (*BNE* i. 44–95; Eng. trans., ii. 44–92).

[39] Second Irish Life of Maedóc, chs. 61, 67.

[40] Latin Life of Macdóc, D text, ch. 49 (*PVSH* ii. 141–63); Martyrology of Oengus, notes on 12 Nov., on Cummean; Latin Life of Carthach alias Mochuda, D text, ch. 30 (*PVSH* i. 170–99); Latin Life of Mochoemóc, D text, chs. 1–6, 8, 14–15, 20. From the 13th cent.: First Latin Life of Brendan, chs. 3, 4, 8, 71, 92 (*PVSH* i. 98–151).

[41] Ita and Killeedy, in the late Latin Lives of Brendan (*Vita I Sancti Brendani*), Carthach, and Mochoemóg. Ita as Mochoemog's teacher, Latin Life of Mochoemóg, chs. 1–6. Cummean Fota also said to have been fostered by her. Life of Maedóc ('Wales Translation') mentions Killeedy, ch. 48. Ita as fostermother of Brendan, probably in early lost Lives of Brendan; earliest extant reference in late Life

was remembered above all for her fostering and humility.[42] The fact that the Ita glosses are particularly rich in hagiographical minutiae may have some significance as to the relations between Killeedy and Tallaght at that time. In the twelfth or thirteenth century Killeedy itself was keen to show how well-connected it was: the Life of Ita portrays the monastery as a house of nuns which was well connected with numerous houses: Glendalough, Clonfert, Clonmacnois, Iona, as well as with a house of virgins at Cuscraid's Derry ('Daire Cusgrid') somewhere in Munster.[43]

Lassair's Churches: Three Killeshers, Kilronan, and Aghavea

Lassair and her churches continue to be mentioned in this era too, though there are some differences in the accounts of her foundations.[44] A place which appears in the earlier texts, Killesher in 'the Gailenga', seems to have closed down. Given the timing of its disappearance from the record it looks to have been a casualty of Viking attacks. Other places come to the fore instead, though, to carry on the saint's memory.

The twelfth-century Martyrology of Gorman gives feast days for some eleven virgins by that name (including this one, identified as 'the daughter of Ronán') which strongly implies that the saint remained popular.[45] Killesher by Lough Macnean in Fermanagh is important in this later period; it features quite strongly in the Life and continued use might be indicated by the fact that it was rebuilt in the seventeenth century for Protestant use. The place is about five miles west of Enniskillen by the Marble Arch on the Cladagh River by Lough Macnean, and its ruins are still visible. Archdall's 1876 guide attributed to it an earthen rath some eighteen feet thick, which would indicate considerable prestige in its heyday.[46]

Another Killesher, also not attested in earlier sources, is further south in the upper or southern part of the plain called Mag Aí, which can be located to the region directly north of modern Roscommon. According to the Life Lassair and her father stayed here for some nine months, and she blessed the church on their departure. The place is not known today.[47]

which is a conflation of the 8th-cent. Voyage (which does not mention Ita) and a now-disappeared Life.

[42] *Carais Pattraic* ['Patrick Loved' or 'Cuimmín's Hymn'], ed. and trans. W. Stokes, 'Cuimmín's Poem on the Saints of Ireland', *ZCP* 1 (1897), 59–73.

[43] Life of Ita, chs. 13, 18, 20, 22, 27, 31, 34, 35.

[44] Martyrology of Gorman, 13 Nov.: *Ioain Lassar lommnán*, glossed with the name of the monastery: *Achaidh Beithe*. Latin Life of Colmán, D text (*PVSH* i. 258–73). Plummer notes the absence of the anecdote in this later version, *PVSH* ii. 263.

[45] Ed. L. Gwynn, 'Beatha Lasrach', *Eriu* 5 (1911), 73–109. A 12th-cent. original composition in the opinion of the editor, who said the 17th-cent. copyist 'probably modernised a late Middle Irish original', which would date the exemplar to the 12th cent. (Gwynn, 73).

[46] Killanan and Duignan, *Shell Guide*, 272; Archdall, *Monasticon*, ii. 169.

[47] Irish Life of Lassair (Gwynn, 'Beatha Lasrach', 86–91).

Her Life also makes Lassair the patroness of the church of Kilronan (Ir. Cill Ronáin), no longer in existence, which was located in the lake district by Lough Arrow and Lough Key on the Roscommon–Sligo border. It claims that she spent her life with her father Ronán as a companion, and it was she who blessed it in his name when they settled there on his patrimony.[48] The Life itself appears to have been composed at Kilronan: most of the events take place there, and it is the one place really prominent in the text; it was for Kilronan that Lassair set her great tax on the surrounding lands. It survived into the later middle ages, for as late as the fourteenth century it still existed in name at least: the Annals of Clonmacnois mention that one David Macdowgennan, who was McDermott's chief chronicler, was 'Cowarb of Virgin saint Lassar' who was buried in its churchyard.[49]

Lassair is absent from the body and notes of the Oengus Martyrology, but a gloss on the Martyrology of Gorman names her in association with a church called Aghavea (Ir. Achad Beithe). Aghavea is named in Lassair's Life as her first foundation, but little is known about this place, for it does not appear in any other sources.

The disjunction of the earlier and later material makes it look very much as if there were two phases to this cult, separated by some centuries. There is also no certainty that the earlier Lassair with assocations to Kildare and Lynally is the same person as Lassair daughter of Ronan, the protagonist of the later Lives and patroness of the churches described above. The former is not identified by patronym, and the latter had no church in the Tethbae region.

Clonbroney

Clonbroney in Longford, the nunnery so impressively brought to fame under abbess Samthann, continued as a major female house. The death of abbess Cocrich ingen Unonn in 1107 was recorded in the annals, as was that of Caillech Domnhaill ingen Naoneanaig in 1163, *banabb* and *comarba Samthainne*.[50] Stories from this era about abbess Samthann's life, collected in later centuries in the Annals of the Four Masters and in this period in the martyrological scholia, include one about her indirect involvement with a local war, at the outset of which she allegedly composed a short rhyme, which was dutifully copied. A poem in honour of her, allegedly composed by the great Áed Allán, is also reproduced in both these collections. A genealogy, significantly, is included, which further suggests the continued political significance of the place into at least the eleventh century.[51] Saint Berach's Life, written in this later era, made a point of claiming a connection with Samthann, in an episode where she cooperated with him in

---

[48] Ibid. (Gwynn, 'Beatha Lasrach', 75–9, for Molaisse; *passim* for Ronán). The site is in the barony of Boyle in the northernmost part of Co. Roscommon (*Onomasticon*).

[49] AClon 1398.   [50] AClon 1107; AFM 1163.

[51] *Samthann fri Soillsi Sainmand*, in AFM 734 and Martyrology of Oengus, notes on 19 Dec.

converting Áed Dub king of Breifne at an assembly, and supported him there when the other saints of Ireland turned against him.[52]

Kildare: Monastery, Abbesses, Relics

As a physical site, Kildare is easier to envision in this period than earlier, thanks to the voluminous scraps of information in the annals and hagiographical glosses. These mention numerous chapels and other features of the site: a great house (*tigh mór*), a bell-church (*clochtech*), a church within the precinct known as 'Cell Ross', a church to the south called 'Cell Brigte'. A ballaun stone was also in the precinct, mentioned first in the thirteenth century but probably from the foundation period.[53] A round tower, reported by Gerald of Wales, was also built at Kildare at some point, doubtless during the ninth or tenth centuries like most of them.[54]

At some point the celebrated wooden church was replaced with a stone one—certainly before Gerald of Wales's day, for by his time the name of the Kildare, 'oak church', was explained not by the type of wood used for the building but by the alleged presence of a wondrous tree nearby. The time of the change of materials may, I think, be narrowed down to between 964, when the annals mention the oak church (*derthaig*), and 1050, when they refer to the stone oratory (*daimliaig*).[55] In any event it was a stone church, in ruins that the Anglo-Norman archbishop of Dublin discovered in the thirteenth century when he came down to visit his new acquisition. In a drive to revive the place, he undertook to build there a Hiberno-Romanesque cathedral of great size. Current scholarly consensus is that none of the old stone building was incorporated into the fabric of the new one. Brigit's and Conlaed's relics, which had been entombed within the main church in the seventh century, had been enshrined (Conlaed's in 800) but had then been carried off by Vikings in the 830s. Conlaed's were gone forever, but Brigit's were spuriously 'discovered' in the twelfth century by an Anglo-Norman lord in Ulster—with Columba's and Patrick's, in Down, in 1185.[56]

One building at Kildare, which appears in the record for the first time, is the 'fire-house', that rectangular stone building which, according to thirteenth-century contemporary reports, housed Kildare's perpetual fire. Its ruins are still

---

[52] Irish Life of Berach, ch. 23.

[53] *Vita IV* of Brigit, book 1, ch. 5; on ballaun stones see Edwards, *Archaeology*, 116, 121.

[54] Discussed in L. Barrow, *Round Towers of Ireland* (Dublin, 1977).

[55] AU 964, 1050; *Ní Car Brigit* scholia; Martyrology of Oengus, notes on 9 Nov.

[56] The main source for the rediscovery of Down is Gerald of Wales, *Topographia*, book 2, ch. 18. The redactor of Brigit's *Vita IV*, 'D', whose intended audience was Anglo-Norman rather than native Irish, made changes in the account so as accommodate the events of 1185—he wrote that Brigit had gone to Ulster to die, as Sharpe notes in his edition (*Vita IV* of Brigit, chs. 91, 96). Equally implausible is the alleged grave of Brigit, 'Brigit's Bed', at St Patrick's Purgatory on Lough Derg: others graves on the site were claimed to be of Patrick, Columba, Molaisse, Brendan, Dabheóc, and Catherine of Alexandria.

visible today, and it is treated as the centre of a surviving Irish vestal cult by many pilgrims of the more neo-pagan and feminist-matriarchal varieties. The perpetual fire and older ethnographers' interpretations of it were touched upon in an early chapter, but here the building itself deserves some remark. Many who believe in a functioning survivalism of Goddess-worship here claim that the building itself, or an earlier layer of it, dates from the pre-Christian era, and that it was in fact a temple.

There are three factors vitiating this interpretation. Firstly, the fire itself does not appear in the textual record until the twelfth century, but notably neither does the enclosing building, though it is evidently a pre-twelfth century construction. Secondly, not only did several male-founded churches have perpetual fires, but two we know each had a fire-house: the monasteries at Cloyne and Molaisse's Inishmurray, excavation of the latter's floor confirming it had been a hearth.[57] Neither of these was among those recorded in the twelfth century as being a place of a perpetual fire. This would suggest either that such fires and their containing building were so common that they were rarely mentioned, or else that the fire-houses were secular rather than religious buildings and the fire, perpetual or otherwise, was a practical rather than a religious one—serving as a need-fire or a metal-working building. A final point to be made is that the date of the Kildare fire-house is architecturally identifiable with the early Christian period, not the late Iron Age—until and unless such buildings are excavated and shown to have pagan-era precursors under their foundations they, like the fires they contained, are best interpreted as a part of general Christian monastic life in Ireland.

In political terms, Kildare is the most fully attested of the female houses in this later period, just as it was in the earlier. By the tenth century it had long been dominated by Leinster's Uí Dúnlainge dynasty, which had replaced the declining Fothairt. The latter did continue their links, though, up to the eleventh century at least: one branch, the Uí Chúlduib, supplied two abbesses, Muirenn (obit 918) and Eithne (obit 1016), and another, the Fothairt Airbrech, supplied the abbess Sebdann (obit 732) and her relative Duirc (obit 750). Many of its other clerics, whose origins are unprovable, may also have belonged to the Fothairt.[58] In this era Kildare, like so many other church centres, was treated as a military site as much as a sacred one, by the Uí Dúnlainge and everyone else.[59] The Scandinavian kingdoms in Dublin and Waterford frequently ravaged it in the wider context of hegemonic aspirations. The Uí Dúnlainge themselves acted out some of their internecine conflicts at Kildare. It was their infighting which prompted an extraordinary event in 1041, one which outraged even the

---

[57] Killanin and Duignan, *Shell Guide*, 166, 308, 318.

[58] M. O'Brien (ed.), *Corpus Genealogiarum Hiberniae* (Dublin, 1962), 80–6; Ó Corráin, 'Early Irish Churches', 329.

[59] Covered in considerable depth in A. Smyth, *Celtic Leinster: Towards an Historical Geography of Early Irish Civilization AD 500–1600* (Blackrock, 1982).

hardened: one faction of the dynasty attacked and raped the incumbent abbess in order to disqualify her and cement their own takeover. The Annals of Tigernach give the fullest account, explaining that Gill Comgaill mac Donn-Cuan mac Dunlaing raped (*saraigh*) the coarb of Brigit and afterwards resided in Kildare; Murchad mac Dunlaing retaliated by dragging him out by force and killing him on the spot where he had committed the outrage.[60] This event not only illustrates the political value of control of the church but also the continued centrality of the abbess's office, symbolically at least, to the notion of its headship. Some ninety years later, in 1127, Uí Failghe and the Uí Faeláin slaughtered each other, on the site, in a struggle for control over the coarbship.[61] Just four years later, in 1131 the Uí Chennselaig moved in and seized Kildare in a manner that leaves no doubt as to the continuing importance of the abbess's office.[62]

Teach n-abadh Cille Dara do ghabhail dibh gCeinnselaigh for chomarba mBrighdi, ocus a loscad, ocus bladh mhór don chill, ocus sochaide do marbad ann, ocus an caillech féin do breith a broid, opcus a tabairt a leabaidh fir.

The abbatial [lit. abbot's] house of Kildare was captured by the Uí Chennselaig from the coarb of Brigit, and burnt, along with a large part of the establishment [lit. Church]; and a great many were killed there, and the nun herself was dragged off as a prisoner and put into a man's bed.

Ecclesiastically, few comments can be made about the place. Kildare's *regula* in the tenth to twelfth centuries was the mysterious 'Placentine' rule. Its legendary origins are recounted in two long glosses, according to which it originated in a church beneath the 'Ictian sea' and was fetched up by a young Kildare boy who went overboard a ship bound for Rome.[63] Evidently Kildare needed to explain why it no longer followed the Roman customs. Placentia is obviously the modern city of Piacenza in northern Italy, the town nearest the Columbanian monastery of Bobbio, which may be of some significance. The church of Piacenza was noted in the Lombard period for its strenuous independence in matters of liturgy and custom, and so it may well be that the Kildare legend had its roots in fact.[64] More than this one cannot say, as Italian sources provide no ready solutions, any more than do the Irish ones. In ecclesiastical terms Kildare's status was destroyed at the Synod of Kells in 1152 when the Irish church was granted formal independence from the English by the papacy and Armagh was made the metropolitan See.[65] In spite of that Brigit continued to be an important figure. Her relics continued to circulate and in Lives she remained

---

[60] ATig; AU 1041.   [61] AU 1127.

[62] AU, C version, 1131; Annals of Loch Cé, 1132. The Uí Chennselaig are also mentioned in 12th-cent. Kildare hagiographic scholia on *Ní Car Brigit*.

[63] Martyrology of Oengus, notes on 1 Feb.; glosses on *Ní Car Brigit*.

[64] The church of Piacenza: R. Schumann, 'Le fondazioni ecclesiastiche e il disegno urbano di Piacenza tra il tardo romano (350) e la Signoria (1313)', *Bolletino storico piacentino* 71 (1976), 159–71.

[65] Flanagan, *Irish Society*, 8–52, esp. 38–42.

eminent: in the late Latin Life of Tigernach, for example, the writer boasted
that Brigit had sponsored Tigernach in baptism, had named him, and had had
him elevated to episcopal orders.[66] Not only did her Irish cult survive, but she
lived on in Continental churches as well. The saint's authority outlived that of
her establishment.

Kildare: A Concentration of Authority?

There is some indication that Kildare's abbess held a special authority over
nuns across Ireland in the tenth, eleventh, and twelfth centuries.[67] The main
body of the Martyrology of Oengus, which is from the ninth century and therefore before the period in question, already called this saint 'Brigit the fair, strong,
praiseworthy chaste head of Erin's nuns': *Brigit bán balc núalann, cenn cáid caillech
n-Erenn.*[68] One gloss on the poem *Brigit Bé Bithmaith* asserted that Brigit and
Patrick had divided authority over Ireland between them geographically, and
another on the same poem elaborates, saying the division was made on the basis
of gender:

Ar mar bad colba ic roind taige sic roroi[n]n Brigit 7 Patraic flathius Herend inter se
conid hi as cen[d] do mnaib Erend, Patraic immorro as chend d'eraib.[69]

For as it were a pillar in a living house, so Brigit and Patrick have divided Ireland between them, so that she is the head to the women of Ireland, Patrick, however, is the
head to the men.

An eleventh-century hymn attributed to Colmán of Lynally reiterates this:

> Bennacht for érlam Patraic · con-nóebaib Herenn impe
> Bennacht forsin cathraig-se · ocus fro chach fil indi
> Bendacht for érlam Brigti · co nógaib Hérenn impe
> tabraid huili cainforgall · bendacht for ordan Brigti.[70]

Benediction on patron Patrick with Ireland's saints around him, benediction on this
monastery and on every one therein. Benediction on fair Brigit, with Ireland's virgins
around her, give all ye fair testimony, benediction on Brigit's dignity.

Several anecdotes in the hagiography of this era claim that Brigit had been ordained bishop at the time of her consecration. That, they claim, justifies a practice in their own day: that of conferring episcopal orders upon the abbess of
Kildare. The ninth-century *Bethu Brigte* is the earliest:

---

[66] Latin Life of Tigernach, chs. 1, 11 (*PVSH* ii. 107–11).
[67] See also Byrne, '*Comarbai Brigte*'.   [68] Martyrology of Oengus, 1 Feb.
[69] *Thes. Pal.* ii. 326. Also Bernard and Atkinson, *Irish Liber Hymnorum*, ii. 193.
[70] 'Colmán's Hymn', Stokes and Strachan, *Thes. Pal.* ii. 301–6. Also in Bernard and Atkinson, *Irish
Liber Hymnorum*, 14–16, 158–60; they felt the language to be consistent with an 11th-cent. date (p. xxxvi).

Ibi episcopus Dei gratia inebreatus non cognovit quid in libro sui cantavit. In gradum enim episcopi ordinavit Brigitam. 'Haec sola', inquid Mel, 'ordinationem episcopalem in Hibernia tenebit virgo'.[71]

The bishop being intoxicated with the grace of God there did not recognize what he was reciting from his book, for he consecrated Brigit with the orders of a bishop. 'This virgin alone in Ireland', said Mel, 'will hold the episcopal ordination'.

This story says that Brigit alone shall have this honour. Yet, when the story then appears in later versions, the honour, or at least its status, is to be enjoyed by the abbess's successors. Brigit's Lismore Life, concludes the episode with the words 'therefore the men of Ireland from that time to the present day give the honour of the bishop to the successor of Brigit' (*conidh anoir espuic doberat fir Eirenn do comarba Brigte o sin ille*).[72] A similar claim is made in the notes to the Martyrology of Oengus:

Rob ail didu do Brigit aithrige do tabairt furri, co rocht co Bri Eli 7 moirseser caillech immailli fria o ro chuala epscop Mél . . . Cid dia tancatar na caillecha? ol epscop Mél. Do thabairt grad n-aithrige for Brigit, ol Mac cailli. Iarsin ro hirlegait grada for Brigit .i. grada epscoip dano dorat epscop Mél fuirri 7 conid annsin rogab Mac cailli caille for a cinn. Conid desin dligis comarba Brigte grada epscuip do thabairt fair.[73]

Now Brigit was fain to have the orders of penitence conferred upon her; so she went to Bri Eile, accompanied by seven nuns, since she heard that bishop Mel was there . . . 'Why have the nuns come?', asked bishop Mel. 'To have the orders of penitence conferred upon Brigit,' says Mac Caille. Thereafter the orders were read out over Brigit, and bishop Mel bestowed episcopal orders upon her, and it is then that Mac Caille set a veil upon (her) head. Hence Brigit's successor is entitled to have episcopal orders conferred upon her.

The glosses on the poem *Ní Car Brigit* relate an almost identical version of the story, in which Brigit again seeks the penitential grade from Mel, and he agrees to grant it, but also gives her the episcopal ordination. Mel asks the reason for the nuns' arrival, to which he is told—

'Do thabairt grad aithrige', ar Mac caille. 'Dober sa on', ar epscop Mél. Iarsein tra doerlegait grada fuirri, 7 is grad epscuip dorala do epscop Mél do thabairt for Brigit, ciarbo grad athrige nama rop ail disi féin; is andsein rochongaib Mac caille caille uas cind Brigte, *ut ferunt periti*; 7 is dosen dliges comarba Brigte do gres grad n-epscuip fuirri 7 honoir epscuip.[74]

'To have the order of penitence conferred', said Mac Caille. 'I will confer it', said bishop Mel. So thereafter the orders were read out over her, and it came to pass that bishop Mel conferred on Brigit the episcopal order, though it was only the order of penitence that she herself desired. And it was then that Mac Caille held a veil over Brigit's head, *ut ferunt periti*. And hence Brigit's successor is always entitled to have episcopal orders and the honour due a bishop.

---

[71] *Bethu Brigte*, ch. 19.
[72] Johnston, 'Transforming Women', 214–15, Homily on Brigit in the Book of Lismore, ch. 40.
[73] Martyrology of Oengus, notes on 2 Feb.   [74] Notes on *Ní Car Brigit*.

This episcopal consecration story first appeared in the ninth century; it is completely absent from the earlier Cogitosus and Brigit's *Vita I*, the source for *Bethu Brigte*. What is of most interest in the *Ní Car Brigit* version is the explicit assertion that the subsequent Kildare abbesses were admitted to the 'grade' or status of bishop. They were entitled to have 'episcopal orders/status' (*gráda epscuip / grád n-epscuip*) bestowed upon them, and were due, the honour of a bishop (*honoir epscuip*). Kildare's political importance underlies these claims, of course and, in the case of the Lismore version at least, so too did ecclesiastical reforms.[75] The extraordinary political and dynastic significance of Kildare, with its female and male heads, came to an end with the synod of Kells-Mellifont. But between the ninth century and 1152, there was an extraordinary female authority, in terms of the ecclesiastical hierarchy as well as political realities, in the Kildare abbess.

In the legal material, too, it appears that the Kildare abbess enjoyed an unusually exalted status. A later gloss in the law tract *Cáin Lánamna*, in the section on *Lánamnas Éicne* (forced or secret couplings) says that if a *mac-caillech* (virginal nun) is raped, one half of her honour price is paid 'to the tanist successor of Brigit' (*tanaist comarba Brigti*). Thurneysen interpreted the *tanist* to be the prioress of Kildare.[76]

If Kildare's authority did increase at this time, with a linked magnification of Brigit's cult to include claims that she was in some way head of the whole island's nuns, this would represent an important change in the widespread balance of ecclesiastical power across Ireland. Additionally, holding the status of bishop might well have given the abbess a supervisory authority over abbesses of subsidiary female communities. According to a leading churchman of the early twelfth century, those who held the grade of bishop could ordain abbesses (*Ordinat episcopus abbatem, abbatissam, sacerdotem et caeteros sex gradus*).[77] It looks very much as if Kildare was asserting that its abbess had an authority over abbesses of other female communities, whether or not they belonged to Kildare's federation or *paruchia*. One may wonder if at Kildare the abbess enjoyed the power of selection, or veto, concerning clergy in the monastery or even throughout the wider network. Unfortunately, the law tracts and their attendant glosses are frustratingly unforthcoming and offer no further elaboration on this case (or even very much on the power of abbesses generally).

Brigidine Relics

There is no doubt about the abundance of Brigidine relics in this period, a strong sign of her cult's influence and Kildare's political prominence in general

---

[75] Johnston, 'Transforming Women', 216.

[76] The main text of this chapter of the tract is ed. and trans. into German in *SEIL*, *ALI* ii. 407 gives a less satisfactory ed. and trans., but does also translate the glosses. R. Thurneysen, '*Cáin Lánamna*', in *SEIL* 1–80, at 73.

[77] Gilla Easpuic, *De Statu Ecclesiae* (*PL* 159, at 1002).

terms. The scholiast on the poem *Ní Car Brigit* mentioned a veil placed on Brigit's head by the bishop Mac Caille before she was presented to Mel for her consecration rite, adding, 'that would be the veil that is venerated' (*comad e sen caille foraithmentar*). The same story appears in the twelfth century as well, adding that the site was 'Moin Faithnig', mod. Croghan, five miles north-west of the town of Tullamore, the same site as appears in the earliest Lives; it too, speaks of a veil there ('that may be the veil which is commemorated there', *cumad esin caille foraithmentar sunn*).[78] Another relic in existence at this time was the beam which supported the altar at Brigit's consecration. Brigit had been touching it during the rite, and afterwards it had ceased to age and had miraculously avoided destruction in spite of the church being burnt down around it—either once or three times, depending on the version. The beam is also mentioned as an extant relic in *Bethu Brigte*, which says its wood at some point had been miraculously transformed into acacia, the wood of the ark of the covenant, which added a Biblical dimension to the relic's cult. The acacia appears only once in the Bible, in Exodus 25: 10 (*arcam de lignis setim compingite*), and the beam's ability to survive fires may have been associated, in people's minds, with that Old Testament account of the ark.[79] Like other relics and their legends, this relic is not particularly 'gendered' or feminine—the ark of the covenant was not especially associated with women but rather the chosen people as a whole.

Another Brigidine wood relic was a wonder-working oak tree at Kildare. It is reported in the early thirteenth-century *Vita IV*, at which time pieces of the stump were much sought after.

Illa iam cella scotice dicitur Killdara, latine vero sonat cella quercus. Quercus enim altissima ibi erat quam multum sancta Brigida diligebat, et benedixit eam; cuius stipes adhuc manet, et nemo ferro abscindere audet, et pro magno munere habet qui potest frangere manibus aliquid inde, sperans per illud Dei auxilium, quia multa patrata sunt miracula per illud lignum per benedictionem beate Brigide.[80]

This church is called in Irish 'Killdara', in Latin 'oak church'. For there was a very tall oak tree there which Brigit loved very much, and blessed, the trunk of which still remains. No one dares chop at it with a weapon, but whoever can break off a part of it with by hand considers it a great advantage, hoping for the aid of God by its means; [this is] because many miracles have been performed by that wood, through Brigit's blessing.

This passage shows the relatively recent origin of the oak tree's significance, as it was based on a failure to understand the real, much more mundane origin of the name of the place—namely, the wood from which the church building had originally been built. It is worth reiterating, lest one should still be tempted to

---

[78] *Ní Car Brigit*, scholia; Martyrology of Oengus, notes on 1 Feb.

[79] Martyrology of Oengus, notes on 1 Feb., where the location cited is Fir Tulach. *Bethu Brigte*, ch. 18; commentary Ó hAodha, *Bethu Brigte*, 48, who noted that Grosjean further suggested that the supposed imperishability of the beam through fire may have owed a debt to an ancient commentary on Exodus.

[80] *Vita IV* of Brigit, book 2, ch. 3. This paragraph, Sharpe has demonstrated, was actually written by the early 13th-cent. redactor who inserted it in the text he was copying (Sharpe, *Saints' Lives*, 161).

link the oak tree with a Brigidine pagan past, that the oak tree was not even mentioned in earlier Lives. Moreover, in the twelfth century a fashion for wonder-working trees appears to have sprung up, for suddenly hagiography is full of them. Ruadán's monastery Lothra had one, as did the new Columban church at Derry, and in 1162 one hears of a yew allegedly planted by Patrick himself.[81]

Brigit's body was miraculously, if dubiously, discovered in 1186 with those of Patrick and Brigit in Down by an Anglo-Norman, De Courcey, an event which cemented the formulation of the three as Irish national saints. The *translatio* rite was attended by papal legates and was conducted with great pomp but nevertheless failed to impress the Irish annalists any more than the finding, for they unanimously fail to report it.[82]

FEMALE SAINTS' CULTS: *MIRACULA MINIMA*?

It has been claimed that the miracles and achievements of female saints, as related by their later hagiographers were mostly domestic, small, or of a 'housekeeping' nature. Lisa Bitel in 1986 proposed that female saints' miracles were considered inferior to those of male saints and that they themselves held a lower esteem than males among the dominant powers in Ireland.[83] This view is unsustainable. Female saints continued to be attributed with real power relevant for male petitioners as well as females, for political groups as well as individuals. Hagiographers at male monasteries were exceptionally keen in this period to claim their patron had been a friend of Brigit's. Brendan, Áed, Ailbe, Maedóc, Mochoemóg, Tigernach, and Monenna were all claimed to have had links with her.[84] Among mortals, abbesses continued to be portrayed with powers often associated with male leaders and foster-mother abbesses continued to be regarded with great esteem. Lives went on relating stories of male saints visiting nunneries and tutoring virgins.

The cult of Monenna is perhaps a particularly striking case. The following of this saint reached even as far as England, as is evidenced in a collection of material on her at Burton-on-Trent dating to the second quarter of the twelfth

---

[81] Cf. Hamlin and Hughes, *Modern Traveller*, 31; Irish Life of Ruadán, ch. 10 (*BNE* i. 317–29; Eng. trans., ii. 308–20).

[82] The enshrined relics remained at Down until 1538 when they were desecrated. Brigit's head was allegedly rescued and taken to Neustadt, Austria, whence it travelled in 1587 to the Jesuit Church in Lisbon. One of her feet made its way to a Brigidine church in Cashel, and in 1900 was among the possessions of the archbishop there. One of her slippers was venerated in the later middle ages, too: the National Museum owns a slipper reliquary from Lochrea dated to 1410, which had been used as a swearing relic. For an anachronistically-inserted account of the event, attributed to a date over a century later, AFM 1293.

[83] Bitel, 'Women's Monastic Enclosures', 30.

[84] Irish Life of Brendan, ch. 56; Latin Life of Áed, D text, ch. 13 (*PVSH* i. 34–45); Latin Life of Ailbe, D text, ch. 26; Martyrology of Oengus, notes on 4 Apr., on Tigernach; Latin Life of Maedóc, D text, ch. 57; Latin Life of Mochoemóg, D text, ch. 20; Life of Darerca, chs. 4–5, 12. The Brigidine presence continued into the 13th cent.: First Latin Life of Brendan, ch. 86; Latin Life of Tigernach, chs. 2, 7.

century.[85] Her wide influence is also exalted in her two Lives. In the Life by Conchubranus, where we are told that she lived on the boundary of the Eastern provinces 'which she claims for herself on the West and North'.[86] In her own day, he asserts, her authority and her possession of lands had been confirmed, after some dispute involving the local king Glunelath and Saint Coemgen, a rival for the monastery and its property. Significantly, the Life recounts a settling of this quarrel and a reconciliation between Monenna and Coemgen. Further, she was responsible for the king's conversion to holy ways and for his nephews becoming clerics.[87] Monenna, it goes on to relate, travelled with her virgins to England and to Scotland, where she founded churches near Edinburgh and on the river Trent, and numerous others in Scotland. After a supposed journey to Rome, the saint also founded a church 'at the foot of Mount Calvus'.[88] At she lay dying (Conchubranus says it was in Scotland), Monenna was visited by various chiefs, who pleaded with her not to die and thus leave them as orphans.[89] They made her offerings to do what she wished with, if she would but ask God to let her live another year, for they were certain that God would not refuse what she asked.

Et appropinquante novissimo die et audita infirmitate eius in populo maximum contulit omnibus luctum. Veneruntque ad illam visitandam Conagal qui erat rex Scotie in illo tempore et Rotheri et Cobo et Bollan et Choilli et omnis maiores natu populi cum cetera multitudine usque adpropinquantes monasterii loca. Miserunt itaque episcopum Ronam fratrem Monenne ad illam ponentes verba hec in ore eius: 'Obsecramus te propter consanguinitatem nostram—nam et ipse rex matrem habuit Conalneam—et germanitatem quam habemus et in carne et in Deo ut etiam uno anno nobiscum maneas et quasi orphanos nos in isto anno non derelinquas. Credimus enim et scimus quia quecumque Dominum rogaveris sine dubio ab illo impetrabis'.[90]

As her last day drew near and people heard of her illness, it caused everyone great sorrow. And there came to visit her Conagall, who was king of Scotland at that time, and of Rotheri Cobo, Bollan and Choille, and all the elders of the people with the rest of the multitude drawing close to the precinct of the monastery. So they sent to her bishop Ronán, Monenna's brother, entrusting him with this message: 'We beg you, by the ties of our blood (for the king's mother was also of the *Conaille*) and because of our relationship both in the flesh and in God, that you stay with us for one year more and not leave us like orphans in that year. For we know that whatever you ask from the Lord you will undoubtedly receive from him.'

---

[85] The USMLS editors suggest that Monenna might have actually founded an English monastery there in the 7th cent., though they offer no more than conjectural evidence for the suggestion (USMLS, 'Life of Monenna', part 3, 426–7).

[86] Book 1, ch. 1.   [87] Book 1, chs. 7–14.   [88] Book 3, chs. 3–8.

[89] Cf. Life of Darerca, ch. 29: *O domina, per nostram te obsecramus consanguinitatem (ibi namque multi de eius gente inerant, ipse etiam rex Eugenius ex parte matris Conallensis erat) perque eam quam carne et anima tenemus affinitatem supplicamus quatenus saltem unius anni curriculo nobiscum in terris cohabitare digneris. Ne ergo hoc anno morte tua nos orphanos esse concedas. Nos etenim certi sumus quia, quicquid a Deo postulaveris, statim obtinebis.*

[90] Book 3, ch. 9.

Monenna refused because, she says, Peter and Paul had already arrived to collect her to take her to Christ. But in reward for their coming to her, she gave the men her leather garment, her sheepskin, and her utensils, which they should carry into battle to attain victory: *victoriam per hec habere Dominus vobis promitit*. They should not, she added, go to war against other peoples beyond the bounds of their lands unless compelled by a greater force, lest the wrath of the Lord come upon them.[91] Certainly this is no domestic, small-time saint speaking. Monenna's anonymous Life in the Codex Salmanticensis also claims major cultic importance for the saint, for in it she was sought out by many people that she might intercede on their behalf.[92]

Frequent visits to Monenna's nunnery by ordinary lay folk are related, and it claimed greatness as an educational centre: she was a *pia magistra* of such note that a nun came from Britain to study psalms and books with her, staying at a hospice near to the saint.[93] Both Lives of Monenna also emphasize her rigorous pursuit of monastic ideals, likening her to John the Baptist.[94] Her authority is repeatedly emphasized: throughout both Lives she autonomously and unilaterally founds monastic houses and hermitages, in some cases overcoming opposition from local rulers. In the Life from the Codex Salmanticensis, Monenna's brother Herbeus helps her overcome one particular ruler, yet here as elsewhere it is Monenna who makes all decisions concerning the foundation and the community. There is no authority over her to which Monenna must answer. Indeed it is hard to overstate her power to conduct herself as she chose, or the esteem accorded to her by the laity, in this text.

Monenna negotiated with a local king for the release of hostages (when her plea for their release was refused, she used miraculous powers to set them free nevertheless) and she intervened in the politicking of the *Connactenses* and the *Techuatenses*, dealing with the kings over hostages.[95] She was visited by a queen, whose infertility she cured, and by a *magister* who sought advice on how to pray.[96] Although she was poor in spirit and possessions (*pauper erat spiritu et rebus*), the hagiographer insists that her lack of land and property was deliberate: her extremely holy asceticism made her refuse the donations of land and goods that people offered to her. One wonders, of course, if in the redactor's day the monastery was in a relatively poor position and this represents an attempt to portray Monenna as powerful nevertheless.

---

[91] Monenna's proviso, namely that success will only be guaranteed when the bearers are defending their own lands and not invading those of others, echoes the peace-keeping tone of abbess saints in lives of the earlier centuries.

[92] Life of Darerca, ch. 20: *Ipsa itaque, degens in latebris, virtutum splendore in cunctis Hybernie partibus fuit celebris. Hinc progressu temporis ab omnibus in circuitu regionibus nobilis matrone eius presentiam adire solebant, genibus in terram flexis petentes ut eius colloquiis uterentur vel orationibus Deo commendarentur. Preterea virginum Christi numerus cotidie crescebat; et non solum de propinquis, verum etiam de remotis regionibus, elemosinis frequenter missis grex Christi pascebatur.*

[93] Ibid., ch. 25.   [94] Ibid., ch. 19.

[95] Ibid., chs. 7, 12, 22. *Techuatensis*, ie. 'the people of Tethbae'.   [96] Ibid., chs. 24, 21.

Ita was represented by her hagiographer as the *matrona* of the Uí Chonaill Gabra, whose leader came to her to donate land for her church, and whose people always gave generous donations to the place.[97] For her part, she gave them many blessings, including raising some noblemen from death.[98] Ita also negotiated with kings for the release of captives in chains and supervised the penance of a warrior who committed murder. In the one case, she was moved to intercede to a king on behalf of a young man condemned to death for the murder of his brother, out of pity for the suffering of the mother.[99] When the Uí Chonaill went to war, she interceded on their behalf, praying to God: *paucis et miseris meis hominibus, qui me benigne in tuo nomine in suis finibus sumpserunt, et me matronam suam receperunt, subveni auxilio.* It was a few against many, but the Uí Chonaill won because of Ita's prayers.[100] When she died, we are told, she was visited by many saints of both sexes who blessed her place and by all the Uí Chonaill people 'who accepted her as their mother' (*que accepit eam matronam suam*).[101]

In her Latin Life Samthann also is called *domina* and, like Monenna in her Lives, she came into conflict with, and showed her power to overrule, the royal rulers of her region.[102] The Life of Lassair asserts that Lassair too exerted power over, and gave blessings to, a *populus*. When she founded a church with her father Rónán, she fixed a tribute for herself upon the lands of Tir Thúathail, 'from the Unshinn to the Shannon, from every townland in the country great or small, on both men and women'.[103] She pronounced that blessings, including entry into heaven, would come to those who would pay, and misery on those who might refuse. Now in all likelihood the saint never did any such thing and the story merely voices a claim more recently asserted by Lassair's church; this is a not-uncommon phenomenon in hagiography. In this case the assertive language attributed to the virgin indicates the great force the Irish felt a woman saint could wield. Four of the stanzas convey this especially well:

> Mo chios aran tírse · Tir Thúathail go ttarbha:
> ainmidhe as gach ceathra · imaire as gach arbar [read *arba*].
> Cidh be bhrisfes an cháinse · dferaibh an bhetha bhuainse:
> ni bhía sliocht ar a lorgsan · is ifrionn ina ordsan úaimse.
> Me Lasair inghen Rónáin · bennaighim an tír go ngloine:
> búadh náithis ara bhfiora · a lathair ghlíadh is ghoile.
> Bennaighim a mná maithe · os ad caoimhe crotha:
> is bennuighim a bpriomhshlúaigh · go madh righbhuan a rat[h]a.

> My tribute upon this land, Tir Thúathail of riches:
> a beast from every herd, a furrow from every cornfield.

---

[97] Life of Darerca, ch. 9.   [98] Ibid., ch. 14.   [99] Ibid., chs. 21, 32.
[100] Ibid., ch. 33.   [101] Ibid., ch. 36.   [102] Samthann called *domina*: Life of Samthann, chs. 5, 11.
[103] In modern terms this territory, of roughly 250 square miles, is bounded on the east by the River Unshin, on the west by the River Shannon, on the north and west by Tirerril, on the south by the River Boyle.

> Whosoever of the men of the everlasting world refuseth my tribute,
> he shall have no posterity after him, but hell thereafter from me.
> I, Lassair Ronán's daughter, I bless the land with purity,
> joyous success for its men in field of valour and conflict.
> I bless its good women, for they are fairest of form,
> and I bless their noble hosts: lasting be their fortune.[104]

To those who refused tribute Lassair literally gave hell. Among female saints, her curse is unique, but not so the scope and tone of the authority she claimed.

Did people really believe that female saints affected political and military outcomes? It would seem so. In 1176, the Anglo-Norman invader Strongbow, much hated by the Irish annalists, died of an infected wound shortly after raiding monasteries, including Kildare. So great was Brigit's perceived spiritual power that as he lay dying he believed he saw himself being killed by the saint herself; so report the Annals of the Four Masters. The Ulster annals report, *tout court*, that Brigit and Columba were responsible for his very welcome death.[105]

Just as a female saint was an appropriate object of supplication for noble males of all grades, for she could offer warriors protection in warfare and rulers favourable outcomes in political and military events, so too might she be supplicated by holy men. The glossator to the poem *Brigit Bé Bithmaith* related a story in which Brendan, having been attacked by a sea monster which would only retreat when Brigit's name was invoked, went to the saint to learn why the creature had honoured her beyond all other saints (*co fessad cid ara tarat in beist in mare onoir do Brigit sech na nóebu archena*).[106] She told him that since she had put her mind on God she had never taken it from Him, at which Brendan exclaimed 'By God, nun, it is right for the monsters that they honour you rather than us!' A gloss on a later stanza of the poem placed Brigit on a par with Patrick as pillars of Christianity in Ireland: as there are wont to be two pillars in the world, so Brigit and Patrick in Ireland (*amal bíte da cholba i ndomun sic Brigit ocus Patraic i nHerenn*).[107] In one Irish Life, Brendan visited Brigit and asked her advice on spiritual matters, acknowledging her superiority as an intercessor for miracle-working.[108]

In the later Lives, as in the earlier *Vita I*, females were on occasion involved in Church affairs, including the settlement of disputes. The Life of Berach relates how, in a disagreement involving a holy man and a druid, both men and women of the Church were called upon to help settle the matter:

[Tunc vir Dei et] magus presentiam illorum iudicum adeunt, cupientes diffinitivam audire ab eis sententiam. Iudices quoque timentes offendere partes, viros sanctos petunt sibi assessores, scilicet sanctum Finnianum et Ultanum, et sanctas virgines Samtannam et Athracteam, cum aliis prelatis, virginibus, ac viris sanctis. Magus vero demonibus

---

[104] Irish Life of Lassair (Gwynn, 'Beatha Lasrach', 96–7).   [105] AFM; AU 1176.
[106] The poem, with glosses, *Thes. Pal.*, ii. 323–6. The story appears, in a more abbreviated form, in the glosses to *Ní Car Brigit*.
[107] *Thes. Pal.* ii. 326. See above.   [108] First Irish Life of Brendan, ch. 56.

immolat, nomina deorum suorum invocans, ut eum in suo certamine contra tot sanctos viros ac sanctas defendant.[109]

Then the man of God and the druid came to their presence, desiring to hear a definitive sentence from them. The judges, fearing to offend the parties, ask holy men to be assessors, namely Finnian and Ultán, and the holy virgins Samthann and Adrochta, with other prelates, virgins and holy men. The druid sacrifices to the demons, invoking the names of his gods, that they defend him in his contest against all the holy men and women.

The fact that some saints were female did not prevent their cults from becoming extensive in this era. Their sex seems to have been no hindrance to their acquisition of a celebrated status, for indeed they could become so famous and sought-after that everyone wanted their own patron, even if male, to have been associated with them. For all this, the period did witness changes. The authors of the tenth to twelfth centuries were markedly more self-conscious about sex than those of the preceding three hundred years. Traces of anxiety about the Church's women, and laywomen, began to emerge, with monks sometimes expressing thoughts on what might be the proper theological and physical relationship between a monk and the female sex. This is reflected in changes, though not revolutionary ones, in attitudes to female saints: it appears that there was a questioning in some quarters of the authority and power of female saints or holy women. What alerts us to this new element is a handful of anecdotes in these later Lives.

The most notable is in that of Ita, which dates from the thirteenth century:

Alio tempore sanctus Luchtichernus et sanctus Lasreanus, abbates, dixerunt ad invicem: 'Eamus visitare famulam Dei, sanctam Ytam.' Tunc quidam adolescens stulte et insipienter dixit eis: 'Quid est vobis, sapientibus et magnis viris, ire ad anum illam vetustam?' Increpantes illum sancti, dixerunt ei: 'Male loquutus es, frater; iam enim prophetissa Dei noverit quod tu dixisti.[110]

Another time St Luchtichernus and St Lasrén, abbots, said to each other, 'Let us go visit the maiden of God, saint Ita.' Then a youth stupidly and foolishly said to them, 'Why would you, wise and great men, go to that old woman?' The holy men, rebuking him, said to him, 'You have spoken badly, brother, for already that prophetess of God knows what you said.'

The youth accompanied the pair and came to Ita 'that she might bless them', ut benediceret eos. When the group arrived, she spoke to the youth, asking somewhat sarcastically, Cur venisti ad anum vetustam, cum dixisti, quid prodesset sanctis venire ad me? He did penance, and the trio stayed with Ita for some days, celebrating and sharing in spiritual things. Now this anecdote has no precedents in earlier hagiography. Earlier Lives contain no apparent trace of questioning the importance of female saints, or the value of visiting them. The hermit who, in Brigit's

---

[109] Latin Life of Berach, ch. 19.   [110] Life of Ita, ch. 31.

Vita I, wished to avoid going to Brigit's community, was said to have done so for ascetic reasons rather than out of a sense that she was, as a woman, unworthy. This episode is the herald of an Irish marginalization of female monastics; it is, though, only the beginnings of such a trend. Significantly, in this case Ita's hagiographer uses the story, and very possibly included it in the first place, in order to reinforce her importance and power. He acknowledges that there is a challenge, and he says that she meets it and proves herself. This, as we shall see in a future section, is a typical Irish resolution or 'handling' of challenges posed by the suspicious, the scorning, and the separatists.

MINOR FEMALE SAINTS

Minor female saints appear in abundance in this era, in lists, genealogies, and later martyrologies. These are often the mothers, sisters, and aunts of male saints, which is significant.[111] As Dorothy Africa showed through her examination of a specific genealogical text, such female relatives were employed by genealogists of the eleventh and twelfth centuries who aimed to aggrandize particular monasteries and dynasties: they used female kinship to establish relationships between given male saints and other pertinent saints, or between those male saints and ancestors of secular lineages with which they wished to be affiliated.[112]

The use and purpose of the lists of minor saints is partially explained by this analysis. Up to a third of the names on the lists and martyrological scholia of female saints followed the simple forename, e.g. Fled, not with a patronym but a church name, e.g. Fled of Tech Fléide. Such mentions could serve no direct genealogical purpose. They could, however, be used as adjunct material in the creation of genealogies: if in his newly-extended genealogy the male saint had become related to Fled, the genealogist could handily check whether claims could be advanced on Tech Fléide.

A particularly rich example is found in a short text in the MS BM Bibl. Reg. 8.D.IX. It lists the disciples and relatives of Columba, giving the names of his twelve disciples and his female relatives. The list of women gives information useful to any Columban genealogist: his mother Eithne was the daughter of Mac Nave; his first blood-sister Cuimne was the mother of the sons of Mac Diciul (named M'Ernocc, Cascene, Meldal, and Bran, the last being buried at

---

[111] Lists include: *Ingenrada Noeb hErenn* (List of the Daughter Saints of Ireland); Comanmand Noebúag Herend (List of the Same-named Virgin Saints of Ireland); *Brigitae Sanctae Subiectae* (List of Those Subject to Saint Brigit); 'Disciples and Relatives of St Columba' (see below, n. 113); 'The Mothers of Irish Saints'; *Secht n-Ingena Dalbronaig* (the Seven Daughters of Dalbroney); *Clann Darerca* ('the family of Darerca').

[112] D. Africa, 'The Politics of Kin: Women and Pre-eminence in a Medieval Irish Hagiographical List' (PhD Thesis; Princeton, 1990) on 'The Mothers of Irish Saints', a list in the Book of Leinster, analysing the use of female kinship claims in the promulgation of the cults of Brigit, Columba, and Patrick.

Derry); his second blood-sister Mincholeth was the mother of the sons of Enan (one of whom was called Calmaan); his third blood-sister Sinech was the mother of the men MocuCein in Cuile Water, i.e. Aidan the monk (buried in Cuile Water) and Chonrii MocuCein (buried in Daurmaig). Last in the list is his grandmother ToCummi MocuCein, who rather confusingly is identified as the ToCummi MoccuCein who grew truly old and finished his (? her) life as a *presbiter sanctus* in Iona.[113]

Members of a religious *familia* could be counted in the extension of claimed ties of kinship and hence privilege, and women were brought into the alleged households of founding saints. Here, the genealogist's project of establishing wider networks of affiliation overrode any possible concessions to extremist anchorites' ascetic virtue of avoiding the opposite sex. Elsewhere the Columban *familia* claimed that a virgin Ercnait had been the saint's dressmaker, 'her name truly Ercnait, "embroideress"', that is to say, cutter and sewer of clothing to Columcille and his disciples'. This was supposedly the same Ercnait who was credited with founding the church of the virgin saint Coch, 'Cell Chóca'.[114] Patrick, too, added three women to his retinue: numerous eleventh- and twelfth-century texts have a list of people in religion with the saint which includes 'his three embroideresses', named as Lupait, Erc daughter of Dáre, and Cruimthiris in Cengoba.[115] Bairre's Irish hagiographer listed the women who had attended his patron's school at Edergole on Gougane Barre Lake at the head of the River Lee in western County Cork. These were his own sister Crothru daughter of Conall, three un-named daughters of Mac Carthainn, Coch of Ross Banagher, Mo-sillán of Rathmore, Scothnat of Clonbec, Lassair of 'Achad Durbcon', and finally the three daughters of Lugaid, namely Dune, Erc, and Brigit of Ernaide.[116] All, it is insisted, had subsequently given their churches to God and Bairre in perpetuity.

Like the earlier ones, the later Lives of male saints mention holy women who had lived at small churches and been buried there. Thus we learn of the 'holy, noble and honourable virgin Midabair, who used to bless at Bumlin' on the Plain of Aí west of the River Shannon in Roscommon. We also hear of a princess Patrick had converted and her holy woman tutor, buried in the cemetery at Cechtumbair of 'Druim Dubain', near Clogher in Ulster.[117] The Meath church of the virgin Scíre (Kilskeer) remains in the record, but now as part of the

---

[113] 'Disciples and Relatives of St Columba' (*Thes. Pal.* ii. 281); *Kenney*, no. 219(i).

[114] Martyrology of Oengus, notes on 8 Jan. 'Cell Chuaca' may be modern Kilcock, Co. Kildare.

[115] Tripartite Life (Stokes, *Tripartite Life*, 266–7); see also Stokes, *Tripartite Life*, i., p. cxxvii, for full references to this list in the Leabhar Breac, Egerton 93, Book of Leinster, Book of Lecan, and AFM 448.

[116] Bairre's school Edergole (Etergabail on Lough Irce) was shown to be at this site, not Addrigoole, by Plummer, *BNE*, ii. 375. Some of the churches are identifiable, of which all are southern: Coch's Minster (Mainister Coinche) in Ross Banagher (Ir. Ros Bendchuir) is identified with Rossmanagher townland north-west of Limerick; Rathmore is on the south coast near Sherkin Island; Clonbec is thought to be in Tipperary; 'Ernaide' presumably refers to the southern place going by that name, Ballyvourney on the Sullane River in Cork, ten miles west of Macroom. 'Achad Durbcon' is not known, but other texts place it in Cork along the River Lee, the 'Muscraige Mittine'.

[117] Irish Life of Berach, ch. 6.

Columban federation; at some point, a late Life tells us, an important assembly was held there.[118] The glosses on the martyrologies also add to the number of known female saints.[119]

For all that their memories, and their names upon the lists recording them, were pawns of political machinations, these less-known females—or at least most of them—were also genuinely regarded as having the power of intercession and thus were saints in the functioning sense of the word. Thus the 'genealogical-pawn' thesis is only a partial one. At the very least they were petitioned by passing visitors to their grave sites, as these places were places of divine power, and the holy dead effective intercessors. But more than this, I think, was the due of many of them. The martyrologies, attest, at bottom that they were formally, liturgically commemorated on their feast days. An eleventh-century Irish lorica prayer addressed invokes the protection Ireland's virgins, and most of those named are almost unknown except for their presence in the notes of one of the martyrologies.[120] In this little-known prayer the petitioner calls upon over a dozen Irish virgins: Coch, Midnat, Scíre, Sinche, Caite, Cuich, Coemill, Craine, Coipp, Cocnat, Ness, Derbfalen, Becnat, Cíar, Crone, Caillann, Locha, Luaithrenn, Rond, Ronnat, Rignach, Sarnat, Segnat, and Sodelb, as well as the better-known Brigit, Monenna, Lassair, and Samthann. The individual who used this prayer believed these now-unknown female saints could provide protection from demons and evil men, sickness and lies, cold and hunger, the plague of the tempestuous doom, and 'the evil of hell with its many monsters'. For him as for many others, these long-dead women were much more than names on an ever-changing family tree, more than historical links between monasteries. They were agents of spiritual power.

CONCLUSION

In sum, nun, nunnery, and female saint were all flourishing in the tenth- to twelfth-century period. The female houses, large and small, continued to exist. The nuns' professions appear to have continued much as before. Female saints, major and minor, continued to be petitioned by worshippers of both sexes. The changes of these centuries are, against this background, initially invisible. They become more apparent, however, when the scholar's gaze turns to the question of relations between the sexes within monastic life, and concentrates particularly on the chronology in the hagiographical corpus.

---

[118] Irish Life of Columba, ch. 38. Columba when at Kells, turned to the south-west and predicted with a smile the '*grafann* of Cell Scíre' at which fifty sons of Life would be born in one night. The church is also mentioned in the charters in the Book of Kells.

[119] e.g. in the notes to the Martyrology of Oengus the virgins Bronach, Cumman the Little, and Aiche ('who raised the dead') appear for the first time.

[120] *Nom Churim ar Commairge*, Plummer, *Irish Litanies*, 92–3.

8

Proximities and Boundaries:
Sexual Anxiety and the Monastery

When we compare the earlier portrayals of male–female relations in the church with the images in the later hagiography, the overriding characteristic is continuity, as it was with the the nuns' professions and the other subjects discussed in the preceding chapter. Yet the issues and problems of sexuality within the monastic world were being addressed more than they had been before, and subtle but important changes were afoot.

In both male and female Lives of these later centuries, the normal course of events remained as it was in the earlier ones. Monks, clerics, and nuns interact in close proximity on account of friendship, collaboration, and mutual support: such arrangements neither scandalized nor puzzled the redactors. In the canon of male Lives, Maedóc of Ferns's second Irish Life is typical: nuns are mentioned neutrally, simply that the saint once took a plough team as alms on a visit to some holy virgins of distinguished chastity.[1] Equally typical is the story from another male Life in which a nunnery borrowed the use of a scribe from a men's house.[2]

The female Lives portray much the same thing. Samthann's Life in particular is characterized by extensive contact between monks and nuns. The nunnery received visitors from male monasteries and gave them hospitality: brothers from Iona brought wool to them, and a cleric came to Samthann to consult with her about going on pilgrimage. Likewise, Samthann went visiting to men's monasteries; Granard is mentioned in this context.[3] Samthann personally organized the carpenters and builders working at the monastery and negotiated the release of prisoners with the local king. Her prioress Nathea also undertook such responsibilities; in fact, Nathea is said to have gone with the builders to the woods and to Connaught, to get the proper wood for building.[4] No explanation or cautions were given by the hagiographer about either the

---

[1] Ch. 114.   [2] Latin Life of Ailbe, D text, ch. 32.   [3] Life of Samthann, chs. 23, 24, 19.
[4] Ibid., going into the woods, ch. 15; Nathea travelling to Connaught, ch. 16.

journey or the going into the forest with these men; no remark was made on the fact of a nun travelling with or working closely with males.

In her Life, Lassair travelled to see parents, to set up churches, and to visit other ecclesiastics, and there is no suggestion that her late redactor had any concerns about her extensive involvement with men. Typical is the passage in which Lassair set out to find her father who had just converted to the religious life and was staying with MacConall some distance away; here as often elsewhere the virgin was very much in the company of men:

Iarsin ceileabhrais Lasair do chléircibh an bhaile 7 rainic roimpe a ccen tséa 7 tsiubhail otha sin go tigh Mic Conaill 7 Espag Aodháin na cuidechta 7 dream eile do chléircibh an bhaile.[4A]

Then Lassair bade adieu to the clerics of the hamlet and set forth walking from there to the house of Conall's son, together with Bishop Aodhán and also a company of clerics of the hamlet.

Just as the person who wrote Lassair's life was unflustered to imagine her on the road amidst a band of priests, so were other authors. Monenna's Life is virtually a travelogue of her wanderings with her virgins, and a homily on Brigit recounts a miracle which occurred once when Brigit was with her virgins at Armagh.[5] Likewise, Monenna's Life, quite typically, has clerics visiting her in friendship: Patrick and Monenna, it seems, were friends, if indeed that is the implication of the chapter which begins, *Quadam die contigit quod octo presbiteri missi a sancto Patricio episcopo venissent ut visitarent sorores in deserto positas et maxime Monennam abbatissam.*[6] Ita and Coemgen were alleged to have had a particularly close affectionate relationship, according to Ita's Life, for the saint was called by a dying Coemgen to come to his monastery: *sanctus abbas Comhganus, cum sciret sue remuneracionis tempus advenire, rogata est a se sancta Ita, ut veniret ad eum.*[7] In this era, as in earlier centuries, sex did not preclude affectionate ties which could be expressed by visits undertaken over long distances.

Male Monasteries Claiming Communities of Nuns

Just as the Lives show monks and nuns engaging with the opposite sex, so too do the pieces of evidence concerning residence and burial habits of the time. Glendalough in the twelfth century and thereabouts was making much of its attractiveness to female devotees. It was a favoured burial place of queens, a boast made in one Life which is supported by the notice in the annals of the burial there in 1098 of the queen mother of the Uí Briain, the lady Derbforgaill.[8] Coemgen's Middle Irish Life refers to a community of nuns at Glendalough, and there

---

[4A] Life of Lassair (Gwynn, 'Beatha Lasrach', 92–3).
[5] Homily on Brigit from the *Leabhar Breac*, in Stokes, *Three Irish Homilies*, 74–5.
[6] Conchubranus, Life of Monenna, book 1, ch. 10.   [7] Life of Ita, ch. 13.
[8] Second Irish Life of Coemgen, ch. 10; ATig 1098.

was a women's church about 150 metres from the monastery's round tower. Its ruins still remain, and one can see that it was situated in a square raised enclosure and that it was rebuilt, or built, in the twelfth century, for there are remnants of the chancel and north door in twelfth-century architectural style.[9] That there may have been a handful of Benedictine nuns in the twelfth century just might be plausible, given a former English presence in the form of one holy man 'Cellach the Saxon of Glendalough' whose ethnic identity was partly English, though somewhat confused in the description, 'he was not English, but was Irish, as he had come from the English to the Irish'.[10]

Armagh for its part became a pilgrimage destination and retirement home for queens *par excellence*. There in 1151 died Derbforgaill daughter of Domhnaill mic meic Lochlainn, king of Ireland, who was wife of Connaught's King Toirdelbaich Ua Conchobhair.[11] It had an oratory 'Recles Brigti', which was one of only two church buildings to survive the Armagh blaze of 1179.[12]

The Columban community promoted abbot Adomnán (floruit *c*.700) as a saint. His Life was written *c*.960, and he also appears in the Middle Irish commentaries on his law of 697, as a saviour of Irish women. In these later commentaries, women were enjoined to give renders to Columba's church whenever his relics were brought to their area on circuit, in gratitude for his promulgating his Law of Innocents: queens should give horses, penitent nuns garments, and lesser women items appropriate to their wealth and status.[13] Confusingly, however, Adomnán's Life appears to denigrate the female sex, commencing as it does with a little homily stressing the idea that women are unsuitable for the rigours of the religious life; it cites the biblical figure of Wisdom whose commandment, 'men, gird up your loins', was said to use the word *vir* rather than *homo* to indicate that Wisdom meant to speak to the male sex in particular; according to the hagiographer, it was as though Wisdom were saying 'I do not speak to women because they who are of unstable mind cannot at all understand my words'.[14] This sort of contradiction in attitude to the female sex, as will be discussed below, is characteristic of Irish writing of this period. Women appear to be very much present in the Columban federation, in other evidence: two Columban houses of this era, Derry and Iona, have traces of female burials.[15] Derry (Ir. Dáire) acquired in the twelfth century a female erenagh,

---

[9] H. Leask, *Glendalough* (Dublin, n.d.); H. Leask, *Irish Churches and Monastic Buildings*, 3 vols. (Dundalk, 1958), i. 74; Killanin and Duignan, *Shell Guide*, 292.

[10] Martyrology of Oengus, notes on 7 Oct.   [11] AFM 1151.

[12] AU, AFM 1179. The other was the Teampull-na-Ferta, the church of the relics. The Brigit church was located thirty yards north-east of the present St Malachy's Church in Chapel Lane (Killanin and Duignan, *Shell Guide*, 60). On the site, see C. Brown and A. Harper, 'Excavations at Cathedral Hill, Armagh', *UJA* 47 (1984), 109–61.

[13] *Cáin Adomnáin*, ch. 24 (Irish Introduction to the core Latin text).

[14] Irish Life of Adomnán (*Betha Adomnáin*), ch. 1 (M. Herbert and P. Ó Riain, *Betha Adamnain: the Irish Life of Adamnan* (Irish Texts Society 54; London, 1986)). On date, background, and purpose of the text see also Herbert, *Iona*, 151–79.

[15] R. Reece, *Excavations on Iona, 1964–1974* (London, 1981).

Bebhinn, daughter of MacConchaille, which could indicate that there was a female community there during her lifetime at least.[16]

It is in the eleventh century that, for the first time, there is proof that Clonmacnois had a women's community: the annals report that 'the cemetery of the nuns was burnt, with its stone church' (*reileacc Chailleach Cluanna mic Nóis do losccad co na daimliaig*).[17] That church was located a third of a mile north-east of the main area, and was rebuilt in the twelfth century by the wife of Tigernan Ua Ruairc of Bréifne, Queen Derbforgaill, who was also involved in the foundation of Mellifont Abbey (1152), the first Cistercian abbey in Ireland.[18]

St Carthach's Lismore was supposedly next to the site of the virgin Coemell's little church (*cellulam*). According to a twelfth-century Life (copied by 'D' in the thirteenth), when Carthach turned up at her church the virgin encouraged him to make his place there, then donated her place to him. At the time the Life was written Lismore was one of the leading monasteries in Munster, and had a group of nuns on the very site where Coemell's little church had allegedly stood all those centuries before.[19] Half of Lismore's *civitas* was enclosed, however, and women were not permitted to set foot inside that part.[20] One guesses that the female component had been continuous through the earlier centuries, and it was doubtless this community which was made into a women's convent of Augustinian canons in the later twelfth century and existed as such until the Reformation.[21]

Other monasteries too were reported in the texts of the tenth- to twelfth-century period to have women. Clones in the thirteenth century boasted that in the founder Tigernach's day the monastery contained a multitude of both sexes.[22] Daig mac Cairrell's Inishkeen had apparently attracted many virgins in the saint's day, but the female community was subsequently disbanded—or so claimed the late Latin Life.[23] Fintán's monastery had nuns in the twelfth or thirteenth century, subject to Inishkeen, and the enclave supposedly had existed

---

[16] AFM 1134.   [17] AFM 1026, 1082.

[18] She was a deeply generous patron: at Mellifont's establishment she presented the abbey with 60 ounces of gold, a gold chalice for the high altar, and with furnishings for sixty other altars. She retired to Mellifont in old age and died there in 1193. A few remains of the Romanesque nave-and-chancel structure survived to modern times; T. Westropp, 'A Description of the Ancient Buildings and Crosses at Clonmacnois, King's County', *JRSAI* 37 (1907), 277–307; C. Manning, *Clonmacnoise* (Dublin, 1994), 18, 32–3; Leask, *Irish Churches*, i. 146–50.

[19] Latin Life of Carthach, D text, ch. 65: *et illa sancta virgo se cum cellula sua sancto Mochutu* [i.e. Carthach] *obtulit, in quo loco monasterium sanctimonialum est hodie in civitate Less Mor . . . Egregia iam et sancta civitas est Less Mor, cuius dimidium est assilum in quo nulla mulier audet intrare.*

[20] Ibid.

[21] The remains at Clones are considerable and feature both early and Romanesque ruins; see W. Wakeman, 'On the Ecclesiastical Antiquities of Cluain-Eois', *JRSAI* 13 (1874–5), 327–40; Killanin and Duignan, *Shell Guide*, 157–8.

[22] Latin Life of Tigernach, ch. 18.

[23] Latin Life of Daig, ch. 16 (*Heist*, 389–94). Religious women in general figure especially prominently in this brief Life. A few ruins of the monastery, which is some seven miles north-east of Carrickmacross, are still visible, including the base of a round tower.

from the time the place was founded.[24] Bairre of Cork's Irish Life claimed that his island monastery of Etergabáil (mod. Edergole) had, or had had, a school which taught many virgins.[25] Seirkieran claimed to have, or have had, an adjacent women's community which Ciarán had founded and put under his mother Liadain's direction.[26]

Other male monasteries contain remains suggesting a female community in the early medieval period. At Offaly's Lemanaghan (Ir. Líath Mancháin) there is a semi-ruined church said to be of Manchán's mother; it is south-east of Manchán's church along a walkway through a marsh, and is surrounded by a small enclosure.[27] The remains of Molaisse's monastery on Inishmurray in Donegal Bay include two chapels to the south-east of the main enclosure, namely Reilic-na-mBan and Teampall-na-mBan ('the women's cemetery', and 'the women's church') with a nearby cross pillar; significantly, in the central sub-enclosure is an oratory known as Teampall-bhFear ('the men's church') where until recently only men were buried.[28] Inishglora, an island off the Mayo coast, had a community allegedly founded by Brendan: its ruins consist of a stone enclosure, a few cross-slabs and pillars and three chapels, one of which is known as Teampall-na-mBan.[29] A woman's church is also found on Inchcleraun in the northern part of Lough Ree, known primarily for its male inhabitants: sources remembered its early saint Diarmait, its saint Sínach (obit AFM 719), and one of its lectors.[30] Carrickmore in Co. Tyrone (Termon-cumaing) had a women's cemetery: a twelfth-century church attests to a small community there, and it subsequently became a parish church.[31]

---

[24] Latin Life of Daig, ch. 12: *in monasterio quoque sanctarum virginum filiarum Fintani, virginem quandam, nocte adventus eius defunctam, vite restituit. Quapropter virgines monasterium suum eius successorumque ipsius dominatui tradiderunt.* There are three Fintáns who were abbots, but Heist considered that this one was Fintán *alias* Munnu, the abbot of Taghmon (Ir. Tech Munnu, in modern Co. Wexford); the others are the abbots of Clonenagh (Ir. Cluain Ednech, Co. Laois) and Doon (Ir. Dún Blesci, Co. Limerick) (*Heist*, 425). There is also, however, a Fintán associated with the very nearby Clonkeen, Co. Louth, of which some eight members are remembered in the martyrologies: perhaps it was nuns of this place instead who were subject to Inishkeen.

[25] Irish Life of Bairre of Cork, ch. 25.

[26] Latin Life of Ciarán of Seirkieran, D text, chs. 8, 24 (*PVSH* i. 200–17). The women's community is also in the Second Irish Life of Ciarán, ch. 6, which according to Sharpe may be based on the same examplar as D. The First Irish Life is derived from D (*BNE* i. 103–12; Eng. trans., ii. 99–108).

[27] Manchán was said to be a pupil of Declán, Latin Life of Declán, D text, ch. 16 (*PVSH* ii. 32–59) but there is to my knowledge no account of his mother. Cf. the adjacent female communities supervised by the mothers of other male saints (Hughes and Hamlin, *Modern Traveller*, 68).

[28] Hughes and Hamlin, *Modern Traveller*, 68; Killanin and Duignan, *Shell Guide*, 308.

[29] Hughes and Hamlin, 68; Killanin and Duignan, 103.

[30] Hughes and Hamlin, 68; Killanin and Duignan, 361; Martyrology of Gorman, 10 Jan., 20 Apr. On the site, F. Bigger, 'Inis Clothrann, Lough Ree: Its History and Antiquities', *JRSAI* 5th ser. 10 (1900), 69–90.

[31] A. Hamlin, 'A Woman's Graveyard at Carrickmore, Co. Tyrone, and the Separate Burial of Women', *UJA* 46 (1983), 41–5.

MALE SAINTS: INTERMITTENT SEPARATISTS

Within the essentially continuous *mundus* of positive nonchalance about relations between the sexes, though, incipient changes become apparent. The Life
of Molua, dating from the late eighth or earlier ninth century, foreshadowed
what becomes in the tenth, eleventh, and twelfth centuries a more frequent
tone. Interspersed among the stories of monks and nuns assisting and visiting
members of the opposite sex are found incongruous messages; these apparent
interpolations are the clues which betray the new preoccupations. When voiced,
they centre on monastic arrangements, namely the proper proximity between
monks and nuns, monks and laywomen, and nuns and laymen.

One way in which this manifests is in statements about the holy saint herself,
or himself, to the effect that he or she personally had followed a separatist
policy. Conchubranus's Life of Monenna exemplifies this clearly. A long text, it
is filled with interactions between the female saint and numerous laymen, all of
which Conchubranus relates without ado. One passage, however, makes a
claim which stands out: Monenna, Conchubranus announces halfway through
the text, avoided the male sex.[32] Qualifying himself, he adds that when, in the
course of her work, she had to deal with men she covered herself:

Narrant ergo certissime de sancta Monenna postquam de peregrinatione Roma re-
vertens in terram venerat sue cognationis sancte sexum virilem numquam intueri. Sed
quando necessitas proficiscendi alibi cogebat infermos visitare aut vinctos precibus sive
muneribus solvere vel captivos redimire illam affirmant in nocte procedere; si autem necessitas cogeret facie operta pallio homines contraire vel appellare semper volens iu-
nioribus exemplum relinquere ne per fenestras ullatenus sineret mortem ad animam
intrare.[33]

Now they say very definitely of saint Monenna that after she had come to the land of her
holy kin on her return from her pilgrimage to Rome she never looked upon the male sex.
But they say that when the need to go forth somewhere caused her to visit the sick or release prisoners by prayers or gifts or redeem captives, she would go out by night; but if
need compelled, she would face or address men with her face covered by a veil, ever
wishing to leave and example to the younger so as not to allow death to enter the soul in
any way through the windows.

The bald assertion stands alone and uncorroborated by either the tone or content of the rest of the Life, especially her death scene in which various noblemen
and kings come to her deathbed. Nevertheless, the point was considered important enough to Conchubranus for him to stress it to his readers. Its tone and
phrasing, combined with its apparent disjunction, suggests that sex-separation of
monks and nuns was a relatively new issue in his day. It is, it could be argued, a
parenthetical insertion whose purpose is to caution the nuns listening to the tale.

[32] Book 3, ch. 5.   [33] Book 2, ch. 16.

This interpretation is strengthened by what we see in another text, a Middle Irish homily on Brigit in the Leabhar Breac. It consists of a retelling of the life and miracles of the saint, and very much resembles a Life, recounting many of the same anecdotes as other Brigidine hagiography: multiplying food, releasing hostages, negotiating with kings on behalf of prisoners, supervising nuns, founding churches, visiting abbots and bishops, and the like. But here we see a new item, a comment not in earlier Lives. 'Now there never hath been any one more bashful or more modest than that holy virgin. She never washed her hands, or her feet, or her head, amongst men. She never looked into a male person's face. She never spoke without blushing.' (*Niroibe tra nech ba nairiu, nabaféli indas innoemógsin. Ni-ronigestar riam alama nach acossa nachacend eter feraib. Nirodfech din riam innguis fersacali. Nirolabra etir cenlossi di*).[34] The purpose of this paragraph is, as in Monenna's Life, to assure the reader or listener that the saint practised certain virtues: avoidance of men, modesty, world-renunciation. Brigit's homilist even wished to convince his readers that she was painfully shy. But Brigit in this sermon acts neither bashful nor retiring. She argues with kings, commands demons, chastises nuns and other abbesses, and gives advice to clerics. What is familiar and demonstrably well-precedented is the majority of stories, in which she is clearly assertive, involved in church affairs and intervening in political matters, and generally given an outspoken personality; what is demonstrably new, on the other hand, is the incongruous claim that she was one of life's coyer maidens.[35]

Male Lives as well, on occasion now make incongruous claims to 'separatism'. Two of them tell of monks who prohibited women from coming near their monastic foundations—the reasons given now, unlike in (say) the seventh-century *Vita I* of Brigit, centre overtly on the women's sexuality. Remarks are made as incidental interjections which say explicitly that for a monk to be in contact with nuns is for him to run a risk of scandal.

The Tutelage of Virgins

It is quite normal for the Lives of this time to recount that in the early days of Christianity in Ireland, some virgins began their religious careers by spending some time under the tutelage of a holy man at his monastic foundation. There was normally no concern expressed about this. Conchubranus, Monenna's hagiographer, was utterly unconcerned about narrating that a young nun was tutored and guided by males. Monenna, he wrote, was consecrated by Patrick, who then gave her religious instruction: *docuit ergo episcopus sanctus sanctam et sponso Christo vero desponsatam filiam diligenter mandata Dei scire et ex corde intelligere.*[36] He then

---

[34] Homily on Brigit in the *Leabhar Breac* (Stokes, *Three Irish Homilies*, 84–5).

[35] A slightly different interpretation is made of gender preoccupations in this Life, based on the anecdote of Orbile, is made by Johnston, 'Transforming Women', 212.

[36] The consecration and education of Monenna are recounted in book 1, chs. 3 and 5, and all subsequent quotes in this paragraph are from these chapters.

placed her under a virgin named Athea, after which he entrusted her to another pious priest (*alius religiosus presbiter*) to teach her the psalms 'and always to nurture her in divine studies' (*in divinis studiis semper nutriret*). After this formative period Monenna returned to her parents' home, to carry on under the instruction of the priest. She then wished to withdraw from the world, but as there were no convents for virgins at this time, she achieved this aim by taking her female followers with her to the holy Bishop Ibar. There, he wrote, she spent much time under the direction of the holy bishop in the service of God, in the strict rule of holy discipline, in severe but just abstinence of life and in great constancy of vigil and reading (*ubi multum temporis in Dei servitio et disciplinarum sanctarum stricta regula et dura vite sed recta abstinentia, in vigiliarum et lectionis assiduitate nimia sub illius episcopi potestate transegit*). Thus Conchubranus was satisfied to write that a young virgin would be away from her parental home under the supervision of male clerics during the time of religious education.

Lassair's hagiographers, too, claimed that their saint had been tutored by a male saint, Molaisse, at whose establishment were found both boys and girls. Molaisse taught wisdom and learning (*laighinn 7 lainegna*), and Lassair had excelled at these so that within three months she had overtaken those who had been there two years.

One redactor of Ciarán's life, who related that this male saint educated a virgin in a one-to-one tutoring arrangement, evidently had some concern about it. His version tells that Ciarán as a young man, while living at Finnian's monastery, was entrusted with the education of a princess who had come to the monastery after dedicating her maidenhood to God; Ciarán was assigned to read the psalms with her, which he did. However, the hagiographer notes carefully, during the whole of her time there the young man would not look upon the princess, but only at her feet (*ni fhaca tra Ciaran do curp na hingine cein batar immale acht a traighthi nama*).[37]

For the hagiographers of this period, the anecdotes of adjacent schools for boys and girls in monasteries occasionally caused concern. Unlike their predecessors of the ninth century and earlier, they would sometimes remark that the proximity of boys and girls could prove problematic. But even when these redactors write down the episodes where the monastic school was the venue of sexual sin among the students, they never blame the institutional structure itself, but rather the individual's shortcomings.[38] The mixed-sex monastic school, or tales thereof, remained in the hagiographic record, then, without being condemned.

---

[37] Homily on the Life of Ciarán in the Book of Lismore, lines 4128–31 (W. Stokes, *Lives of the Saints from the Book of Lismore* (London, 1890), 117–34, 262–80).

[38] Carthach's lapse as a student with a young virgin, described below.

Foster-mothers

In this era male saints were portrayed, more than ever before, as being 'related' to female saints through the bonds of fosterage. Many were said to have been fostered and educated by nuns. To cite but a few examples, Mochoemóg was said to have studied twenty years with Ita, and Brendan spent his first five years with her. Brigit tended Tigernach, and Lassair took on an unnamed youth who wanted to receive learning and instruction. Through the period, the esteem for the foster-mother remains strong, and there is no apparent anxiety about monks being in contact with the virgins who raised them. Indeed, devotion to one's virginal foster-mother is considered a virtue, and Lives often mention saints going in adulthood to visit and care for these women. The first Irish Life of Ciarán of Seirkieran, for example, relates how the saint faithfully returned to visit his foster-mother Cuinche (a holy widow), to give her communion and pray with her, even though it was a long way from his monastic community; and his second Life says he used to go and plough for her.[39]

Even after their charges had grown up, virgin foster-mothers offered advice and spiritual guidance, and good foster-sons followed it. In the poem *A Chrínoc*, a monk addresses the virgin with whom he spent his childhood, lauding her with words 'your advice is ever prompt' (*erlam do chomairle chóir*) and admits, 'if I followed your teaching I should safely reach stern God' (*dia seichmis cech día do dán ro-seismis slán co Día ndían*).[40] In a similar vein Brendan, returning from one of his voyages, dutifully went to his own foster-mother. Ita on one occasion scolded him: 'Ah, dearly beloved son, why did you go on your journey without first taking counsel from me?'[41] But Ita comes across with the most breathtakingly paradoxical advice, for when Brendan was a young man about to leave her to go out in the world for the first time, she had counselled, 'Do not learn of women or of virgins, lest you be reproached in regard to them' (*'na dena foghlaim ag mnaibh na acc oghaibh; 7 na derntar hécnach friu. Imtigh si' olsi '7 teiccemaidh laech suaitnidh soicenelach duit foran slicchid'*).[42] In the Latin Life, this advice was formulated in a wry rhyming couplet: *noli enim discere a virginibus, ne scandalum incurras ab hominibus.*[43] So Brendan was to ignore the counsel of women, including virgins, yet he dutifully carried on visiting his virgin foster-mother and was rightly reproached for failing to ask her advice on religious matters. Both hagiographers were inconsistent beyond this, for in other episodes of these two Lives Brendan sought counsel from the virgin Brigit on several occasions, and he met, aided, and counselled other women. Like its equivalents in other Lives, this anecdote promoting female-avoidance sits somewhat uneasily amidst a wealth of other stories where male saints have easy relations with women.

---

[39] First Irish Life of Ciarán, chs. 35–6.

[40] Greene and O'Connor, *Golden Treasury*, 168–9. Text discussed in *Kenney*, no. 606. The poem is commonly agreed to be a *double entendre* addressing a psalter as though it were a woman; see below, Ch. 9.

[41] First Irish Life of Brendan, ch. 62.   [42] Ibid., ch. 19.   [43] First Latin Life of Brendan, ch. 8.

Nuns, Abortions, and Absolutions

In this period, the Lives of both male and female saints show an increasing concern with matters of sexuality. Certainly there is much continuity of the older nonchalance about contact between the sexes, but the stories of lapses, particularly those of nuns, are greater in number and increasingly detailed.

Among female Lives, it is Ita's that contains the greatest proportion of material concerned with nuns' sexuality. In the Life of thirty-six chapters, four concern sexual lapses of nuns and a fifth treats a nun who was beset by temptation. In the anecdote in chapter 16, a *sanctemonialis* 'fornicated in secret'; confronted by the clairvoyant Ita she confessed, did penance under Ita's hand, and was *sanata*. In chapter 17, another virgin had sex with a man whilst she was away in the province of Connaught; Ita sent for her, heard her confession, supervised her penance, and the nun's soul was restored. Chapter 27 relates that a thieving nun who failed to confess or repent eventually left her community and became a degenerate harlot, *frons meretricis facta est . . . et illa infelix, deserens habitum suum, apud silvaticos in fornicatione consuprata permansit*. In chapter 34 Ita's hagiographer tells that one day the saint gathered her nuns and announced that she knew (prophetess that she was) that one of them had sinned. Each was asked to admit or deny the sin. Ita approached the nun whom she identified as the fornicator, saying to her: *tu hodie in fornicatione peccasti*. Unfortunately she did not repent, nor confess (*non penituit illa, nec confessa est; set cum peccati ignomenia recessit*). She left the community, and wandered to many places, eventually ending up as a slave in Connaught and giving birth to a baby girl. One day, some time later, Ita announced to her *familia* that she knew clairvoyantly that the errant nun was to be found in Connaught in the house of a druid, and that she had repented of her sin; furthermore if she were freed, she would faithfully amend her ways. Ita sent for her and she returned with her baby, to be received with rejoicing. She did penance and lived at Killeedy in sanctity for the rest of her days, raising her daughter in the nunnery (*et ipsa agens penitentiam, in sanctitate usque ad obitum suum cum filia sua in monasterio piisime matrone Yte mansit*). Thus in spite of a new preoccupation with nuns' sexual lapses, this Life like others also promoted the message that, through confession and penance, redemption was possible and desirable. What comes across is the importance of confession and penitence for such a sin, and the ability of the saint and God to forgive these lapses. Against this background is the Tripartite Life's story (absent from earlier versions) that Patrick's sister Lupait, a religious, sinned with a man so she became pregnant; Patrick, when he discovered the fact, killed her in a rage, but softened somewhat to pronounce that he would not damn the child and its descendants. Two things are striking: firstly the harshness of Patrick's response, which must owe something to the Armagh environment in which it was composed, a time when Armagh was increasingly seeking foreign approval and positioning itself for appointment as Ireland's metropolitan See. But secondly even this Life, containing as it does

the most shockingly severe response, fails to condemn Lupait: the anecdote concludes by saying that Patrick buried her and sang her requiem, and she rose to
heaven on the spot; she persuaded Patrick not to condemn the man and his off-
spring, so that that race (the Uí Faeláin and the Uí Duib Dare) was eligible to
enter heaven, though they would always be a sickly stock.[44] Elsewhere the Tripartite Life recounts another episode on the theme: a holy virgin named Ercnait
daughter of Dáre, who was madly in love with the holy man Benignus, died of
an illness. Benignus came and raised her from the dead with the help of some
Patrician relics, and after she sprang up alive it was evident that a miracle had
happened, for now she just loved Benignus spiritually. It is as obvious as it is surprising that in the eyes of Patrick's hagiographer Ercnait's sainthood was uncompromised by her having fallen in love.

As has already been demonstrated, the Lives of this era continue to show
nuns travelling and undertaking journeys for a variety of reasons. Even junior
nuns were shown doing this: for example, Lassair, when a young nun and a pupil
of Molaisse, got his permission to go home to see her parents, and did so.[45] Yet
for one hagiographer journeys did become an occasion for worry. The redactor
of Ita's Life tells of the abbess Rychena's visit to Killeedy over a matter concerning a foster-son: when Rychena is about to set off for home, Ita warns the nun
that she ought to travel back with a bishop as her chaperone, lest she be overcome by demons. *Ancilla Dei, iter tuum prosperum non esset, nisi episcopus tecum veniret,
quia multum demones insidiantur nostro sexui.*[46] Here for the first time a nun travelling
alone is described as being at risk from her own weakness, presumedly of
sexual lust.

The Life of Samthann has two cases of fornicating nuns. In the first anecdote
two nuns lived next to the monastery of the abbot Cainnech; as the result of a
diabolical temptation, one became pregnant: *erant due moniales iuxta monasterium
Kynnechi abbatis, quarum una diabolica suggestione concepit, et postea peperit filium.* To
avoid the damage this would cause to the reputation of the monastery, the two
nuns decided to take the baby to Samthann, having heard of the great saint.
Samthann took pity on the nun and undertook the fostering of the child at her
place, and raised him herself.[47] A second episode of sexual exploits took place
amongst Samthann's own community. A monk entered the precinct and, as a
result of gazing on a particularly beautiful nun, fell in love with her, and she responded. Having arranged to meet the monk outside the walls of the nunnery
to elope with him, the nun got permission to leave on an errand and met
her lover. The affair was aborted by a miraculous if brutal intervention on
the saint's part, and the monk swore never to visit a nunnery again: *itaque*

[44] The political agenda of the episode is self-evident, but this discussion concentrates on its form of expression (Stokes, *Tripartite Life*, i. 234–5); on Benignus (Ir. Benén) and Ercnait, whose church is here specified as Tamlacht Bó in Ulster (possibly mod. Taulagdarn near Armagh), ibid. 232–3.

[45] Irish Life of Lassair (Gwynn, 'Beatha Lasrach', 79).

[46] Life of Ita, ch. 24.   [47] Life of Samthann, ch. 18.

vexacio dans sibi intellectum, ad monasterium virginum se nunquam iterum venturum cum iuramento promisit.[48]

The Leabhar Breac homily on Brigit has but one sexual episode, and it is hardly a scandal. It recounts that the saint met a demon at a nunnery she was visiting, and asked him why he had come among 'our nuns' (*dixit brigit fria demon. cid diatanacaise chucainde inarcaillechu*). He replied that it was because he was accompanying one of the virgins, so Brigit instructed this virgin to perform the sign of the cross over her eyes, whereupon she saw the demon, repented, and was healed of the devil of gluttony and lust that had dwelt in her company (*dorígne inóg athrige iarsin. 7 rohictha dondemon craís ocus etraid bói inacomitecht*).[49]

A story in two versions, both written during this era, relates that St Carthach as a student at Seirkieran fell in love with a girl in the women's community, and she with him, so they arranged a tryst. In the first, the two did not consummate their desire thanks to a last-minute attack of fear of God, after which they separated without saying a word. The girl was blinded by the event and the text goes on to moralize (in what may be an addition by redactor 'D') that this punishment was fitting: since the girl had been blinded morally in her sin she was then blinded physically in her rescue from it. Carthach was punished too, though only in the sense that he performed a penitential pilgrimage.[50] In the second version the couple did make love and a child was conceived, and the baby was to grow up to be known as Molua mac Ochae. It related that Ita allegedly composed the following rhyme on the matter:

> Ticfa Carthach cugaib · fer co n-arthrach creidim
> berthar mac do Carthach (.i. Molua mac Ochae) · nocha marthar etir.[51]

> Carthach will come to you, a man with the appearance of belief
> A son will be born to Carthach (i.e. Molua mac Ochae); he is not at all magnified.

As in earlier Lives, male saints sometimes produced miraculous abortions for pregnant nuns, as a reward for their contrition. In a variation on this compassionate response, one saint instead pronounced that the child would be born, but shame would still be averted because it would grow up to be the monastery's abbot.[52] The incidence of saint-induced abortions does decline, and there is reason to believe that redactors of the twelfth and thirteenth century edited some of them out of the narratives.[53]

---

[48] Ibid., ch. 11. [49] Homily on Brigit from the *Leabhar Breac* (Stokes, *Three Irish Homilies*, 74–5).

[50] Ciarán of Seirkieran, D text, ch. 24; it also appears in the derivative Latin Life of Ciarán of Seirkieran in the Codex Salmanticensis, ch. 15 (*Heist*, 346–53).

[51] Martyrology of Oengus, notes on 5 Mar.

[52] Miraculous abortions: Latin Life of Ciarán of Seirkieran in the Codex Salmanticensis, ch. 5. Abbatial successor: Latin Life of Búite, ch. 29 (*PVSH* i. 87–97).

[53] As did redactor 'D' in some cases (Sharpe, *Saints' Lives*, 213).

SEDUCING THE CONFESSORS

Another change is also evident. A new *topos* is that of the woman who attempts to seduce the monk or cleric. The rise of this subject in ecclesiastical writing is hardly surprising, given the events and trends in England and the Continent. In England, the Benedictine reforms were proceeding apace, influencing not only writing but practice. On the Continent, from the eleventh century the papal reforms, one of whose platforms was reform of the clergy to a celibate norm, were also creating a stir. Both movements framed women as clerics' seducers.

Although some later male Lives promoted separation of monks from all females (including nuns) this feature is neither consistent nor preoccupying. One of the Lives of Coemgen illustrates particularly well just how closely the writers of this period could juxtapose the message of sexual asceticism on the one hand, and the nonchalance of friendships with nuns on the other. It relates that Coemgen used to work in the fields with his brothers in a place visible to the women of the neighbourhood. One ardent young woman watching the monks became smitten when she saw the saint. Filled with uncontrollable desire for him, she gave frantic chase with the intention of ravishing him. He managed to beat her off with stinging nettles and thus saved his virtue, but having defended himself Coemgen neither cursed her nor ran away. Instead he talked with her and persuaded her to become a nun, whereupon she promptly took the veil and promised her virginity to God and to Coemgen. Thereafter, we are told, the woman served Coemgen loyally: *illa autem iuvencula deinceps prudens et sancta virgo effecta est, que sancta monita beati Coemgeni diligenter servabat.*[54] It is significant that Coemgen did not treat his passionate admirer as an envoy of the devil; rather, his reaction recalls Tírechán's seventh-century memoirs which had mentioned calmly that the virgin Comgella had been 'a nun to Cethiacus'. Perhaps more surprisingly, this author goes on to say this maiden 'diligently served' Coemgen, and, given the ambiguity of the language, it is possible that he meant to imply that she lived with him. This type of legend was not unique, for other saints were said to have virgins attending to their close needs as was noted earlier in the legends that Patrick's three embroidresses 'were in orders with him'.[55]

The instruction to show compassion towards lusty women is found in another of Coemgen's Lives as well. This tells of the monk Berchán who went on a mission from Glendalough to the monastery of Abbot Cronán. On the journey Berchán came across a woman wanting to accompany him to his destination; he agreed and they went together. Then she was seized with love for him, 'for he was handsome', so she set about seducing him, finding an excuse to undress in front of him. Just as Berchán was about to succumb, he pulled away and began

---

[54] Latin Life of Coemgen, D text, ch. 4.
[55] Their names are given as Lupait, Erc the daughter of Dare, and Cruimthiris in Cengoba (Stokes, *Tripartite Life*, i. 266–7); Martyrology of Oengus, notes on 8 Jan.

beating her with his bachall. This event was seen clairvoyantly, from a distance, by the two abbots Coemgen and Cronán, and their respective responses launch the moral of the story. Cronán cheered him on, encouraging him in his beating the strumpet (*impudica*) so manfully, but Coemgen had the spiritually superior response. He told him to have mercy: '*O fili carissime Berchane, indulgens parce, et noli miseram flagellare.*' Berchán obeyed Coemgen, and the result was the hagiographer's ideal: the woman repented, took the monk to where he was going, and changed her ways, doing penance and magnifying the Lord.[56]

There are other stories which encourage the would-be seducer of monks or clerics to think of God instead, to love God instead, or even to marry God instead. In fact, this is the Irish standard response. In a Life of Carthach the saint healed a princess, Flandnait, of her withered arm, and at this her exultant father, King Cuanu of Fermoy, said she could marry any man she chose, of all the royal males of Munster. She replied, 'I choose no man other than the one who healed my arm.' Carthach, rather than running away, took advantage of her desire. 'Give her to me and I shall give her to the Son of God, who healed her', he said. This was done and she established with her inheritance (*hereditatem*) a church on the River Blackwater in Fermoy.[57] A similar act is reported in Carthach's Irish Life: being so extraordinarily handsome, it relates, he attracted the passionate, irrepressible love of no less than thirty maidens. In distress he prayed to God about them—asking that their love should turn into a spiritual love (*guidhis Día imón seirc sin do thinntodgh hi sierc spiritalta*). God obliged, and Carthach made then all into nuns (*caillecha*) who served God until death.[58]

'The Temptation of a Confessor' is a little story found in several manuscripts, dated to the twelfth century or just possibly the thirteenth.[59] In it a woman has a monk for her confessor and attempts to seduce him. First she simply propositions him. This does not work: the monk tells her that he is vowed to God since youth and has never known a woman. She should, he says, approach instead her husband if she is lacking sex, for it is right that he, and not himself, be approached that way. And besides, he adds, he is just a poor monk serving God, and it is not suitable for him to be sleeping with her. It is nothing personal, of course. Upset, the woman threatens to make a scene and accuse him of sexual harassment unless he gives in; if he does sin with her, though, she will give him all manner of gifts and wealth. Seemingly caught by the threat, the monk agrees to have sex with her. 'All right', he says, inviting her to follow him into a walled

[56] Latin Life of Coemgen, D text, ch. 43.

[57] Latin Life of Carthach, D text, ch. 39; Irish Life of Mochuda, ch. 19. Flandnait's place is called 'Cluain Dallain at Feic'.

[58] Irish Life of Carthach *alias* Mochuda, ch. 15 (*BNE* i. 291–9; Eng. trans., ii. 282–90).

[59] *Foscél ar Bannscail* ('Short Tale of a Woman'), also sometimes called 'The Temptation of a Confessor', in the *Leabhar Breac*, Bodl. Rawl. B.512, BM Egerton 92, and Bib. Nat. *Fonds celtique* I. *Kenney*, no. 624. This loose translation based on Vendryes's edition, J. Vendryes, 'Trois historiettes irlandaises', *Revue Celtique* 31 (1910), 302–6; also, H. Gaidoz (ed. and trans.), 'La tentation d'un confesseur', Κρυπτάδια 4 (1888), 262–81.

garden adjacent to the monks' quarters where he says they will make love. When the two step out, however, the woman is astonished to discover the garden filled with people. Wandering about among the trees and flowers are members of royal and noble families, including her own husband. She blushes deep red:

'Why have we come here, with all these people around us? And why did you not know this great crowd would be here?', she asks.

'I knew they would be here. Indeed it was I who opened the doors for them all.'

'Quick, let us leave immediately', she says.

'Not until we have done what we came for.'

'That's impossible! Not with all these people around us, who would be staring at us! And truly, when you give me "life from East to West", I simply shan't be able to do it, out of modesty and discretion, what with all these people surrounding me as they are.'

'Alas, noble lady,' he replies, 'they are as nothing compared to the other witnesses who will see you if you do the deed.'

'What do you mean?', she asks.

'Look up', he says. The woman raises her eyes towards the sky, and behold what she sees: the doors and windows of heaven open, and Christ himself is carrying his bleeding cross on his back, with his sacrificial wounds and sores. Mary surrounded by virgins is at another window. The apostles, angels, and nine orders of heaven and all the others look down at the monk and the woman where they stand.

'Do you see, noble lady?'

'I certainly do.' And the woman falls to the ground and begins to weep and beat herself, repenting of her sins.

'It is a sad thing, noble lady, that you were ashamed to commit a sin in the presence of a crowd of people, but you didn't mind the presence of the Lord and the nine orders of heaven whilst committing this act against God's will. Me, I don't mind at all the presence of anyone, living or dead, being around me at my misdeeds as much as I mind a single angel of the Lord's family. So get up, noble lady. Take your husband as your consoler and do penance for this evil action you have attempted. And as for me,' he went on, 'I shall give up dealings with women so long as I live.'

The woman turned to penitence so assiduously that she succeeded in becoming a master of devotion (*súi chrabhaigh*), so that after her death they went together up to heaven.

In much the same spirit, though without the twist at the end, is a poem of the tenth(?) century commonly known as 'Daniel Úa Liathaide's Reply to a Woman'.[60] The narrator, Daniel Úa Liathaide, was the confessor, and the woman a lady who came to him regularly. As the poem opens, he has evidently just received a sexual proposition from her: the poem itself is his reply. As in the

---

[60] *A Ben, Bennacht Fort* ['O Woman, A Blessing on You' or 'Sell Not Heaven for Sin']. *Kenney*, no. 604. K. Meyer (ed. and trans.), 'Daniel Úa Liathaide's Advice to a Woman', *Ériu* 1 (1904), 67–71. Also, Murphy, *Early Irish Lyrics*, 16–17. Meyer thought it might possibly date from as early as the 9th cent., and Murphy agreed. The supposed author, Daniel Úa Liathaide, abbot of Lismore, died in AD 861 according to the Annals of the Four Masters.

other texts discussed, the holy man does not harangue his would-be seductress as a demon or harlot, but instead urges her to change her mind. Significantly, Daniel sends her away with not a curse, but a blessing: 'O woman, a blessing on you! Do not speak! Let us meditate on the doom of eternal judgement! . . . In God's safeguard go to your house, And take a blessing from me, O woman.'

If a sexually-minded approach from a woman ideally required a firm but polite refusal from a holy man, then an innocent approach demanded even more strongly a chivalric response. This is the explicit message in the Lismore Homily on the Life of Brendan. Written in Middle Irish and dating to the eleventh or twelfth century, it recounts that once, when the young Brendan was sitting alone on his chariot, singing his psalms, a 'full-grown girl' jumped up on the chariot and attempted to play with him. He responded by beating her severely; his fosterer Bishop Erc saw the entire transaction and harshly rebuked Brendan, making him do penance for behaving so cruelly to the 'blameless maiden'.[61] The episode recalls one in Cassian's *Conlationes*, the moral of which was also the importance of regarding women as fellow-members of humanity.[62]

In sum, the Irish were evidently responding to issues of celibacy, seduction, and clerical relations with women in a way which was subtle and complex, and their new attitude to the female sex cannot be classed as either 'avoidance' or as 'demonization'. In fact, as will be discussed in the following two chapters, the Irish handling of these issues was markedly different from that of English and Continental ecclesiastical writers in other ways too. There is still, however, the issue of the single-sex male hermitage to consider.

MEN'S SINGLE-SEX MONASTERIES

This chapter began with an enumeration of examples in which men and women were portrayed in the later Lives as living together at monasteries, and these are important to bear in mind when exploring the exceptions. Indeed there had long been places at which men dedicated to God had lived apart from women: in Brigit's early *Vita I* and the (probably) late-eighth or early-ninth century Latin Life of Molua we encountered the male-only hermitage which refused them. In this later period we also meet several such places, and they seem to be increasing in number. Moreover, when they did mention them, hagiographers now went on to offer some justification as to the motive and the theological basis for their policy of segregation. For those who wanted to maintain an all-male environment, women of the laity rather than those of the church were the target of any abuse,

[61] Homily on the Life of Brendan mac Finnlug, lines 3403–26 (Stokes, *Lismore Lives*, 247–61, 99–116).
[62] Cassian, *Conlationes*, book 7, ch. 26, in which Abbot Paul ran away from women because he confused the avoidance of familiarity with the opposite sex (a virtue) with hating the very form of that sex (a sin) (*PL* 49. 477–1328).

yet even lay women were attacked in the Lives by the monks only when they encroached onto the proscribed territory. In all Lives with such episodes, elsewhere in the same text the monks and saints gladly succour lay women in need.

Among the writers whose texts survive, it seems that the desire to separate nuns from monks, when it did arise, was rooted not in misogyny but in a sense of propriety. The reason for separation, the Lives imply, is not that there is anything wrong with the nuns themselves, but rather that people might think there was sexual misconduct going on. In the the Irish Life of Daig, for example, virgins were part of the Inishkeen community, but for some reason the abbot of Clonmacnois was scandalized when he heard it, and sent a messenger to voice his disapproval, but the latter on his arrival was placated by miracles wrought by the virgins. In spite of their vindication, Daig sent the nuns away to various monasteries of their own.[63]

A late Life of Senán explores the justifications of a mixed-sex monastery more explicitly and with greater eloquence. Furthermore, it does something the much earlier Brigidine *Vita I* and the Lives of Daig and Carthach did not do, namely deal directly with the theological issues such exclusion raises, teasing out some of the deeper issues of gender, sexual temptation, and ritual purity. In it, the holy virgin Canair of Bantry on the south-west coast was drawn by a vision to Senán's hermitage on Scattery Island, at the mouth of the Shannon river.[64] She travelled north on pilgrimage to get there, and when she came to the edge of the river she walked across the water to the island. From the surface of the water just off the shore she spoke with the saint, who had come out to meet her.

First she introduced herself, saying she was seeking hospitality from him and wished to receive the sacrament from him. He replied by offering her hospitality at an adjacent island where the nuns stayed who lived under his rule, and agreeing to give her the eucharist 'from his hand'. She replied that she wanted to stay not on the nearby isle but on *his* island. At this, Senán explained that they did not have women on this particular island. The refusal prompted Canair's remarkable speech:

'Cid dia ta latsa sin?' ol Canair. 'Ni messa Crist, ar ni lugha thainic do thathcreic ban inás do thathcreic fher. Ni lugha roces ardaigh ban inás ardaigh fher. Robhatar mná oc umaloid 7 oc timterecht do Crist 7 dia aps[t]alaib. Ní lugha, dano, thiaghuit mná isin bhflaith nemhdha inait fir. Cidh, dano, arna gebhthasa mná cucat at indsi?'[65]

'How can you say that?', said Canair. 'Christ is not worse than you. Christ came to redeem women no less than men. No less did he suffer for the sake of women than for men. Women have served and administered to Christ and his Apostles. Indeed, no less than men do women enter the heavenly kingdom. Why then shouldn't you take women on your island?'

---

[63] Latin Life of Daig, ch. 66.

[64] On the site (Ir. 'Inis Cathaig') see Leask, *Irish Churches*, i. 72.

[65] Irish Homily on the Life of Senán in the Book of Lismore, lines 2416–35 (Stokes, *Lismore Lives*, 54–74).

Senán thereupon told Canair she was stubborn. He would nevertheless offer her a place at the shore of his island, on the brink of the wave, though he was afraid she would be washed away. Canair took up his offer, came ashore, received the eucharist from Senán, and then died and went straight to heaven.

Lisa Bitel, Kathleen Hughes, and Ann Hamlin have all cited the above extract from Senán's Life as evidence for an Irish suspicion of women and, in Bitel's case, for a belief that women were impure. But such a conclusion is insufficient. It loses sight of the fact that Canair, even though not admitted, was deemed neither lustful nor unworthy because of her sex.[66] The saint was clearly acting properly in offering the female pilgrim hospitality and a personal administration of the eucharist. It is explicit that the saint, and probably his other monks too, attended to the nuns nearby, and that they were under his care; his only stipulation was that she should not come onto one particular island, and on even this he gave in to her. That Senán was not a shunner of women is confirmed by the Life's later episodes, which recount that when he knew he was soon to die he was determined to visit for one last time his sister and also the group of nuns who lived under his rule.

Misogyny was on the upsurge, though, and we can see that progression in what happened to the story of Canair as it was recounted in the thirteenth-century. Senán's thirteenth-century poetic Life recounts the same encounter, and by then assertion that women were impure went unchallenged:

> Et ecce adest angelus,   qui elevatam protinus
> Deo devotam feminam   transportavit in insulam.
> Cui presul: 'Quid feminis   commune est cum monachis?
> Nec te nec ullam aliam   admittemus in insulam.'
> Tunc illa ad episcopum: 'Si meum credis spiritum
> posse Christum suscipere,   quid me repellis corpore?'
> 'Credo,' inquit, hoc optime,   sed nulli umquam femine
> huc ingressum concedimus,   esto salvet te Dominus.
> Redi iterum ad seculum,   ne sis nobis in scandalum.
> Etsi es casta pectore,   sexum habes in corpore.'
> 'Spero,' ait, 'in Dominum   quod prius meum spiritum
> de hac carne eiiciat   quam me reverti faciat.'
> Nec mora, reddit spiritum   diemque claudit ultimum.
> A fratribus insolite   celebrantur exequie.
> Sic sancti patris precibus   utrumque complet Dominus,
> et id quod virgo dixerat   et id quod sanctus voverat.[67]

And behold an angel approaches, who raised her up at once and transported the woman, dedicated to God, onto the island. The bishop said to her, 'What do women have in common with monks? We shall admit neither you nor any other [woman] onto the island.' The said she to the bishop, 'If you believe that my spirit can receive Christ

---

[66] Bitel, 'Women's Enclosures', 31; Hughes and Hamlin, *Modern Traveller*, 8.
[67] Latin Life of Senán, ch. 18.

into it, why do you repel me in the flesh?' 'I believe this completely', he said, 'but we have never allowed access here to any woman, so be it, may the Lord save you. Return again to the world, lest you be to us a source of scandal. Even if you are chaste in heart, you have sex in your body.' 'I have faith in the Lord', she said, 'that he shall cast out my spirit from this flesh before he makes me turn back.' Without delay he restored her spirit and closed her final day. An exceptional funeral was celebrated by the brothers. Thus with the prayers of the holy father, the Lord fulfils each of the two [requests], both what the virgin had said and what the saint had vowed.

Only in this version does Senán say anything like 'even if you have no lust in your heart you still have sex in your body'. Neither hagiographer, however, wished his readers to feel they could justify demonizing women dedicated to God, even if they themselves lived at a place which refused residence to nuns, for Christ had redeemed women as much as he had redeemed men. Even if a male house had a God-given right to turn away nuns, it should nevertheless be remembered that women's spirits too can receive Christ. The danger of scandal, combined with the argument of traditional practice, was deemed a valid reason for segregation in the eleventh and twelfth centuries: misogyny was not.

All-Male Cemeteries

Senán's Scattery Island is but one of several places, recounted in the texts of this period, where females could not go. If they alighted on these sites, which were often islands, they would die, go mad, or humiliate themselves. This trope is a new one.

Adomnán's tenth-century Life mentioned that the saints were offended by the burial of a pregnant woman on Tory Island off the west coast of Donegal.[68] Gerald of Wales spoke of an island in a north Munster lake which no woman or female animal could enter without immediately dying: 'this has been proved many times by instances of dogs and cats and other animals of the female sex.' A similar island, possibly the same one, was recorded earlier in verse by the Irish-born eleventh-century bishop Patrick of Dublin.[69] St Féchín's church and rock-cut mill in Fore (Co. Westmeath) was also a place no woman could enter.[70] Though Fore is not an island, two other places Féchín allegedly founded are,

---

[68] Irish Life of Adomnán, ch. 11. On the place, Ir. Tóraig Island, see D. Kelly, 'The Crosses of Tory Island', in Smyth, *Seanchas*, 53–63, with references. The saint of this place, Ernaine, is commemorated in the Martyrology of Donegal, 17 Aug.

[69] Bishop Patrick, 'Verses', verse 21, *De insula quadam satis admiranda*, on which female birds do not land (A. Gwynn (ed. and trans.), *The Writings of Bishop Patrick, 1074–1084* (Scriptores Latini Hiberniae 1; Dublin, 1955), 58–69).

[70] Fore, Co. Westmeath, near present-day Castlepollard, was an early monastery founded by St Féchín, alias Mo Fhéca, renowned for his harsh asceticism. It was large and wealthy enough to suffer repeated Viking attack. Some ruins, including those of the graveyard, can still be seen. Fore is still a pilgrimage site today; and monastic ruins remain, with the early church still standing, with a chancel added *c*.1200; there is also a plain stone cross and a nearby holy well (Leask, *Irish Churches*, i. 64 with plans; Killanin and Duignan, *Shell Guide*, 144, 154; Harbison, *Pilgrimage*, 136).

i.e. Omey Island and Hish Island in Cleggan Bay, Co. Galway.[71] The grave of St Critán, *alias* Mac Rustaing in Russagh (Ir. Ross Ech) in Westmeath must be the most memorable of the lot, however, for no woman could approach it without losing her dignity. As one scribe elucidated in a little ditty:

> Lighe maic Rustaing raidhe · i Ros ech cen imnaire,
> mar atchi cach ben baighid · briaghid ocus banghairidh.[72]

> Mac Rustaing's grave in Russagh, you say without shame—
> if she sees it, every women talks, farts, and laughs aloud.

Bishop Patrick of Dublin wrote a short poem on this or another such grave, for the effect on women of the grave he describes was the same; in his account, though, the un-named owner of the grave was not a saint but a man who had raped many good women.[73]

The sudden rise in popularity of this type of folklore was arguably, due to the new atmosphere emanating from the Continent, in which women might be derided, combined with the native tradition of the anchoritic male-only retreat. It fed into the rising interest in 'wonders' which so characterized the twelfth century as a whole. The origin and meaning of these sites may lie in an earlier use by anchorites who had taken the vow not to have contact with women. Recalling the episode of the anchorite in Brigit's early *Vita I* serves to highlight the usefulness of island dwellings for such hermits and may indicate a long-standing general preference among them. Presumably when they died they were buried on their islands or in their hermitages, and the tradition of excluding the female sex would continue long after there ceased to be an eremitic community on the sites. It seems likely that in the tenth, eleventh, and twelfth centuries the rule blocking females from single-sex anchoritic retreats survived in folk custom.

CONCLUSIONS

As will be already apparent to some readers, the foregoing interpretation of hagiographic evidence on the sexes in the Irish Church differs considerably from that of many ecclesiastical scholars of an older generation. With very few exceptions they used the 'anxiety episodes' treated in this chapter to illustrate their general assertion that the 'Isle of Saints and Scholars' was one whose clerics had unimpeachable, indeed scrupulous morals. That era was less aware of the dating of the hagiography and its method of evolution and redaction,

---

[71] Gerald of Wales, *Topographia*, book 2, chs. 37, 81 (J. Dimock, *Topographia Hibernica et Expugnatio Hibernica* (Rolls Series; London, 1867).
[72] Martyrology of Oengus, notes on 14 Sept. Russagh is mentioned in AFM 614, 821, 896. Critán appears in the story *Aislinge maic Conglinne*, ch. 6 (K. Meyer, *Aislinge maic Conglinne* (London, 1892)).
[73] Bishop Patrick, 'Verses', verse 13, *Continet hec hominis*.

which permitted them to cherry-pick the ascetic episodes in relatively good conscience. Much as the survivalist ethnographers and folklorists of the same generation took a twelfth-century report of a Kildare fire as a sign of enduring paganism in preference to earlier accounts which suggested discontinuity, these scholars took accounts of woman-shunning over earlier, non-separatist ones. Both found only in the later sources the evidence which best described their beliefs about early Irish Christianity. It is hoped that the present interpretation is built from the empirical evidence, rather than imposing itself upon it.

9

The Virgin Consort in Hagiography

If the Irish attitudes were increasingly mixed on the subject of men and women sharing space in the religious life, this ambivalence is nowhere clearer than in one new and most extraordinary type of narrative. It both epitomizes the issues and reveals the underlying common lines of thinking and rationalization. There is no better way to introduce it than by example. The tale below is embedded in the notes to the Martyrology of Oengus, and makes up part of the extensive scholia. Holy Saint Scothíne of Tisscoffin, the tenth- or eleventh-century writer explains, had had rather unusual nocturnal habits.

No laigdis dano da ingin chorrchíchecha immi cach n-aidchi comad móide in cath dó fri Demon, cor' himraided a ailiugud trit-sin. Co tainic Brénaind dia derbad, co nderbairt Scoithin: Loighed am lepaidsea in cleirech anocht, ar se. O ro siacht iarum co huair chumsanta and tecait na hingena issin tech a raibe Brenaind 7 a n-utlaige do grissaig ina caslaib, 7 ní ro loisc in teine iat, 7 doirtid i fiadnaisi Brénaind 7 tiagait issin lepaid chuice. Créd so? ol Brénaind. Is amlaid dogniam cach n-aidchi, ar na hingena. Loighit im Brénaind, 7 ní choemnacair sidhe cotlad etir lasin élscoth. Is anforbthe sin, a cleirig, ar na hingena: intí bis sunn cach n-aídchi ní mothaig ní etir. Cid tái nach eirge isin dabaig, a cleirig, damad usuaidhe duit? Is minic athaigis in cleirech .i. Scothín. Maith, tra, ol Brénaind, is cair duind in derbad so, is ferr intí seo itamni. Doniat a n-aentaid 7 a cotach iarsin, 7 scarait feliciter.[1]

Now two maidens with pointed breasts used to lie with him every night that the battle with the Devil might be the greater for him. And it was proposed to accuse him on that account. So Brendan came to test him, and Scothíne said, 'Let the cleric lie in my bed tonight'. So when he reached the hour of resting the girls came into the house in which was Brendan, with their lapfuls of glowing embers in their chasubles; and the fire burnt them not, and they spill the embers in front of Brendan and go to bed. 'What is this?', asks Brendan. 'We do this every night', say the girls. They lie down with Brendan, and nowise could he sleep for longing. 'That is imperfect, O cleric', say the girls: 'he who is here every night feels nothing at all. Why do you not go into the tub [of cold water] if it be easier for you? Often the cleric, even Scothíne, visits it.' 'Well', says Brendan, 'it is wrong to make this test, for he is better than we are.' Thereafter they make their union and their covenant, and they part happily.

The Irish consort stories have perplexed historians for nearly a hundred years, and the discussions have so far produced no plausible explanation. In 1894 T. Olden published an article, 'On the Consortia of The First Order of Irish

[1] Martyrology of Oengus, notes on 2 Jan.

Saints', which argued that the Irish practised syneisactism throughout the whole of the early medieval period.[2] The 1902 publication of a book entitled *Virgines Subintroductae* saw the assertion restated, with the author Hans Achelis going so far as to assert that the Celtic Church was actually characterized by the practice, but he, unlike Olden, believed that it had died out there by the sixth century.[3] Kuno Meyer in 1918 stated his conviction that syneisactism had reached and had survived in Ireland, on the basis of an Irish monastic poem seemingly written by a monk to a consort nun.[4] Louis Gougaud followed Meyer's view.[5] But these three scholars were in a minority. Even at this early date most historians preferred to say that the texts did not reflect actual Irish practice. When they did concede that the actuality was possible, they took Achelis's line, namely that it had died away very quickly. Literary discussions have since appeared about individual texts, notably the poem *A Chrínóc*, but these have not taken on the question of Irish syneisactism as a whole, and neither the debate (minor though it is) nor the body of texts on which it rests have been studied in the succeeding years.

There is, however, one partial exception. In 1968 Roger Reynolds treated the matter in a short article published in the *Harvard Theological Review*, in which for the first time many of the relevant texts were brought together and considered in the light of their wider Christian context.[6] He concluded that it was indeed likely that female consorts lived with holy men in early medieval Ireland. Indeed, 'far from being a Celtic skeleton-in-the-closet, Celtic syneisactism represented one of the most primitive aspects of Christianity to survive in medieval Western Europe.'[7] Reynolds's article did not explore the dating of the Irish texts on which he built his case, but it did bring as many as possible together so they could be seen as a corpus. Their number and their presence across a variety of sources, combined with the panoply of late antique and European references to the same practice, were sufficient to convince him that the Irish were indeed participating in the practice.

Reynolds was surely right to draw scholarly attention to the fact that consort relations have a real and meaningful history in Christianity, and that the Irish accounts must be seen in their broader historical context. But his argument was flawed in two ways. First, he did not distinguish other sorts of male–female monastic association (joint journeys, opposite-sex students, etc.) from syneisactism *per se*, whose definition bears repeating: the situation in which 'female

---

[2] T. Olden, 'On the Consortia of The First Order of Irish Saints', *PRIA* 3 (1894), 415–20.

[3] H. Achelis, *Virgines Subintroductae* (Leipzig, 1902), see esp. 124, 223.

[4] K. Meyer, 'An Crínóg: Ein altirisches Gedicht an eine Syneisakte', *Sitzungberichte der königlich preussischer Akademie der Wissenschaften* 18 (1918), 361–74.

[5] L. Gougaud, '*Mulierum Consortia*: étude sur le syneisaktisme chez les ascètes celtiques', *Ériu* 9 (1923), 147–56.

[6] R. Reynolds, '*Virgines Subintroductae* in Celtic Christianity', *Harvard Theological Review* 61 (1968), 547–66, at 548.

[7] Reynolds, '*Virgines Subintroductae*', 548.

Christian ascetics . . . lived together with men, although both parties had taken the vow of continence, and were animated with the earnest desire to keep it'.[8] He also included without distinction texts referring to married clergy, which is a different albeit related matter; thus his data was skewed, containing as it did inapplicable evidence. The second problem with the article is that he did not (and in some cases could not, given the state of scholarship at the time), consider the dates of the sources.

Reynolds's imprecise typology and inattention to chronology shaped his conclusions. When one considers the relevant material in relationship to when it was written, a different set of conclusions about consorts in Ireland becomes more convincing. It is now evident that all the texts which self-consciously address the practice of syneisactism *per se* date from the tenth century or later. We know too that in Ireland all along it had not been unusual for consecrated women to live in proximity to monks and clerics, and that these relations might be marital or proto-marital—to wit, a cleric's female companion was sometimes called *caillech*, and in the ninth century the virgin Perpetua was remembered as St Peter's *coniunx*. Considering this, it becomes apparent that for some reason Irish religious writers in the tenth, eleventh, and twelfth centuries drew upon the *topos* of the *virgo subintroducta*, which they knew from patristic literature and possibly, post mid-eleventh century, from Continental reformist writings. Their deliberate engagement with this motif strongly suggests there was pressure, located possibly within Ireland as well as outside it, to remove clerics and monks from the presence of their women intimates.

THE TEXTS AND THEIR STORIES

The Scothíne story follows a more general pattern: at its most basic, the holy man's spiritual power is proved to doubters by his ability to successfully go to sleep while between two naked virgins. Scothíne can thus handle the temptation, but Brendan, who doubts him, cannot. Brendan must therefore abandon the temptation and must not live with female companions. The moral of the story? Those clerics who cannot maintain chastity, or even peace of mind, whilst sharing quarters with women, need to live separately. It is important to note also what is not said; the author makes no criticism of the women involved. The virgins are no seducing harlots, no new Eves holding up apples of sinful lust. Nor is St Scothíne criticized—having transcended his own lust, he need not shun women, nor need he change his living arrangement into one which is sex-segregated.[9]

---

[8] Clark, '*Subintroductae*', 265.

[9] Johnston sees these females as liminal figures, embodiments of a symbolic female sexuality which the church perceived as dangerous, a view with which I in large part disagree ('Transforming Women', 209–10).

Patrick's Tripartite Life contains another such story. Bishop Mel, although he does not practise the ascetic gymnastics which Scothíne undertakes, is found to be living with a woman. Though called *siur* ('sister') the woman here is probably not a blood relative.[10]

Olaili aimsir atchúas doPatraic cin doepscop Mel fria fiair, tre comrorcoin indaescarsluaig, ar nobitis in aentegdais oc ernaigthe frisinCoimdi[d]. Otconnairc epscop Mél Patraic chucai día cairiugud do Ardachad, dochúaid epscop Mél do aclaid etrache for a fer flechod. Otchúas do Patraic gabail bratán do fonninnassin, roráidi Patraic inderbáruscc nairdirc '"ar aroi (.i. ar na immaire) adclaiss linne". Fortés Mél du thocad, ar ni fortachtaig[i] Día nach mifhir meirb, id est, non temptabis Dominum Deum tuum'. Dodechaid dano siur epscuip Mél, ocus tene lea innacasa[i]l. Rofitir Patraic natbói cin, eturra, dicens: 'Seorsum viri [et] seorsum feminae, ne occasionem dare infirmis inveniemur, et ne nomen Domini per nos blasfemaretur, [quod] absit a nobis'. Et sic relicit eos, .i. Bri (.i.mons) Leith eturru: sisi in Druimm Chea fri Brí leith indíar, eissium friss anair inArddachud.[11]

At a certain time Patrick was told, through the error of the rabble, that Bishop Mel had sinned with his kinswoman [sister], for they used to be in one habitation a-praying to the Lord. When Bishop Mel saw Patrick coming to him, to Ardagh, in order to reproach him, Bishop Mel went to angle in the furrows whereon rain had poured. When Patrick was told that he was catching salmon in that wise, Patrick uttered the renowned proverb '"On his field, i.e. on the ridges he angled for salmon". I will help Mel to luck, for God assists not a feeble ignorant man i.e. thou shalt not tempt the Lord thy God.' Then bishop Mel's kinswoman [sister] came having fire in her chasuble [And her raiment was not injured. Then] Patrick knew that there was no sin between them, saying, 'Let men and women be apart, so that we may not be found to give opportunity to the weak, and so that by us the Lord's name be not blasphemed, which be far from us!' And thus he left them, with Bri Leith between them. She in Druim Chea, to the west of Bri Leith. He is in the east of it, in Ardagh.

The virginity of Mel's consort is demonstrated symbolically by the fact that she can carry coals in her skirt or apron: the author is alluding to Proverbs 6: 25–8, which deals with lust for women generally: 'For the price of a harlot is scarce one loaf: but the woman catches the precious soul of a man. Can a man hide fire in his bosom, and his garments not burn? Or can he walk upon hot coals, and his feet not be burnt?' This symbolism had been utilized by patristic authors in their own discussions of consort relationships: Jerome had used it in his diatribe against clerical consorts of his own day (see below).[12] The

---

[10] The term *siur* could be used for those related by the Christian faith rather than by blood; the term *derb-siur* ('true sister') was sometimes used by writers to specify blood-sisters. Stokes translated it as 'kinswoman', though the literal and better translation is 'sister'. Olden held that the *siur* came to mean a sister living in *consortium*, an interpretation which is not maintainable ('On the Consortia', 415–20). Nonetheless, as Reynolds has observed, the Irish used 'sister' to mean 'consort' in their phrasing of the third canon of the Council of Nicaea ('*Virgines Subintroductae*', 555).

[11] Tripartite Life (Stokes, *Tripartite Life*, 88–91). Gwynn and Hadcock tentatively located Druim Chea at a site only about five miles to the west of Ardagh in Co. Longford (*Religious Houses*, 231).

[12] Jerome, *Ep*. 22, ch. 14.

Irish knew Jerome's *Epistolae* by the seventh century, in which the analogy is made between coals and lust, and Jerome had the view that in fact it was impossible to carry coals in one's lap and not be burned. It is evident that the Irish were very familiar with the passage, and its applications, by the time the Tripartite Life was written. But here the symbolism has a different twist, and the 'harlot' overtones are left aside; instead, the carrying of hot coals shows that the accused is innocent of lust. Mel and his sister, though innocent of fornication and even of lust, are instructed to live separately. Indeed, henceforth, all holy men and women must do so. The reason? To avoid scandal. The author acknowledges that saintly men and women are capable of living together without sin, but the danger of scandal makes it impracticable.

There is an underlying sense in these two Middle Irish texts that the male–female proximities of the past were to be considered admirable, not 'degenerate'. Ireland's saints of the fifth and sixth century, they suggested, had been able to mingle, love, and share quarters with women without diminution of their holiness, or indeed their reputations. But, they seem to say, times are changing and those days are gone. This conclusion was also drawn by the redactor of Daig's Life, who also used the image of the burning coals. This saint, the story goes, had taken on the care and supervision of a group of holy virgins who wished to live under his rule. The abbot of Clonmacnois heard of this and, scandalized, sent inspectors to investigate Inishkeen, as he suspected illicit relations between them. The burning coals vindicated them.

Post hec, divulgata beati Daygei per totam Hyberniam sanctitate, confluxerunt undique ad eum sancte virgines, ut sub eius regula degerent: quedam Cannea; alia Lassara, sancti Daygei soror; alia Dalvina. Hoc audiens Cluonensis abbas, nomine Oenu, ad beatum misit Daygeum, ut eum de susceptione virginum obiurgaret. Ille autem, nunciorum presciens negotium, monialibus ut humiliter illis ministrarent precepit. Quarum quedam in sinu suo ignem sine ulla vestis lesione, quedam aquam velut in vase firmissimo, ad eos portavit. Quod hospites videntes, penitentiam egerunt. Beatus autem Daygeus moniales illas versus septentrionem ducens, in diversis locis diversa monasteria, in quibus cum aliis virginibus seorsum Deo servirent, eis prout decuit construxit.[13]

After the sanctity of Daig was proclaimed across all Ireland, there gathered to him from all over holy virgins wishing to live under his rule: one was Cannea, another was Daig's sister Lassair; another was Dalvina. Hearing this the abbot of Clonmacnois, named Oenu, sent to blessed Daig, to correct him from receiving/fostering virgins. He, then, foreknowing the business of the messengers, told the nuns to minister to them humbly. One of them carried fire in her breast without any burn to her clothes, one [carried] water to them as though it were in a solid container. The guests, seeing this, did penance. Then holy Daig leading them [the virgins] to the west, built various monasteries in diverse places for them to serve God with other virgins, as was seemly.

---

[13] Latin Life of Daig, ch. 16.

The Irish writers knew well the familiar canon of stories about the historical saints who had such close friendships with nuns and they knew other aspects of the Irish tradition which accepted close male–female relationships in the Church. By picking up and utilizing a long-extant motif in the Christian canon, some churchmen were attempting to find an inner reconciliation for themselves and their changing community.

Another anonymous writer of this period, the author of the *Catalogus Sanctorum Hiberniae* or 'Catalogue of Irish Saints', also saw the issue in terms of a decline in the level of sanctity amongst clerics. During Christianity's initial period in Ireland (up to AD 544), he writes, the men in the Church were so holy that women were permitted to administer, minister, and consort with them without it posing any danger of temptation. The first 'order' or age of Christianity in Ireland had been characterized by close male–female relations in the Church:

Primus ordo catholicorum sanctorum erat in tempore Patricii. Et tunc erant episcopi omnes clari et sancti et Spiritu Sancto pleni, CCCL numero, ecclesiarum fundatores. . . . Et mulierum ministrationem et consortia non respuebant, quia super petram Christum fundati, ventum tentationis non timebant.[14]

The first order of catholic saints was in Patrick's time. At that time they were all bishops famed and holy and filled with the holy spirit, 350 in number, founders of churches . . . and they did not reject the ministration and consort of of women because, founded on the rock of Christ, they did not fear the blasts of temptation.

The male saints of the second era, the *ordo sanctior* (544–98), fled the ministrations and company of women and excluded them from their monasteries (*mulierum quoque consortia ac administrationes fugiebant, atque a monasteriis suis eas excludebant*).[15] The *Catalogus*, a tenth-century pseudo-history of the Irish Church, is patently and egregiously inaccurate on other matters, and historians now dismiss it as useless: it avers that the early Church was unified under the leadership of Patrick, celebrated one mass, had one tonsure, and celebrated one Easter. Nor do the sources indicate that in the later sixth century the Irish drove nuns out of the monasteries. Nevertheless, as an indicator of gender ideas at the time of composition, the *Catalogus* is singularly useful. We note that the author asserts that early male saints had consorted with women. Now he could have gained this view from seventh- and eighth-century saints' Lives, which speak casually of close relationships between male saints and holy virgins. Alternatively, as with his assertions on other items of the early Church, he may have been more purely

[14]   *Catalogus Sanctorum Hiberniae*, recension U, ch. 1 (P. Grosjean, 'Edition et commentaire du *Catalogus Sanctorum Hiberniae*', *Analecta Bollandiana* 73 (1955), 197–213, 287–322, at 209–10).
[15]   *Catalogus*, S recension, ch. 2. The A recension is very similar: *abnegabant mulierum ministrationem, separantes eas a monasteriis* (Grosjean, '*Catalogus*', 206–10, 298). The assertion that in this era men ejected women from their monasteries is not attested in the Lives or in any other source.

'creative'. Whichever is the case, we can be certain he was writing in an environment with a history of openness about nuns and their relations to men. The question of the author's aim in making this claim is thus raised. After all, his other assertions, though historically untrue, represent his notion of an idealized Irish Golden Age of Christianity. In this ecclesiastical Utopia men and women of God work side by side, and can live together. There is regret that such close relationships cannot be sustained now; the men are no longer holy enough to manage them chastely. This writer, one may reasonably infer, was writing in response to someone or some group who was in his own day promoting a stricter separation of the sexes. He sadly acknowledged that, though this is a necessity, it is a regrettable one. If only clerics were what they used to be, the 'old system' could have continued.

Not all the romanticizing of the chaste consort friendships by the writers of the tenth to twelfth centuries places them in the distant past. The most famous of the consort texts places the relationship in the present tense. The celebrated poem *A Chrínóc*, attributed to Mael Ísu Ó Brolcháin, differs from the texts discussed so far in that it is more lyrical and is not hagiographic. Furthermore there is some question as to the identity of the speaker: is it the poet himself? In other words, is the poet speaking of practices he himself knew in his own day, or is he pretending (as it were) to be living in the distant past, in that era when clerics and monastics were thought to have had consorts?

> A Chrínóc, cubaid do cheól · cenco bat fíróc at fíal;
> ro-mósam túaid i tír Néill · tan do-rónsam feis réid ríam.
>
> Rop hí m'áes tan ro-foís lem · a bé níata in gáesa grinn,
> daltán clíabglan cáem nád camm · maccán mall sech mbliadan mbinn.
>
> Bámar for bith Banba bailc · cen éilniud anma ná cuirp,
> mo lí lasrach lán dot seirc · amal geilt cen aslach uilc.
>
> Erlam do chomairle chóir · dóig nos-togamne in cech tír
> is ferr rográd dot gaeis géir · ar comrád réid frisin Ríg.
>
> Ro-foís la cethrar íar sin · im díaid cen nach methlad mer;
> ro-fetar, is beóda in blad · at glan cen pheccad fri fer.
>
> Fo deóid dom rúachtais do-rís · íar cúartaib scís, gleó co ngaeis;
> do-dechaid temel tart gnúis · cen drúis is dered dot aeis.
>
> At inmain lem-sa cen locht · rot-bía mo chen-sa cen cacht;
> ní léicfe ar mbadud i péin · fo-gabam crábud léir lat.
>
> Lán dot labrad in bith búan · adbal do rith tar cach rían;
> día seichmis cech día do dán · ro-seismis slán co Día ndían.
>
> Do-beire do thimna in toí · do chach co himda ar bith ché;
> síthlai dúin uile in cech ló · ní gó guide díchra Dé.
>
> Do-rata Día dellraid dúin · a ré frit ar menmain mín
> rop rolainn frinn gnúis Ríg réil · íar n-ar léimm ór colainn chrín.

Crinoc, lady of measured melody,
      not young but with modest maiden mind,
together once in Niall's northern land
      we slept, we two, as man and womankind.

You came and slept with me for that first time,
      (skilled wise amazon annihilating fears)
And I a fresh-faced boy, not bent as now,
      a gentle lad of seven years.

There we were on that firm Irish earth
      desirous, but in pure and mystic sense;
burning with love my flesh, still free from fault
      as fool of God in smitten innocence.

Your counsel is ever there to hand,
      we choose it, following you in everything;
Love of your word is the best of loves
      our gentle conversation with the King.

Guiltless are you of sin with any man,
      fair is your name, and bright, and without stain
although I know that when you went from me
      each in his turn, four lay where I had lain.

And now you come, your final pilgrimage,
      wearied with toil and gravel, grimed with dust,
wise still but body not immaculate,
      time it is that ravished you, not lust.

Again I offer you a faultless love,
      a love unfettered for which surely we
will not be punished in the depths of hell
      but together ever walk in piety.

Seeking the presence of elusive God
      wandering we stray, but the way is found
following the mighty melodies that with you
      throughout the pathways of the world resound.

Not ever silent, you bring the word of God
      to all who in the present world abide,
and then through you, through finest mesh,
      Man's earnest prayer to God is purified.

May the King give us beauty back again
      who ever did his will with quiet mind,
may he look on us with eagerness and love,
      our old and perished bodies left behind.[16]

[16] J. Carney, *Medieval Irish Lyrics* (Dublin, 1967), 74–9.

Kuno Meyer in 1918 argued the case for the poem's application to a real consort nun, and for a tenth-century composition date.[17] In this he was followed by Louis Gougaud. James Carney refuted this interpretation repeatedly, and most strongly in 1965 in 'Old Ireland and Her Poetry', in which he dated the poem later than had previous scholars, to about 1100, and this date, he argued, made the poem's composition too distant in time from the Council of Nicaea to speak of actual contemporary syneisact practice.[18]

Reynolds, writing in the sixties, astutely observed that Carney's criticisms did not take into account other late Irish references to syneisactism, such as the *Vita Tripartita* and the story of Scothíne.[19] He presumed that the contemporary Continental sources described actual practice, and that it was therefore absolutely reasonable to conclude that *A Chrínóc* spoke of Irish syneisactism in the poet's own day. Reynolds was unaware, however, that Continental uses were allegorical not literal (as will be shown below) and that the other Irish examples were inspired by literature, not practice. Bearing this in mind, one may not join in Reynolds's conclusions, but one is unlikely to agree with Carney in dismissing the consort theme in *A Chrínóc* as no more than a 'donnish joke. Certainly there was some joking going on, as Carney suggested, but it was black humour aimed at those who would force clerics to shun their *caillecha*: the Irish did not hesitate to voice their dislike and disagreement to the Englishmen who attempted to persuade them to change their practices. In addition, the Irish scholarly mind was traditionally engaged in wordplay and clever puns, and it did not cease to engage in it when matters of the church were being considered. A good example is the correspondence between a leading reformer in England, Archbishop Lanfranc of Canterbury, and an Irish churchman. During a heated debate conducted by correspondence on the issue of child baptism, Lanfranc attempted to make the Irish institute it and met resistance. Bishop Domhnall Ua Henna's response included a series of pertinent puzzles and riddles. Lanfranc's return letter scaldingly derided the Irishman's theology, and said of the riddles: 'When we were children that amused us; but the administration of a diocese has led us to renounce such games.'[20] Surely the double entendre in *Á Chrínóc* is another such 'game' which, like Ua Henna's riddles, was a sardonic commentary on a deadly serious issue.

CONSORTS IN THE CHURCH'S HISTORY

The writers of the Irish consort texts drew on patristic and conciliar antecedents. The virgin consort had been a formally acknowledged personage in the early

[17] Meyer, 'An Crínóc' (1908), 266; id. (ed. and trans.), *Selections from Ancient Irish Poetry* (London, 1911), 37–8; 'An Crínóg: Ein altirisches Gedicht', 361–74.

[18] J. Carney, 'A Chrínóc, Cubaid do Cheól', *Éigse* 4 (1944), 280–3; id., 'Old Ireland and her Poetry' in R. McNally (ed.), *Old Ireland* (1965), 147–72, at 157. Carney's position is discussed in Greene and O'Connor, *Golden Treasury*, 167. For earlier comments on the text, see *Kenney*, no. 606.

[19] Reynolds, '*Virgines Subintroductae*', 555.   [20] Bethell, 'English Monks', 128, with references.

Mediterranean churches. Formally called *virgines subintroductae*, they have been aptly defined as 'female Christian ascetics who lived together with men, although both parties had taken the vow of continence, and were animated with the earnest desire to keep it.'[21] The earliest references to the practice of Christian holy men living with ascetic women are from the second century. Irenaeus, who lived *c.*130–200 mentions that the Valentinians occasioned scandal by allowing 'brothers' and 'sisters' to live together, and says that it became apparent that the chastity had been violated when some of the so-called sisters became mothers.[22] Around the turn of the second and third centuries 'Pseudo-Clement' wrote two letters on virginity, warning brethren against dwelling with maidens, and Tertullian (160–220) and Cyprian (bishop of Carthage, 248–58) both refer to it.[23] Eusebius of Caesarea (260–339) wrote in his *Church History* that one of the accusations made against Paul of Samosata was that he had scandalized the Church by living with young girls, a practice which contributed to his condemnation by the Synod of Antioch in AD 267–8.[24] It was clearly a pressing issue in 325 at the Council of Nicaea, which banned the practice in its third canon. The prohibition was copied and adopted widely and immediately.

Interdixit per omnia magna synodus, nec episcopo nec presbytero nec alicui prorsus, qui est in clero, licere subintroductam habere mulierem, nisi forte matrem aut sororem aut amitam vel eas tantum personas quae suspicionem effugiunt.[25]

The great Synod has stringently forbidden any bishop, presbyter, deacon, or any one of the clergy whatever, to have a subintroducta dwelling with him, except only a mother, or sister, or aunt, or such persons only as are beyond all suspicion.

Through this council, *mulier subintroducta* became another term for the chaste religious consort, entering common parlance across the early medieval West. Another name for them, *gynaikes syneisaktoi*, was coined by the early Antiocheans and was cited at the Synod of Antioch (267–8), and it is this phrase which gives rise to the English term for the practice—'syneisactism'.

The fourth century saw an all-out war against it, and the Church Fathers of this time rallied all their passion, reason, logic, and even sarcasm in the effort. John Chrysostom (347–407) wrote two tracts in the 380s or early 390s which 'contain the most extensive discussion of syneisactism to be found anywhere in early Christian literature'.[26] One, 'On the Necessity of Guarding Virginity', is addressed to women: in it he takes them to task for agreeing to, and

---

[21] E. Clark, 'John Chrysostom and the *Subintroductae*', in id. (ed.), *Ascetic Piety and Women's Faith: Essays on Late Ancient Christianity* (Studies in Women and Religion 20; New York, 1986), 265–90, at 265.

[22] Irenaeus, *Adversus haereses*, ed. W. Harvey, 2 vols. (Cambridge, 1857), book 1, ch. 6.

[23] Pseudo-Clement, *Ep.* 1–2; Tertullian, *De exhortatione castitatis*, ch. 12; *De monogamia*, ch. 16. Cyprian, *Ep.* 6. Cited in E. Clark, *Jerome, Chrysostom and Friends: Essays and Translations* (Studies in Women and Religion 1; New York, 1979), 162.

[24] Clark, 'Chrysostom and the *Subintroductae*', 267.

[25] Council of Nicaea, canon 3 (G. Alberigo (ed.), *Conciliorum oecumenicorum decreta* (Freiburg, 1962), 6).

[26] Clark, *Jerome, Chrysostom*, 158.

participating in, this lifestyle: 'if you want to have men live with you, then you ought not to choose virginity but proceed on to matrimony, for it is far better to marry in that fashion than to be a virgin in this.'[27] Addressing men in his second treatise, Chrysostom accuses *the men* of bad motives.[28] Jerome (c.342–420) also took the practitioners of religious cohabitation to task. His Epistle 22 is probably the most scathingly eloquent piece written on the subject, which also serves to describe what exactly the practice consists of:

Unde in Ecclesias Agapetarum pestis introiit? Unde sine nuptiis aliud nomen uxorem? Imo unde novum concubinarum genus? Plus inferam: unde meretrices univirae? Eadem domo, uno cubiculo, saepe uno tenentur et lectulo, et suspiciosos nos vocant, si aliquid aestimemus. Frater sororem virginem deserit, caelibem spernit virgo germanum, fratrem quaerit extraneum, et cum in eodem proposito esse se simulent, quaerunt alienorum spiritale solatium, ut domi habeant carnale commercium. Istius modi homines Salomon in Proverbiis spernit, dicens *Alligabit quis in sinu ignem et vestimenta eius non comburentur? Aut ambulabit super carbones ignis, et pedes illius non ardebunt?*[29]

How comes this plague of the 'dearly beloved sisters' to be in the church? Whence come these unwedded wives, these novel concubines, these harlots, so I will call them, though they cling to a single partner? One house holds them and one chamber. They often occupy the same bed, and yet they call us suspicious if we fancy anything amiss. A brother leaves his virgin sister; a virgin, slighting her unmarried brother, seeks a 'brother' in a stranger. Both profess equally to have but one object, to find spiritual consolation from those not of their kin; but their real aim is to indulge in sexual intercourse. It is on such people that Solomon in the book of proverbs heaps his scorn. 'Can a man take fire in his bosom,' he says, 'and his clothes not be burned? Can one go upon hot coals and his feet not be burned?'

Jerome's writings on the subject influenced subsequent literature through the early Middle Ages. Three features he mentions here recur throughout later writings: the concept of the sister who is not a blood relation, the word 'stranger', and the reference to Proverbs 6: 27–8. Other Christian writers who engaged in this holy war included Gregory Nazianzen (323–89), Gregory of Nyssa (c.335–95), Basil of Caesarea (c.330–79), Eusebius of Emesa, and 'Pseudo-Cyprian',[30] along with a variety of synods and councils.[31]

---

[27] 'On the Necessity of Guarding Virginity', ch. 4.

[28] See esp. his 'Introduction and Refutation Directed Against Those Men Cohabiting with Virgins', ch. 1: 'There are certain men who apart from marriage and sexual intercourse take girls inexperienced with matrimony, establish them permanently in their homes, and keep them sequestered until ripe old age, not for the purpose of bearing children (for they deny that they have sexual relations with them) nor out of licentiousness (for they claim they keep them inviolate). If anybody asks the reason for their practice they have plenty and start rehearsing them; however I myself think that they have not found a single decent, plausible excuse . . .' (trans. Clark, *Jerome, Chrysostom*, 164).

[29] Jerome, *Ep.* 22, ch. 14.

[30] Gregory Nazianzen, Epigrams 10–20. Gregory of Nyssa, 'On Virginity'. Basil of Caesarea, *Ep.* 55. Eusebius of Emesa, Homilies 7, 20, and 22. Pseudo-Cyprian, *De singularitate clericorum.* All cited in Clark, *Jerome, Chrystostom*, 162.

[31] Pierre de Labriolle cites some twenty-four councils and synods between 267 and 787 that forbid clerics to live with unrelated women ('Le "mariage spirituel" dans l'antiquité chrétienne', *Revue Historique* 137 (1921), 204–25, at 222).

This résumé of the patristic literature serves not only to illustrate the wide base of writing which informed the Irish authors, but also to show that the subject was a serious one, a struggle in which the question at stake was the very nature of the clergy. These writings had been the propaganda of the Church Fathers pushing for ascetic separation among the ordained and the monastic. At the time of writing, they had not yet won the theological battle, though in the long term theirs became the 'official' Christian position. The passage in Proverbs on the coals in the clothing was clearly meant rhetorically: no one can carry them without being burnt, and it was in this way that the passage was normally interpreted in the West during the fourth-century controversies. After that time its use died out almost completely. The only exception I know is an instance that foreshadows the Irish use: Gregory of Tours's case of the Gaulish bishop Simplicius (obit 420) and his wife, who proved the chastity of their marriage by standing in front of a crowd for an hour with coals in their unburnt garments.[32] When the Irish composed stories about the domestic arrangements of their saints, it was upon the imagery used in the material of these fourth- and fifth-century controversies that they drew. It seems reasonable to conclude it was because it spoke to issues they faced in their own day.

Related to the theme of cohabitation is that of ascetic challenge—the act of placing oneself in a situation of great sexual temptation in order to test or prove's one's spiritual mastery. This *topos*, too, is traceable to the very early Church. The anonymous 'Similitudes of Hermas' speaks of an ascetic spending the night with beautiful virgins 'as a brother not a husband'.[33] This image was called upon but very rarely, the early medieval West embracing for its asceticism instead the language of withdrawal, 'the desert', and the *monach* or 'solitary one'. It is found in Cassian's *Conlationes*, which seems to be the direct source of the image for the Irish writers of this period, since it appears to be wholly absent from Western writings, including Irish ones, of the intervening centuries. Cassian's tale is that of the holy man Paphnutius who, after subduing many demons and achieving great holiness, was one day burnt by a little fire. This prompted self-questioning, for he wondered why he could still be burnt by a physical flame after he had overcome so many spiritual fires of temptation. At this the Lord appeared and suggested that he had not overcome the deeper roots of his carnal emotions, and if he wished to test it he should undertake the following experiment: 'Go, take a naked and most beautiful virgin, and if while you hold her you find that the peace of your heart remains steadfast, and that carnal heat is still and quiet within you, then the touch of this visible flame also shall pass over you gently and without harming you as it did over the three children in Babylon.'[34] Paphnutius was chastened and of course 'did not try the dangers of the experiment divinely shown to him, but asked his own conscience and examined the purity of his

[32] Gregory of Tours, *Gloria Confessorum*, ch. 75.   [33] 'Similitudes', chs. 9–10.
[34] Cassian, *Conlationes*, book 15, ch. 10.

heart'. The experiment was never meant to be tried: it was a rhetorical suggestion. Elsewhere Cassian is very clear that to his mind chastity is not strengthened by temptation, for he specifically addresses the matter and rules against
it.[35] The Irish of this time, however, made their early saints take up this rhetori-
cally-set test in a literal way, and made them pass it with flying colours, just as
they did with the biblical test of the burning coals.

Consorts Abroad: The Crackdown on Nicolaitism

The earlier phase of the Gregorian reforms focused on the two vices of simony
and nicolaitism, the latter of which is of interest here. Nicolaitism, an evil sect
named in Revelations 2: 6, was a term the reformers attached to clerical marriage (although the Bible mentioned nothing of priestly incontinence among
them). The biblical Nicolaitans had, however, been charged with fornication.
The reforming theologian Humbert therefore felt free to apply the term to the
married clergy of his own day. Through a biblical sleight-of-hand the reformers
had clerical marriage made into a formally-recognized heresy, on the grounds
that 'it' (nicolaitism) was deemed by scripture to be a heresy. In their campaign
to eradicate clerical marriage Humbert and others combed the Church Fathers
for other antecedents which could be brought to bear. In particular, they took up
as ammunition the patristic writings against *virgines subintroductae*. One important decree used directly the language of fourth-century syneisactism as expressed by Jerome, and alluded to the late-antique problem as a parallel to the
problems they were facing in their own day. Canon 3 of a 1058 synod under
Nicholas II ruled that 'no one shall attend the Mass of a priest whom he knows
for certain to have a *subintroducta mulier*'.[36]

Other reformers followed suit, and the *subintroducta* material of Jerome and
other Church Fathers was adopted by a wide range of writers in their works on
clerical relations with women. In the twelfth century William of Malmesbury
gave a picture of the temptation of Aldhelm taken from the second-century
'Shepherd of Hermas' which is very similar to that of Scothíne in his Life.[37] Gerald of Wales, too, warned against following the example of Aldhelm who lay
inter duas puellas, unam ab uno latere, alteram ab altero, singulis noctibus.[38] The twelfth-
century monastic leader Robert of Arbrissel, accused of nicolaitism, was told
with no admiration but much disapproval by Bishop Marbod of Rennes that *has
etenim solum communi accubitu per noctem, ut referunt, accubante simul et discipulorum grege,
ut inter utrosque medius iacens, utrique sexui vigiliarum et somni leges praefigas*.[39]

[35] Ibid., book 19, ch. 16.
[36] Frazee, 'Origins of Clerical Celibacy', 164. J. Mansi (ed.), *Sacrorum Conciliorum nova et amplissima collectio* (Paris, 1901–6), v. 19, 907.
[37] *De gestis pontificum Anglicorum*, ch. 5 (ed. N. Hamilton, in Rolls Series; London, 1870).
[38] Gerald of Wales, *Gemma ecclesiastica*, book 2, ch. 15 (trans. J. Hagen, *The Jewel of the Church* (Leiden, 1979)).
[39] Marbod of Rennes, *Epistola* 6 (*PL* 171. 1480–6, at 1481), cited in Elliott, *Spiritual Marriage*, 111.

The fourth-century patristic condemnation of consorts, so graphically painted in the 'Hermas' text, provided the pro-separatist faction with a handy parallel. By claiming as analogous the priest's wives of their own day and the *virgines subintroductae* of old they created for themselves, ever so conveniently, a patristic precedent. Even chaste marriages of clerics, to which the church had until the eleventh century acceded, could be justifiably forbidden, providing the analogy could be maintained.[40]

All of this material must be considered in the analysis of that strange, small corpus of Irish consort material. Reynolds did just that, using in particular the eleventh-century Continental and English parallels.[41] But he took the Continental material at face value, presuming it to describe a literal truth about practice at that time in those places. Thus he believed that syneisactism was current in England and Europe in the eleventh and twelfth centuries. A closer study would have shown that Robert of Arbrissel, and even Aldhelm, probably never lay between naked virgins, or at least not in the manner thus described. Reynolds's presumptions led him to conclude that the Irish consort stories, although appearing in a more literary guise, proved that such practices were actually occurring in Ireland in these later centuries. Such a conclusion rested on faulty foundations.

The Continental reformists derogated the men of antiquity who had lived with consorts—they were examples of sinners, not heroes. What is amazing is that the Irish did not. Though they were familiar with Jerome and many of his fellows, they did not accept his view that the practice was inherently wrong. Syneisacts, for the Irish, were successfully doing something which proved their holiness. In the Tripartite Life, Bishop Mel and his consorts explicitly meet Jerome's challenge. Who, Jerome had asked rhetorically, can carry burning coals in their apron? Mel's virgins could, came the Irish answer. If we must give up our consorts, the writers imply, it is only to avoid gossip or because nowadays few men have the will-power to keep the relationship platonic—not because it is wrong in principle. One can almost see the Irish hagiographers and poets gently persuading people to get used to the idea that co-habitation of churchmen with women was no longer acceptable, but they themselves were struggling internally against the criticisms of such closeness.

Because the churches on the Continent were tackling the same questions using the same motif in roughly the same period, i.e. the eleventh and twelfth centuries, it is reasonable to wonder if perhaps this framing language was transmitted from there to Ireland. However, the chronology of the texts tells us this cannot be so. The *Catalogus* is now definitely dated to the tenth century, well before Humbert and his associates were writing. This part of the Tripartite Life may even be from the tenth, if we follow Richard Sharpe. Nor is transmission necessary to explain the Irish use. The Irish knew Jerome, they knew other early

---

Christian apocrypha in which the practice was demonstrated and praised, and they had a long tradition of using conjugal language to describe virgin-friendships; we may again recall the ninth-century Oengus describing the Roman virgin Perpetua as St Paul's *coniunx*. The *topos* of the saint living *in consortium* rose in Ireland, as it did elsewhere, because it was useful in highlighting the issues of clerical marriage, cohabitation, and celibacy, as well the matter of monastic friendships between the sexes. This indeed seems the most feasible explanation for their roughly simultaneous appearance, and is pursued in the next chapter.

CLERICAL MARRIAGE

The Continental preoccupation in the eleventh and twelfth centuries with ancient consort practices was part and parcel of the campaign to make clerics renounce even their chaste wives; how then did the Irish Church deal with the matter of the married priest?

Apart from the consort stories in the hagiography, the source material for Irish clerical marriage and celibacy is minute by comparison with the quantity extant for the Continent or even for England. But among that small amount, the consort *topos* does figure, and that evidence is both telling and significant. It suggests that the attitudes of the Irish towards priests' wives mirrored those held towards nuns: a rising anxiety about scandal, a new concern about sex, but an enduring affection for women generally and a respect for those great holy men of the past who had cherished them.

Two extant texts from this period deal explicitly with clerical marriage. Thus it seems safe to say that the subject *per se* was not a major concern in the tenth, eleventh, and twelfth centuries much more than it was in earlier times. Nevertheless, at least some Irish in this period considered a priest's celibacy or lack of it important. A poem contained in the (tenth- or eleventh-century) notes to the Martyrology of Oengus informs us:

> Sacart ic denam comna · ic baisded, bec a tarba
> ni con tic baisted de · iar taistel a cailligi.[42]

> A priest, practising coition, small is his profit in baptizing;
> baptism comes not from him, after visiting his nun.

In addition to urging clerical celibacy, the poem also raises the issue of ritual purity, a question affecting both priests who were married and those who were supposed to be celibate. Asserting the invalidity of the baptism of the priest lately risen from the bed of his sexual partner, the poem suggests that its Irish author adhered to the belief (learned rather than popular) that 'it was inappropriate for clergymen to rush from the fleshly passions of the marriage bed to officiate at the

---

[42] Martyrology of Oengus, notes on 27 Oct., relating to a priest named Odrán.

sacred rites'. The notion of the clergy's ritual defilement through marital intercourse had, in earlier centuries, given rise to many councils which strove to coerce
married clerics into abstinence. Penances and punishments, including excommunication, were meted out for those who continued sexual activities.[43] The en-
forcement of this prohibition was 'neither uniform nor successful', Brundage
observes, and it was extremely common in rural areas across the West for the care
of the parish to pass from father to son for generations.[44] Certainly this was as true
of Ireland as elsewhere, and more so if one believes the fulminations of the likes of
St Bernard, who claimed Ireland was being especially errant in this regard.[45] The
existence of married clergy in Ireland is well evidenced and is not disputed
throughout the early medieval period and even into the post-1170 era.

A curious but very important feature of the Martyrology poem is its use of the
term *caillech* (lit. 'veiled one') for the priest's sexual companion. The parallels
with the eighth century *Berrad Airechta* text should be noted, for there the sexual
companion (possibly wife) of the priest is also called his *caillech*, his 'nun', and
there her rights are acknowledged, but it was expected that the marriage was to
be chaste once the husband was in orders. As Máirín Ní Dhonnchadha has
shown, there is a long history of the priest's partner *caillech*, and it is also the standard Irish term for nun which is equally used for consecrated virgins and female
saints (Brendan addresses Brigit *A chaillech*, 'O nun', for example).[46] It is possible
that at this time priests' partners like that in this poem enjoyed the legal rights
accorded wives by Irish law but that their status also had a religious quality.

Evidently the Irish themselves in this period did not draw those distinctions
between wife and nun that the twentieth century does. The very fluidity of language demonstrates it. Though the parameters around these relationships remain unclear to us, it is of course likely that the Irish at the time knew perfectly
well their position and status: we simply do not have an appropriate categoriz-
ing system, nor do we have the details that would allow us to draw one. Instead
we are tempted to try to put these women into one or the other of two boxes, neither of which is appropriate.

We should note that, while the poem says that a priest who had sex with his
caillech could not administer valid sacraments, the *caillech* was of no concern to
the author; he did not interest himself in condemning her. The last chapter explored the attitudes to nuns in the later Lives of the saints and found them to be
somewhat more concerned about sex than earlier ones, but still free from any
demonization of even the sexually lapsing ones. In Ireland, those who were
companions to clerics, too, escaped the lashes of condemnation, at least those
evidenced in the surviving sources.

---

[43] J. Brundage, *Law, Sex, and Christian Society in Medieval Europe* (London, 1987), 150. In particular he
cites the Second Council of Toledo (AD 527), the Council of Lérida (546), and the Council of Orleans
(538), and the Visigothic laws.
[44] Brundage, *Law, Sex*, 150.   [45] Bernard of Clairvaux, Life of St Malachy, esp. books 1, 6.
[46] Ní Dhonnchadha, '*Caillech*'. Scholia on the poem *Brigit Bé Bithmaith*.

The second text on clerical 'wives' to be considered is doubtless the most vivid and moving illustration of this point. 'Arise, O King's Daughter' (*Eirigh, a Ingen an Rígh*) is a Middle-Irish poem in which Cormac, bishop-king of Cashel, sends away his wife Gormlaith, daughter of Flann mac Maele Sechnaill, because he has decided to adopt an ascetic single life as befits his office.[47] Cormac calls upon the memories of saints of earlier days who resisted sexual temptation in order to strengthen his resolve in sending his wife away from their shared home. It is a long poem, and only a selection of the relevant stanzas is repeated here.

[1] Éirigh a ingen an rígh · ná bíd h'aigneadh a n-imsnímh
atá bean ele it' aghaidh · a bélcorcra banamail.
[2] As í bean atá 'com chrádh · ecclas Dé dá ndéntar dán;
acus smúaintigte ele · ima ndénta aithrige.
[5] Do smúainius Bairre Búadach · 'ga fuil in t-aignedh úallach,
dár ob an rígain rebaigh, · ingen Dúngail d'Uíb Eanaigh.
[6] Do smúainius Cíarán Clúana, · mór dá crábadh at-chúala,
dár ob Aillinn ingin Broin · is fo cígaibh ro codail.
[7] Do smúaineas in crábad cóir · Scuithín Sléibe Mairge móir,
luigedh—grádh Dé fo-dera, · sé iter aindrib uchtgeala.
[8] Do smúainius Colum Cille · ar grádh rígh na firinne,
dár obb sé, gér mór a cáil, · ingena áille Aedáin.
[11] Do radus-[s]a ingin Floinn · meic Maoil tSeachloinn meic Domnaill;
tugus trí chét mbó mbennach · 'na connradh, 'na cétcheannach.
[12] Tugus fichit uingi óir · acus fichit corn comóil,
nochon featur a deimin · in neoch rug úaim d'innelaibh.
[13] Dar in anmain atá im chorp, · nocha dearnus-sa ría d'ulc
acht mad énpóg re n-éirge · do dénamh na híarmérghe.
[14] Do gabus trí caícta psalm · i tipraid Locha na Tarb,
ticfadh rim, manbadh m'óighe, · adailge na hénpóigi.
[15] Do-gén-sa do dáil co bog, · úair ní tusa ríamh ro ob,
is fris do-géantar do dáil · re Cearball mac Muireagáin.
[16] Nochar cuvaidh d'ingin Flainn, · m'inar ro-indigh-si fo coim,
in corp 'ma fuil an t-inar · go nglana Día a cuid cinad.
[17] Mithig duit-si feis ra fer, · a ingen, luchair láingeal,
tuccus m'óighi do Día dil, · gab imat acus érigh.[48]

[47] According to the AClon, Cormac was indeed married to Gormlaith, but she was married to two other kings as well, at least one of whom came after Cormac. This story, i.e. Cormac's renunciation of his wife, finds no confirmation in AU, but Gormlaith's obit in AD 948 (AU 949) says that she 'died in penitence' as did many queens; Cormac's death is listed as taking place in battle in 907 (AU 908). It is of course irrelevant whether the historical Cormac indeed sent away his wife in order to embrace a more ascetic life appropriate for a bishop. See most recently on her marriages Ní Dhonnhadha, 'On Gormfhlaith'; also D. Ó Cróinín, 'Three Weddings and a Funeral: Rewriting Irish Political History in the Tenth Century', in Smyth, *Seanchas*, 212–24.

[48] M. Ní Dhonnchadha's edition and translation, used here, 'On Gormfhlaith'. Previously published in Irish with short commentary by A. Von Hamel, 'Poems from the Brussels MS 5100–4', *Revue Celtique* 37 (1917–19), 349–51. Translated poorly into English with brief comments by Seán O'Faóláin, *Revue Celtique* 47 (1930), 197–9.

[1] Arise, O king's daughter, let your mind not be perplexed
There is another woman in rivalry with you, O red-lipped womanly one.
[2] The woman who torments me is God's church, for whom poetry is composed,
—and other thoughts too for which penance should be done.
[5] I thought about victorious Bairre, on him of the lofty mind,
When he turned down the the spirited queen, the daughter of Dúngail Uí Eanaig.
[6] I thought about Ciarán of Cluain [Clonmacnois], much have I heard of his piety,
when he turned down Aillenn, the daughter of Bran; it was under her breasts he slept.
[7] I have thought also of the great piety of Scóthín of Slaibh Mairce Móir,
who used to lie (God willed it in his love) between the white breasts of women.
[8] And I thought about Columcille, who for the love of the King of Truth
denied, for all their great fame, Aidan's lovely daughters.
[11] I married the daughter of Flann son of Máel Sechnaill,
I paid a hundred horned cattle in covenant, as a bride-price, for her.
[12] I gave twenty ounces of gold and twenty drinking horns,
I do not know the exact amount of possessions she took from me.
[13] By the soul in my body, I have done nothing wrong with her,
except for a little kiss before rising to say matins.
[14] I recited thrice fifty psalms in the well of Loch na Tarbh,
That kiss would have a hold over me were it not for my virginity.
[15] I will make a match for you easily, for you are not one who ever refused;
The one with whom your match will be made is Cerball mac Muirecáin.
[16] It was improper for Flann's daughter; she wore my wedding tunic secretly;
that body which my tunic covers, may God cleanse it of its sins.
[17] The time is come for you to love another man, O radiant shining maiden;
I have given my virginity to dear God; come, clothe yourself, and arise.

Though his poem is ascribed to the tenth-century Cormac, the language dates
it to the twelfth or thirteenth century. Its most recent editor feels the focus on
Cormac makes preferable a twelfth-century date.[49] The theme of clerical separation from the spouse would strengthen that inclination. The poet's error in the
queen's lineage could be used as an argument for a later date, but for the fact
that the error is a very easy one to make, even in the twelfth, given Gormlaith's
genealogy.[50]

   It is the treatment of the wife which is so unexpected, especially for those
scholars more familiar with the writings of this era composed by the likes of
Peter Damian. This piece is less surprising in the context of other Irish texts, but
its exalted language of love nevertheless cannot fail to grip the historian. The
king-bishop's wife is a 'good maiden' (ingen fíal), and he has thoughtfully arranged
a new marriage for her, to another man. The poet focuses on the moment when
the man is in the process of sending away his wife, because he can no longer live

---

[49] For Ní Dhonnchadha's observations and comments on the dating of the text on linguistic and
politico-historical grounds, see 'On Gormfhlaith', 234. The poem's first editor made no attempts to date
it apart from commenting that on the basis of the linguistic forms it could not be as old as the 10th cent.
  [50] I am grateful to Ann Connon for this observation.

with her and also remain on good terms with God. The message is that Cormac is the ideal married cleric; though he struggles, he nevertheless sends his wife away. Chaste marriage is not adequate, only actual separation will do.

Cormac's recollection of the consort-keeping saints (Mel, Scothíne, and others) shows that the poet made an association between clerical marriage and chaste *consortium*, the practice of syneisactism. Though he invokes Scothíne, modelling his life on that saint's *consortium* is (paradoxically) unacceptable; Scothíne had not sent his consorts away, it will be recalled. With all its contradictions, the example helps reconcile him to the right course of action. Cormac is here voicing a new moral code in which duties to God were now to preclude the producing of heirs and the enjoyment of privileges of power, but acknowledging the emotional wrench involved.

A Chrínóc, as we saw earlier, was not frivolous just because it was clever. Similarly we can perhaps look at the funny side of *Eirigh*—the man leaving his wife is recalling erotic imagery, stanza after stanza, to give him strength to leave the marital bed. For all that, the poet did not necessarily see it in a light-hearted manner. But certainly the issues of politics and proper clerical behaviour were not, for the Irish, subjects which had to be handled only in tracts and essays or not at all. By the twelfth century, the Irish were certainly aware of their bad reputation amongst the papal reformers. Some wanted to go along with the changes in clerical behaviour; others were not so keen. Even those who favoured sex separation could deploy the very language and symbolisms central to the reform in a subversive way.

CONCLUSIONS

It is to be wondered whether this gentle, sympathetic approach was responsible for the failure of the campaign to abolish clerical marriage, as it survived and remained relatively widespread in Ireland into the central Middle Ages, whereas on the Continent, where women were viciously demonized, the practice was more efficiently repressed. There is a pronounced poignancy throughout the Middle Irish literature that touches on cleric–female relations. A new culture is indicated by the texts, but the writers affirmed the rightness of close inter-sex relations in the heroic past, in the Golden Age of holiness.

The pattern seen in the Irish consort texts is unsurprising when we bear in mind the *mundus* in which they were written. Consecrated Christian women had always lived in a variety of milieux, many of which placed them in close proximity to men of the clergy and of the laity. Religious women in nunneries had always been visited by men. Nuns might share their monastic precinct with a bishop and possibly even monks. In male monasteries which featured female adherents there could also be extensive contact with men. In the countryside there had always been nuns on their own and in pairs who were in touch with men. Communication in dual-sex monasteries might have been restricted amongst more junior members, as indicated in the Customs of Tallaght, but some religious men did live with women in proto-marital relationships. Finally, they knew at first hand about a priesthood which might sometimes live with women who went under the name *caillech*, in the eighth and ninth centuries certainly, and probably in their own day as well. All of this was well documented to have a long history: the ecclesiastical writers of the eleventh and twelfth centuries knew of (and probably believed) the accounts in Tírechán, the *Vita I*, Cogitosus, and the *Liber Angeli*, all of which showed men and women following holy, indeed monastic, lives which could include friendship between the sexes. The consort anecdotes mark changes in female monasticism and, inextricably linked to them, in male monasticism as well.

10

'Generous Eve' and the Echoes of Reform

If the changes in Irish material are best explained as a response, albeit an am-
bivalent and resistant one, to reform ideas flourishing beyond its shores, there
are further enquiries to be made. First there are the reforms themselves—the
language, imagery, and methods used, a few points of which have already been
encountered. Then there is the vexed question of transmission, for it is commonly asserted that Ireland was largely insulated from overseas movements; in
fact it is standard to say that the Gregorian reforms only reached Ireland in the
twelfth century, and the English Benedictine reforms are generally thought to
have made no impact on Ireland at all. If the first two issues can be explained
satisfactorily, the final question remains: does the thesis work, in a broader way,
for Irish writing on the female sex as a whole?

REFORMERS AND THE FEMALE SEX

Both reform movements—Benedictine and Hildebrandine—aimed to introduce monastic standards of life to the clergy. Ritual purity was cited as a reason,
though concerns of property and inheritance are seen by historians to have
motivated the reformers to enforce the sexual standard which had been 'on the
books' of canon law for centuries. The reformers had to convince Western
Christendom of two things: first that it was wrongheaded to tolerate a sexually-
active clergy, and secondly, beyond this, that it was wrong for clerics to have even
a chaste marriage. The former was easier to achieve than the latter. That sex
was improper for those close to God was not too hard to put across: as one character in an Italian Life of a Patarene reformer said, 'Who is so stupid as not to be
able to lucidly consider that the life of those I call upon to bless my house ought
to be different and more elevated than mine?'[1] The second item was the more
difficult of which to convince people. To undo the celibate marriages of priests
and to promote separation of the sexes, a range of tools were used and for the
later Hildebrandine reforms scholars have studied in considerable depth the use
of theology, history, canon law, and emotive polemic. Certainly historians have
long recognized the implications of that movement on perceptions of the female

---

[1] Sermon of Ariald (d. 1066), a clerical leader of the Patarene reform movement in Milan, cited in
Elliot, *Spiritual Marriage*, 101.

sex. Christopher Brooke, who has covered this subject well, commented, 'At the heart of the movement lay the notion that women were a temptation and a danger.'[2] On the Continent the eleventh century certainly did see the rise of a misogyny, and it is recognized that this era saw a clerical and monastic flight from womankind. Historians see this trend's roots in the reformers' determination to eradicate clerical marriage and concubinage.[3] Dyan Elliott wrote of the eleventh-century clerical reforms, 'It is inevitable that with a campaign which aimed at nothing less than completely purging a male clergy of their female companions, women in general would become the enemy.'[4]

But in the earlier Benedictine reform, at least in England, we see it too. Aelfric was a great disseminator of the tenth-century reform ideas. His homilies, scrutinized by Katie Cubitt, point out women as a sexual danger, and even cross the line into misogyny.[5] Another was the fact of human weakness, including that of monks and clerics. Frailty was highlighted and, with scaremongering tactics, reformers could argue that lapses by religious men were preventable only by shunning women. This technique was employed in both reforms. In the earlier English reform movement, for example, we can note with Cubitt an addendum to the movement's key text, the *Regularis Concordia*, saying that no male might enter a female house.

England's tenth-century reformers aimed to accomplish a number of things, perhaps most notably to limit the ecclesiastical power of the laity, though scholars have made historians revise the old view that nobles were being simply attacked. For all its monastic focus, the leadership of the movement was heavily episcopal: Dunstan, Aethelwold, and Oswald were all bishops, and this fact gave the programme a strong pastoral element, most clearly seen in the second generation of the movement. As a result there were implications for the secular clergy as well. As Cubitt summarized, 'The Benedictine ideal in the hands of the bishops was to inform all aspects of religious life.'[6] One such aspect was clerical celibacy. Aethelwold commissioned a pastoral letter from Aelfric which attempted to impose the celibacy of the monks on his parochial clerics, and used satire to try to shame them into changing. Cubitt pointed out another, sharper

[2] C. Brooke covers this subject in his *Medieval Idea of Marriage* (Oxford, 1989), 68–77, quote from 69. Important also is his 'Gregorian Reform in Action: Clerical Marriage in England, 1050–1200', *Cambridge Historical Journal* 7 (1956), 1–21, 187–8. Others writing on this subject include J. Russell, *Dissent and Reform in the Early Middle Ages* (Berkeley, 1965), esp. 137–43; Barstow, *Married Priests*; J. McNamara, 'The Herrenfrage*: The Restructuring of the Gender System, 1050–1150', in C. Lees (ed.), *Medieval Masculinities: Regarding Men in the Middle Ages* (Medieval Cultures 7; Minneapolis, 1994), 1–30; M. Dortel-Claudot. 'Le prêtre et le mariage: évolution de la législation canonique des origines au XII siécle', *L'année canonique* 17 (1973), 319–44.
[3] G. Duby, *The Three Orders: Feudal Society Imagined*, trans. Arthur Goldhammer (Chicago, 1990).
[4] Elliot, *Spiritual Marriage*, 102.
[5] C. Cubitt, 'Virginity and Misogyny in Anglo-Saxon England', paper delivered March 1998 to the York Centre for Medieval Studies Thirtieth Anniversary Quodlibet Conference on 'Virginities: Post-Classical to Counter-Reformation'.
[6] Cubitt, 'Reforms', 85.

theological tool: Aelfric's letter to Wulfstan stresses the fundamentality of virginity to mankind's salvation and promotes the idea that sex and sexual licence are a sign of bondage to the devil. In this project Aelfric repeatedly cited the threefold schema of humanity which virgins and celibates ranked above the sexually active rest, interestingly using the trope so popular with the Irish but directed to an aim they certainly did not yet share. In Cubitt's assessment virginity in this context can be confirmed as having been essentially a male pursuit, with the Aelfric material strengthening earlier scholarly assertions that women were marginal to the Benedictine reforms.[7]

The *Regularis Concordia*, backbone of the English reforms, is to my knowledge not known to have been in Ireland in the tenth or earlier eleventh century. This in itself is not significant, due to the scarcity of surviving manuscripts known to have been written on the island at the time, but one tantalizing fact might suggest that the English Benedictine reformers hoped their ideas would travel westward: the *Regularis Concordia* opens with a statement that King Edgar is 'by Christ's grace the king of the English and all the peoples living in the ambit of the British island'.[8] The work of Janet Nelson, James Campbell, and Marie-Thérèse Flanagan has demonstrated that there is valid evidence that the English kings viewed themselves in the tenth century (not just the twelfth and projecting backwards) as rulers in some sense over the whole of the British isles.[9] Denis Bethell outlined many of the provable connections between the Irish and the English in the ecclesiastical sphere, a few of which bear repeating here. Firstly, the English Dunstan was brought up by Irish scholars, and his surviving classbook from Glastonbury contains Irish material. Dunstan must also have met Irish scholars at the court of Athelstan. Furthermore, according to the *Vita Wulfstani* Irish kings wrote to Wulfstan.[10] At Worcester in the tenth and eleventh centuries, Bethell reports, copies were made of Irish texts: the writings of Patrick, Bishop Duncaht's commentary on Martianus Capella, Bishop Israel's work on metre, the Irish canon collection, and a handful of others.[11] Nor were Irish–English connections new. Kathleen Hughes demonstrated that the Irish influenced English prayer and devotion in the ninth as well as tenth centuries.[12] To summarize with Bethell on the Irish and the English: 'up to 1066 we can still say that the English and the Irish shared a common cultural world in which the Irish could still be teachers.'[13]

[7] Cubitt, 'Virginity and Misogyny'.

[8] *Regularis Concordia*, ch. 1 (T. Simons, *Regularis Concordia* (London, 1953)). Flanagan, *Irish Society*, 42, with references.

[9] Flanagan has argued that the earlier Anglo-Saxon see at Canterbury was not attempting to interfere in the Irish Church, but she did find it plausible that Cnut might have felt Dublin to be part of his Anglo-Danish empire, as Bethell had suggested (Flanagan, *Irish Society*, ch. 1, esp. at 10).

[10] D. Bethell, 'English Monks and the Irish Reform', *Historical Studies* 8 (1971), 111–35, at 116, with references.

[11] Ibid. 117, with references.

[12] Hughes, cited in ibid. 118.   [13] Ibid. 125.

THE GREGORIANS

The propagandist of the aims and methods of the Gregorians, who gained increasing force from the middle of the eleventh century, included the theologian Peter Damian, who was a great promoter of clerical celibacy. No one was more passionate about the matter than he, and he reserved his especial wrath for the cleric's wife. He famously addressed them with, 'I speak to you O the clerics' charmers, Devil's choice tidbits, expulsion from paradise, you virus of the mind, you sword of souls, you wolfbane to drinkers, you poison to companions, you substance of sin, you occasion of death. . . . And so come, hear me whores, prostitutes, lovers, wallowing pools of greasy hogs, chambers of filthy spirits . . .'

Although this tone is far from anything found in Ireland, the Irish did know much of what was happening in Rome and its ecclesiastical environs. After 1066, in particular after 1070, the links were strong. From 1070 Lanfranc of Bec was in the seat of the see of Canterbury, and he was an active promoter of the next wave of reforms originating from Rome. As Archbishop of Canterbury he took to consecrating Irish bishops, a practice of which Irish kings demonstrably approved. And as for direct connections with Rome, Germany, and France, these were greater than has often been realized. Scholarship owes a great debt to Aubrey Gwynn for starting to correct a serious misapprehension inadvertedly created by Kenney, namely that Ireland had little to do with European movements until the twelfth century. His many articles repeatedly demonstrate that it was very much in touch with ecclesiastical matters in England, Germany, France, and Rome in the tenth and eleventh centuries. To cite but a few examples, a number of Irish kings went on pilgrimage to Rome in the decades up to the 1060s.[14] Probably it was in the late eleventh century there was established a community of Irish monks in Rome, whose membership is recorded in a single manuscript a short letter from Gregory VII himself to 'Terdelvacus, king of Ireland, and all the archbishops, bishops, abbots, nobles, and other faithful Christians who dwell in Ireland' in the 1080s, inviting them to consult him directly on matters of the church on which they might be seeking guidance. In addition to Rome, the German parts of the Empire also had extensive contact with Ireland, a point which is relevant given the conflict and debate which the reforms generated there. The Irish scholar David Scotus, for example, was in the Emperor Henry V's retinue during his famous expedition to Rome in 1110.[15] The connections were longstanding: Irish scholars had been at Charlemagne's court in the ninth century; under the Ottonians in the tenth Irish monks had set up communities at Metz, Cologne, Verdun, Fulda, and Ratisbon; and during the

---

[14] Flanagan, *Irish Society*, 10, with references.
[15] For all these events and foundations, see A. Gwynn, *The Irish Church in the Eleventh and Twelfth Centuries*, ed. G. O'Brien (Dublin, 1991), 34–45, 85–95, with references.

twelfth there was a group of Irish monasteries subject to the Irish community of St James at Ratisbon.

Peter Damian must have been read in Ireland by the twelfth century, if not earlier, because, among other things, he was one of the sources for the Middle Irish litany, *A Muire Mór*. In spite of the model he provided them, the Irish produced no rival to Peter Damian as a polemicist for isolating the church's men from women. In fact, by the middle of the twelfth century, the English and the Western churches in general saw Ireland as no longer the *insula sanctorum* but rather an *insula barbarorum*: its marriage customs were uncanonical, its baptismal practices were non-conformist, and in general its practices were lax.

That was the view we see in a wide range of sources including the correspondence with the papacy and with the English archbishops of Canterbury, Bernard of Clairvaux's Life of Malachy, and Gerald of Wales's *Topographia*. Not only had the Irish church failed to produce a reforming propagandist of the forcefulness of Peter Damian or the effectiveness of Lanfranc, it had failed even to keep up with the reforms. The reformers knew what the Irish situation was, and they misliked it.

IRISH WRITING ON WOMEN

There is a great deal of truth in Dyan Elliot's assertion about the reforms, that 'women in general would become the enemy'.[16] It is true that attitudes concerning the relations between clerics and monks on the one hand, and women, including nuns, on the other, do not exist in a vacuum. There is likely to be a resonance between them and their wider beliefs about women. If the conclusions made in the previous chapters are valid, the contemporary literature on the theology of womanhood generally should corroborate and mirror those seen in the more limited sphere of the ecclesiastical domain. Furthermore, they may add to our understanding of the context in which the female monastics and clerical consorts lived and pursued their vocations.

The literature in which the Irish generalize about womankind took its theme from the Bible for the most part. In Christian writing, woman traditionally carried a typological value, so women of the Bible were often used as starting-points for exploration of various aspects of femaleness. In medieval Ireland, as elsewhere, female biblical characters served as *bonnes à penser*, 'goods to think with', and this included thinking about gender and its contours. In Ireland, a few only were really taken up: these are Eve and Mary, John the Baptist's nemesis Herodias, and the queen of the great king Solomon. Irish mentalities concerning womanhood come to life in these women.

---

[16] Elliot, *Spiritual Marriage*, 102.

'O Generous Eve of Fair Shape'

Eve has no rival as the most celebrated sinner in Christendom. Tempted by the serpent in the Garden of Eden, she took of the apple and gave it to Adam to eat. When God confronted Adam, asking why he had eaten the forbidden fruit, the man replied, 'the woman, whom thou gavest me to be my companion, gave me of the tree, and I did eat' (Gen. 3: 12). As the Church taught that all women are 'daughters of Eve', the medieval woman was believed to share in Eve's sin, not only her sin of disobedience but her tendency to lure men into wrongdoing, and sexual wrongdoing at that. Ever since Augustine formalized this interpretation, the Western Church had seen the offering of that forbidden fruit in terms of sexual allurement and temptation.

Eve made her mark on early medieval Ireland as she did on other Christian communities. From the Irish high crosses sculpted at monasteries in the Viking era she peers out from under the Tree of Good and Evil, hand outstretched clutching the forbidden fruit. She stands on the left, the distaff side of the branching arbour, and her companion Adam, who took what she offered, is always to the right. Between them the serpent, Satan, curls up the trunk. Their naked bodies peer out amidst the many Biblical characters who populate these monuments, a testimony both to humanity's origins and to its fallen state.[17]

How the Irish perceived and wrote about Eve reveals much about how they viewed women in their own society. Fortunately, the Irish did leave textual material on the Fall, and from the two main texts on the theme we can gain insights into the Irish understanding of the relationship between woman and sex, woman and man, and woman and sin. Yet it needs to be noted that Eve was not a major character for the Irish in their exegetical and apocryphal writings, which date as far back as the seventh century. There is nowhere near the focus on her that there is on the Virgin Mary, whose Irish cult was both early to develop and widespread in its extent. Before the tenth century she is hardly evident at all, and even the theological glosses (most of which are from the seventh century) show little interest in her. Genesis was not a favourite topic and within that Eve even less so: only a couple of examples can be found. Indeed the scholar combing these writings searches in vain to find even passing mentions of Eve, whereas one is continually tripping over references to Mary.

Not only is Eve rarely taken up as a theme in herself, women are not likened to her. When we do find her in the earlier material, she is not held up as an archetypal female: the seventh-century exegetical text, *De Mirabilibus Sacrae Scripturae*, for example, does comment on the Fall but in ungendered terms, with no mention made of Eve or womankind; it is *homo* who falls; furthermore, it is the serpent, not Eve, who is cast in the role of the seducer.[18] From the same century,

[17] F. Henry, *Irish Art During the Viking Invasions, 800–1020 AD* (London, 1967), plates 81, 83, 96.
[18] *De Mirabilibus Sacrae Scripturae*, book 1, ch. 2 (*PL* 35. 2151–2200). This Irish text in three books is falsely

the anonymous exegetical tract on Creation, *Liber de Ordine Creaturarum*, mentions Adam briefly as the eater of the apple, but not Eve: '[the Bible] does not show satisfactorily from which tree Adam ate' and 'Lord Jesus . . . accepted death for Adam's transgression.'[19] A ninth- or tenth-century prayer written by an Irish nun in the Antiphony of Bangor makes no mention of Eve, nor the Virgin Mary, though many other saints are invoked; there is nothing notably gendered about the prayer, in fact it is only evident that the author is female from a few lines such as *ut pro me dei famula oretis*.[20]

It is in the late tenth century, in a long poetical adaptation of an apocryphal Genesis, that we first really see the Irish Eve. The *Saltair na Rann* is a composition of 150 cantos to which another twelve cantos were later added.[21] The subject matter of the *Saltair* is the sacred history of the world, starting with Creation. The inspiration for the main part of the composition, the first 150 quatrains, is the apocryphal *Vita Adae et Evae* along with what must have been a Latin version of the Greek *Apocalypsis Mosis*. The *Vita Adae* was a late antique composition popular enough in the early middle ages to spawn several vernacular versions, including an Anglo-Saxon and a German one. The Genesis account in the *Saltair na Rann* can be compared against that in the *Vita Adae* (its primary source) and other variants. Because it is possible to detect the points at which the Irish author departed from the Latin source inspiring him, we can see where the Irish notions of female sin were at variance from it. Murdoch's commentary does this on a line-by-line basis and, as a further exercise, notes the Anglo-Saxon and German departures as well.

The *Saltair* story, like the *Vita Adae* on which it is based, is remarkable in its almost lover-like praise for the first woman. She first appears in canto 6, created from Adam's side.

> Dianid commainm Eua án,
> crichid, corcarda, coemnár,
>> dil, delb[d]a, toga rainni,
>> fotha febda fírc[h]lainne.
> Iar sain as-raracht Ádom
> assa súan cen imgábud,
>> con-facca in mnaí, mín a dath,
>> ségda, súaichnid, sochruthach.

attributed to Augustine, the author usually referred to by scholars as 'Augustinus' or 'the Irish Augustine'. For more see Lapidge and Sharpe, *Bibliography*, no. 291.

[19] *Liber de Ordine Creaturarum*, ch. 1 (*PL* 83. 913–54).
[20] F. E. Warren, ed. *The Antiphony of Bangor*, 2 vols. (Henry Bradshaw Society 4, 10; London: 1893/5); the prayer, which commences *Estu mihi sanitas*, is in ii. 83–9.
[21] W. Stokes (ed.), *The Saltair na Rann: A Collection of Early Middle Irish Poems* (Anecdota Oxoniensia 1, pt. 3; Oxford, 1883). The relevant section has more recently been edited by F. Kelly, B. Murdoch, and D. Greene, *The Irish Adam and Eve Story*, 2 vols. (Dublin, 1976). Textual and manuscript discussion: McNamara, *Apocrypha*, 10–11; *Kenney*, no. 609. It is written in early Middle Irish and found in complete form in a sole manuscript, Bodl. MS Rawl. B502, fos. 19–40. It is generally assumed to have been composed in 988, possibly by Aibertach mac Coisse, head of the school of Ros Ailithir in south-west Cork.

> Amal ro déccai a ggnúis,
> dos-roega sech cach nderbdúis,
>> do-rarngert di, éraim nglé,
>> combad sainserc sochaide.
> 'Is orot rirfes cen cleith
> cách a máthair 's a athair;
>> óndiu tria bithu, buaid néin,
>> bíaid cech oen úain dit ógréir.'

Whose name was noble Eve, prudent, bright, fair and modest, dear, shapely, the best of the dividing, the excellent foundation of true children. After that Adam arose out of his sleep without danger, and saw the woman of fair complexion, noble, famous, shapely. And he saw her dear face, he chose her above every true prize, he promised her, clear wisdom, that she would be the especial love of hosts. 'It is for you, without concealment, that every man will abandon his mother and his father; from today forever, triumph . . ., all of us will be completely at your disposal.'[22]

After Adam ate of the apple, he berated Eve for her foolishness. 'Who tempted you?', he asks. She replies that the serpent had promised that if she ate she would know evil, so she could know the difference between good and evil: she took it because she did not know what evil was. God banished them from the Garden of Eden, and they fell into poverty, cold, and hunger. Yet Adam speaks of the transgression as a shared thing: 'It is not God who failed us, o bright fair Eve; it is we who outraged the Prince' (*Ní Dia robo lochtach frind, a Eua chorcra c[h]aemfind; is sinn ro sáraig in flaith*).[23] Eve, in misery, blames herself. Why, she asks, doesn't Adam kill her. 'It is I who broke the law . . . it is right for you to kill me for that, my lord Adam' (*is mé do-chóid darsin smacht, is mé do-róni in tarmthecht, cóir duit mo marbad di sain, a mo thigerna, a Ádaim*).[24] She reasons that God is more likely to show mercy to Adam, her beloved husband, if she dies for the crime. He protests that he will not kill his own kin, no matter how bad matters have got, and even though her fault was great, he will not outrage God even further by killing her.

Adam hits on the idea that they should do penance to cleanse some of the sin. She is to stand thirty-three days in the river Tigris, and he forty-seven days in the Jordan. They go their separate ways to undertake this act, and well before the time was completed, God forgave Adam and his descendants. The devil, hearing of this, rushed to where Eve stood in the river so as to sabotage the absolution: to exploit her weakness and entice her to cut short her act of penance, to 'destroy something of her work and disturb her devotion' (*coro bádur ní dia mud, 'ma crábud do chumscugud*).[25] Disguised as an angel he arrives at the Tigris and tells her that God has taken pity on her and she should come out of the river. Not spotting the trick, Eve gets out of the river and goes with the 'angel' to give the good news to Adam. She did not recognize Lucifer with all his disguises, the

---

[22] *Saltair na Rann*, lines 1061–72 (F. Kelly *et al.*, *Adam and Eve Story*, 2 vols. (Dublin, 1976)).
[23] Lines 1521–4.   [24] Lines 1529–32.   [25] Lines 1667–8.

poet explains, it was a difficulty for the excellent woman, her mind was in doubt.[26] Adam, still standing neck deep in the water doing penance, sees his wife approach with the Devil (whom he recognizes as such) and is furious and horrified. Realizing that Eve has been led astray, he asks what possessed her to get out of the river without God's command, and tells her the true identity of the 'angel' beside her. At his outburst she falls to the ground. 'Lucifer, Devil, why are you persecuting us?', she cries, and goes on for the next thirty lines to protest his campaign against them. It was not they who cast him out of heaven, nor took away his wealth, nor deposed his sovereignty; his argument was with God, not them. It was, she tells him, his own rebellion and vainglory that is to blame. So why was he attacking them, having robbed them of their purity and put them into error?[27] Though it is not specified, it is presumed that they finished their penance. They subsequently went out into the world and begat their children and lived out their long lives.

This section of the *Saltair* has been recounted here in such detail because it brings to life an Irish author's understanding of Eve's character and thus the relationship between women, original sin, and the essence of femininity. First to be noted is the description of Eve at her creation: she is the fair mother of all future generations, and is praised as such. Motherhood enjoys high esteem, and Eve partakes of that. She is beauteous, too, another quality the Irish held in high regard. When it comes to the Fall, the absence of a sexual tone here also requires note: Adam and Eve do not sin carnally, nor is the forbidden knowledge portrayed as being sexual. Eve is not a wilful temptress; she was deceived. Eve does give Adam the apple, but she does so out of a rather dim-witted conviction that it would be a good thing for him and her both. At no point does she wish harm to her husband. She is not his scheming nemesis but rather his beautiful and cherished helpmate, whose naïve stupidity causes repeated tragedy but whose devoted loyalty is deeply touching. When Adam briefly loses his temper at Eve she becomes overwrought with sorrow. In his turn Adam is heroically steadfast towards her; never does he turn against her, but rather he does his best to help them get out of their predicament together.[28]

The sympathetic treatment accorded to Eve is remarkable. She receives no special punishment from God, nor is there any special curse upon future generations of women to pay for her transgression. The women of the future are in no way, it suggests, going to share in her particular guilt. Indeed, Eve's desperate self-reproach can elicit in the modern reader a feeling of compassion, and it is hard to imagine it not having a similar effect on the early medieval reader as

---

[26] Ibid., lines 1681–700.   [27] Ibid., lines 1721–38.

[28] In the Anglo-Saxon version also stupidity is Eve's overriding shortcoming. See e.g. R. Finnegan, 'Eve and "Vincible Ignorance" in *Genesis B*', *Texas Studies in Literature and Language* 18 (1976), 329–39; A. Renoir, 'Eve's I.Q. Rating: Two Sexist Views of *Genesis B*', in H. Damico and A. Olsen (eds.), *New Readings on Women in Old English Literature* (Bloomington, Ind., 1990), 262–72; J. Vickery, 'The Vision of Eve in Genesis B', *Speculum* 44 (1969), 86–102.

well. The notion of shared responsibility, the man taking at least partial blame for his woman's deeds, suggests an Irish notion of honour and responsibility. One may recall that the law texts insist that every woman has a 'head' who is responsible for her actions. Perhaps this is part of the underlying moral in the sequence of the fall.

In the *Saltair*, Eve is the mouthpiece of a form which recurs in Irish texts written in a woman's voice, namely the lament. When she berates herself for her and Adam's downfall and then, at greater length, when she despairingly reproaches the Devil for undoing them, Eve is a shedder of tears for the way of the world. She is also, like other Irish female literary figures, a voice of outraged justice. Eve eloquently takes the Devil to task for making her and Adam pay for his own misfortune. Ireland at this time gives women the role of the lamenter, and gives woman also a voice against injustice. The famed Lament of Deirdre, for example, contains both heartbreaking sorrow and outspoken criticism, as does 'The Massacre of the Innocents', written as though spoken by the infants' mothers, and the poem 'Eve's Lament'. In this regard Eve resembles the sorrowing woman, not a Jezebel.

The *Saltair* and the prose 'Creation and Fall' quite closely resemble the *Vita Adae* which inspired them. It is interesting that the Irish were drawn to adopt a female-friendly interpretation of Genesis, and that in adapting it they did not make it more misogynistic (as did one German writer, Lutwin, who wrote a vernacular version).[29] In fact when the Irish author did depart from the Latin story it was never to magnify blame or criticism of Eve. The *Saltair* in particular is distinctly more laudatory of Eve than the Latin *Vita Adae*. The latter does not treat the Creation, commencing instead immediately after the expulsion from Paradise, and the *Liber Mosis* was not followed in the episodes under consideration here. The *Saltair's* account of the creation of Eve, then, is to the best of our knowledge a wholly Irish composition. It was an Irishman who composed that lengthy and loving description of the new-sprung woman: noble, prudent, bright, fair, modest, shapely, excellent, famous, and of fair complexion. He gushes unabashedly that from the day of woman's creation man would be completely at her disposal.[30]

Once the story progresses to the expulsion, it is possible to compare the Latin original and the Irish variant. Though it deals sympathetically with Eve, the *Vita Adae* at no point has any similar speech, or any equivalent to the eulogy in the Irish version, so it was almost certainly the Irish who interspersed the laudatory adjectives we see in their version ('beloved Eve', 'modest Eve of bright form', and so forth).

There is an interesting divergence also at the point at which the disguised Devil comes to Eve standing in the Tigris. In the Latin version, he tells her: *Dominus . . . misit me, ut educerem vos de aqua et darem vobis alimentum.* In the Irish, by

---

[29] Kelly *et al.*, *Adam and Eve*, ii. 117.   [30] *Saltair na Rann*, lines 1061–72.

contrast, the Devil explicitly tells her that God has had pity on her; thus he is made to imply that God has considered her penance sufficient: 'your strong king has sent me on a journey, it is from him I have come to show pity on you' (*do rí rúad rom faíd for fecht, úad tánac dott' airchissecht*).[31] This textual change has the effect of making Eve seem more devoted to her task; she is here clearly *not* leaving off her penance simply because she wants something to eat. Murdoch sees in this passage that the Devil makes Eve believe she has overdone the penance or at least that she has done enough. Overall, in fact, his opinion was that the Irish version places a stronger emphasis on redemption through penance than others do.[32] An additional point may be made, namely that there is a gendered angle to this message: womankind too achieved redemption.

The Irish and Latin texts diverge at another point of the encounter by the river. In both versions Eve is said not to recognize Satan. But the *Saltair* alone expands on this, adding 'it was a difficulty for the excellent woman, her mind was in doubt' (*don banscáil febdai bá hairc, bae a menmai i cumtabairt*).[33] Eve's state of mind is not described in the *Vita Adae*, and only rarely in any other vernacular version (Anglo-Saxon, Slavic, etc.). Only Lutwin, noted Murdoch, addresses himself to Eve's state of mind in his German version. But Lutwin had at this point digressed into a misogynistic homily which named other weak and evil women of the Bible. Comparing the Irish and the German versions, Murdoch observes 'the two texts . . . are entirely different in spirit'.[34] This difference in spirit highlights the fact that vernacular writers of different backgrounds could and did 'twist' the tone of this apocryphal story to make it more closely resemble their own views of womankind. The Irish variant was the kindest one of the lot. It is only partially rivalled by the somewhat sympathetic Anglo-Saxon version, known as the *Genesis B*, whose content is compared against the others in Murdoch's commentaries in volume two of *Adam and Eve*.

A prose version of the section on the creation and fall is found in RIA MS 25, the Leabhar Breac, and the Yellow Book of Lecan. It is extremely similar to the *Saltair*, both in content and tone. The creation of Eve, however, is glossed over in this version and she only comes to the fore as she meets the serpent. Nor is she given the illustrious epithets accorded to her in the poem, but is still very much the naïve: she tells Adam that she was aware of no harm resulting from eating the apple until she saw herself naked. This author, too, made it clear that Eve is not to take too much of the blame: at the interrogation by God, Adam tells God it is all Eve's fault and he pleads that if he has violated God's command it was the woman bestowed on him who tempted him. God does not accept the excuse, saying that Adam will now be punished, and his children after him, for his failure to acknowledge his guilt. Though man might try to pass the buck God will not accept this, and will castigate those who try to avoid their responsibility.

---

[31] Lines 1681–4.   [32] Kelly *et al.*, *Adam and Eve*, ii. 38, 116.
[33] *Saltair na Rann*, lines 1687–8.   [34] Kelly *et al.*, *Adam and Eve*, ii. 117.

Another Irish text of this period delves into the nature of womankind through the character of Eve, and thus gives another view of attitudes to the female sex in a theological or ontological sense. *Mé Eba Ben* ('I am the Woman Eve') is a poem inspired by Genesis apocrypha and dated by Meyer to around the late tenth or early eleventh century.[35] Structured as a dramatic monologue in verse, it seems at first glance to contradict the spirit we encountered in the *Saltair*. The poet places into Eve's mouth a most woeful self-excoriation for her sin and for its effect on humankind. But quite rightly, scholars have treated the poem as a lament, nicknaming it 'Eve's Lament'. She is here, as she is in the *Saltair*, and as Deirdre is in the tales, a tragic figure.

> Mé Eba, ben Adaim uill; mé ro sháraig Ísu thall;
> me ro thall nem ar mo chloinn; cóir is mé do-chóid sa crann.
>
> Ropa lemm ríched dom réir, olc in míthoga rom thár;
> olc in cosc cinad rom chrín; fo-rír, ní hidan mo lám.
>
> Mé tuc in d-uball an-úas, do-chúaid tar cumang mo chraís;
> in céin marat sain re lá, de no scarat mná re baís.
>
> Ní bíad eigred in cach dú, ní bíad geimred gaethmar glé,
> ní bíad iffern, ní bíad brón, ní bíad oman, minbad mé.

I am Eve, the wife of noble Adam; it was I who violated Jesus in the past;
it was I who robbed my children of heaven; it is I who by right should
   have been crucified.

I had heaven at my command; evil the bad choice that shamed me;
evil the punishment for my crime that has aged me; my hand is not pure.

It was I who plucked the apple; it went past the narrow of my gullet;
as long as they live in daylight women will not cease from folly on
   account of that.

There would be no ice in any place; there would be no bright and windy winter;
there would be no hell, there would be no grief, there would be no terror
   but for me.[36]

But for Eve's 'bad choice' (*olc in míthoga rom thár*) there would be no winter, no hell, no grief, no terror, no sorrow, writes the poet. In spite of this damning blame, the poem is intended to cause the reader to pity Eve, for she voices a heavy world-weary sorrow which is once poignant and existential—a universal lament for the pains of life. These texts show what looks to be a typical Irish view, namely that Eve has a pivotal role in the grand drama of the sacred history of the world. The Irish acknowledged her as their prime mother, and as such the *Saltair* praises her greatly. At the same time she was the one who brought upon her beloved children the pains of life and the agonies of the fallen world. Eve

---

[35] *Kenney*, no. 610.
[36] Greene and O'Connor, *Golden Treasury*, 157–8, which in turn is based on the edition of Kuno Meyer, *Ériu* 3 (1907), 148.

was humanity's mother, whose torment at her own evil folly was both heroic and saddening.

Neither the *Saltair* nor *Mé Eba Ben* links Eve's fall to carnal, sexual lust. Eve's sin was not a sexual one, and the primary weakness of her daughters is not of the concupiscent variety. When we turn to see if biblical women other than Eve were epitomized for the Irish sinfulness of sex, we are similarly disappointed. Mary Magdalen, the biblical repentant harlot, was largely ignored by the Irish. In one of the extremely rare instances when she is mentioned she is remembered not for her harlotry but rather for her weakness and her tears of penance. The Middle Irish (probably tenth-century) poem 'A Prayer for Tears' contains a line in which the poet cries that, alas, even a little stream of tears is not forthcoming onto his cheek 'as thou gavest a flood of tears to the weak, wretched woman' (*feib tucais in linn don banscáil thimm thrúaig*). The woman in question is glossed as Mary Magdalen. She is weak, wretched, and repentant, indeed characterized by many of the same traits Eve is accorded. As with Eve, the sexual angle is not taken up.[37] This is very much in tune with what was observed in the hagiography concerning attitudes to nuns and clerics. There we saw that the nun was not painted a sexual temptress, nor were clerics or monks imaged as being victimized by voracious female lust. It must be said that Molua's early hagiographer had seen the threat of women in sexual terms: that saint, it will be recalled, had problems finding a place to settle away from women.[38]

Women in this later theological material suggest that woman's greatest hindrance to spiritual *virtus* was her propensity to folly. Eve in the lament says foolishness is the legacy she bestows on womankind 'for as long as they live in daylight': *in céin marat sain re lá, de no scarat mná re baís.*[39] In the *Saltair*, the same trait is at the root of Eve's first taking of the apple. And so too is it responsible for her cutting short her penance in the river Tigris, for which Adam reproaches her with—

> Cia rot brathaig, a ben báith,
> rot rathaig narbsat firgaith,
> don-rat fri sním saethraich seis,—
> rot baíthig, rom baethigeis![40]

Who betrayed you, foolish woman, who perceived that you were not truly wise, who has put us into painful torment?—he deceived you, you deceived me.

[37] K. Meyer (ed. and trans.), 'Four Religious Poems', *Ériu* 6 (1911–12), 12–13. Mary Magdalen is treated in the glosses to the Martyrology of Oengus, which relate the story of the oil, her forgiveness by Christ, and the upbraiding given to Christ by a Pharisee for allowing a harlot near him (Martyrology of Oengus, notes to 6 July).

[38] Life of Lugaid *alias* Molua, Φ text, ch. 32.

[39] *Báes*: normally foolishness, levity, but also referring to incapacity at law; in a few later texts it is found with the meaning of 'lust' or wantonness, but I think that in this instance the sexual connotation is not at the fore, if present at all.

[40] *Saltair na Rann*, lines 1317–20.

This view, too, is in line with the material relating more specifically to nuns, to the women in the ecclesiastical establishment of the time. The later female saints' Lives, concerning themselves as they did with the highest possible attainment of women, agree. One episode in the Life of Monenna in particular is of interest in this light. The Life makes no suggestion that women are impure or salacious, but they can be, it says, prone to weakness and foolishness. One of Monenna's virgins saw a vision and, frightened, came to her in a trembling state.

Cui sancta Monenna clementer respondit: 'Signa diligenter tuum cor. Forsitan bestiarum vel demonum horrorem invenistis que omnia desertis solent accidere et sexum feminarum potest modicum commovere.'[41]

St Monenna calmly replied, 'Make the sign of the cross over your heart; perhaps you came upon horrible beasts or devils, all of them things which tend to turn up in lonely places—and a little thing can upset a woman.'

Despite the propensity to folly, woman is deemed capable of deep feeling, of touching loyalty, and of that very important thing, motherhood. For this she is honoured, and whatever her idiocies, womankind is not to be shunned. The two Eve texts avoid any suggestion that man should renounce woman. It may be that Eve is repeatedly falling into acts and oversights of an innocently imbecile nature, but man should emulate Adam and forgive womanly foolishness; to harm her would anger God. He must needs be a good 'head' and not shirk his duty of looking after her, and with male help and her own commitment, a woman repenting of folly can achieve real insight and wisdom. Man and woman must stick together and share the burden of living in a fallen world.

The Virgin Mary

Another biblical woman through whom the Irish worked out ideas about womanhood was the Virgin Mary, who was in early medieval Ireland the patroness of virgins especially. The observations made here on the figure of Mary are necessarily more cursory than exhaustive, for a full-scale study of the Irish cult of the Virgin would fill a book on its own. The rise of her cult elsewhere in the West in the eleventh and twelfth centuries has been linked to the simultaneous demonization of 'real women' in the reform era. According to many scholars, the virgin mother of Christ was promoted at this time in a campaign to instate a fully chaste and utterly untouchable female ideal, the likes of which no mortal woman could match. Mary was held up as a contrast to Eve, the two together serving as the two sides of the coin of femininity, the good and the bad. Mary, it was taught, had overcome the legacy of Eve: where Eve was sexual, Mary was chaste; where Eve was disobedient, Mary was wholly and willingly compliant to God's instructions. Mortal women—especially laywomen—were

---

[41] Conchubranus, Life of Monenna, book 3, ch. 6.

of course closer in nature to Eve than to Mary, but they could reach up beyond their natural state through divine grace and the application of ascetic will.

This pattern does not fit for Ireland. There the cult of the Virgin rose in the seventh century, earlier than almost anywhere else in Western Christendom.[42] At that time, as Marian devotion began to flourish, the evidence of the voluminous sources makes it clear that there was no nosedive in women's status or theological position. However, in the later period, the era under discussion in this chapter, one can only just barely perceive an escalation in Mary's already-established cult. As evidenced in the sources from the tenth to twelfth centuries, the Marian cult says little about the nature of womankind *per se*. Rather Mary represents all that is best about women: beauty, nobility, honour, modesty. This alone is hardly good fodder for incisive analysis. It is hard to put a finger on what the Irish Mary reveals about the Irish understanding of womankind. Only a few general points may be made which may indirectly shed some light on the matter. At this time Mary was considered one of, if not the, most powerful of intercessors. According to the apocryphal account of the Virgin's assumption, *Transitus Mariae*, she even intercedes with Christ to grant respite to those in hell.[43] Prayers and litanies to her abound. Mary's womanhood offered no obstacle in Irish eyes to her enjoyment of a high celestial status. She was believed to be a powerful spiritual ally, and reverence for her was clearly deep-felt and widespread.

The litany *A Muire Mór* ('O Great Mary') represents the sole known case of the Virgin Mary being contrasted to Eve. Found in the Leabhar Breac, this Middle Irish text is of uncertain date: Stokes attributed it to the twelfth century, a date with which Carney was inclined to agree.[44] It recites the Virgin's many epithets, and her power seems limitless. She is paragon of women, queen of the angels, lady of heaven, mother of the eternal glory, mother of the church in heaven and earth, beauty of virgins, lady of nations, breast of infants, handmaid of God, mother of Christ, spouse of the Lord, queen of the world. She is beauteous as a dove, lovely as the moon, as elect as the sun. The epithet of interest here is the one that calls Mary the 'repulse of Eve's reproach' (*dichor aithisse Eua*). It is a Continental import, almost certainly. This and almost all the other invocatory titles in the litany have been shown to derive from Continental sources, namely from Peter Damian, Anselm (both eleventh-century), and from pseudo-Anselm and pseudo-Ildephonsus (dates uncertain). Perhaps significantly, the litanist was not even well versed in earlier Irish poems on the Virgin.[45]

---

[42] The earliest known devotions to her are evidenced in the *Versiculi Familia Benchuir* in the Antiphony of Bangor, dated to *c*.600.

[43] *Transitus Mariae*, ch. 54 (St John Seymour, 'Irish Versions of the *Transitus Mariae*', *Journal of Theological Studies* 23 (1922), 36–43). For more on this text see McNamara, *Apocrypha*, no. 97.

[44] Discussion of dating in O'Dwyer, *Devotion to Mary*, 70.

[45] G. C. Meersseman, *The Acahistos Hymn* (Freiburg, 1958), 166–70; O'Dwyer, *Mary*, 72. Given the sources, a 12th-cent. date for the litany seems most reasonable; however, it may be that Anselm and Damian in turn used earlier sources, which the Irish litanist was himself using.

For the Irish, Mary was a redeemer of Eve's sin only in a very inexplicit way. This was in the sense that she encouraged women to go beyond their innate foolishness which, according to the Eve texts, was Eve's legacy to them. In the *Transitus Mariae*, a prose tale most probably composed in the twelfth century relating the death of the Virgin, she is shown living with a group of *virgines* of whom she was the spiritual mother.[46] As death drew near, a great fear seized the virgins and they pleaded with her not to leave them, for when she had gone the Devil might overtake them.[47] She was their protector against him: she was the shepherd, they the sheep. This reinforces the role of Mary as the protector of virgins, but implies that women, even virgins, are weak in the face of diabolical threat. They are weak, but Mary is strong. The Virgin's reply is as telling as the pleading of the girls, for she tells them sternly and tersely, 'Be quiet and do not disobey God'. Mary, the patroness of virgins, speaks with the voice of sensible clarity.

'. . . After the Murder of John'

If Eve and Mary were not linked icons of evil and good femininity respectively, and if a sin no more dramatic than foolishness was woman's prime inheritance from Eve, it is feasible to wonder to what extent the Irish expressed hostility to woman through other biblical women. We do find, however, two New Testament women who were on the receiving end of whatever Irish misogyny did exist. The death of John the Baptist (Matt. 14: 2–11) was a popular story among the Irish. John, was executed at Herod's orders through the trickery of two women. Herod loved Herodias, wife of his brother, but John pointed out that it was illegal for him to marry her, so Herod had him imprisoned. He had a mind to put John to death, but dared not do so because the people revered him as a prophet. On Herod's birthday Herodias's daughter danced for Herod. Well pleased, he offered the girl 'whatsoever she would ask of him'. Prompted by her mother, the girl asked for the head of John the Baptist on a plate. Herod was caught in an inextricable bind and honour forced him to something he did not want, so to keep his word he ordered John to be beheaded in prison. His head was then, as requested, brought forth on a platter to the mother and daughter.

The Irish had a native tradition in which catch-22s and *gessa* (taboos) figure strongly, as is seen in the *Táin* and other vernacular tales, and it thus unsurprising that they were fond of this story. In fact, they developed a legend which claimed the beheading was performed by an evil Irish druid named Mag Roth. And so too the Irish developed an interest in the two women, the evil mother and daughter. *Pais Eoin Bautist*, 'The Passion of John the Baptist', is found earliest in the Leabhar Breac but also appears in the Yellow Book of Lecan, the

---

[46] *Transitus Mariae*, chs. 2–6.   [47] Ibid., ch. 6.

Liber Flavus Fergusiorum, and five other manuscripts.[48] In some Irish versions the story is changed and John's death is requested by the two daughters of Herodias, named as Salvisa (or Salia) and Neptis. The wickedness of the girls' deed is repeatedly stressed. In a late Middle-Irish poetic version of the story John enquires who is going to actually behead him: 'Which of you undertakes to behead me for evil women?' (*Cúich ocaib gabas do láim mo díchennad do drochmnáib?*)[49] The notes to the Martyrology of Oengus, which also refer to the death of John, offer the most vivid expression of how the women tricking Herod into executing John are expressions of evil womanhood. 'The world's women, save a few of them, burn in the fire of doom: to speak of them is unmeet after the murder of John' (*Mná in domuin acht mad bec dib, i tinid brathat breoid: labra fríu nocha techta, indegaid echta Eoin*).[50] John is a martyr to womanly evil.

The story of John turns on its head the widespread notion that women are weak and foolish, and instead obliquely suggests that they can have a cunning power on account of men's love for them. Such a view is expressed even more strongly in another short Irish apocryphal story, the probably ninth-century 'The Power of Women'. This story was popular enough to have been copied into several collections, including the Book of Leinster and the Yellow Book of Lecan.[51] Like many others it uses biblical characters, here the great king Solomon and his wife.

One day a tribal king held a great feast for the great king Solomon, which he attended and everyone got very drunk. Before going to bed Solomon set three faithful retainers to guard him, fearful as he was of being attacked in the night. To pass the time the guards play a game, each to suggest what was the most powerful thing in the world. One suggests wine, 'for it is wine which gladdens the host till they be without reason, without sense' (*Air is fín romedair is slúag combátar cen chond, chen chéill*). The second says no, it is the power of the ruler. 'Strongest of men is the sovereign. Senior of creatures is man. It is his power which has made us be without drunkenness, without sleep though we are here drinking wine' (*Tressa flath feraib. Sruithiu dúilib duine. Is a chumachtae sidi do-nrigni-ni cen mesca cen chotlud ce no-n fil oc o[u]l fina*). The third man, whose name was Nemiasserus, said no, the greatest power is the power of women and the next day he would prove it. The next day the three were in the company of Solomon and his queen and their retinue. They related their conversation to the

[48] For full manuscript details of all Irish versions see McNamara, *Apocrypha*, no. 55. The Leabhar Breac version is in Bernard and Atkinson, *Passions and Homilies*, 64–8, 304–9. The story is virtually the same as that in *Acta Sanctorum* (1867 edn.), under 'June', v. 615–17.
[49] The poem commencing *Abstalón, adba na ríg*, ed. B. Ó Cuív in 'Two Items from Irish Apocryphal Tradition', *Celtica* 10 (1973), 87–113.
[50] Martyrology of Oengus, notes on 29 Aug.
[51] Textual and manuscript details in McNamara, *Apocrypha*, no. 10B. The text was originally edited with an English trans. by K. Meyer, 'Anecdota from Irish Manuscripts 9: the Book of Leinster p. 282a', *Gaelic Journal (Irisleabhar na Gaedhilge)* 4 (1893), 216–17. Also ed. J. Pokorny, *A Historical Reader of Old Irish* (Halle, 1923), 12–14, 36–48. Meyer identified it as a garbled version of Esdras 3: 3–4.

company. Various men chimed in with their opinion. One thought it wine, another the sovereign. The queen suddenly struck Solomon, knocking his crown off his head so it fell on the floor, and said, 'What, am I without power then?'

'A mmarbad!' ol cách. Do-sn-écai in rí sechae. Tibid ind rígain. La sodain tibid in rí fochétóir. 'Niloitfider in ben', ol in rí. 'A sin ille', ol Nemiasserus, 'is trén a chumachtae sin.' 'Is fir' ol in rí. 'Is tressa cumachtae mná, oldá[a]s cach cumachtae. Ol is in[n]a étun biid di a Satain comaitechtae 7 timgaire 7 chumachtai conacumangar a aithber forrae cachadénae di ulc.'

'Her death!', cried everyone. The king looked at her sideways. The queen smiled. Thereupon, suddenly the king smiled too. 'The woman will not be harmed' said the king. 'From that, then' said Nemiasserus, 'strong indeed is her power.' 'It is true' said the king. 'The power of women is greater than any other power, because in her brow is her companion Satan, so she cannot be reproached for whatever she does of evil.'

With that line, the little story ends. The power of women, then, lies in men's soft spot for them, for the love and indulgence extended to them. In their adoration of women men make promises to them, binding themselves to women's wills. This view is seen more widely in other literature such as in the tales of the *Táin*, where men are sometimes impelled, through love or through vows arising from love, into performing dangerous or tragic courses of action. Furthermore, here we are given a theological explanation of sorts: it is a sort of devilish power that women have that makes men so soft-hearted towards them, that dissipates their rage against them. Without being too heavy-handed about it, the author of the tale of Solomon's wife attributes men's inability to recriminate against the female sex to the Devil.

IMPLICATIONS FOR THE CLERICAL SPHERE

The four characters discussed epitomized womankind for the Irish authors. Eve, Mary, Herodias, and Solomon's wife are about the only ones utilized in this way, even though in other areas authors used many more as *bonnes à penser*, as 'goods to think with', on sexual issues. In Ireland one finds no lyrical exegeses on many of the other obvious candidates. Delilah, for example, received little attention, and Mary Magdalen similarly drew little interest at this time, though she had earlier been linked with the grade of repentant widows. Nor are there useful commentaries on such women as Sarah, Raab, or any of the other female characters the Bible presents and which medieval writers in other regions used as fodder on which to chew over concepts of gender and sexuality. This absence in the Irish material goes back long before the commencement of the late period under consideration here, back in fact to the very beginning of such writings in the seventh century. It seems the Irish never took up this practice of using biblical females as stereotypes, or theoretical types, with much enthusiasm, and when they did so it was late and involved only a few figures.

This longstanding reluctance or lack of interest is reflected also in the portrayal of holy women. For example, the Irish female saints' lives are notably more grounded and considerably less formulaic than many surviving from other areas of Christendom. The hagiographical material on nuns and the apocryphal/exegetical material on womankind combines to provide a strong indication that in early medieval Ireland women were treated by the literate ecclesiastical establishment in a quite down-to-earth way, more as people than as beings onto which notions and fantasies could be projected.

The Irish image of female nature that emerges from the biblical and exegetical material in many ways resonates with what is found in the hagiographic texts. This is most evidently so in the case of Eve, whose sympathetic treatment is similar to the treatment of nuns by clerics, even though the plot details are not mirrored. When it comes to the picture of womankind seen in Irish texts on John the Baptist's passion, the parallels are harder to see: it is from this story that the Irish give us the line 'The world's women, save a few of them, burn in the fire of doom'.[52] In that tale the evil deed was due to her cunning stubbornness, a will to carry on with a marriage deemed illegal by canon law. It is probably reading too much into this text to think that its author intended it to speak to the issue of clerical marriage. Nevertheless it is interesting that the subject in question is Judeo-Christian marriage statutes, and it is much more likely to be related to contemporary attempts to regularize the marriage practices of the laity: the Irish practices of serial marriage and multiple wives were at this time inspiring great criticism from abroad; the Irish aristocracy, including its kings, were particularly guilty of the practice. This sort of attitude we do not find in the texts which speak to the proper relations between clerics, monks, and nuns, nor is there much apparent similarity between Herodias and her daughters and the queen in the story 'The Power of Women', except that they both emphasize that women could wield immense psychological power over men, including kings. A female saint's power lay in her intimate relationship with God, and a queen's in her enchantment to mortal men.

As shown in an earlier chapter, the female saints were highly regarded in the tenth to twelfth centuries, but it is in this very same era that we increasingly find the normal laywoman being typified as silly and weak. In a great virgin, the female flaws had been overcome and she possessed *virtus*, manliness. Even so, the Irish considered now that mortal nuns could also be prone to some of the weaknesses of their sex—triviality, timidity, and foolishness. The misogyny evident in the 'Passion of John the Baptist' may well be connected with the trend which increasingly pressed for the separation of the sexes within churches in monasteries. To paraphrase Dyan Elliot's statement, if a campaign to purge clerics of

---

[52] Martyrology of Oengus, notes on 29 Aug.

their female companions would inevitably make the latter 'the enemy', then a cautious movement towards that same end portrayed women thus only partially and only sometimes.

BOUNDARIES OF INCLUSION AND EXCLUSION: *DE STATU ECCLESIAE*

One theological piece of this period, however, does explicitly address the question of women's role in God's great scheme of humanity, and, within that, their role within the church. This early twelfth-century text, *De statu ecclesiae*, written by Gilbert (Gilla Easpuic), bishop of Limerick, to all intents and purposes vindicates the position argued in the last three chapters. In particular, it confirms that for a leading cleric of that day, women were important enough to include explicitly in a schema describing Christian society, a schema whose Continental version (received by the bishop) omitted them. It is with an examination of this text, and its wider implications, that we conclude our treatment of women in the tenth to twelfth centuries.

On the Continent, the first half of the eleventh century saw the growth of a concept of a society which was to be influential in shaping the mentalities surrounding social order. According to this model, society should be seen as being made up of three distinct types of person, between whom there should be clear and meaningful boundaries. There were those who pray, those who fight, and those who plough: *oratores, bellatores, and aratores*. This schema, witnessed in a range of writing but owing a great deal to the formulation of Adalbero of Laon, was explored in detail by Georges Duby in *The Three Orders*. It heralded and encouraged real social changes, the most important of which was the creating of a sharp division separating the laity from clergy.[53] In this project the promulgators of the 'three-order cosmology' emphasized that the critical factor distinguishing the order of 'those who pray' was the absence of sexual activity. The promoters aimed to create a general social acceptance of the idea that clerics were sexually chaste, and lay people were not, and indeed to inculcate a general belief that God had created the human race in this manner.[54] One is therefore not surprised to learn that the three-order social model was one of the instruments in the campaign for the abolition of clerical marriage.

A second important feature of this model has to do more directly with its impact on women. Some historians at least have seen it as a creation which had a very negative effect on them. Duby himself observed that this formulation leaves out women entirely. He asserts that the threefold hierarchy of believers

---

[53] Duby, *Three Orders*, esp. 82–3. See also Adalbero of Leon, *Carmen ad Robertum regem* (C. Corozzi (ed. and trans.), *Poème au roi Robert* (Paris, 1979)); C. Corozzi, 'Les fondaments de la tripartition sociale chez Adalbéron de Laon', *Annales E.S.C.* 33 (1978), 683–702; R. I. Moore, 'Family, Community and Cult on the Eve of the Gregorian Reform', *TRHS* 5th ser. 30 (1980), 49–69, esp. 55–6.

[54] On the demarcation of clergy and laity, see Duby, *Three Orders*, 81, 108, 209–10, 255–6.

(virgins, widows, and the married) of the Latin Church underwent a change in the centuries leading up to the eleventh, which gave rise to a three-way division of the social sphere: the older classic model had included women, but this new version betrayed, he felt, an increased marginalization of womankind.[55] It corresponded to the clergy's flight from women in their drive to develop a celibate priesthood, although, Duby points out, the Gregorian ideology did not adopt the trifunctional postulate.[56]

In all this it is important to remember that the new functional schema is not framed in a gendered way and women were excluded only by implication. This is because a leading Irish reformer of the twelfth century, one with ties to both Rome and England, subverted both these objectives (i.e. eliminating clerical celibacy and marginalizing women) when presenting the cosmology to the Irish. Gilbert of Limerick (obit 1145) was consecrated as bishop in about 1106 in Ireland under the auspices of the powerful high king Muirchertach Ua Briain. His appointment was met with approval by Anselm, who was Archbishop of Canterbury, a leading reformer, and a personal acquaintance of Gilbert's— they had met in Rouen.[57] The Irish reforming Synod of Cashel of 1101 was held under the auspices of Ua Briain, and some five years after the synod, the method of selection of the archbishopric of Armagh was changed.[58] Gilbert subsequently presided over the next reform synod, Ráith Bressail in 1111, in the capacity of papal legate. He wrote *De statu ecclesiae* some time between 1107 and 1110, at a time when he was exceptionally influential in the Irish Church.[59] In this tract on the structure of church and society, he reiterated the three-order schema in a modified, indeed more complex form. In it the general pyramid of the three orders, a standard diagrammatic description, contained two sub-pyramids. It was in that context that he introduced his assurances about the inclusion of the female sex:

Ex quibus superiores in pyramide oratores intellege; et quia quidam ex eis coniugati sunt, ideo viros et feminas nominavimus. Sinistrales vero in pyramide aratores sunt, tam viri quam feminae. Dextrales quoque bellatores sunt, viri atque feminae. Nec dico feminarum esse officium orare, arare aut certe bellare; sed tamen his coniugatae sunt atque subserviunt, qui orant, et arant, et pugnant. Nec seiunctas ab Ecclesia putamus praesenti, quas Christus cum matre sua collocat in coelesti.[60]

The highest of these in the pyramid are understood to be those who pray, and since some of these are married, therefore we have nominated men and women. Indeed, on the left

---

[55] Ibid. 80–1. [56] Ibid. 211. [57] Flanagan, *Irish Society*, 20–2.

[58] Flanagan suggests that the Irish may have held Cashel in response to what they saw happening to Anselm in England. They knew and appeared to like Anselm: in 1096 he had requested (but not insisted) that Irish ecclesiastics seek recourse to Canterbury when they had issues to resolve; he had consecrated the bishop of Dublin and had written to the high king about the need to observe canon law in regard to marriage and episcopal consecrations: Flanagan, *Irish Society*, 21–2. For a fuller treatment of the synod see Gwynn, 'First Synod of Cashel'.

[59] *Kenney*, no. 651. [60] Gilbert, *De statu ecclesiae* (*PL* 159. 997).

in the pyramid are those who plough, as many men as women. Those on the right are those who fight, men and women. I am not saying that it is an official duty of women to pray, plough or certainly [not] to fight, but they are married to, and serve under, those who pray and plough and fight. Nor do we think of them [i.e. women] as separated from the present church, whom Christ placed in heaven along with his own mother.

First and most striking is his explicit inclusion of women in the category of 'those who pray' and, indeed, are there as wives of clerics; in that alone he under-mined the model as a tool for promoting clerical celibacy. On the second issue, that of the general exclusion of women from the cosmology, Gilbert was equally subversive, though probably unwittingly. For him women have an important place in the divine plan: they were linked with the grace and divinity of the Vir-gin Mary, the personage through whom female sanctity was most strongly em-bodied, and this place, to his way of thinking, needed to be made explicit. To my knowledge, the only version of the model which explicitly mentions the female half of the population was the Irish one, and it is almost certainly unique in including wives of 'those who pray'. It may be that Gilbert as a reformer did promote a stricter boundary between the laity and those in orders, but we can-not simply say that the structure of society, as he envisioned it, reflected a cler-ical flight from women, either as part of a drive to develop a celibate priesthood or for any other reason. Though we do not see in Gilbert any evidence of a doctrine of separation, in all respects his writings are considered orthodox. So while he promoted an orthodox Western-style Church in *De statu* he was not pre-occupied with separating nuns from monks, nor clerics from consorts. If he was copying a non-Irish source for this section, and it appears he was, it is then rea-sonable to surmise that the native Irish ecclesiastical *mundus* influenced him. Certainly the other textual evidence from that era would support such a notion: his writing falls within a pattern which is by now familiar. The evidence of this text is important to an argument which asserts that women of the Irish Church were not marginalized or shunned, even in the reform era of the twelfth century, and in the eyes of one of its most influential reformers, one who had extensive contacts with both England and Rome.

IRELAND IN CONTEXT

In the mid-eleventh to mid-twelfth centuries Western Europe underwent a pro-found change in attitude regarding the respective roles of men and women in the social and spiritual orders. McNamara has said that at this time the structure of gender altered, and women began to be excluded from areas of social life in which they had had a long presence. The same marginalization of women in the social framework about which Duby wrote was epitomized in the tri-functional model. For McNamara men in the Christian West experienced a psychological crisis of sorts; at its crux was the question 'how can men redefine manhood to prove women's incapacity to carry out professional responsibilities?'[61] Ireland does not fit exactly the patterns described by McNamara or by Duby. The literature of the tenth to twelfth centuries which elucidates the Irish understanding of the female sex shows other changes, bearing some resemblances but with important differences. Women were liable to have certain sorts of shortcomings, but the Irish saw this as no cause to demonize them. The treatment of such characters as Eve, Mary, Herodias, and Solomon's queen, used as exemplars of femaleness, shows this clearly and repeatedly, though the amount of extant material is admittedly small. Newly ascendant notions about the right ordering of society, which elsewhere saw women marginalized, in Ireland were adapted to include women and to restate their value and their centrality in the corporate entity of the human community. Irish views show a consistent pattern: womankind as a whole, though prone to folly and capable of scheming evildoing, was not made into 'the enemy'—either of the male sex generally or of the clergy in particular. We saw earlier that even the cleric's wife, much maligned elsewhere, could in Ireland be the object of a sort of love poem, as in the Cormac verses. As for Ireland's nuns, they, like its laywomen, for the most part escaped being cast as diabolical sexual snares for men.

The Irish holy women of the tenth to twelfth centuries enjoyed the company of their brothers more than is to be expected. The ecclesiastical writers of Lives continue to portray them as partners of clerics and monks in the business of bringing God's grace, redemption, and miraculous wonders to humankind; and it is in Ireland that male saints' hagiographers insistently claim that their protagonists met (for example) the great Brigit or the great Ita. On those occasions when nuns and other religious women were to be separated from the monks with whom they had previously enjoyed fraternal contact, the justifications, when given, normally centred around the need to avoid rumours of scandal, rather than around supposed feminine evil. The process was gentler and more respectful than one might have expected, given the reputation of Ireland among some contemporary medievalists as a place of strict asceticism as regards sex. In Ireland, a separatist such as Senán, dwelling on an all-male island, could be challenged (in his own Life, no less) by a pilgrim nun demanding, 'Women have served and administered to Christ and his Apostles. Indeed, no less than men do women enter the heavenly kingdom. Why then shouldn't you take women on your island?' Ireland gave us the author of Molua's sardonic line *ubi fuit mulier, ibi peccatum; ubi vero peccatum, ibi erit dyabolus*, but it also gave us Conchubranus, who cited Corinthians to write of Monenna that the Lord did not disdain to act through her because *in Christus . . . neque masculus neque femina sed omnia in omnibus Christus.*[62]

---

[61] McNamara, '*Herrenfrage*', 4.
[62] Conchubranus, Life of Monenna, book 3, ch. 2.

Bibliography

PRIMARY SOURCES: COLLECTIONS

Alberigo, G. (ed.), *Conciliorum oecumenicorum decreta* (Freiburg, 1962).

Atkinson, R. (ed. and trans.), *The Passions and the Homilies from the Leabhar Breac* (Dublin, 1887).

Bernard, J., and R. Atkinson (eds. and trans.), *The Irish Liber Hymnorum*, 2 vols. (Henry Bradshaw Society 13, 14; London, 1898).

Bieler, L. (ed. and trans.), *Four Latin Lives of St. Patrick* (Scriptores Latini Hiberniae 8; Dublin, 1971).

—— (ed. and trans.), *The Irish Penitentials* (Scriptores Latini Hiberniae 5; Dublin, 1963).

—— (ed. and trans.), *The Patrician Texts in the Book of Armagh* (Scriptores Latini Hiberniae 10; Dublin, 1979).

Binchy, D. (ed.), *Corpus Iuris Hibernici*, 6 vols. (Dublin, 1978).

Brosnan, D. (ed.), *Archivium Hibernicum, or Irish Historical Records* (Maynooth, 1912).

Carney, J. (ed. and trans.), *Medieval Irish Lyrics* (Dublin, 1967).

Cross, T., and C. Slover (trans.), *Ancient Irish Tales* (London, 1936).

De Clerq, C. (ed.), *Concilia Galliae A.511–A.695* (*CCSL* 148a; Turnhout, 1963).

Elliott, J. (ed.), *The Apocryphal New Testament: A Collection of Apocryphal Christian Literature in an English Translation* (Oxford, 1993).

Fouracre, P., and R. Gerberding, *Late Merovingian France: History and Historiography, 640–720* (Manchester, 1996). [Merovingian saints' Lives].

Gantz, J. (trans.), *Early Irish Myths and Sagas* (Harmondsworth, 1981).

Greene, D., and F. Kelly (eds. and trans.), *Irish Bardic Poetry* (Dublin, 1970).

—— and F. O'Connor (ed. and trans.), *A Golden Treasury of Irish Poetry, AD 600 to 1200*, (London, 1967).

Gwynn, A. (ed. and trans.), *The Writings of Bishop Patrick, 1074–1084* (Scriptores Latini Hiberniae 1; Dublin, 1955).

Hancock, W., T. O'Mahony, A. Richey, W. Hennessy, and R. Atkinson (eds.), *Ancient Laws of Ireland*, 6 vols. (Dublin, 1865–1901).

Heist, W. (ed.), *Vitae Sanctorum Hiberniae ex Codice olim Salmanticensi nunc Bruxellensi* (Subsidia Hagiographica 28; Brussels, 1965).

Herbert, M., and M. McNamara (trans.), *Irish Biblical Apocrypha: Selected Texts in Translation* (Edinburgh, 1989).

Hood, A. (ed. and trans.), *Patrick: His Writings and Muirchú's Life* (London, 1978).

Kinsella, T. (trans.), *The Táin* (Oxford, 1979).

Mansi, J. (ed.), *Sacrorum Conciliorum nova et amplissima collectio*, 5 vols. (Paris, 1901–6).

Meyer, K. (ed. and trans.), *Selections from Ancient Irish Poetry* (London, 1911).

Migne, J.-P. (ed.), *Patrologiae [latinae] cursus completus . . .*, 221 vols. (Paris, 1844–64).

—— (ed.), *Patrologiae [graecae] cursus completus . . .*, 161 vols. (Paris, 1857–66).

Munier, C. (ed.), *Concilia Galliae A.314–A.406* (*CCSL* 148; Turnhout, 1963).

Murphy, G. (ed. and trans.), *Early Irish Lyrics, Eighth to Twelfth Century* (Oxford, 1956).

O'Brien, M. (ed.), *Corpus Genealogiarum Hiberniae* (Dublin, 1962).

Ó Riain, P. (ed.), *Corpus Genealogiarum Sanctorum Hiberniae* (Dublin, 1985).

Plummer, C. (ed. and trans.), *Bethada Náem nÉrenn*, 2 vols. (Oxford, 1922).

—— (ed. and trans.), *Irish Litanies: Text and Translation* (Henry Bradshaw Society 62; London, 1925).

—— (ed.), *Miscellanea Hagiographica Hibernica* (Subsidia Hagiographica 15; Brussels, 1925).

—— (ed.), *Vitae Sanctorum Hiberniae*, 2 vols. (Oxford, 1910).

Stevenson, J. (ed.), *Creeds, Councils and Controversies: Documents Illustrative of the History of the Church AD 337–461* (London, 1966).

Stokes, W. (ed.), 'The Irish Verses, Notes and Glosses in Harl. 1802', *Revue Celtique* 8 (1887), 346–69.

—— (ed.), *Lives of the Saints from the Book of Lismore* (London, 1890).

—— (ed.), *Three Irish Glossaries* (London, 1862).

—— (ed. and trans.), *Three Middle-Irish Homilies on the Lives of Saints Patrick, Brigit and Columba* (Dublin, 1880).

—— and J. Strachan (eds.), *Thesaurus Palaeohibernicus: A Collection of Old Irish Glosses, Scholia, Prose and Verse*, 2 vols. (London, 1901/3).

Walker, G. (ed. and trans.), *Sancti Columbani Opera* (Scriptores Latini Hiberniae 2; Dublin, 1957).

Warren, F. (ed.), *The Antiphony of Bangor*, 2 vols. (Henry Bradshaw Society 4, 10; London, 1893–5).

PRIMARY SOURCES: INDIVIDUAL TEXTS

A Ben, Bennacht Fort ['O Woman, A Blessing on You', or 'Sell Not Heaven for Sin'], ed. and trans., K. Meyer, 'Daniel Úa Liathaide's Advice to a Woman', *Ériu* 1 (1904), 67–71. Also in Murphy, *Early Irish Lyrics*, 16–17.

A Chrínóc, ed. J. Carney, 'A Chrínóc, Cubaid do Cheól', *Éigse* 4 (1944), 280–3. Also in Greene and O'Connor, *Golden Treasury*, 167–9; (ed.), K. Meyer, 'An Crínóc', *ZCP* 6 (1908), 266; Meyer, *Selections from Ancient Irish Poetry*, 37–8.

A Muire, min maith-ingen ['O Mary, Kind and Gentle Maid'], in Plummer, *Irish Litanies*, 96–9.

A Muire mór ['O Great Mary'], in Plummer, *Irish Litanies*, 48–51.

A Sláinicidh ['O Saviour'] in Plummer, *Irish Litanies*, 20–3.

Abstalón, adba na ríg ['Abstalón, the dwellings of the kings'], ed. B. Ó Cuív, 'Two Items from Irish Apocryphal Tradition', *Celtica* 10 (1973), 87–113.

Adalbero of Laon, *Carmen ad Robertum regem*, ed. and trans. C. Corozzi, *Poème au roi Robert* (Paris, 1979).

Adomnán, *De locis sanctis*, ed. D. Meehan, *Adamnan's De Locis Sanctis* (Scriptores Latini Hiberniae 3; Dublin, 1958).

—— Life of Columba *alias* Columcille [Latin], ed. and trans. A. and M. Anderson, *Adomnán's Life of Columba* (Edinburgh, 1961). Also in R. Sharpe (trans.), *Life of Columba*, with introduction (New York, 1996).

Aislinge maic Conglinne ['Mac Conglinne's Dream'], ed. and trans. K. Meyer, *Aislinge maic Conglinne* (London, 1892).

Ambrose, *De institutione virginis, PL* 16. 319–48.

—— *De virginibus, PL* 16. 197–243.

—— *De virginitate, PL* 16. 319–48.

Annals of Clonmacnois, ed. and trans. D. Murphy, *The Annals of Clonmacnoise* (Dublin, 1896).

Annals of the Four Masters, ed. and trans. J. O'Donovan, *Annals of the Kingdom of Ireland by the Four Masters*, 7 vols. (2nd edn.: Dublin, 1856).

Annals of Inisfallen, ed. and trans. S. MacAirt, *The Annals of Inisfallen* (Dublin, 1951).

Annals of Tigernach: Continuation, trans. W. Stokes, 'The Annals of Tigernach: The Continuation, AD 1088–AD 1178', *Revue Celtique* 18 (1897), 9–59, 150–97, 267–303.

Annals of Ulster, ed. S. MacAirt and G. MacNiocaill, *The Annals of Ulster*, 2 vols. (Dublin, 1983/4).

Antiphony of Bangor, ed. F. E. Warren, *The Antiphony of Bangor*, 2 vols. (Henry Bradshaw Society 4, 10; London, 1893/5).

Ateoch Frit ['I entreat Thee', or 'Litany of Jesus'], in Plummer, *Irish Litanies*, 30–45.

Athanasius, *Apologia ad Constantium, PG* 25. 593–642.

Audite fratres facta, ed. M. Esposito, '*Conchubrani Vita Sanctae Monennae*', appendix B, *PRIA* 28C (1910), 242–4.

Audite sancta studia, ibid., appendix A, 239–42.

Augustine, *De bono coniugali, PL* 40. 373–96.

—— *De sancta virginitate, PL* 40. 395–428.

Augustinus (the 'Irish Augustine'), *De mirabilibus sacrae scripturae, PL* 35. 2151–200.

Basil of Caesarea, *Epistolae*, trans. R. Deferrari, *St Basil: Letters*, 4 vols. (Loeb Classical Library; Cambridge, Mass., 1961/2).

Bede, *Historia ecclesiastica*, ed. C. Plummer, *Historia Ecclesiastica Gentis Anglorum* (Oxford, 1896).

Berrad Airechta ['The Shearing of the Court', on suretyship], *CIH* 591.8–599.38, trans. R. Stacey, '*Berrad Airechta*: An Old Irish Tract on Suretyship', in T. Charles-Edwards, M. Owen, and D. Walters (eds.), *Lawyers and Laymen: Studies in the History of Law* (Cardiff, 1986), 210–33.

Bernard of Clairvaux, Life of St Malachy of Armagh, ed. and trans. H. Lawlor, *St Bernard of Clairvaux's Life of St Malachy of Armagh* (London, 1920).

Bethu Brigte. See 'Life of Brigit [Irish and Latin]'.

Blathmac, *Maire máthair in maic bic* ['Mary Mother of the Little Boy'], ed. and trans. J. Carney, 'Two Old Irish Poems', *Ériu* 18 (1958), 1–43, at 26–7. Also in J. Carney (ed.), *The Poems of Blathmac son of Cú Brettan, together with the Irish Gospel of Thomas and A Poem on the Virgin Mary* (Irish Texts Society 47; Dublin, 1964), 108–11.

—— *Tair Cucum, A Maire boíd* ['Come to Me, Loving Mary', or 'To Mary and Her Son'], ibid. 2–87.

Bobbio Missal, ed. E. Lowe, *The Bobbio Missal* (London, 1920).

Book of Armagh, ed. J. Gwynn, *Liber Ardmachensis: The Book of Armagh* (Dublin, 1913).

Book of Leinster, ed. R. Best *et al.*, *The Book of Leinster, formerly Lebar na Núachongbala*, 6 vols. (Dublin, 1954–83).

Bretha Crólige ['On Blood-lying'], *CIH* 2286.24–2305.3. Also ed. D. Binchy, 'Bretha Crólige', *Ériu* 12 (1938), 1–77.

Bretha im Fuillema Gell ['Judgements on Pledge-interests'], *CIH* 462.19–477.30. Also in *ALI* v. 377–423.

Bretha Nemed déidenach ['The Last *Bretha Nemed* '], *CIH* 1111–38. Also ed. E. Gwynn, 'An Old Irish Tract on the Privileges and Responsibilities of Poets', *Ériu* 13 (1942), 1–60, 220–32.

Bretha Nemed Toísech ['The First *Bretha Nemed* '] *CIH* 2211–32. Also in L. Breatnach, 'The First Third of *Bretha Nemed Toísech*', *Ériu* 40 (1989), 1–40.

Brigit bé Bithmaith ['Brigit Ever-Excellent Woman'], in *Thes. Pal.* ii. 323–6.

Brigitae Sanctae Subiectae [List of Those Subject to Saint Brigit], Ó Riain, *Corpus Genealogiarum*, 112–18. Book of Leinster version: *Book of Leinster*, vi. 1580–1.

Caesarius of Arles, Rule for Virgins, ed. and trans. M.-J. Delage, *Sermons au Peuple* (Sources chrétiennes 243; Paris, 1978), 219–25.

Cáin Adomnáin ['The Law of Adomnán'], ed. and trans. K. Meyer, *Cáin Adamnáin: An Old Irish Treatise on the Law of Adamnán* (Anecdota Oxoniensa 12; Oxford, 1905).

Cáin Adomnáin's Guarantor List, ed. M. Ní Donnchadha, 'The Guarantor List of Cáin Adomnáin', *Peritia* 1 (1982), 178–215.

Cáin Lánamna ['The Law of Connections'], *CIH* 502.29–519.35. Also ed. and trans. R. Thurneysen, in Binchy *et al.* (eds.), *Studies in Early Irish Law*, 1–80.

Cantemus in omni die [or 'Cuchuimne's Poem on the Virgin Mary'], in Bernard and Atkinson, *Irish Liber Hymnorum*, i. 32–4.

Carais Pattraic ['Patrick Loved', or 'Cuimmín's Hymn'], ed. and trans. W. Stokes, 'Cuimmín's Poem on the Saints of Ireland', *ZCP* 1 (1897), 59–73.

Catalogus Sanctorum Hiberniae, ed. P. Grosjean, 'Edition et commentaire du *Catalogus Sanctorum Hiberniae*', *Analecta Bollandiana* 73 (1955), 197–213, 287–322.

Christus in nostra insula [or 'Ultán's Hymn'], in Bernard and Atkinson, *Irish Liber Hymnorum*, i. 14–15.

Ps.-Clement, *Epistolae ii ad virgines PG* 1. 350–452.

Cogitosus, Life of Brigit [Latin], ed. J. Colgan, *Triadis thaumaturgae acta* (Louvain, 1658), 135–41. Also in *PL* 72. 775–90; trans. S. Connolly and J.-M. Picard, 'Cogitosus' Life of St Brigit', *JRSAI* 117 (1987), 5–27.

Collectio Canonum Hibernensis, ed. H. Wasserschleben, *Die irische Kanonensammlung* (Leipzig, 1885).

Columbanus, *Epistola* I, ed. and trans. G. Walker, *Sancti Columbani Opera* (Scriptores Latini Hiberniae 2; Dublin, 1957), 2–13.

Conchubranus, Life of Monenna [Latin], ed. M. Esposito, 'Conchubrani Vita Sanctae Monennae', *PRIA* 28C (1910), 197–251. Also ed. and trans. Ulster Society for Medieval Latin Studies (USMLS), 'The Life of Saint Monenna by Conchubranus', *Seanchas Ard Mhacha*: 9.2 (1979), 250–73; 10.1 (1980–1), 117–41; 10.2 (1982), 426–53.

Comanmand Noebúag Herend ['The Same-Named Virgin Saints of Ireland'], Ó Riain, *Corpus Genealogiarum*, 153–6. Also in Brosnan, *Archivium Hibernicum*, 353–60.

Concilium Eliberitanum, *PL* 84. 301–10.

Cormac, Glossary, ed. W. Stokes, *Cormac's Glossary, translated and annotated by the late John O'Donovan* (Calcutta, 1868).

Córus Béscnai ['The Regulation of Proper Behaviour'], *CIH* 520.1–536.27; 903.37–905.9; 1812.33–1821.27. Also in *ALI* iii. 3–79.

'The Creation and Fall from the Leabhar Breac', in Herbert and McNamara, *Irish Biblical Apocrypha*, 5–6.

Clann Darerca ['The Family of Darerca'], in *Book of Leinster*, vi. 1591.

Críth Gablach ['Branched Purchase'], *CIH* 777.6–783.38. Also ed. D. Binchy, *Críth Gablach* (Medieval and Modern Irish Series 11; Dublin, 1941); trans. E. Mac Neill, '*Críth Gablach*', *PRIA* 36C (1923), 281–306.

Cummean, Penitential, in Bieler, *Irish Penitentials*, 108–35.

Customs of Tallaght, ed. and trans. E. Gwynn and W. Purton, 'The Monastery of Tallaght', *PRIA* 29C (1911), 115–79.

Cyprian, *De habitu virginum*, *PL* 4. 451–78.

Pseudo-Cyprian, *De singularitate clericorum*, ed. G. Hartel (*CSEL* 3, part 3; Vienna, 1871).

Damian, Peter, *Opera*, *PL* 144 and 145.

De Arreis [Old Irish Table of Commutations], ed. and trans. D. Binchy. 'The Old-Irish Table of Commutations', in Bieler, *Irish Penitentials*, 277–83. Also ed. K. Meyer, 'An Old Irish Treatise *De Arreis*', *Revue Celtique* 15 (1894), 484–98.

Di Astud Chirt 7 Dligid ['On the Confirmation of Right and Law'], *CIH* 223.22–244.22. Also in *ALI* 426–93.

Di Chetharslicht Athgabála ['On the Four Divisions of Distraint'], *CIH* 352.25–422.36; 1438.36–1465.27; 1723.11–1755.16. Also in *ALI* i. 65–305; ii. 3–118.

Din Techtugad ['On Legal Entry'], *CIH* 205.22–213.37. Also in *ALI* iv. 3–33.

Díre Text [untitled Honour-Price Text], ed. and trans. R. Thurneysen, *Irisches Recht, Aus den preussischen Akademie der Wissenschaften* (Jahrgang, 1931), 1–37. Also in D. Binchy *et al.*, (eds.), *Studies in Early Irish Law*, 213–14.

'Disciples and Relatives of St Columba', in *Thes. Pal.* ii. 281.

Egeria, *Peregrinatio*, trans. G. Gingras, *Egeria: Diary of a Pilgrimage* (New York, 1970).

Eirigh, a Ingen an Rígh ['Arise, O King's Daughter'], ed. M. Ní Dhonnchadha. 'On Gormfhlaith Daughter of Flann Sinna and the lure of the Sovereignty Goddess', in A. Smyth (ed.), *Seanchas: Studies in Early and Medieval Irish Archaeology, History and Literature in Honour of Francis J. Byrne* (Dublin, 2000), 225–37. Also ed. A. Von Hamel, 'Poems from the Brussels MS 5100–4', *Revue Celtique* 37 (1917–19), 349–51; trans. S. O'Faóláin, 'Eirigh, a Ingen an Rígh', *Revue Celtique* 47 (1930), 197–9.

Estu mihi sanitas (ed.) F. Warren, *The Antiphony of Bangor* (Henry Bradshaw Society 10; London, 1895), ii. 83–9.

Expositio quattuor evangeliorum, *PL* 30. 531–90.

Eusebius of Emesa, Sermons, ed. E. Buytaert, *Eusèbe d'Émèse: Discours conservés en latin* (Spicilegium Sacrum Lovaniense 26; Louvain, 1953).

Finnian, Penitential, in Bieler, *Irish Penitentials*, 74–95.

First Synod of St. Patrick, in Bieler, *Irish Penitentials*, 54–9.

Foscél ar Bannscail ['Short Tale of a Woman' or 'The Temptation of a Confessor'], ed. and trans. J. Vendryes, 'Trois historiettes irlandaises', *Revue Celtique* 31 (1910), 302–6. Also H. Gaidoz (ed. and trans.) 'La tentation d'un confesseur'. Κρυπτάδια 4 (1888), 262–81.

Geoffrey of Vendôme, *Epistolae*, *PL* 157. 33–212.

Gerald of Wales, *Topographia Hibernica*, ed. J. Dimock, *Topographia Hibernica et Expugnatio Hibernica* (Rolls Series; London, 1867). Trans. J. O'Meara, *Topography of Ireland* (Dundalk, 1951).

—— *Gemma ecclesiastica*, trans. J. Hagen, *The Jewel of the Church* (Leiden, 1979).

Gérard de Cambrai, *Gesta episcoporum cameracensium*, *MGH* 55, part 7.

Gilbert of Limerick (Gilla Easpuic), *De statu ecclesiae*, *PL* 159. 994–1004.

Gildas, *De excidio Britanniae*, ed. and trans. M. Winterbottom, *Gildas: The Ruin of Britain and Other Works* (Arthurian Period Series 7; London, 1978), 13–79.

—— Fragments of Lost Letters, ibid. 80–2.

Gregory of Nazianzus, *Epigrammata*, *PG* 38. 81–130.

Gregory of Nyssa, 'On Virginity', ed. M. Abineau, *Grégoire de Nysse: Traité de la virginité* (Sources chrétiennes 119; Paris, 1961).

Gregory of Tours, *Liber in gloria confessorum*, ed. B. Krusch, *MGH, Scriptores rerum Merovingicarum* 1, part 2 (Hanover, 1885), 744–820.

Gúbretha Caratniad ['The False Judgements of Caratnia'], *CIH* 2192–9. Also ed. and trans. R. Thurneysen, 'Aus Dem Irischen Recht III. Die falschen Urteilssprüche Caratnia's', *ZCP* 15 (1925), 302–70.

Homily on the Life of Brendan mac Finnlug in the Book of Lismore [Irish], in Stokes, *Lives of the Saints*, 99–116, 247–61.

Homily on the Life of Brigit in the Book of Lismore, ibid. 34–53, 182–200.

Homily on the Life of Brigit in the Leabhar Breac ['On the Life of Saint Brigit'], in Stokes, *Three Middle Irish Homilies*, 50–89.

Homily on Life of Ciarán of Clonmacnois in the Book of Lismore [Irish], in Stokes, *Lives of the Saints*, 117–34, 262–80.

Homily on the Life of Senán in the Book of Lismore, ibid. 54–74.

Impide Maire ['Litany of the Virgin and All Saints'], in Plummer, *Irish Litanies*, 26–7.

Ingenrada Noeb Herenn [List of the Maiden Saints of Ireland] Ó Riain, *Corpus Genealogiarum*, 159–60. The Book of Leinster version: *The Book of Leinster*, vi. 1678–81.

Irenaeus, *Adversus haereses*, ed. W. Harvey, 2 vols. (Cambridge, 1857).

Isidore of Seville, *De ecclesiasticis officiis*, ed. Christopher Lawson (*CCSL* 113; Turnhout, 1989).

Ísucán ['Little Jesus'], ed. and trans. E. Quin, 'The Early Medieval Irish Poem *Ísucán*', *Cambridge Medieval Celtic Studies* 1 (1981), 39–52. Also in Greene and O'Connor, *Golden Treasury*, 102–3; Murply, *Early Irish Lyrics*, 26–9, 183–4; Carney, *Medieval Irish Lyrics*, 66–7.

Jerome, *Adversus Iovinianum*, *PL* 23. 221–352.

—— *Commentarium in Mattheum*, ed. D. Hurst and M. Adriaen (*CCSL* 77; Turnhout, 1956).

—— *Epistola 22* ['To Eustochium'], *PL* 22. 394–425.

—— *Epistola 54* ['To Furia'], ibid. 550–60.

—— *Epistola 130* ['To Demetria'], ibid. 1107–24.

John Cassian, *Conlationes*, *PL* 49. 477–1328.

—— *Institutes*, *PL* 49. 54–476.

John Chrysostom, 'Instruction and Refutation Directed Against Those Men Cohabiting with Virgins', in E. Clark, *Jerome, Chrysostom, and Friends: Essays and Translation* (Studies in Women and Religion 1; New York, 1979), 164–208.

Jonas, Latin Life of Columbanus, ed. B. Krusch, *MGH, Scriptores rerum Merovingicarum*, iv (1902), 1–152.

'Lament of the Caillech Béirre', ed. and trans. D. Ó hAodha, 'Lament of the Old Woman of Beare', in D. Ó Corráin, L. Breatnach, and K. McCone (eds.), *Saints, Sages and Storytellers: Studies in Honour of Professor James Carney* (Maynooth, 1989), 308–31. Also in Greene and O'Connor, *Golden Treasury*, 48–55.

'Liadain and Curithir', ed. and trans. K. Meyer, *Liadain and Curithir: An Irish Love Story from the Ninth Century* (London, 1902).

Liber Angeli ['Book of the Angel'], in Bieler, *Patrician Texts*, 185–91. Also in K. Hughes, *The Church in Early Irish Society* (London, 1966), 275–81.

Liber de ordine creaturarum, *PL* 83. 913–54.

Life of Abbán of Moyarny [Latin], D text, *PVSH* i. 3–33.

Life of Adomnán of Iona [Irish], ed. and trans. M. Herbert and P. Ó Riain, *Betha Adamnain: the Irish Life of Adamnan* (Irish Texts Society 54; London, 1986).

Life of Áed mac Bricc [Latin], Φ text, *Heist*, 167–81.

Life of Áed mac Bricc [Latin], D text, *PVSH* i. 34–45.

Life of Ailbe of Munster[Latin], Φ text, *Heist*, 118–31.

Life of Ailbe of Munster [Latin], D text, *PVSH* i. 46–64.

Life of Bairre of Cork [Irish], *BNE* i. 11–21; Eng. trans.: ii. 11–22.

Life of Berach [Latin], *PVSH* i. 75–86.

Life of Berach [Irish], *BNE* i. 23–43; Eng. trans.: ii. 22–43.

Life of Brendan I [Irish], *BNE* i. 44–95; Eng. trans.: ii. 44–92.

Life of Brendan [Latin, *Vita I Brendani*] *PVSH* i. 98–151.

Life of Brendan [Latin; *Vita II Brendani*, a latinization of an Anglo-French poem], *PVSH* ii. 270–92.

Life of Brigit [Latin] by Cogitosus. *See under* 'Cogitosus'.

Life of Brigit [Latin; *Vita I Brigitae*], ed. J. Colgan, *Triadis thaumaturgae acta* (Louvain, 1647), 527–42. Also trans. S. Connolly, 'Vita Prima Sanctae Brigitae', *JRSAI* 119 (1989), 5–49.

Life of Brigit [Irish and Latin; *Bethu Brigte*], ed. and trans. D. Ó hAodha, *Bethu Brigte* (Dublin, 1978).

Life of Brigit[Latin; *Vita IV Brigitae*], ed. Sharpe, *Saints' Lives*, 139–208.

Life of Brigit[Latin, Metrical; not Irish], ed. D. N. Kissane, '*Vita Metrica Sanctae Brigidae*: A Critical Edition', *PRIA* 77C (1977).

Life of Brigit in the Book of Lismore, *see under* 'Homily'.

Life of Brigit in the Leabhar Breac, *see under* 'Homily'.

Life of Búite of Monasterboice [Latin], *PVSH* i. 87–97.

Life of Cainnech of Aghaboe [Latin], Φ text, *Heist*, 182–98.

Life of Carthach *alias* Mochuda of Lismore in the Codex Salmanticensis [Latin], *Heist*, 334–40.

Life of Carthach *alias* Mochuda of Lismore [Latin], D text, *PVSH* i. 170–99.

Life of Carthach *alias* Mochuda of Lismore [Irish], *BNE* i. 291–9; Eng. trans.: ii. 282–90.

Life of Carthach *alias* Mochuda of Lismore, 'The Expulsion of Mochuda' [Irish], *BNE* i. 300–11; Eng. trans.: ii. 291–302.

Life of Ciarán of Clonmacnois [Latin], D text, *PVSH* i. 200–17.

Life of Ciarán of Clonmacnois in the Book of Lismore [Irish], *see under* 'Homily'.

Life of Ciarán of Seirkieran [Latin], D text, *PVSH* i. 217–33.

Life of Ciarán of Seirkieran, I [Irish], *BNE* i. 103–12; Eng. trans.: ii. 99–120.

Life of Ciarán of Seirkieran, II [Irish], *BNE* i. 113–24; Eng. trans.: ii. 109–120.

Life of Ciarán of Seirkieran in the Codex Salmanticensis [Latin], *Heist*, 346–53.

Life of Coemgen of Glendalough [Latin], D text, *PVSH* i. 234–57.

Life of Coemgen of Glendalough, I [Irish], *BNE* i. 125–30; Eng. trans.: ii. 121–6.

Life of Coemgen of Glendalough, II [Irish], *BNE* i. 131–54; Eng. trans.: ii. 127–50.

Life of Coemgen of Glendalough, III [Irish], *BNE* i. 155–67; Eng. trans.: ii. 151–62.

Life of Colmán of Lynally [Latin], Φ text, *Heist*, 209–24.

Life of Colmán of Lynally [Latin], D text, *PVSH* i. 258–73.

Life of Columba *alias* Columcille of Iona [Latin], *see* Adomnán.

Life of Columba [Irish], ed. and trans. M. Herbert. 'Betha Coluim Cille', in Herbert, *Iona, Kells*, 217–88. Also ed. and trans. A. Kelleher, 'Betha Coluimba Chille', *ZCP* 11 (1917), 114–47.

Life of Daig mac Cairill of Inishkeen [Latin], *Heist*, 389–94.

Life of Darerca *alias* Monenna of Killevy [Latin], *Heist*, 83–95. Also trans., 'The Life of St Darerca, or Moninna, the Abbess', in L. de Paor, *Saint Patrick's World*, 281–94.

Life of Declán of Ardmore [Latin], D text, *PVSH* ii. 32–59.

Life of Enda of Aran [Latin], *PVSH* ii. 60–75.

Life of Finán of Kinnity [Latin], Φ text, *Heist*, 153–60.

Life of Fintán of Clonenagh [Latin], Φ text, *Heist*, 145–53.

Life of Fintán *alias* Munnu of Taghmon [Latin], Φ text, *Heist*, 198–209.

Life of Ita of Killeedy [Latin], *PVSH* ii. 116–30.

Life of Lassair of 'Cell Lasrae' [Irish; *Beatha Lasrach*], ed. L. Gwynn, 'Beatha Lasrach', *Ériu* 5 (1911), 73–109.

Life of Lugaid *alias* Molua of Clonfertmulloe [Latin], Φ text, *Heist*, 131–45.

Life of Lugaid *alias* Molua of Clonfertmulloe [Latin], D text, *PVSH* ii. 206–25.

Life of Maedóc of Ferns (formally named Áed, but that name not used) [Irish], *BNE* i. 191–290; Eng. trans.: ii. 184–265.

Life of Maedóc of Ferns, II [Irish], *BNE* i. 191–290; Eng. trans.: ii. 184–281.

Life of Maedóc of Ferns [Latin], D text, *PVSH* ii. 141–63.

Life of Maedóc of Ferns in the Cotton MS [Latin], 'The Wales Translation', *PVSH* ii. 295–311.

Life of Melania the Younger, ed. D. Gorse, *Vie de Sainte Mélanie* (Sources chrétiennes 40; Paris, 1962). Also trans. E. Clark, *The Life of Melania the Younger* (New York, 1984).

Life of Mochoemóg (formally named Comgallus, but that name not used) [Latin], D text, *PVSH* ii. 164–83.

Life of Moling *alias* Dairchellus of St Mullins [Latin], D text, *PVSH* ii. 190–205.

Life of Moling *alias* Dairchellus of St Mullins in the Codex Salmenticensis [Latin], *Heist*, 353–6.

Life of Monenna *alias* Darerca of Killevy [Latin, Anonymous], *see* 'Life of Darerca'.

Life of Monenna *alias* Darerca of Killevy [Latin]. See 'Conchubranus'.

Life of Patrick [Latin and Irish; 'The Tripartite Life of Patrick', or *Vita Tripartita*] ed. and trans. W. Stokes, *The Tripartite Life of Patrick, with Other Documents Relating to that Saint*, 2 vols. (Rolls Series 88; London, 1887).

Life of Patrick [Latin]. *See* Muirchú.

Life of Ruadán of Lorrha [Latin], Φ text, *Heist*, 160–7.

Life of Ruadán of Lorrha [Irish], *BNE* i. 317–29; Eng. trans.: ii. 308–20.

Life of Samthann of Clonbroney [Latin], *PVSH* ii. 253–61.

Life of Senán of Scattery Island in the Book of Lismore [Irish], *see under* 'Homily'.

Life of Senán of Scattery Island [Latin], *Heist*, 301–24.

Life of Tigernach of Clones [Latin], *PVSH* ii. 107–11.

List of Abbesses of Killevy, Esposito, 'Conchubrani Vita', Appendix C, *PRIA* 28C (1910), 244–5.

Marbod of Rennes, *Epistolae*, *PL* 171. 1465–92.

Martyrology of Gorman, ed. and trans. W. Stokes, *Félire húi Gormain* (Henry Bradshaw Society 9; London, 1895).

Martyrology of Oengus, *see* 'Oengus the Culdee'.

Martyrology of Tallaght, ed. R. I. Best and H. J. Lawlor, *The Martyrology of Tallaght, from the Book of Leinster and MS 5100–4 in the Royal Library, Brussels* (Henry Bradshaw Society 68; London, 1931).

Mé Eba Ben ['I Am Eve', or 'Eve's Lament'], ed. and trans. K. Meyer, 'Eve's Lament', *Ériu* 3 (1907), 148. Also in Greene and O'Connor, *Golden Treasury*, 157–8.

'Mothers of Irish Saints', in O'Sullivan, ed., *Book of Leinster*, vi. 1692–7.

Muirchú, Life of Patrick [Latin], in Hood, *Patrick*, 61–81. Also in Bieler, *Patrician Texts*, 61–121.

Ní Car Brigit ['Brigit Loved Not', or 'Broccán's Hymn'], in *Thes. Pal.* ii. 327–49. Also in Bernard, and Atkinson, *Irish Liber Hymnorum*, ii. 189–205.

Nom churim ar commairge ['I Place Myself Under the Protection', or 'Litany of the Virgins'], in Plummer, *Irish Litanies*, 92–3.

Oengus the Culdee, Martyrology of Oengus, ed. W. Stokes. *Félire Oengusso Céli Dé: The Martyrology of Oengus the Culdee* (Henry Bradshaw Society 29; London, 1905). Earlier version: *On the Calendar of Oengus* (Dublin, 1880).

Old Irish Penitential, trans. D. Binchy, 'The Old Irish Penitential', in Bieler, *Irish Penitentials*, 258–76. Also ed. E. Gwynn, 'An Irish Penitential', *Ériu* 7 (1914), 121–95.

Pais Eoin Bautist ['The Passion of John the Baptist'], in Atkinson, *Passions and Homilies* 64–8, 304–9.

Palladius, The Lausiac History, trans. R. Meyer, *The Lausiac History, by Palladius* (Warminster, 1965).

Patrick [Saint Patrick], *Confessio*, in Hood, *Patrick*, 23–34.

—— *Epistola*, ibid. 35–8.

Patrick [Bishop of Dublin], ed. and trans. A. Gwynn, *The Writings of Bishop Patrick, 1074–1084* (Scriptores Latini Hiberniae 1; Dublin, 1955).

Pelagius, Expositions on the Thirteen Epistles, ed. A. Souter, *Pelagius' Expositions of Thirteen Epistles* (Texts and Studies 9; Cambridge, 1922–31).

'The Power of Women', ed. and trans. K. Meyer, 'Anecdota from Irish Manuscripts, 9: the Book of Leinster, p. 282a', *Gaelic Journal (Irisleabhar na Gaedhilge)* 4 (1893), 216–17. Also in J. Pokorny, *A Historical Reader of Old Irish* (Halle, 1923), 12–14, 36–48.

'A Prayer for Tears', ed. and trans. K. Meyer, 'Four Religious Poems', *Ériu* 6 (1911–12), 12–13.

Ropadh maith lem ['I Should Like', or 'St Brigit's Alefeast'], ed. and trans. D. Greene, 'St. Brigid's Alefeast', *Celtica* 2 (1952–4), 150–3.

Rule of the *Céli Dé* in the *Leabhar Breac*, ed. and trans. W. Reeves. 'On the Culdees', *Transactions of the Royal Irish Academy* 24 (1873).

Rule of the Céli Dé in a Franciscan Dublin MS, ed. and trans. E. Gwynn, 'The Rule of Tallaght', *Hermathena* 44, 2nd supplemental vol. (1927), 64–87.

Rule of Patrick [*Ríagail Phátraic*], ed. and trans. J. O'Keeffe, '*Ríagail Pátraic*: The Rule of Patrick', *Ériu* 1 (1904), 216–24.

Rule of Tallaght, ed. and trans. E. Gwynn, 'The Rule of Tallaght', *Hermathena* 44, second supplementary vol. (1927), 2–63.

Saltair na Rann [Psalter of the Quatrains'], ed. and trans. W. Stokes, *The Saltair na Rann: a collection of Early Middle Irish Poems* (Anecdota Oxoniensia 1, pt. 3; Oxford, 1883). Also ed. and trans. (in part) F. Kelly, B. Murdoch, and D. Greene, *The Irish Adam and Eve Story*, 2 vols. (Dublin, 1976).

Sanas Cormaic ['Cormac's Glossary'], ed. K. Meyer, *Sanas Cormaic: An old Irish glossary, compiled by Cormac Úa Cuilennáin . . . Edited from the copy in the Yellow Book of Lecan* (Halle, 1912).

Secht n-Ingena Dalbronaig ['The Seven Daughters of Dalbroney'], in O'Sullivan, ed., *Book of Leinster*, vi. 1589–91.

Second Synod of St. Patrick, in Bieler, *Irish Penitentials*, 184–97.

Sen Dé ['Colmán's Hymn'], in *Thes. Pal.* ii. 301–6. Also in Bernard and Atkinson, *Irish Liber Hymnorum*, ii. 14–16, 158–60.

Slán seiss, a Brigit ['Sit Safely, Brigit', or 'To St Brigit'], in Greene and O'Connor, *Golden Treasury*, 67–71. Originally ed., with commentary, by K. Meyer, *Hail Brigit: An Old-Irish Poem on the Hill of Alenn* (Halle, 1912).

Stowe Missal, ed. G. Warner, *The Stowe Missal*, 2 vols. (Henry Bradshaw Society 32; London, 1906).

Teagasg Maoil Ruain ['Teaching of Mael Ruain']. *See* 'Rule of Tallaght'.

Tertullian, *De oratione*, ed. G. Diercks, *CCSL* 2. 255–74.

—— *De exhortatione castitatis*, ed. E. Kroymann, *CCSL* 2. 1013–36. Also *PL2*, 913–30.

—— *De monogamia*, ed. E. Dekkers, *CCSL* 2. 1227–54. Also *PL2*, 929–54.

Tírechán, Memoirs, with Additamenta, in Bieler, *Patrician Texts*, 122–80.

Transitus Mariae, ed. St John Seymour, 'Irish Versions of the *Transitus Mariae*', *Journal of Theological Studies* 23 (1922), 36–43.

Triads, ed. K. Meyer, *The Triads of Ireland* (Royal Irish Academy Todd Lecture Series 13; Dublin, 1906).

Tripartite Life of Patrick. *See* 'Life of Patrick'.

Versiculi Familiae Benchuir, in P. O'Dwyer, *Mary: A History of Devotion in Ireland* (Dublin, 1988), 35–43.

William of Malmesbury, *De gestis pontificum Anglorum*, ed. N. Hamilton (Rolls Series; London, 1870).

SECONDARY SOURCES

Achelis, H., *Virgines Subintroductae* (Leipzig, 1902).

Adler, M., *Drawing Down the Moon* (2nd edn.: Boston, 1986).

Africa, D., 'The Politics of Kin: Women and Pre-eminence in a Medieval Irish Hagiographical List' (Ph.D. Thesis; Princeton, 1990).

—— 'St Malachy the Irishman: Kinship, Clan and Reform', *Proceedings of the Harvard Celtic Colloquium* 10 (1985), 103–27.

Andrieu, M., *Les 'Ordines Romani'*, 6 vols. (Louvain, 1931–61).

Archdall, M., *Monasticon Hibernicum, or, A History of the Abbeys, Priories, and Other Religious Houses* (Dublin, 1786).

Bamberger, J., 'The Myth of Matriarchy: Why Men Rule in Primitive Society', in M. Rosaldo and L. Lamphere (eds.), *Woman, Culture and Society* (Stanford, 1974), 263–80.

Barrow, L., *Round Towers of Ireland* (Dublin, 1977).

Barstow, A., *Married Priests and the Reforming Papacy: the Eleventh-Century Debates* (Texts and Studies in Religion 12; New York, 1982).

Bateson, M., 'Origin and Early History of Double Monasteries', *Transactions of the Royal Historical Society*, NS 13 (1899), 137–98.

Benham, P., *The Avalonians* (Glastonbury, 1993).

Bernhards, M., *Speculum virginum: Geistigkeit und Seelenleben der Frau im Hochmittelalter* (Cologne, 1955).

Bethell, D., 'English Monks and the Irish Reform', *Historical Studies* 8 (1971), 111–35.

Bieler, L., 'The Celtic Hagiographer', in id., *Ireland and the Culture of Early Medieval Europe*, ed. R. Sharpe (Variorum Reprints; London, 1987).

—— 'The Classics in Celtic Ireland', in R. Bolgar (ed.), *Classical Influences on European Culture AD 500–1500* (Cambridge, 1971).

—— 'Interpretationes Patricianae', *Irish Ecclesiastical Record* 107 (1967), 1–13.

—— 'The Island of Scholars', in id., *Ireland and the Culture of Early Medieval Europe*, ed. R. Sharpe, article 7 (Variorum Reprints; London, 1987).

—— *The Life and Legend of St Patrick: Problems of Modern Scholarship* (Dublin, 1949).

—— 'Patrick's Synod: a Revision', in anon. (ed.), *Mélanges offerts a Mlle Christine Mohrmann* (Utrecht, 1963), 96–102.

—— 'Recent Researches in Irish Hagiography', *Studies* 33 (1946), 230–8, 236–44.

—— 'Studies on the Text of Muirchú, II: The Vienna Fragments', *PRIA* 59C (1959), 181–95.

—— 'Trias Thaumaturga', in T. O Donnell (ed.), *Father John Colgan, OFM* (Dublin, 1959).

Bigger, F., 'Inis Clothrann, Lough Ree: Its History and Antiquities', *JRSAI* 5th ser. 10 (1900), 69–90.

Binchy, D., 'An Archaic Legal Poem', *Celtica* 9 (1971), 152–68.

—— 'Family Membership of Women', in *SEIL*, 180–6.

—— 'The Legal Capacity of Women in Regard to Contracts', ibid. 207–34.

—— 'Patrick and His Biographers, Ancient and Modern', *Studia Hibernica* 2 (1962), 7–123.

—— 'The Pseudo-Historical Prologue to the *Senchas Mór*', *Studia Celtica* 10 (1975), 15–28.

—— 'St Patrick's "First Synod"', *Studia Hibernica* 8 (1968), 49–59.

—— *et al.* (eds.), *Studies in Early Irish Law [SEIL]* (Dublin, 1936).

Binford, S., 'Myths and Matriarchies', in C. Spretnak (ed.), *The Politics of Women's Spirituality* (Garden City, 1982).

Bischoff, B., 'Turning Points in the History of Latin Exegesis in the Early Middle Ages', trans. C. O'Grady, in M. McNamara (ed.), *Biblical Studies: The Medieval Irish Contribution* (Dublin, 1976), 74–160.

Bitel, L., *Isle of the Saints: Settlement and Christian Community in Early Ireland* (Ithaca, NY, 1990).

—— *Land of Women* (Ithaca, NY, 1996).

—— 'Women's Monastic Enclosures in Early Ireland: A Study of Female Spirituality and Male Monastic Mentalities', *Journal of Medieval History* 12 (1986), 15–36.

Blair, J., and R. Sharpe (eds.), *Pastoral Care Before the Parish* (Leicester, 1992).

Bonwick, J., *Religion of the Ancient Celts* (London, 1894).

Bowen, E., 'The Cult of St. Brigit', *Studia Celtica* 8–9 (1973–4), 33–47.

Bowman, M., 'Cardiac Celts: Images of the Celts in Contemporary British Paganism', in Harvey and Hardman, *Paganism Today*, 242–51.

—— 'Contemporary Celtic Spirituality', in A. Hale and P. Payton (eds.), *New Directions in Celtic Studies* (Exeter, 2000).

Bradley, I., *The Celtic Way* (London, 1993).

Bradley, M. Z., *The Mists of Avalon* (New York, 1982).

Bray, D., 'The Image of Saint Brigit in the early Irish church', *Études Celtiques* 24 (1987), 209–15.

—— 'Motival Derivations in the *Life of St Samthann*', *Studia Celtica* 20–1 (1985–6), 78–86.

Breatnach, L., 'Canon Law and Secular Law in Early Christian Ireland: the Significance of *Bretha Nemed*', *Peritia* 3 (1984), 439–59.

—— 'The First Third of *Bretha Nemed Toísech*', *Ériu* 40 (1989), 1–40.

Breen, A., 'The Date, Provenance and Authorship of the Pseudo-Patrician Canonical Materials', *Zeitschrift für Rechtsgeschichte der Savigny-Stiftung*, Kanonistische Abteilung 112 (1995), 83–129.

Brenan, M., *Ecclesiastical History of Ireland* (Dublin, 1864).

Brennan, B., '"Episcopae": Bishops' Wives Viewed in Sixth-Century Gaul', *Church History* 54 (1985), 311–23.

Bromwich, R., *Medieval Celtic Literature: A Select Bibliography* (Toronto, 1974).

Brooke, C., 'Gregorian Reform in Action: Clerical Marriage in England, 1050–1200', *Cambridge Historical Journal* 7 (1956), 1–21, 187–8.

—— *The Medieval Idea of Marriage* (Oxford, 1989).

Brown, C., and A. Harper, 'Excavations at Cathedral Hill, Armagh', *UJA* 47 (1984), 109–61.

Brown, P., *The Body and Society: Men, Women and Sexual Renunciation in Early Christianity* (New York, 1988).

Browne, G., 'The Importance of Women in Anglo-Saxon Times', in id., *The Importance of Women in Anglo-Saxon Times . . . And Other Addresses* (London, 1919), 11–39.

Brundage, J., *Law, Sex and Christian Society in Medieval Europe* (London, 1987).

Budapest, Z., *The Holy Book of Women's Mysteries* (San Francisco, 1980).

Bugge, J., *Virginitas: An Essay in the History of a Medieval Ideal* (Archives internationales d'histoires des idées, series minor, 17; The Hague, 1975).

Bullock, J., 'Early Christian Memorial Formulae', *Archaeologia Cambrensis* 105 (1956), 133–41.

Bulst, N., 'Irisches Mönchtum und cluniazensische Klosterreform', in H. Löwe (ed.), *Die Iren und Europa im Früheren Mittelalter* (Stuttgart, 1982), ii. 958–69.

Burrus, V., *Chastity As Autonomy: Women in the Stories of Apocryphal Acts* (Studies in Women and Religion 23; Lewiston, NY, 1987).

Bury, J., *The Life of Saint Patrick and His Place in History* (London, 1905).

—— 'Sources of the Early Patrician Documents', *English Historical Review* 19 (1904), 493–503.

—— 'The Tradition of Muirchú's Text', *Hermathena* 28 (1902), 172–207.

Byrne, F., 'Comarbai Brigte', in T. W. Moody and F. J. Byrne (eds.), A New History of Ireland, ix. Maps, Genealogies, Lists (Oxford, 1984), 259–62.

Byrne, M., The Tradition of the Nun in Medieval England (Washington DC, 1932).

Cabré y Pairet, M., '"Deodicatae" y "deovotae": La regulación de la religiosidad femenina en los condados catalanes', in A. Muñoz Fernández (ed.), Las mujeres en el cristianismo medieval: Imágenes teóricas y cauces de actuación religiosa (Madrid, 1989), 169–82.

Candon, A., 'Barefaced Effrontery: Secular and Ecclesiastical Politics in Early Twelfth Century Ireland', Seanchas Ardmhacha 14 (1991), 1–25.

Carey, J., 'Notes on the Irish War Goddess', Éigse 19 (1983), 263–75.

Carney, J., Studies in Irish Literature and History (Dublin, 1955).

—— 'Old Ireland and her Poetry', in R. McNally (ed.), Old Ireland (New York, 1965), 147–72.

—— 'On the Dating of Early Irish Verse', Éigse 19 (1982–3), 177–216.

Carville, G., The Occupation of Celtic Sites in Medieval Ireland by the Canons Regular of St Augustine and the Cistercians (Kalamazoo, Mich., 1982).

Caton, J., Manifestaciones asceticas en la iglesia hispano-romano del siglo IV (León, 1962).

Chadwick, O., John Cassian: A Study in Primitive Monasticism (2nd edn.: Cambridge, 1968).

Charles-Edwards, T., 'The Church and Settlement', in Ní Chatháin and Richter, Irland und Europa, 167–75.

—— 'Review Article: The Corpus Iuris Hibernici', Studia Hibernica 20 (1980), 141–62.

—— 'The Pastoral Role of the Church in the Early Irish Laws', in Blair and Sharpe, Pastoral Care, 63–80.

—— 'The Social Background to Irish Peregrinatio', Celtica 11 (1976), 43–59.

—— Early Irish and Welsh Kinship (Oxford, 1993).

Clancy, T., 'Women Poets in Early Medieval Ireland: Stating the Case', in C. Meek and K. Simms (eds.), The Fragility of her Sex? (Dublin, 1996), 43–72.

Clark, E., 'Ascetic Renunciation and Feminine Advancement: A Paradox of Late Antique Christianity', Anglican Theological Review 63 (1981), 240–57.

—— 'Introduction to John Chrysostom, "On Virginity; Against Remarriage"', in id. (ed.), Ascetic Piety and Women's Faith: Essays on Late Ancient Christianity (Studies in Women and Religion 20; New York, 1986), 229–55.

—— Jerome, Chrysostom and Friends: Essays and Translations (Studies in Women and Religion 1; New York, 1979).

—— 'John Chrysostom and the Subintroductae', in id. (ed.), Ascetic Piety and Women's Faith (above), 265–90.

Condren, M., The Serpent and The Goddess: Women, Religion and Power in Celtic Ireland (San Francisco, 1989).

Connolly, S., 'The Authorship and Manuscript Tradition of Vita I Sanctae Brigidae', Manuscripta 16 (1972), 67–82.

Connon, A., 'The Banshenchas and the Uí Néill Queens of Tara', in Smyth, Seanchas, 98–108.

Corish, P., The Christian Mission (Dublin, 1972).

Corozzi, C., 'Les fondaments de la tripartition sociale chez Adalbéron de Laon', Annales E.S.C. 33 (1978), 683–702.

Cubitt, C., 'The Tenth-Century Benedictine Reforms', Early Medieval Europe 6 (1997), 77–94.

Davies, S., *Revolt of the Widows: The Social World of the Apocryphal Acts* (Carbondale, Ill., 1980).

Davies, W., 'Celtic Women in the Early Middle Ages', in A. Cameron and A. Kuhrt (eds.), *Images of Women in Antiquity* (London, 1983), 145–66.

—— 'Clerics as Rulers: Some Implications of Ecclesiastical Authority in Early Medieval Ireland', in N. Brooks (ed.), *Latin and the Vernacular Languages in Early Medieval Britain* (Leicester, 1982), 81–97.

—— 'The Myth of the Celtic Church', in N. Edwards and A. Lane (eds.), *The Early Church in Wales and the West: Recent Work in Early Christian Archaeology, History and Place-names* (Oxbow Monograph Series 16; Oxford, 1992), 12–21.

—— 'Protected Space in Britain and Ireland in the Middle Ages', in B. Crawford (ed.), *Scotland in Dark Age Britain* (Aberdeen, 1996), 1–19.

—— *Wales in the Early Middle Ages* (Leicester, 1982).

De Labriolle, P., 'Le "mariage spirituel" dans l'antiquité chrétienne', *Revue historique* 137 (1921), 204–25.

De Paor, L., 'The Aggrandisement of Armagh', *Historical Studies* 8 (1971), 95–110.

—— *Ireland and Early Europe* (Dublin, 1997).

De Vries, J., *Keltische Religion* [*La religion des Celtes*, trans. L. Jospin] (Paris, 1977).

de Waal, E., *The Celtic Vision* (London, 1988).

Dillon, M., 'The Relationship of Mother and Son, of Father and Daughter, and the Law of Inheritance with Regard to Women', in *SEIL*, 129–79.

Doherty, C., 'The Irish Hagiographer: Resources, Aims, Results', in T. Dunne (ed.), *The Writer as Witness: Literature as Historical Evidence* (Historical Studies 16; Cork, 1987), 10–22.

—— 'The Use of Relics in Early Ireland', in Ní Chathain and Richter, *Irland und Europa*, 89–101.

Dortel-Claudot, M., 'Le prêtre et le mariage: évolution de la législation canonique des origines au XII siécle', *L'Année canonique* 17 (1973), 319–44.

Doyle, P., 'The Latin Bible in Ireland: Its Origins and Growth', in M. McNamara (ed.), *Biblical Studies: The Medieval Irish Contribution* (Dublin, 1976), 30–45.

Duby, G., *The Three Orders: Feudal Society Imagined*, trans. Arthur Goldhammer (Chicago, 1990).

Duchesne, L., 'Lavocat et Catiherne, prétres bretons du temps de Sta Merlaine', *Revue de Bretagne et de Vendée* 57 (1885), 5–21.

Duchesne, M., *Christian Worship: Its Origins and Evolution* (London, 1927).

Dumville, D., 'Biblical Apocrypha and the Early Irish: A Preliminary Investigation', *PRIA* 73C (1973), 299–338.

—— (ed.), *Saint Patrick AD 493–1993* (Studies in Celtic History 13; Woodbridge, 1993).

—— 'British Missionary Activity in Ireland', ibid. 133–45.

—— 'Church-Government and the Spread of Christianity in Ireland', ibid. 179–81.

—— *Councils and Synods of the Gaelic Early and Central Middle Ages* (Quiggin Pamphlets on the Sources of Mediaeval Gaelic History 3; Cambridge, 1997).

—— 'The Dating of the Tripartite Life of St Patrick', in id., *Saint Patrick*, 255–8.

—— 'The Floruit of St. Patrick—Common and Less Common Ground', ibid. 13–18.

—— 'Gildas and Uinniau', in M. Lapidge and D. Dumville (eds.), *Gildas: New Approaches* (Studies in Celtic History 5; Woodbridge, 1984), 207–14.

Dumville, D., 'Late Seventh- or Eighth-Century Evidence for the British Transmission of Pelagius', *Cambridge Medieval Celtic Studies* 10 (1985), 39–52.

—— 'St Patrick at his "First Synod"?', ibid. *Saint Patrick*, 175–8.

—— 'St Patrick's Missing Years', ibid. 25–8.

—— 'Some British Aspects of the Earliest Irish Christianity', in Ní Chatháin and Richter, *Irland und Europa*, 16–24.

Duncan, A., *The Elements of Celtic Christianity* (Shaftesbury, 1992).

Eckenstein, L., *Women Under Monasticism: Chapters on Saint-Lore and Convent Life between AD 500 and AD 1500* (Cambridge, 1896).

Edwards, N., *The Archaeology of Early Medieval Ireland* (London, 1990).

Elliot, D., *Spiritual Marriage: Sexual Abstinence in Medieval Wedlock* (Princeton, 1993).

Ellis, P. Berresford, *Celtic Women: Women in Celtic Society and Literature* (London, 1995).

Esposito, M., 'Notes on Latin Learning and Literature in Mediaeval Ireland, I', *Hermathena* 45 (1930), 225–60.

—— 'On the Earliest Latin Life of St. Brigid of Kildare', *PRIA* 30C (1912), 307–26.

—— 'On the Early Latin Lives of St Brigid of Kildare', *Hermathena* 49 (1935), 120–65.

—— 'The Sources for Conchubranus' Life of St Monenna', *English Historical Review* 35 (1920), 71–8.

Etchingham, C., 'Bishops and the Early Irish Church: A Reassessment', *Studia Hibernica* 28 (1994), 35–62.

—— 'The Early Irish Church: Some Observations on Pastoral Care and Dues', *Ériu* 42 (1991), 99–118.

Farrar, S., *The Witches' Way* (London, 1984).

Fell, C., C. Clark, and E. Williams, *Women in Anglo-Saxon England and the Impact of 1066* (London, 1984).

Ferguson, S., 'On the Ceremonial Turn Called Desiul', *Proceedings of the Royal Irish Academy*, 2nd ser. 1 (1877).

Fernandez Caton, J., *Manifestaciones asceticas en la iglesia hispano-romano del siglo IV* (León 1962).

Firey, A., 'Cross-examining the Witness: Recent Research in Celtic Monastic History', *Monastic Studies* 14 (1983), 31–49.

Foot, S., 'Parochial Ministry in Early Anglo-Saxon England: the Role of Monastic Communities', in W. Shiels and D. Wood (eds.), *The Ministry: Clerical and Lay* (Studies in Church History 26; Oxford, 1989), 43–54.

—— *Veiled Women* (forthcoming, 2001).

Ford, P., 'Celtic Women: The Opposing Sex', *Viator* 19 (1988), 417–38.

Fox, M., *Original Blessing: A Primer in Creation Spirituality* (Santa Fe, N.Mex., 1983).

Frazee, C., 'The Origins of Clerical Celibacy in the Western Church', *Church History* 41 (1972), 149–67.

Fry, S., *Burial in Medieval Ireland, 900–1500* (Dublin, 1999).

Gardner, G., *Witchcraft Today* (London, 1954).

Gougaud, L., *Christianity in Celtic Lands: A History of the Churches of the Celts*, trans. M. Joynt (rev. edn.: Edinburgh, 1932).

—— '*Mulierum Consortia*: étude sur le syneisaktisme chez les ascètes celtiques', *Ériu* 9 (1923), 147–56.

Graves, R., *The White Goddess: A Historical Grammer of Poetic Myth* (London, 1948).

Green, D., 'Brigid's Ale-Feast', *Celtica* 11 (1952), 150–3.

Green, M., *Celtic Goddesses: Warriors, Virgins, Mothers* (London, 1995).

Grosjean, P., 'Hagiographica Celtica', *Analecta Bollandiana* 55 (1937), 96–108.

Gwynn, A., 'The First Synod of Cashel', *IER* 66 (1945), 81–92; 67 (1946), 109–22.

—— *The Irish Church in the Eleventh and Twelfth Centuries*, ed. G. O'Brien (Dublin, 1991).

—— *The Twelfth-Century Reform* (Dublin, 1968).

—— and R. Hadcock, *Medieval Religious Houses, Ireland* (London, 1970).

Gwynn, E., 'The Irish Glosses', in Ní Chatháin and Richter, *Irland und Europa*, 210–17.

Halsall, G., 'Female Status and Power in Early Merovingian Central Austrasia: the Burial Evidence', *Early Medieval Europe* 5 (1996), 1–24.

Hamilton Thompson, A., 'Double Monasteries and the Male Element in Nunneries', Appendix 8 to *The Ministry of Women: Report Commissioned by a Committee Appointed by the Archbishop of Canterbury* (London, 1919), 145–64.

—— 'Northumbrian Monasticism', in id., *Bede: His Life, Times and Writings* (Oxford, 1935), 60–101.

Hamlin, A., 'The Early Irish Church: Problems of Identification', in N. Edwards and A. Lane (eds.), *The Early Church in Wales and the West* (Oxbow Monograph Series 16; Oxford, 1992), 138–44.

—— and C. Foley, 'A Women's Graveyard at Carrickmore, County Tyrone, and the Separate Burial of Women', *UJA* 46 (1983), 41–6.

Hamp, E., '*Imbolc, oimelc*', *Studia Celtica* 14 (1979), 106–13.

Hanson, R., *Saint Patrick: His Origins and Career* (Oxford, 1968).

Harbison, P., *Pre-Historic Ireland: From the First Settlers to the Early Celts* (London, 1988).

—— *Pilgrimage in Ireland: the Monuments and the People* (London, 1991).

Harding, E., *Women's Mysteries* (London, 1929).

Harris, D., 'Saint Gobnet, Abbess of Ballyvourney', *JRSAI* 68 (1938), 272–7.

Harrison, J., *Prolegomena to the Study of Greek Religion* (Cambridge, 1903).

Harvey, G. (ed.), *Contemporary Paganism* (New York, 1997).

—— and C. Hardman (eds.), *Paganism Today* (London, 1995).

Haskins, S., *Mary Magdalen: Myth and Metaphor* (New York, 1993).

Healy, J., *Insula Sanctorum et Doctorum: Ireland's Ancient Schools and Scholars* (Dublin, 1893).

Heineken, A. H., *Die Anfänge der sächsischen Frauenklöster* (unpub. Phil. Diss.; Göttingen, 1909).

Henry, F., 'Decorated Stones at Ballyvourney, Cork', *Journal of the Cork Historical and Archaeological Society* 57 (1952), 18–61.

—— *Irish Art During the Viking Invasions, 800–1020 AD* (London, 1967).

Herbert, M., *Iona, Kells and Derry: the History and Hagiography of the Monastic Familia of Columba* (Oxford, 1988).

—— 'Goddess and King: the Sacred Marriage in Early Ireland', in L. Fradenburg (ed.), *Women and Sovereignty: Cosmos* 7 (1992), 264–75.

—— 'Transmutations of an Irish Goddess', in S. Billington and M. Green (eds.), *The Concept of the Goddess* (London, 1996), 141–51.

—— and M. McNamara, *Irish Biblical Apocrypha: Selected Texts in Translation* (Edinburgh, 1989).

Herity, M., 'The Layout of Early Christian Monasteries', in Ní Chatháin and Richter, *Irland und Europa*, 105–16.

Herren, M., 'On the Earliest Irish Acquaintance with Isidore of Seville', in E. James (ed.), *Visigothic Spain: New Approaches* (Oxford, 1980), 243–50.

—— 'Mission and Monasticism in the Confessio of Patrick', in D. Ó Corráin, L. Breatnach, and K. McCone (eds.), *Saints, Sages and Storytellers: Celtic Studies in Honour of Professor James Carney* (Maynooth Monographs 2; Maynooth, 1989), 76–85.

Hillgarth, J., 'The East, Visigothic Spain and the Irish', *Studia Patristica* 4 (1961), 442–56.

—— 'Visigothic Spain and Early Christian Ireland', *PRIA* 62C (1962), 167–94.

Hilpisch, S., *Die Doppelklöster; Entstehung und Organisation* (Münster, 1928).

Hlawitschka, E., 'Beobachtungen und Überlegungen zur Konventsstarke im Nonnenkloster Remiremont während des 7.–9. Jahrhunderts', in G. Melville (ed.), *Secundum regulam vivere: Festschrift für P. Norbert Backmund* (Windberg, 1978), 31–9.

Hochstetler, D., 'The Meaning of Monastic Cloister for Women According to Caesarius of Arles', in T. F. X. Noble and J. Contreni (eds.), *Religion, Culture and Society in the Early Middle Ages: Studies in Honour of Richard E. Sullivan* (Kalamazoo, Mich., 1987), 27–40.

Hodgson, A., 'The Frankish Church and Women, From the Late Eighth to the Early Tenth Century: Representation and Reality' (unpub. PhD thesis; University of London, 1992).

Hogan, E., *Onomasticon Goedelicum: Locorum et Tribuum Hiberniae et Scotiae* (Dublin, 1910).

Hollis, S., *Anglo-Saxon Women and the Church: Sharing a Common Fate* (Woodbridge, 1992).

Hughes, K., 'The Changing Theory and Practice of Irish Pilgrimage', *Journal of Ecclesiastical History* 11 (1960), 143–51.

—— *The Church in Early Irish Society* (London, 1966).

—— *Early Christian Ireland: Introduction to the Sources* (London, 1972).

—— 'Sanctity and Secularity in the Early Irish Church', in D. Baker (ed.), *Sanctity and Secularity: the Church and the World* (Studies in Church History 10; Oxford, 1973), 21–37.

—— 'Synodus II S. Patricii', in J. O'Meara and B. Nauman (eds.), *Latin Script and Letters AD 400–900* (Leiden, 1976), 141–7.

—— and A. Hamlin, *The Modern Traveller to the Early Irish Church* (London, 1977).

Hutton, R., 'The Neolithic Great Goddess: A Study in Modern Tradition', *Antiquity* 71 (1997), 91–9.

—— *Pagan Religions of the Ancient British Isles: Their Nature and Legacy* (Oxford, 1991).

—— *The Triumph of the Moon* (Oxford, 1999).

Jackson, K., 'The Date of the Tripartite Life of St Patrick', *ZCP* 41 (1986), 5–45.

James, E., 'Ireland and Western Gaul in the Merovingian Period', in D. Whitelock, R. McKitterick, and D. Dumville (eds.), *Ireland in Early Medieval Europe: Studies in Memory of Kathleen Hughes* (Cambridge, 1982), 362–86.

Jaski, B., 'Marriage Laws in Ireland and on the Continent in the Early Middle Ages', in C. Meek and K. Simms (eds.), *The Fragility of her Sex?* (Dublin, 1996), 16–42.

Jenkins, D., and M. Owen (eds.), *The Welsh Law of Women: Studies Presented to Professor Daniel A. Binchy* (Cardiff, 1980).

Johnston, E., 'Transforming Women in Irish Hagiography', *Peritia* 9 (1995), 197–220.

Junod, E., and J.-D. Kaestli, *L'Histoire des Actes Apocryphes des apôtres du II au IX siècle: le cas des Actes de Jean* (Cahiers de la Revue de théologie et de philosophie 7; Geneva, 1982).

Kehnel, A., *Clonmacnois, the Church and Lands of St Ciarán: Change and Continuity in an Irish Monastic Foundation (6th–16th Century)* (Munster, 1995).

Kelly, D., 'The Crosses of Tory Island', in A. Smyth (ed.), *Seanchas: Studies in Early and Medieval Irish Archaeology, History and Literature in Honour of Francis J. Byrne* (Dublin, 2000), 53–63.

Kelly, F., *A Guide to Early Irish Law* (Dublin, 1988).

Kelly, J., 'Hiberno-Latin Theology', in H. Löwe (ed.), *Die Iren und Europa im Früheren-mittelalter* (Stuttgart, 1982), ii. 549–67.

—— 'Pelagius, Pelagianism and the Early Christian Irish', *Medievalia* 4 (1980 for 1978), 99–124.

Kendrick, T., *The Druids: A Study in Keltic Prehistory* (London, 1928).

Kenney, J. F., *The Sources for the Early History of Ireland: Ecclesiastical* (New York, 1929).

Killanin, Lord, and M. Duignan, *The Shell Guide to Ireland* (London, 1962).

Klein, E., *Feminism Under Fire* (Amherst, NY, 1996).

Kraemer, R., 'The Conversion of Women to Ascetic Forms of Christianity', in J. Bennett, E. Clark, J. O'Barr, *et al.* (eds.), *Sisters and Workers in the Middle Ages* (Chicago and London, 1976), 198–207.

Lapidge, M., 'Gildas's Education and the Culture of Sub-Roman Britain', in id. and Dumville, *Gildas* (below), 27–50.

—— and D. Dumville (eds.), *Gildas: New Approaches* (Studies in Celtic History 5; Woodbridge, 1984).

—— and R. Sharpe (eds.), *A Bibliography of Celtic-Latin Literature 400–1200* (Dublin, 1985).

Leask, H., *Glendalough* (Dublin, n.d.).

—— *Irish Churches and Monastic Buildings*, 3 vols. (Dundalk, 1958).

Legrand, L., *The Biblical Doctrine of Virginity* (London, 1963).

Leibell, H., *Anglo-Saxon Education of Women: From Hilda to Hildegarda* (New York, 1922).

Leyser, Karl, *Rule and Conflict in a Medieval Society: Ottonian Saxony* (London, 1979).

Loth, J., 'Un Ancien Usage de L'Église Celtique', *Revue Celtique* 15 (1894), 92–3.

Lucas, A. T., 'The Sacred Trees of Ireland', *Journal of the Cork Archaeological and Celtic Society* 68 (1963), 16–54.

—— 'The Social Role of Relics and Reliquaries', *JRSAI* 116 (1986), 5–37.

Luhrmann, T., *Persuasions of the Witches' Craft* (Oxford, 1989).

Lynch, J., *Godparents and Kinship in Early Medieval Europe* (Princeton, 1986).

Macalister, R. A. S., *The Archaeology of Ireland* (2nd edn.: London, 1949).

McAll, C., 'The Normal Paradigms of a Woman's Life in the Irish and Welsh Law Texts', in D. Jenkins and M. Owen (eds.), *The Welsh Law of Women: Studies Presented to Professor Daniel A. Binchy on his Eightieth Birthday* (Cardiff, 1980), 7–22.

MacCana, P., 'Aspects of the Theme of King and Goddess in Irish Literature, *Études Celtiques* 7 (1955–6), 76–114, 356–413, and 8 (1958–9), 59–65.

—— *Celtic Mythology* (Feltham, 1983).

McCone, K., 'Brigit in the Seventh Century: A Saint With Three Lives?', *Peritia* 1 (1982), 107–45.

—— 'An Introduction to Early Irish Saints' Lives', *The Maynooth Review* 11 (1984), 26–59.

—— *Pagan Past and Christian Present in Early Irish Literature* (Maynooth, 1990).

MacCulloch, J., *The Celtic and Scandinavian Religions* (London, 1948).

—— *Religion of the Ancient Celts* (Edinburgh, 1911).

Mac Curtain, M., and D. Ó Corráin (eds.), *Women in Irish Society: the Historical Dimension* (Dublin, 1978).

MacDonald, A., 'Notes on Monastic Archaeology and the Annals of Ulster, 650–1050', in D. Ó Corráin (ed.), *Irish Antiquity: Essays and Studies Presented to Professor M. J. O'Kelly* (Cork, 1981), 304–19.

—— 'Notes on Terminology in the Annals of Ulster, 650–1050', *Peritia* 1 (1982), 329–33.

MacDonncha, F., 'Dáta Vita Tripartita Sancti Patricii', *Éigse* 18 (1980–1), 124–42, and 19 (1982), 254–72.

—— 'Middle Irish Homilies', *Proceedings of the Irish Biblical Association* 1 (1976), 59–71.

MacEoin, G., 'The Dating of Middle Irish Texts', *Proceedings of the British Academy* 68 (1982), 109–37.

MacLeod, F. [pseud. Sharpe, W.], *The Immortal Hour: A Drama in Two Acts* (Portland, Me., 1907).

MacLeod, N., *Early Irish Contract Law* (Sydney Series in Celtic Studies 1; Sydney, 1992).

McNamara, J., 'The *Herrenfrage*: The Restructuring of the Gender System, 1050–1150', in C. Lees (ed.), *Medieval Masculinities: Regarding Men in the Middle Ages* (Medieval Cultures 7; Minneapolis, 1994), 1–30.

—— 'Muffled Voices: The Lives of Consecrated Women in the Fourth Century', in J. Nichols and L. Shank (eds.), *Distant Echoes: Medieval Religious Women*, i (Kalamazoo, Mich., 1984), 11–31.

McNamara, M., *The Apocrypha in the Irish Church* (Dublin, 1975; repr. with corrections, 1984).

—— *Biblical Studies: The Medieval Irish Contribution* (Dublin, 1976).

—— 'Hiberno-Latin Biblical Studies: an Addendum', *Irish Theological Quarterly* 40 (1973), 364–70.

—— 'A Plea for Hiberno-Latin Biblical Studies', *Irish Theological Quarterly* 39 (1972), 337–53.

—— 'The Text of the Latin Bible in the Early Irish Church', in P. Ní Chatháin and M. Richter (eds.), *Irland und die Christenheit: Bibelstudien und Mission* (Stuttgart, 1987), 7–58.

McNamee, J., *History of the Diocese of Ardagh* (Dublin, 1954).

MacNeill, E., 'Ancient Irish Law: The Law of Status or Franchise', *PRIA* 36C 16 (1923), 265–316.

—— *Celtic Ireland* (Dublin, 1921).

—— 'Dates of Texts in the Book of Armagh Relating to St Patrick', *JRSAI* 58 (1928), 85–101.

—— 'The Earliest Lives of St Patrick', *JRSAI* 58 (1928), 1–21.

—— *Early Irish Laws and Institutions* (Dublin, 1935).

—— 'The Vita Tripartita of St. Patrick', *Ériu* 11 (1930), 1–41.

MacNiocaill, G., 'Christian Influences in Early Irish Law', in Ní Chatháin and Richter, *Irland und Europa*, 151–6.

—— *Ireland Before the Vikings* (Gill History of Ireland 1; Dublin, 1972).

Mackey, J. (ed.), *An Introduction to Celtic Christianity* (Edinburgh, 1989).

Maher, M. (ed.), *Irish Spirituality* (Dublin, 1981).

Manning C., *Clonmacnoise* (Dublin, 1994).

Markale, J., *La Femme celte: mythe et sociologie* (Paris, 1973).

Markus, R., 'Pelagianism: Britain and the Continent', *Journal of Ecclesiastical History* 37 (1986), 191–204.

Martindale, J., 'The Nun Immena', in J. Shiels and D. Wood (eds.), *Women in the Church* (Studies in Church History 27; Oxford, 1990), 27–42.

Massey, M., *Feminine Soul: The Fate of an Ideal* (Boston, 1985).

Massingham, H. J., *Through the Wilderness* (London, 1935).

Maund, K., *Ireland, Wales and England in the Eleventh Century* (Studies in Celtic History 12; Woodbridge, 1991).

Meersseman, G., *The Acahistos Hymn* (Freiburg, 1958).

Metz, R., *La Consécration des vierges dans l'église romaine: Étude d'histoire de la liturgie* (Paris, 1954).

—— 'Le statut de la femme en droit canonique médiéval', *Recueils de la Societé Jean Bodin* 12 (1962), 59–113.

Meyer, K., 'An Crínóg: Ein altirisches Gedicht an eine Syneisakte', *Sitzungsberichte der Königlichen Preussischen Akademie der Wissenschaften* 18 (1918), 361–74.

Mohrmann, C., *The Latin of Saint Patrick: Four Lectures* (Dublin, 1961).

Moore, R. I., 'Family, Community and Cult on the Eve of the Gregorian Reform', *TRHS* 5th ser. 30 (1980), 49–69.

Morin, D., 'Un passage énigmatique de S. Jérome contre la pèlerinage espagnole Eucheria?', *Revue Bénédictine* 30 (1913), 181–4.

Morris, J., 'Pelagian Literature', *Journal of Theological Studies* NS 16 (1965), 26–60.

Motz, L., *Faces of the Goddess* (Oxford, 1997).

Murray, D., 'A Forgotten Saint', *County Louth Archaeological Journal* 5 (1923), 155–60.

Mytum, H., *The Origins of Early Christian Ireland* (London, 1991).

Nelson, J., 'Women and the Word in the Earlier Middle Ages', in W. Shiels and D. Wood (eds.), *Women in the Church* (Studies in Church History 27; Oxford, 1990), 53–78.

Ní Brolcháin, M., 'Women in Early Myths and Sagas', *Crane Bag* 14 (1980), 12–19.

Ní Chatháin, P., and M. Richter (eds.), *Irland und Europa: die Kirche im Frühmittelalter* (Stuttgart, 1984).

Ní Dhonnchadha, M., '*Caillech* and Other Terms for Veiled Women in Medieval Irish Texts', *Éigse* 28 (1994–5), 71–96.

—— 'The Guarantor List of *Cáin Adomnáin*', *Peritia* 1 (1982), 178–215.

—— 'The *Lex Innocentium*: Adamnán's Law for Women, Clerics and Youths, 697 AD', in M. O'Dowd and S. Wichert (eds.), *Chattel, Servant or Citizen: Women's Status in Church, State and Society* (Historical Studies 19; Belfast, 1995), 58–69.

—— 'On Gormfhlaith Daughter of Flann Sinna and the lure of the Sovereignty Goddess', in Smyth, *Seanchas*, 225–37.

Nicholson, J., '*Feminae Gloriosae*: Women in the Age of Bede', in D. Baker (ed.), *Medieval Women* (Studies in Church History, Subsidia 1; Oxford, 1978), 15–29.

Ó Briain, F., 'Brigitana', *ZCP* 36 (1977), 112–37.

Ó Corráin, D., 'The Early Irish Churches: Some Aspects of Organisation', in id. (ed.), *Irish Antiquity: Essays and Studies Presented to Professor M. J. O'Kelly* (Cork, 1981), 327–41.

—— 'High Law and Canon Law', in Ní Chatháin and Richter, *Irland und Europa*, 157–66.

—— 'Historical Need and Literary Narrative', in D. Evans *et al.* (eds.), *Proceedings of the Seventh International Congress of Celtic Studies* (Oxford, 1983).

Ó Corráin, D., *Ireland Before the Normans* (Gill History of Ireland 2; Dublin, 1972).

—— 'Marriage in Early Ireland', in A. Cosgrove (ed.), *Marriage in Ireland* (Dublin, 1985), 5–24.

—— 'Nationality and Kingship in Pre-Norman Ireland', in T. W. Moody (ed.), *Nationality and the Pursuit of National Independence* (Historical Studies 11; Belfast, 1978), 1–35.

—— 'High Kings, Vikings and Other Kings', *Irish Historical Studies* 21 (1979), 283–323.

—— 'Women and the Law in Early Ireland', in M. O'Dowd and S. Wichert (eds.), *Chattel, Servant or Citizen: Women's Status in Church, State and Society* (Historical Studies 19; Belfast, 1995), 45–57.

—— 'Women in Early Irish Society', in M. Mac Curtain and D. Ó Corráin (eds.), *Women in Irish Society: The Historical Dimension* (Dublin, 1978), 1–13.

—— L. Breatnach, and A. Breen, 'The Laws of the Irish', *Peritia* 3 (1984), 382–438.

Ó Cróinín, D., *Early Medieval Ireland, 400–1200* (London, 1995).

—— 'Three Weddings and a Funeral: Rewriting Irish Political History in the Tenth Century', in Smyth, *Seanchas*, 212–24.

O'Dwyer, P., *Devotion to Mary in Ireland, 700–1100* (Dublin, 1976).

Ó Fiaich, T., 'The Church of Armagh Under Lay Control', *Seanchas Ard Mhacha* 5 (1969–70), 75–127.

Ó hAodha, D., 'The Early Lives of St Brigit', *County Kildare Archaeological Society Journal* 15 (1971–6), 397–405.

Ó hEaluighthe, D., 'St Gobnat of Ballyvourney', *Journal of the Cork Historical and Archaeological Society* 57 (1952), 43–60.

O'Kelly, M., 'Church Island near Valencia, Co. Kerry', *PRIA* 59C (1958), 57–136.

—— 'St Gobnat's House', *Journal of the Cork Historical and Archaeological Society* 57 (1952), 18–40.

Olden, T., 'On the Consortia of the First Order of Irish Saints', *PRIA* 3 (1894), 415–20.

O'Leary, P., 'The Honour of Women in Early Irish Literature', *Ériu* 38 (1987), 27–44.

O'Rahilly, T., *Early Irish History and Mythology* (Dublin, 1946).

Ó Riain, P., 'St. Finnbarr: A Study in a Cult', *Journal of the Cork Historical and Archaeological Society* 82, no. 236 (1977), 63–82.

—— 'The Irish Elements in Welsh Hagiographic Tradition', in D. Ó Corráin (ed.), *Irish Antiquity: Essays and Studies Presented to Professor M. J. O'Kelly* (Cork, 1981), 291–303.

Ó Riain-Raedel, D., 'Aspects of the Promotion of Irish Saints' Cults in Medieval Germany', *ZCP* 39 (1982), 220–4.

Parisse, M., 'Les chanoinesses dans l'Empire germanique (ixe–xie siècles)', *Francia* 6 (1978), 107–26.

Patai, D., and N. Koertge (eds.), *Professing Feminism: Cautionary Tales from the Strange World of Women's Studies* (New York, 1996).

Patterson, N., 'Brehon Law in Late Medieval Ireland: "Antiquarian and Obsolete" or "Traditional and Functional"?', *Cambridge Medieval Celtic Studies* 17 (1989), 43–63.

Payer, P., 'Early Medieval Regulations Concerning Marital Sexual Relations', *Journal of Medieval History* 6 (1980), 353–76.

Picard, J.-M. (ed.), *Ireland and Northern France, AD 600–850* (Dublin, 1991).

—— 'The Purpose of Adomnán's *Vita Columbae*', *Peritia* 1 (1982), 160–77.

Plummer, C., 'A Tentative Catalogue of Irish Hagiography', in id. (ed.), *Miscellanea Hagiographica Hibernica* (Brussels, 1925), 171–285.

Power, N., 'The Classes of Women Described in the *Senchas Mór*', in *SEIL*, 81–108.

Pryce, H., 'Early Irish Canons and Medieval Welsh Law', *Peritia* 5 (1986), 107–27.

—— 'Pastoral Care in Early Medieval Wales', in Blair and Sharpe, *Pastoral Care*, 41–62.

Quin, E. G., 'The Irish Glosses', in Ní Chatháin and Richter, *Irland und Europa*, 210–17.

—— 'The Early Medieval Irish Poem *Ísucán*', *Cambridge Medieval Celtic Studies* 1 (1981), 39–52.

Radford, C., 'The Earliest Irish Churches', *UJA* 40 (1977), 1–40.

Reade, G., 'Cill-Sleibhe-Cuillinn', *Journal of the Historical Association of Ireland* (forerunner of *JRSAI*) 1 (1868–9), 93–101.

Reece, R., *Excavations on Iona, 1964–1974* (London, 1981).

Rees, B., *Pelagius: A Reluctant Heretic* (Woodbridge, 1988).

Reynolds, R., '*Virgines Subintroductae* in Celtic Christianity', *Harvard Theological Review* 61 (1968), 547–66.

Roe, H., *The High Crosses of Kells* (Dalkey, 1959).

Royal Irish Academy, *Dictionary of The Irish Language* (compact edition) (Dublin, 1983).

Russell, J., *Dissent and Reform in the Early Middle Ages* (Berkeley, 1965).

Ryan, J., *Irish Monasticism: Origins and Early Development* (Dublin, 1931).

—— 'The Cáin Adomnáin', in *SEIL*, 269–76.

Salisbury, J., *Church Fathers, Independent Virgins* (London, 1991).

Schäfer, K. H., *Die Kanonissenstifter im deutchen Mittelalter: Ihre Entwicklung und innere Einrichtung im Zusammenhang mit dem altchristlichen Sanctimonialentum* (Stuttgart, 1907).

Schneider, D., 'Anglo-Saxon Women in the Religious Life: A Study of the Status and Position of Women in an Early Medieval Society' (unpub. PhD thesis; Cambridge, 1985).

Schulenberg, J., 'Female Sanctity, Public and Private, 500–1100', in M. Erler and M. Kowaleski (eds.), *Women and Power in the Middle Ages* (Athens, Ga., 1988), 102–25.

—— 'Strict Active Enclosure and its Effects on the Female Monastic Experience (ca. 500–1100)', in J. Nicholls and L. Shank, *Medieval Religious Women I: Distant Echoes* (Kalamazoo, Mich., 1984), 51–86.

Schumann, R., 'Le fondazioni ecclesiastiche e il disegno urbano di Piacenza tra il tardo romano (350) e la Signoria (1313)', *Bolletino storico piacentino* 71 (1976), 159–71.

Sharpe, R., 'Armagh and Rome in the Seventh Century', in Ní Chatháin and Richter, *Irland und Europa*, 58–72.

—— 'Churches and Communities in Early Medieval Ireland: Towards a Pastoral Model', in Blair and Sharpe, *Pastoral Care*, 81–109.

—— 'Gildas as a Father of the Church', in Lapidge and Dumville, *Gildas*, 193–205.

—— *Medieval Irish Saints' Lives: An Introduction to Vitae Sanctorum Hiberniae* (Oxford, 1991).

—— 'The Patrician Texts', *Peritia* 1 (1982), 363–9.

—— 'St Patrick and the See of Armagh', *Cambridge Medieval Celtic Studies* 4 (1982), 33–59.

—— 'Some Problems Concerning the Organization of the Church in Early Medieval Ireland' *Peritia* 3 (1984), 230–70.

—— 'Vitae S. Brigitae: The Oldest Texts', *Peritia* 1 (1982), 81–106.

Simms, A., with K. Simms, *Kells* (Irish Historic Towns Atlas 4; Dublin, 1990).

Sims-Williams, P., 'Thought, Word and Deed: An Irish Triad', *Ériu* 29 (1978), 78–111.

Sjoo, M., and B. Mor, *The Great Cosmic Mother: Rediscovering the Religion of the Earth* (San Francisco, 1987).

Smith, J., 'Oral and Written: Saints, Miracles and Relics in Brittany', *Speculum* 65 (1990), 309–43.

—— 'The Problem of Female Sanctity in Carolingian Europe, *c*.780–920', *Past and Present* 146 (1995), 1–37.

Smith, J., 'Robert of Arbrissel: *Procurator Mulierum*', in D. Baker (ed.), *Medieval Women* (Studies in Church History, Subsidia 1; Oxford, 1978), 175–84.

Smyth, A., *Celtic Leinster: Towards an Historical Geography of Early Irish Civilization AD 500–1600* (Blackrock, 1982).

—— *Seanchas: Studies in Early and Medieval Irish Archaeology, History and Literature in Honour of Francis J. Byrne* (Dublin, 2000).

Souter, A., 'The Character and History of Pelagius' Commentary on the Epistles of St. Paul', *Proceedings of the British Academy* 7 (1915/16), 261–96.

Spence, L., *The Mysteries of Britain: Secret Rites and Tradition of Ancient Britain* (London, 1911).

Spretnak, C. (ed.), *The Politics of Women's Spirituality: Essays on the Rise of Spiritual Power within the Feminist Movement* (Garden City, NJ, 1982).

Stafford, P., *Queen Emma and Queen Edith: Queenship and Women's Power in Eleventh-Century England* (Oxford, 1997).

—— 'Gender, Religious Status and Reform in England', *Past and Present* 163 (2000), 1–35.

Stählin, O., 'Chéra', in G. Friedrich (ed.), *Theological Dictionary of the New Testament* (Grand Rapids, 1974), ix. 448–65.

Starhawk, *The Spiral Dance: A Rebirth of the Ancient Religion of the Great Goddess* (New York, 1979).

Stevenson, J., 'Introduction', in F. Warren, *The Liturgy and Ritual of the Celtic Church* (2nd edn.: Woodbridge, 1987).

—— 'Irish Hymns, Venantius Fortunatus and Poitiers', in J.-M. Picard, *Ireland and Aquitaine* (Dublin, 1995), 81–110.

Stokes, G., *Ireland and the Celtic Church* (London, 1892).

Stone, M., *The Paradise Papers*, later repr. as *When God Was a Woman* (London, 1976).

Tiffany, S., 'The Power of Matriarchal Ideas', *International Journal of Women's Studies* 5, no. 2 (1982), 138–47.

Thomas, C., *Celtic Britain* (London, 1986).

—— *The Early Christian Archaeology of North Britain* (Oxford, 1971).

—— 'Imported Pottery in Dark-Age Western Britain', *Medieval Archaeology* 3 (1959), 89–111.

—— 'The Irish Settlements in Post-Roman Western Britain: A Survey of the Evidence', *Journal of the Royal Institution of Cornwall*, ns 6 (1972), 251–74.

—— *Christianity in Roman Britain to AD 500* (London, 1981).

Thurston, B., *The Widows: A Women's Ministry in the Early Church* (Minneapolis, 1989).

Thurneysen, R., 'Cáin Lánamna', in *SEIL* , 1–80.

—— *A Grammar of Old Irish* (rev. edn., Dublin, 1946).

Toulson, E., *The Celtic Alternative* (London, 1987).

Vendryes, J., 'Imbolc', *Revue Celtique* 41 (1924), 241–4.

Vogel, C., *Medieval Liturgy: An Introduction to the Sources* (Spoleto, 1981).

Wagner, H., 'Origins of Pagan Irish Religion', *ZCP* 38 (1981), 1–28.

Wailes, B., 'Dun Ailinne: An Interim Report', in D. Harding (ed.), *Hillforts: Later Prehistoric Earthworks in Britain and Ireland* (New York, 1976).

Wailes, B., 'Irish Royal Sites in History and Archaeology', *Cambridge Medieval Celtic Studies* 3 (1982), 1–29.

Wait, G. A., *Ritual and Religion in Iron Age Britain* (British Archaeological Reports 149; Oxford, 1985).

Wakeman, W., 'On the Ecclesiastical Antiquities of Cluain-Eois', *JRSAI* 13 (1874–5), 327–40.

Warren, F., *The Liturgy and Ritual of the Celtic Church*, 2nd edn., with introduction and bibliography by J. Stevenson (Woodbridge, 1987).

Watson, A., 'The King, the Poet and the Sacred Tree', *Études Celtiques* 18 (1981), 165–80.

Watt, J., *The Church in Medieval Ireland* (Gill History of Ireland 5; Dublin, 1972).

Wemple, S., *Women in Frankish Society: Marriage and the Cloister 500 to 900* (Philadelphia, 1981).

Westropp, T., 'A Description of the Ancient Buildings and Crosses at Clonmacnois, King's County', *JRSAI* 37 (1907), 277–307.

Whitelock, D., *et al.* (eds.), *Ireland in Early Mediaeval Europe: Studies in Honour of Kathleen Hughes* (Cambridge, 1982).

Winterbottom, M., 'Columbanus and Gildas', *Vigiliae Christianae* 30 (1976), 310–17.

Witherington, B., *Women in the Earliest Churches* (Society for New Testament Studies 59; Cambridge, 1988).

Wood-Martin, W., *Traces of Elder Faiths of Ireland* (London, 1902).

Yeats, W. B., *The Celtic Twilight* (London, 1893).

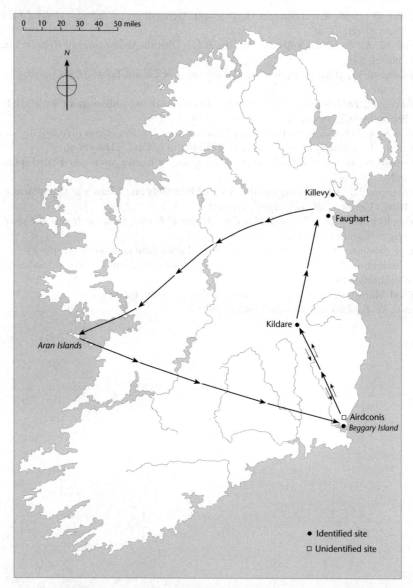

MAP. I   Saint Monenna's Travels in her Anonymous Life (Life of Darerca)

Monenna was of the people of the Conaille Muirthemne in the Plain of Coba (Ir. Mag Coba) in mod.
north-west Co. Down. (1) Went from Conaille homelands to Aran Islands (Ir. Tríarna) to Bishop Ibar.
(2) Followed Ibar from Aran Islands to his next site on Beggary Island (Ir. Béc Ériu). (3) Visited Brigit's
Kildare for some time. (4) From Kildare went back to Airdconis, near Beggary, where she headed a group of
nuns under Ibar's rule (exact location unidentified). (5) A second visit to Kildare. (6) From Kildare she took
her nuns north to her Conaille homeland and set up a community at Faughart. (7) Moved the community
from Faughart to Killevy on the north side of Slieve Gullion. According to the annals she died c.519.

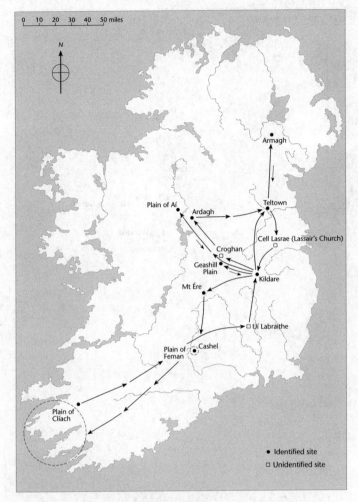

MAP. 2   Saint Brigit's Travels in her *Vita I*

Brigit was born among the Fothairt peoples of Leinster, to a druid and his slavewoman. (1) First she went from Fothairt to a church of Bishops Mel and Melchú in Meath, prob. Croghan, north-west of mod. town of Tullamore. (2) Then from Meath to the bishops' large church of Ardagh in Tethbae. (3) From Ardagh through the Plain of Brega to 'Tailtiu', i.e. Teltown, mod. Donoughpatrick. (4) From Teltown to St Lassair's church, 'Cell Lasrae'. (5) From Lassair's Church to Kildare. (6) A journey from Kildare to Geashill Plain ('Campum Gesilli') and back again. (7) A long journey from Kildare to Armagh with Saint Patrick; side journeys when there to Plain of Macha and Plain of Inis. (8) She came back from Armagh via the Plain of Brega, settling a dispute of two sons of Niall Noígiallach. (9) A long trip to Munster with Bishop Erc, starting at Kildare and stopping at Mount Ére, probably Ard Eirinn in Slieve Bloom mountains. (10) From Mount Ére they went on to the Plain of Feman, near Cashel (Ir. Mag Femin) to a synod. (11) From Plain of Feman to Erc's church (unidentified, in Kerry) and she lived close by, near the sea, with a community of nuns for some years. (12) From Erc's church to Plain of Clíach in Kerry (Ir. Mag Clíach), where she stayed for some time. (13) Back to Kildare stopping at the Uí Labraithe lands on the Leinster borders. (14) A journey to the Plain of Aí (Ir. Mag Aí) in Connaught, and back again to Kildare. According to the annals, she died in the 520s.

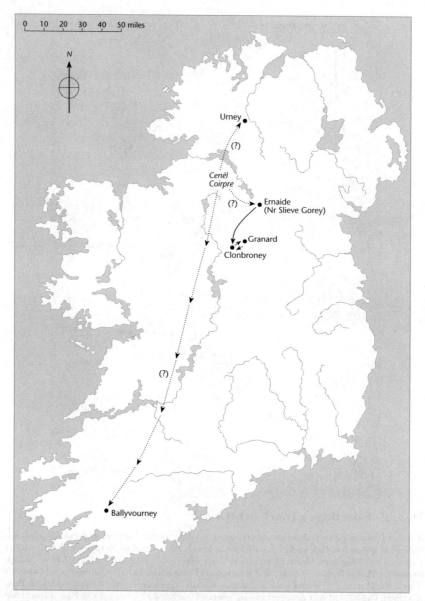

MAP. 3   Saint Samthann's Travels in her Anonymous Life

Born in Ulster, fostered by king of the Cenél Coirpre people. (1) She went from the Cenél Coirpre
territory to female monastery of 'Ernaide', where she held the post of prioress. This could be any of three
places that went by that name: [A] St Gobnat's Ballyvourney in western Co. Cork; [B] the virgin Féme's
Urney in the north on the River Mourne; or [C] the virgin Findsech's 'Ernaide' near Slieve Gorey, Co.
Cavan which seems the most likely. (2) Left 'Ernaide' for Clonbroney on account of a dream, and became
abbess there. (3) Often went to and from the men's monastery of Granard. Died at Clonbroney in 734.

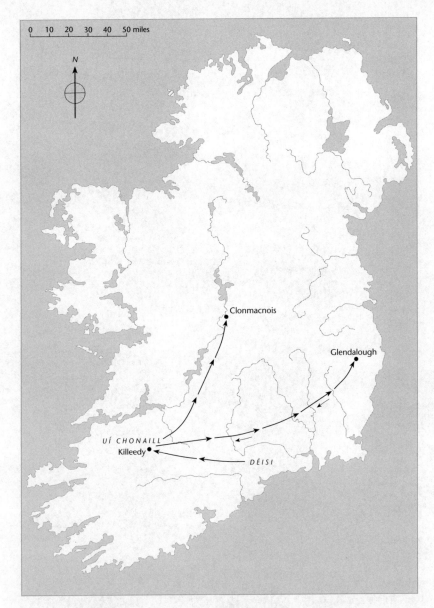

0 10 20 30 40 50 miles

N

Clonmacnois

Glendalough

UÍ CHONAILL
Killeedy

DÉISI

MAP. 4   Saint Ita's Travels in her Anonymous Life

Saint Ita was of the Déisi people in the south. (1) She left home to be consecrated, but the location and performing bishop are unspecified. (2) Left her homeland for the lands of the Uí Chonaill Gabra in the south-west and settled the community of Killeedy among them. (3) She was called by St Coemgen to Glendalough to tend him as he died. (4) On another occasion she journeyed secretly to Clonmacnois to receive the host from the hand of a worthy priest. (5) She went to the court of the Uí Chonaill king to plead for the release of prisoners. According to the annals she died in the 570s.

Index